IN DEATH'S
DARK SHADOW

A SOLDIER'S STORY

Cleve C Barkley

11-22-2014

Copyright © 2006
Cleve C. Barkley
Updated 2013

ISBN: 1-59872-487-8

Printed in the USA by Instantpublisher.com

Pfc. Harold G. Barkley

First Scout, Company G, 38th Infantry

Photo taken in Paris, France, October, 1944

IN DEATH'S DARK SHADOW

A SOLDIER'S STORY

As told to

Cleve C. Barkley

PHOTO CREDITS

All photographs by U.S. Army Signal Corps (National Archives) with the following exceptions:

Harold Barkley: frontispiece and pages 1, 24

Imperial War Museum, London; (photo HU 28965): page 28

Author's collection: pages 170, 209

Dan Styles: page 317, 318

Robert Capa; Magnum Photos: page 334

Detail from "Love in the Ruins" by Tony Vaccaro: page 379

INTRODUCTION
AND
NOTES ON SOURCES

Although written in the style of a novel, I assure you that the events depicted in this narrative are factual, backed up by exhaustive research and eye-witness testimonials from those who were there. However, due to the chronic fatigue experienced by combat soldiers during those harrowing days, and the ravages of time since, placement of certain episodes may not be set in their precise chronological order. This holds especially true for the period covered by the Normandy Campaign, where men were so exhausted that even then they may have had difficulty recalling if a certain event occurred several days previous, or weeks before. Lack of sleep has a numbing effect. Nonetheless, the incidents detailed did occur. I have endeavored through my research to insert those stories into the most likely setting possible, and I feel they do not detract from the facts of that grueling campaign.

Obviously, the primary source for this story is the man who lived it, my father, Harold Barkley. Throughout my life I've listened to his stories, not as one chronologically ordered narrative, but in snippets now and then as he related his wartime experiences over the years. Yet all through the decades that have passed since I first heard these accounts, one fact remained: the stories never changed. Whether told forty-some years ago, or yesterday, the details were identical and never enhanced, and therein lays the seed of truth. Dad was never one for telling tall tales. He told it like it was, or at least how he saw it as a teenage warrior, so many years ago.

Although he often told of heroics by his comrades, he saw himself as neither hero nor villain. I recall an incident years ago when my parents were entertaining guests and the subject of World War II arose. At this, my mother proudly stated that Dad was a war hero. No sooner had the words left her mouth, than Dad "blew up", saying how he was NOT a hero, that all of the heroes were dead. He believed in the self evident truth that he was simply a soldier doing what he was ordered to do. I have since discovered that this is a sentiment shared by other men who have served in combat. I, for one, contest that thought, for I see them all as a true American heroes. Their modesty only reinforces that image.

Numerous letters to and from my father during the war also proved valuable. Although few were written during his time in combat, they did by their omissions shed light on the hardships and fatigue experienced in battle. For obvious reasons his letters home told nothing of the horrors of combat, for he did not wish to unduly alarm his parents.

A number of the letters he received during battle were also absent, as they were often used as kindling to warm cold rations. Other letters, especially those written while at Camp Wolters in Texas, Wind Whistle Hill in England, and during Dad's stint with the Army of Occupation are extensive.

Other primary sources came from personal interviews with those who were there -- Dad's own "band of brothers". Indispensable were fellow members of Company G: Frank Balchunas of Chicago, Illinois; Bill Dudas of Grandville, Michigan; Command Sergeant Major Percy Imbody, (retired), of San Antonio, Texas; Wayne Parker of Mathis, Texas; John Savard of St. Paul, Minnesota; and John Wheeler of Hamilton, Ohio. I must also mention the contributions of Mrs. Anthony (Alice) Bartas of Chicago, Illinois; and Mrs. Joe (Josephine) Guajardo of Corpus Christi, Texas -- both of their husbands were good friends of Dad's. I also offer thanks to Ralph Barrella, junior, of Pennsylvania, who, through a telephone conversation, helped determine the severity of his father's final wound. Although Ralph senior had served in Company F, he had been a close friend of Dad's in England prior to the invasion.

Of considerable help were correspondences with Colonel Robert O. English, (retired), of Punta Gorda, Florida, who had been a lieutenant at Wind Whistle Hill in England, and later assigned to the 38th Infantry's First Battalion after the invasion of France. His knowledge of the regiment's actions was very helpful. Despite the great difference in their wartime ranks (i.e. Dad leaving service as a Pfc.; English years later as full colonel) they always regarded each other simply as fellow soldiers, combat men who had survived the storm. They, too, were brothers in arms.

Another contributor was Colonel Jack Norris, (retired), of Payette, Idaho, the wartime commander of the Second Battalion, Thirty-Eighth Infantry. I had contacted Colonel Norris by telephone, and without hesitation the colonel offered to mail me his personal copy of a very limited unpublished manuscript entitled: "The History of the Second Battalion, Thirty-Eighth Infantry in World War II". He did so not knowing me from the proverbial Adam and the act displays the honor and trust associated with the caliber of men that made his generation great.

Another big "Thank You" goes out to Al Heintzleman of Littleton, Colorado. Al was a member of the 741st Tank Battalion which often supported the attacks of the 2nd Infantry Division in World War II. His input, as well as his unit's history booklet "D-Day to V-E Day and the Story of Vitamin Baker" shed more light on the battles fought. The men of the 2nd Infantry Division will never forget the aid given them by the valiant tankers of the 741st in Normandy, as well as the epic struggle for the Twin Villages of Rocherath and Krinkelt in Belgium during the crucial early days of the Battle of the Bulge.

In my quest for knowledge, I traveled to the National Archives in Washington, DC, and later College Park, Maryland, where I personally conducted weeks of research with the extraordinary help of their excellent staffs. The documents provided verified facts and helped put certain incidents in their most probable order. Also vital to keeping the story in chronological sequence were my trips to the National Personnel Records Center, in St. Louis, Missouri, where I examined every Morning Report of Company G, Thirty-Eighth Infantry, for the period concerning its service during the war. Again, their staff was extremely cooperative.

I've poured over the pages of the volumes of the Official History of the U.S. Army in World War II, as well as many general histories of the war and its battles as guides to my endeavor. Various unit histories have also been useful.

All-in-all, I've been absolutely amazed at how accurate my father's recollections of those terrible years have been. All of his stories have been supported by the sources listed above. As one veteran put it: "These things are burned so deeply into one's memory that they are impossible to forget." So they are with my father.

Finally, I take full responsibility for any errors that may appear in the telling of this story, for it is I who have put it to words and made decisions regarding the placement and nature of the events described. For any such discrepancies, I apologize, for it is not my intent to discredit history, but to tell the story of one old soldier as he recalls his service in a war that was bigger than life itself.

To all our veterans, past and present, I am deeply indebted.

Cleve C. Barkley
Loraine, Illinois
January, 2006

PROLOGUE

In 1933 Adolf Hitler rose to power in Germany. Fanatic support for his Nazi Party was demonstrated in monstrous theatrical exhibitions such as the massive Party Rallies held in Nuremberg. Typically, multitudes of Germans were whipped into an hysteria of patriotic and ethnic vanity, culminating in a frenzy of stiff-armed salutes and a resounding chorus of "Sieg Heil! Sieg Heil!" Hitler beamed smugly, the proud father of the 1,000 Year Reich.

In Asia, Japan was exercising its military muscle by invading Manchuria in China. Setting up a puppet state there, the Japanese looked southward to the remainder of China and greedily licked their lips.

The United States was in the throes of the Great Depression.

That same year, in Quincy, Illinois, 8-year old Harold Gene Barkley, only child of Harry and Nettie Barkley, loaded his toy wagon with home-made stuffed animals that had been lovingly stitched together by his mother. He then paraded them throughout the neighborhood as he pretended to be the ringmaster of a circus. The local children would gather for the show and Harold would command the animals to perform. The kids called Harold "Circus Man".

The Barkleys were poor, but Harold was rich in imagination. At home he would retrieve a great jar of metal buttons his mother kept and sort out the different colors. The various colored buttons represented Indians; the blue ones were always cavalrymen who slept beneath creased cardboard tents and resided in a paste-board fort. When sending his "troops" out on campaign Harold always pushed two blue buttons far in advance of the others to act as scouts to warn the troops of impending danger.[*]

---

[*] Little did he know how this small act of sending scouts forward would be played out in his own life in future years.

By the mid-1930's Japan was conducting savage warfare in China.

Benito Mussolini had come to power in Italy and created a fascist state. Pompous and vain, Mussolini pictured himself as a modern day Caesar and lusted for empire, and longed to recapture the glory that was Rome. His visions of conquest became reality when he sent his modern legions to the backward African nation of Ethiopia in October of 1935. The undisciplined tribesmen were subdued in a matter of months and Mussolini had his glorious "empire". Shortly thereafter, Adolf Hitler had coaxed Mussolini into an alliance -- the Rome-Berlin Axis.

In 1936 civil war erupted in Spain. Communists and international volunteers supported the Loyalists while the Germans and Italian fascists bolstered the rebels. The fascists proved triumphant by 1939.

Before 1938 came to a close Austria was coerced into joining the Nazi German Reich and Germany had "annexed" the Sudetenland of Czechoslovakia. The Germans snatched the remainder of Czechoslovakia the following year while the balance of Europe watched nervously, but did nothing.

Throughout this era, Harold Barkley was waging a "war" of his own. He and his neighborhood pals ambushed each other from alleyways and backyard sheds using notched wooden rifles that launched thick rubber bands cut from old inner-tubes.

When not playing with his friends, young Harold could be found with his nose stuck in a book. One day his father, Harry, took him to the Public Library to get a library card -- it was *free!* Harold started for the children's department but his father reached out and stopped him, saying, "You don't want that. Get a regular library card!" and signed up his son for an adult card. Harold read voraciously -- mysteries and adventure novels were his favorites. He also enjoyed the rhyme and rhythm of poetry and was soon experimenting with prose of his own.

About this time Harold became fascinated with stamp collecting, too.

September 1, 1939 -- World War II began as German Stuka dive bombers and panzers invaded Poland. Two days later France and England declared war on Germany but were unable to help the Poles. Unaided, Poland fell quickly to a new kind of warfare called "Blitzkrieg" -- Lightning War.

After months of inactivity, the Nazi war machine faced west and swept across the Low Countries in May, 1940, totally defeating the Anglo-French armies. The heroic evacuation of Allied troops at Dunkirk was completed as the Nazi hordes occupied most of France within a month. The gallant Battle of Britain raged in the skies above England. Miraculously, England had been saved by the heavily outnumbered Royal Air Force, but the remainder of Europe was lost when Nazi jackboots marched through the Balkans and didn't stop until the island of Crete fell to Hitler's dark legions in May, 1941.

The following months the Germans, flushed with victory, launched several armies against Russia and were at the gates of Moscow by December, 1941. The Nazi war machine seemed unstoppable.

No longer a viable force in Europe, British and Allied forces had withdrawn from Greece and Crete to North Africa where they struggled to maintain a tenuous hold on their base in Egypt.

In German occupied Europe, Hitler initiated the unthinkable -- the mass extermination of all Jews. In the following years, sinister black clouds hung over camps with names like Auschwitz, Treblinka, and Chelmno where humans were incinerated wholesale. In other camps, Jews and other undesirables were forced into slave labor until death.

Meanwhile, the famed Flying Tigers, American mercenary pilots, were downing Japanese Zeroes in the China skies.

During this same period, Harold Barkley, now about 15-years old, was camping out on overnight fishing trips south of Quincy with his school chums. They swam in a flooded quarry called Hidden Lake.

Harold acquired an interest in cave exploring and enrolled in the National Speleological Society, lying about his age in order to obtain membership Once he and a buddy were deep within a cave when their flashlight went out; to their horror they discovered that their back-up batteries were dead and although they had a candle, all of their matches were too damp to ignite. So, for four long hours they groped in total darkness until they found their way out.

December 7, 1941 -- Japanese warplanes attacked the U.S. Pacific Fleet at Pearl Harbor, Hawaii. America was at war.

Strategic Wake Island was lost. The Japanese achieved another naval victory when they sank a number of Allied warships in the Battle of the Java Sea. Then the Philippine Islands fell to the Japanese in the spring of 1942 and the grueling Bataan Death March saw American servicemen brutalized and murdered on their way to prison camps.

U.S. Naval victories at the battles of Coral Sea and Midway in the Pacific Ocean stanched Japanese aggression, and by August, 1942, the United States went on the offensive as Marines stormed ashore on a steamy, unknown island called Guadalcanal in the South Pacific.

While American forces struggled to gain the advantage in the Pacific, German submarines continued to prowl the east coast of the United States and sank merchant ships within view of citizens watching from shore.

In the spring of 1942 a carnival arrived at Quincy and when it pulled up its stakes to depart, 17-year old Harold Barkley was riding with them. He had signed on as a concession "barker" and worked with them through his summer vacation.

By September, Harold was back in Quincy to continue high school, but he had no interest in that -- his summer adventure had given him a taste of freedom and a glimpse of the world. The first day at school he tore up his class assignments and walked out the door. Another carnival was in town and much to his parents' discord, he joined it. Heading southward as weather became colder, they eventually arrived at Paragould, Arkansas, but due to low crowd turnout Harold quit the carnival since he was not making any money.

At this time be became an avid hitch-hiker and traveled as far as southern Texas.

In November, 1942, the Americans and British had invaded the western region of North Africa as they commenced their long march toward the liberation of Europe. The slaughter at Stalingrad in Russia was in progress and American airmen had joined their English comrades in the bombing of Germany.

As 1943 dawned, the Army, Navy and Marines were continuing their bitter island-hopping campaigns in the Pacific while the Allies wrested Sicily from the Germans in the Mediterranean Sea that summer.

Harold Barkley was again in Quincy, Illinois, in early 1943. He had turned 18-years old on March 1st and tried to enlist in the service but was told that he was classified 1-A and would soon be drafted. Meanwhile, a friend had told him of work in Davenport, Iowa, and he was off again, finding employment in a candy factory.

September, 1943 -- The Allies invaded Italy. That same month Harold Barkley finally received his induction notice. For him it was a call to adventure -- he was excited and anxious to go…

IN DEATH'S DARK SHADOW

ACQUAINTANCE

Yes, I know you.
I've felt you near
So many times
Throughout the year.
And all around I've seen the sign
That you had passed throughout our line.
Sometimes you came so close to me
That I could feel your breath;
I've heard you whisper in my ear…
I know you, Mr. Death.

H. Barkley
(Written on the battlefield)

IN DEATH'S DARK SHADOW

CHAPTER 1

CAMP WOLTERS

Harold Barkley gazed through the window of a train car as it rocked and swayed through the flat Illinois countryside and listened to the rhythmic clacking of the wheels as they swept across the rail joints. Outside, the fall scenery passed, washed in colors of bright reds and yellows. Vast fields of ocher-colored corn, ready to harvest, were interrupted by dull green pastures where cattle grazed, dumbly ignorant of their inevitable demise at the slaughter house.

Towns came and went... Camp Point... Golden... Macomb... Galesburg. Small towns; large ones; each marking one step closer to Harold's destination: Chicago.

He was eighteen years old when he received notice that he had been inducted into the Armed Forces of the United States. That was on the 29th of September, 1943. Now, a few weeks later, he was on his way to report to the Induction Station located in Chicago.

At the Induction Station he was herded through the various testing stations with a throng of other prospective soldiers. Being a wiry five feet, six inches tall and of average intelligence, he easily passed the necessary tests and physical and was sent to Camp Grant, near Rockford, Illinois, where he was mustered into the United States Army on the 20th of October.

At Camp Grant he was stripped of his clothes and issued uniforms -- there would be no need for civilian garb in the near future. His old clothes were boxed up and shipped home to his parents. More medical examinations followed and Harold found himself clutching in white-knuckled horror to a dentist's chair as his teeth were scraped and prodded with sinister implements. Shuffling down another long line of disgruntled young men he was soon at the mercy of needle-wielding medics who dutifully harpooned each recruit with a series of inoculations. Harold hated needles.

Staying only briefly at Camp Grant, he was transported by rail with other draftees to the Infantry Training Center at Camp Wolters, Texas, arriving in late October. This camp was located near the town of Mineral Wells, lodged in the rolling hills of north-central Texas. Harold had told his folks back home that he hoped to get into an anti-tank unit -- he now had his chance as this training was given at Camp Wolters.

The train wheezed to a halt, then disgorged its consignment of recruits. The passengers assembled loosely, an odd mix of civilians masquerading as soldiers who were greeted by a real soldier with a stack of chevrons sewn to each sleeve. This awesome figure barked his charges into formation and gave them a brief "you're-in-the-Army-now" speech, then marched them through camp, passing street after street of barracks. Each barrack was identical to the next -- two-storied, white washed, wooden structures. Eventually the recruits were halted and ordered to enter one such building. Inside were orderly rows of steel-framed beds with a shelf above each for personal items. Long ranks of windows allowed daylight to grace the room. This would be their home for the duration of their training.

Harold Barkley was assigned to the 1st platoon of Company C, 53rd Infantry Training Battalion, 12th Regiment. His company commander was First Lieutenant Roy Roughton, but the man who oversaw every detail of his life from this point on was his platoon sergeant, Sergeant McKay.* McKay was a small man who had seen action against the Japanese in the Pacific. He believed in the dictum of "tough but fair" when it came to training his men, and in return they came to respect him, and in time even grew to like him and considered him a hell of a good guy.

After receiving rifles, Company C began its actual training on the first day of November, 1943. Initially they learned the rudiments of elementary soldiering, chiefly military bearing and courtesy, discipline and close order drill. But as days wore one, and days evolved into weeks, the recruits became familiar with other aspects of their deadly new trade. When not drilling or wearing themselves out in physical conditioning they were learning the hazards of the obstacle course where they leaped barriers, swung over pits on ropes and wriggled prone through long culvert pipes. Marching was done with rifles and full field packs. They were becoming fit. After only three weeks at Camp Wolters, Barkley had gained six pounds of muscle.

As future infantrymen, they discovered that their primary battle weapon was the M-1 rifle, the famous Garand. This was the only semi-automatic rifle used as the basic infantry weapon by troops of any country during the war. When the time came to actually fire this weapon, the entire company formed up and marched several miles to the firing range. Once there they blasted away at distant targets, taking advice from instructors whenever they did something wrong and did their best to make corrections. Private Barkley really liked the M-1, but long stretches on the firing line became tedious. When the company was finished on the range they reassembled and marched back to the barracks.

---

* McKay is a fictitious name The sergeant's real name is long lost to memory.

It seemed that any spare time was spent by pulling KP duty at the mess hall or cleaning the barracks. Earlier, during Barkley's brief sojourn at Camp Grant, he learned to take these tasks seriously. One of the few chores he had then was KP duty. A number of inductees had been ordered to report to the mess sergeant who assigned Barkley and several others as dishwashers. One of the other draftees lost his grip on a slippery coffee mug and it crashed to the floor and shattered. A suppressed moan arose from the cooks. *"The Major's cup!"* someone gasped. Apparently the mug was the personal property of some officer. Now it was broken. The perpetrator was singled out by the mess sergeant and given a royal butt-chewing -- it was the *Major's* cup! The poor fellow was thoroughly shaken and worried sick about the impending consequences.

The recruits were young. Most were eighteen and nineteen year old kids with a sprinkling of older men tossed in. Nearly all were drafted men. The majority were away from home for the first time and were eager to form friendships during these early weeks of Army life. In their off duty time they'd gather in impromptu "bull sessions" where they discovered details about each other's pre-Army life:

There was William Ackle, a swell kid from Louisiana, long-faced and friendly.

Ralph Anderson picked up the nickname "Andy", naturally.

Frank Balchunas was a bespectacled 36-year old Postal Clerk from Chicago. He was on his second tour of basic training, being recycled after getting some needed dental work and replacements for broken glasses. Of all the recruits, he knew his way around camp best since he had been there awhile longer than the others. Being 18 years Barkley's senior, he was amazed to find himself in the infantry. His family was of Lithuanian stock -- his mother spoke only her native tongue. He was the last of three brothers to enter the Army.

Anthony Bartas, like Balchunas, hailed from Chicago. One of the older men, he was quite overweight and reminded Barkley somewhat of the comedian Oliver Hardy of "Laurel and Hardy" fame. But he also resembled the character "Major Hoople" of the Sunday comics, so his buddies christened him "The Major", a name which would stick with him for the duration of his Army life. A married man, he was a pleasant fellow who enjoyed razzing the others in a good natured way.

Elmer Antonelli was another Chicago boy and as his name indicated, was the very picture of an Italian-American lad. Young and husky, he had black hair and big, dark eyes. In troubled situations his eyes would grow even wider and he'd ask, "What are we going to do?" Usually Barkley gave his standard answer, "Whatever we have to." Antonelli hated to be called by his given name, Elmer, and "Major" Bartas picked up on this, needling him incessantly with phrases like, "What ya gonna do, El-l-mer?", drawing out the "l" with a billy-goat flutter.

Walter Augustus was another Illinoisan, a sturdy, twenty-five year old country boy who hailed from the eastern part of the state.

Irwin Bourgeois was a Louisiana Cajun whose name was soon corrupted to "Bushwa".

Carlo Flossi was another youngster of Italian heritage.

Grant Bell sported dark hair and a long, lantern jaw. Whenever he wore his helmet Barkley noticed that it sat low on his head just above his eyes which peered spookily from beneath its rim.

George Arndt, though a draftee like the others, was enthusiastic about military service. A hard-charging, gung-ho young man, he later volunteered for the paratroops.

As the bull session evolved, Barkley told them of his experiences hitch-hiking through the States, cave exploring and working two seasons with traveling carnivals. Several of the fellows snickered doubtfully, prompting "Major" Bartas to lean forward and ask, "*How* old are you?" not believing that an 18-year old could have done all of that.

Barkley went by the simple moniker of "Bark".

Meanwhile, life went on as usual back home, in Quincy, Illinois. Harold's mother would write and declare how proud she and his father were of him. She noted how all of a sudden her son was a "grown up man." She thought Harold was the finest soldier in the land and had bought a nice service flag to display in her window -- the blue star indicating that her only child was in the military.

5

She always managed to include sage advice, too. "Keep your lips closed, your eyes and ears open and you'll be a good soldier", she wrote, and, "Darling, watch your spelling. Improve yourself where ever you can in education." She also implored Harold not to spend his money foolishly.

She said she was still recovering from an operation that had removed a tumor from her side some time ago and was not capable of doing much work. Harold's father, Harry, was still employed at Dayton-Dowd, a factory, but was feeling sick and had missed some work. This hurt them financially as money was scarce -- times were still hard. She urged her son to try to get a matching allotment in order to help out back home.

Harold learned that his dad was now the local "Block Warden", charged with the wartime security of the neighborhood. He was supposed to study flash cards depicting silhouettes of various aircraft to aid him in identifying any planes that might pass overhead. Allegedly, he was to give warning in the highly unlikely event that the planes were German or Japanese raiders, and then ensure that all the neighbors' windows were blacked out. It was an extreme precaution to say the least, but it demonstrated the prevailing spirit of "We're all in this together", so therefore served some purpose. But young Harold found it almost comical in light of the fact that there were no aircraft capable of making the monumental journey half-way across the continent to bomb Quincy.

On the lighter side, he was told that his dog, Spotty, had given birth to six pups, so now, along with Tippie, they had eight dogs running around. The old black cat, Kits, was jealous of the dogs and would take a random swipe at them whenever the opportunity was ripe.

Harold's long-time friend, Ernie Hemmings, wrote of local happenings from the viewpoint of a teen-ager, keeping him up to date on friends back home, including the issuance of report cards at High School. He had also told Harold that Pete, the ticket taker at the Orpheum Theater, was still able to slip the guys into the movies for free.

The movies... how Barkley missed them.

Camp Wolters, Texas, late November, 1943 -- A shrill whistle pierced the crisp morning air and men came clambering down the barracks steps to assemble for roll call in the company street. Barkley was already in ranks when a chorus of guffaws and derisive laughter drew his attention back to the barracks. There, tumbling down the steps, came a figure with his arms entangled in the legs of his newly issued long underwear as he struggled to pull them over his head and wear them on the outside of his uniform as if a sweater. What a sight! It was the Company "Jonah"[*]. This poor creature had a tendency to foul up nearly everything he endeavored to do and was always slow to catch on to any new skills. As the recruits were called to attention the Jonah still had his long johns draped over part of his head and shoulders and was immediately chewed out by Sergeant McKay. Everyone wondered if he was really a bit retarded or only playing the part to obtain a discharge from the Army through a Section Eight.[**]

The training escalated. The company set out on 20-mile marches across the rolling Texas hills with full field packs and rifles. The route proved strenuous and Barkley's new buddy "The Major" (Bartas) would always become winded after only three or four miles and would eventually fall out and wait for the trucks that followed to pick up stragglers. Although the marches were grueling, Barkley always came through okay. Frank Balchunas, despite his advanced age over the rest of the platoon, also managed to complete the entire march.

As training intensified they learned how to set up and fire a machine gun and battered each other in bayonet drill. They were taught the correct way to toss a hand grenade with each man taking his turn under the critical eye of an instructor. When the Jonah's turn came, his comrades watched with marked interest, for they knew he was apt to do something foolish. Their fears were realized when, to their utter horror, he fumbled the grenade and dropped it at his feet. Only the lightning reaction of the instructor averted a disaster as he quickly retrieved the grenade and pitched it down range where it exploded. The boys began to worry more seriously about the Jonah

---

[*] Jonah -- a misfit.
[**] Section Eight – a medical discharge for those mentally incapable of performing military duties.

after that. He had goofed up before, but this was serious -- maybe he really wasn't cut out for Army life.

As training progressed, the art of war became more personal as they were taught what Barkley called "dirty fighting". They were given basic instruction in the use of commando skills where they learned how to disarm an attacking soldier or catch an opponent off balance and toss him with the aid of their hips. They practiced hand-to-hand fighting using knives and fists. Private Barkley expressed his views on this type of training to his Grandma Tryon[*] in Missouri: "That is pretty rough and a lot of the boys get hurt that way. I expect to get a few bruises from it but it will teach us to take care of ourselves." They were becoming aggressive. They were learning how to be effective killers.

One day Barkley had a difference of opinion with a young lieutenant who was notorious for arrogantly slapping his thigh with a riding quirt. The lieutenant thought eighteen-year-old Barkley needed to shave. Barkley didn't think so. It was a decidedly one-sided argument. The end result -- Private Barkley got extra KP duty all afternoon the following Sunday.

Company C shouldered their rifles and marched out of camp. In time they arrived at an open field that was crisscrossed with barbed wire. This was the infiltration course.

They were told that they were to crawl beneath the wire, following pre-determined lanes, until they reached the opposite end of the course. While attempting to do this they would be subjected to live machine gun fire which would be leveled about two feet above their heads. They were cautioned to keep low. Also, there would be explosions from pre-set charges along the course, safely placed, but located close enough to simulate incoming artillery.

Barkley's squad was to initiate the exercise. Many of the boys were noticeably nervous as they approached the obstacle. But Barkley felt otherwise. He knew the machine guns were supposed to be firing

---

[*] Grandma Tryon was the mother of Harold Barkley's father, Harry. Twice widowed, Charlie Tryon was her third husband.

only two feet overhead, but reasoned they had been told that to scare them and reckoned they would probably shoot higher than that. But even at two feet one had plenty of crawl space to maneuver under. The dynamite charges were clearly marked so no one with any sense at all would get near them. *This should be a piece of cake!*

The signal was given to go. Barkley wriggled on his belly with his rifle cradled in his arms and began to crawl the distance. Bullets snapped overhead and the charges belched fire, sending clods of dirt cascading all around, but he kept going, slithering rapidly beneath the barbed wire. Before long he emerged from the opposite end of the course. Rising, he looked left and right to see how many of the other "infiltrators" had made it. He was the first one through.

What he didn't know was that General Magruder, the camp commander, and a group of officers were observing the trainees tackle the course. They noticed Private Barkley standing there all alone and the general summoned him as the other soldiers began to clear the wire.

"Let me see your rifle," the general barked. Barkley presented his weapon for inspection. Apparently the general thought anyone completing the course so quickly had to have gotten his rifle dirty. It was clean. Impressed, the general returned the weapon, saying, "Very good," and dismissed him.

Later, rumor had it that one of the recruits chanced upon a rattlesnake in his lane, panicked, sprang up and was killed by a burst of machine gun fire. This was serious business!

One day the company was marched to another open field and ordered to dig foxholes. They were advised to dig them plenty deep, for a tank would soon be rolling over the top of each one. Holes completed, the men hunkered down.

Before long a powerful engine roared from afar. Then a creaking and clanking and a trembling of earth announced the gargantuan's approach. Barkley crouched deeper in his hole as the rumbling intensified and suddenly a great shadow loomed over his foxhole -- and then it was dark.

Although he knew it was a training exercise, he was a little nervous as the treads ground soil into his hideout. Then the darkness turned to light as the tank churned on, seeking other trainees' holes. Somehow, despite the degree of danger involved, it was a thrilling experience for Barkley and even seemed like fun.

When the tank had completed its mission word was passed that all was clear and everyone crawled from their shelters. Assembling in clusters, young men chattered excitedly about their ordeal. Some of the fellows appeared shaken by the experience and a few had actually been terrified.

Later, back at the barracks, Barkley gave the experience a lot of thought. He carefully analyzed the situation from the viewpoint of both the infantryman and the tanker. What did he find most horrifying as the man in the foxhole? And if he were a tanker, how would he be able to eliminate the enemy soldier in the hole?

After weighing the possibilities he came up with an idea. *What if the tank had a machine gun mounted in the floor?* With such an apparatus as this one could drive over a foxhole and kill the poor wretch below with a quick burst of machine gun fire. Therefore the occupant would be unable to spring up after the tank rolled over his position and attack it from the rear with anti-tank weapons.

It sounded good. He wrote up his suggestion, complete with diagrams, and mailed it to the War Department in Washington. He concluded his introductory letter with, "…it could stand some improvement but I will leave that to you and your office." He believed he was doing his part to help win the war.

Throughout their training Barkley and his friends were subject to the orders and commands of their superiors. The non-commissioned officers (sergeants and corporals) were generally a pretty good lot of fellows. They were tough but never cruel.

The officers, too, for the most part, were respectable and conscientious men, performing their duty while maintaining the gap that separated the castes of enlisted men from officers. As in everything, though, there are exceptions to the rule. For the men of Company C this exception was a young "Brown Bar", a freshly commissioned Second Lieutenant anxious to demonstrate his newly acquired powers. He was, to use a simple term, a real prick. Pompous and arrogant, he strutted about the camp slapping his leg with a riding quirt, emitting an aura of supremacy over the trainees.

He was always on the alert for anything that wasn't exactly per regulations and quick to make the offenders suffer for any such infraction. Lack of military bearing and courtesy seemed to be the lieutenant's pet peeves. It was not uncommon to see a soldier spring to attention and give a hand salute as Lieutenant "Quirt" approached. Invariably, Lieutenant Quirt would stop and spout, "That's not good enough, soldier," as he tapped the man with his crop. "Do it again!" The recruit would repeat the salute to the lieutenant's satisfaction. Barkley had already had one encounter with this pompous ass concerning his shaving habits. He was destined to have more.

During the course of their training the men would be given lectures by Lieutenant Quirt on tactics or perhaps the proper placement of certain types of weapons. At the conclusion of his speech he would ask if there were any questions. Occasionally a solider might ask what one was to do in a particular tactical dilemma. The lieutenant would reply with his pat answer: "Well, it depends on the situation and the terrain," and leave it at that, not really giving a satisfactory explanation. With Lieutenant Quirt, it *always* depended on the situation and the terrain. The trainees didn't learn much from that.

On one occasion the company was assembled on some bleachers, receiving another lecture prior to tackling a field problem. As Lieutenant Quirt droned on with his monotonous monologue he abruptly aimed his quirt at Barkley and asked, "What would *you* do in that situation, soldier?"

After a moment, Barkley answered wryly, "Well, that depends on the situation and the terrain, sir." Suppressed chuckles rippled through the gallery.

Lieutenant Quirt saw no humor in the mimicry and the laughter abruptly ceased beneath his icy stare. "Well, soldier, I want you to get down here and run twice around this field with your rifle held over your head. And leave your pack on," he sneered.

The pack was full and heavy. But Barkley was fit after weeks of physical conditioning and he was tough. "I can do that!" he answered brazenly, and promptly took off on his two lap tour of the field.

The training was not limited to the destruction of the enemy. There were also the more tedious chores of every day Army life. Inspections were frequently held and the platoon bustled with activity in preparation. The barracks had to be kept spotlessly clean. Trainees were kept busy outside as well, policing the company area, keeping it free of litter. Uniforms had to be in good condition, pressed and clean; shoes polished. Beds were to be made up smooth and tight. Weapons were field stripped with each piece meticulously scrubbed, cleaned and oiled, then re-assembled, ready for eagle-eyed scrutiny.

When inspection day came, Platoon Sergeant McKay would bellow, "Atten-SHUN!" and the recruits would stand rigidly at the foot of their beds as a bevy of officers surged into the barracks. The officers scrutinized each man and his equipment, bed, etc. If something was amiss, they'd bring it to the attention of Sergeant McKay. Once the inspection was completed, the officers would leave and the violators would be promptly chewed out by the sergeant. Corrections were made and the entire platoon would often find themselves scrubbing vigorously with buckets and tiny brushes to extricate whatever miniscule particles of dirt had been allowed to desecrate their barracks.

The threat of KP duty loomed over everyone. If a soldier was unfortunate enough to find his name on that duty roster he was doomed to long, drawn out hours of boring work in the mess hall. A private might be assigned the time-honored peeling of potatoes or similar food processing duties. More than likely the soldier would endure the drudgery of washing all of the cooks' pots and pans. Even the garbage cans were scrubbed bright.

On one occasion, Lieutenant Quirt decided that the length of Private Barkley's hair was un-military. It was two inches long. But for Barkley, money didn't come easily and he didn't want to spend the 40 cents required for the clipping. Again he lost the argument and found himself with another stint of extra KP duty the following Sunday. Fortunately the mess sergeant was sympathetic and Barkley was designated a table waiter, a less toilsome job.

Camp Wolters had all the amenities of a small city. The Post Exchange, or PX, was similar to a general store where a soldier could find items that were not strictly GI. The post also held the basic medical services, including an optometrist who determined that Barkley needed glasses to correct the vision in his left eye. As a consequence, he received two pairs of spectacles, but when he put them on he couldn't see a damned thing, so threw them away! He could see fine as it was.

There was a chapel to serve the soldiers' spiritual needs. When needed, a trainee could get a haircut at the camp barber shop. The post also sported a theater where trainees could take in a movie and a Service Club where off duty personnel could unwind after the grind of training.

However, there existed some forms of entertainment that were not offered at the camp. For this the men looked to the nearby town of Mineral Wells. If one could wangle a pass he could get into town for a night of civilian diversions. To each soldier this meant different things -- maybe just to get a real cheeseburger at a real restaurant; or perhaps a different movie was playing. There were beer halls where a soldier could slake his thirst. And of course there was always someplace to go dancing, and dancing meant girls. Being an Army post town, Mineral Wells had all types of girls, good and bad. As Frank Balchunas noted: "We call the town 'Venereal Wells.'"

As for Barkley, he didn't dance and didn't care to drink, either. After all, he was only eighteen years old. He did love the movies, though, and he and young Ackle or Balchunas or perhaps one of the other fellows would take in a show in town and maybe get a Coke and a sandwich afterwards. They didn't have much spending money.

On one trip to Mineral Wells, Frank Balchunas visited a local tattoo parlor and had his left forearm engraved with an ornate design and the word "Mother" scrolled across it. (Later, when home en route for overseas, his mother saw it and gave it a big kiss.)

Whatever the diversion a soldier was seeking, he had to be satisfied with whatever Mineral Wells had to offer since one needed a special pass to go to Fort Worth, the big city. And special passes were not readily available.

However, Barkley's buddy, Frank Balchunas, managed to get a pass to Fort Worth once and steered for one of its many saloons. Frank liked his beer and could handle it as well as the next Joe. He had a beer and then another and the next thing he knew he was sitting on the street curb with a fuzzy head, having no idea how he got there. Some MPs came along and picked him up. He couldn't give any reason for his stupor since he only had a couple of beers. He surmised that someone must have slipped him a Mickey Finn -- knock-out pills. It was back to camp for Frank.

Anthony Bartas, the hefty man dubbed "The Major", got a pleasant surprise when he received word that his wife, Alice, was coming for a two week visit. She found accommodations in Mineral Wells. Whenever he could, Bartas got a pass and met her in town. A number of the boys paid their respects to the couple and even pitched in to buy them two bottles of whiskey before she had to leave. They all liked The Major -- he was such a friendly guy. On their last night together, a Saturday, The Major told his wife to be sure and wake him as he had to report back to camp on Sunday. When morning came they embraced in a fond, sad farewell. And then she was gone.

Of course passes weren't available for the asking. Usually the men had to make use of their free time in camp as best they could. Barkley had always written stories, and also had an inherent flair for poetry. He utilized some of his off-duty time jotting down poems and then sent them home in letters. His mother really liked one in particular. In time she sent it to a publishing company, Westmore Music Corporation, and it was published with accompanying music in a song book. It was entitled "HOW FAR IS IT TO HEAVEN?", and was to be aired on NBC's "The Million Dollar Band" radio program. There was even talk of incorporating it into a Hollywood movie.

Naturally, the only contact with home was through the mail. Barkley's friend, Ernie, wrote that back in October he and several of the fellows had put some soap to good use the night before Halloween and that their pal, Pete, had given a couple of the boys tickets for the movies. All in all, it sounded as if the fellows back home were having a grand time.

Barkley's mother, Nettie, did most of the writing for herself and his father, reporting that Grandpa Courtney had come over from Missouri and had stayed with them for a few days in November.

December found both of his parents down with colds. Barkley also learned that his mother was supposed to return to the doctor for a check-up after her operation but she just couldn't face him without any money. Meanwhile she had been selling the pups for one dollar each, but gave a couple away, too. They decided to keep the one referred to as the midget. They named him "Pig".

She and Harry were tired of receiving shipments of various slot machines. Barkley had been buying them since his carnival days and hoped that they would prove to be a good investment as well as a source of entertainment after he got out of the Army. But now his mother complained that their house was taking on the appearance of a gambling hall!

Christmas was coming. Nettie thought that she and Harry would stay at home and not cross over to Missouri for the holiday. She told her son that Grandma Tryon, Harry's re-married mother, had sent Harry a wool sweater and some tobacco for Christmas; she sent Nettie two handkerchiefs and two candy bars.

Harold's parents were sending him a new fountain pen for Christmas. "We can't afford much", his mother wrote, "too many Dr. bills, but if we are well and know you are alright that's all that counts." Harry added a few lines, saying that he thought that his son should receive a good Christmas dinner. He recalled that during the last war "we shure had a good dinner when I was in the Army we all had passes in the Company that were not on special duty from day before Christmas untill New Yr Day."

His mother also sent a box of home-made candies. She summed up her Holiday message this way: "Hope you keep well and have a nice Christmas… I'd hang up my sock if I could find you in it… With Love from Mother and Dad."

Christmas came and went. The weather at Camp Wolters steadily worsened as winter swept across Northern Texas and by January it was not uncommon to see the troops training in the sleet and snow.

By then, Barkley and his friends had graduated to another plateau of their training -- anti-tank school. This is what he had had hoped for. He was finally learning the skills necessary to destroy enemy tanks.

They became acquainted with the 37mm anti-tank gun, designated by the Army as the M-3. Mounted on a two-wheeled gun carriage and weighing 912 pounds, it fired a light shell whose projectile weight just under two pounds. It was capable of penetrating only about 2 ½ inches of armor at a distance of 500 yards, even though the maximum range was better than 12,000 yards. The M-3 was obsolete before America entered the war. Nonetheless, it made a good training tool for future anti-tank gunners. If they mastered this piece of ordnance they would be given instruction on the more powerful 57mm gun.

Barkley enjoyed operating the 37mm gun. The men took turns learning the different positions required to set up and fire the weapon. Five men manned each gun: a gunner, the loader, and three ammunition handlers.

Once the basics of the weapon were understood the boys were trucked to the field with their guns bucking along in tow. Arriving at the gunnery range, each gun crew worked as a team as they unlimbered their cannon, swung it around to face the target, then stabilized the gun by spreading the split trail. Kneeling behind the weapon, the gunner would then use the sighting device and crank the barrel to track a target while ammunition handlers passed shells from the truck to the loader. When the weapon was loaded and properly sighted, the gunner fired its projectile toward the target.

In time the men learned how to hit a moving "tank" as plywood silhouettes cruised along tracks some distance away. Barkley was becoming a pretty good gunner.

Having become proficient with the tiny 37mm gun, the students moved on to master the larger 57mm gun, called the M-1 (designating the first model of this caliber of weapon).

Weighing in at 2700 pounds, it was nearly three times heftier than the old M-3. With a maximum range of 10,260 yards it could smash through nearly three inches of armor at 1,000 yards. The warhead of each shell weighed about 6 ½ pounds, not counting the brass casing which contained the propellant gunpowder. The overall length of casing and shell was almost two feet.

This gun had some kick to it! Barkley knew that he could do some serious damage with this one. The training continued in the same manner as with the 37mm piece -- each man learning and understanding the stations needed to successfully operate this tank killer.

Through the winter weeks the training concentrated primarily on gunnery practice and maintenance of the gun. By mid-January the apprentice gunners were ready to fire for the record. Their scores would determine if they would qualify as anti-tank gunners. On the first day of the course thirty targets were presented to each trainee.

When Barkley's turn came he carefully sighted the cannon on each silhouette and methodically blew away twenty-five out of thirty "tanks", blasting neat holes in the traversing plywood targets. Thirty more targets were to be offered the following day -- of these he only had to hit nine to qualify.

The second day on the range was a great success. Barkley was elated with his marksmanship with the 57mm gun. Calmly aiming and firing, he easily destroyed the targets necessary to achieve a First Class Gunner's rating. He proudly wrote home that "it means I will ship out as a gunner 1st class and I will be probably a anti Tank man from now on till I eather come home or my dog tag is shipped home in a letter."

BULL SESSION
(Several men, squad area)

"I just heard that the batch that trained here just before us is overseas already."

"Boy! They didn't stay stateside very long!"

"Yeah, but before we go over we're supposed to get a seven-day furlough enroute to our embarkation point."

"Seven days ain't much time…"

"Hell, I'd only have time to say 'hello' and 'good-bye'!"

"Seven days sure ain't much time!"

"'Heard that there's a bill before Congress that they'll extend the furlough to fourteen days."

"I told my folks about that. My mother sure hopes we get the fourteen days."

"What do you think, El-l-l-mer?"

"Antonelli! Call me Antonelli!"

"Awright, El-l-l-mer."

The platoon had completed its anti-tank schooling, and although not everyone qualified, all continued with their regular infantry training. They had already learned about marching, camping and surviving in the field. They could fire a variety of weapons, take them apart for cleaning and reassemble them. They had practiced patrolling and infiltration of enemy positions at night. Each knew how to defeat another soldier man to man. Now the time had come, after almost three months of training, to put all of these elements of soldierly skills together in combined field exercises.

It was late January and the icy winds howled through the Texas hills. The frigid climate was made worse by occasional bone-chilling rain, sleet or snow. The trainees of Company C braced for the ordeal of the next few weeks.

First they were dumped off at a place called Dry Gulch where they made camp and bivouacked for four days. Dry Gulch was a misnomer -- it rained every day that they were there -- a cold, cold rain that soaked through their clothing and set their teeth to chattering. The men did their best to resolve the field problems presented them while coping with the inclement weather. Before they left the Gulch they were sleeping in a blizzard!

After the frozen bivouac at Dry Gulch the trainees were allowed to return to their barracks for one day in order to recover. Much of their time was expended by cleaning rifles and equipment in preparation for the second stage of the program.

Baker's Hollow was next on the agenda. During the next four days Company C stalked through a combat course, alert for "enemy soldiers" that took the form of pop-up dummies that sprang into view from the cover of heavy brush or from behind trees. The fledgling warriors blasted away at their "enemies" with blank cartridges from their M-1's. If the dummies were close enough, they'd thrust at them with bayonets or club them with rifle butts.

The following four days were spent at Hell's Bottom where the familiar infiltration course awaited them. Again machine gun bullets snapped overhead as men wormed their way beneath barbed wire. As before, dynamite charges showered them with clumps of earth.

Also at Hell's Bottom, they were instructed in the proper method to advance behind an artillery barrage. As the men went forward, artillery shells burst before them, sending fragments of steel screaming through the air. The distance between the skirmish line and the impacting shells was carefully calculated to give the trainees a taste of what it might be like in combat, yet kept them safe from actual harm.

Immediately after completing the course, the company strapped on field packs, slung their other equipment and stepped off on a 25-mile hike. At the conclusion of this grueling march they conducted night maneuvers where rival platoons skirmished and ambushed each other in cold darkness. Aggressive spirits surfaced throughout the gloomy night and a number of men came away with cuts and bruises and a few nursed broken bones.

Weary after two weeks of intensive training, the men returned to the warmth of their barracks.

Rest, however, was not in store for them. On the heels of the field exercises came extensive instruction on mine detection where the recruits learned how to probe the earth with bayonets until metal was struck. The trick was to insert the blade into the soil at such a sharp angle that it would not trigger the mine!

The training program at Camp Wolters appeared to be very comprehensive. There didn't seem to be anything that the trainees couldn't cope with.

Back at the barracks the men anxiously read the war news, which was printed in news briefs posted on the bulletin board. It seemed that the dominant theme was the war against Japan in the Pacific Theater. There were clips of the fighting in Italy and other paragraphs on "side show" actions, but the focus of the news appeared riveted on the island warfare in the Pacific.

It was mid-February and the men were about to receive orders concerning their next duty station after completion of their training. Although no one really knew when or where they were going, they all realized that it would be soon. The news briefs helped fan the flames of rumor -- the boys were certain that they would be up against the Japs.

Barkley wrote home: "I just signed my shipping papers. Only 14 men out of our plattoon is shipping out and I get 7 days at home. I know where I am going but I can't tell you for shure untill I get home but I will be positively on a banana boat on the way accross when I finnish my 7 days at home. Incidentally I am going to..." and following this he drew a half-page illustration of a South Seas Island complete with palm trees, beaches, grass huts and a hula girl. A word balloon had the girl saying: "Me hulla a ta wa." Then, in the ocean surrounding the island was depicted a shark and two natives in an out-rigger canoe saying: "Me a hulla. Hulla-tu-a-wa-wa", and "Southea Pacificia". Young Barkley was certain that he was heading for the islands -- and he'd only get a seven day furlough en route before he went over. The bill before Congress for the fourteen days had apparently failed.

The mail from home kept coming in regularly. His pal, Ernie Hemmings, had seen the collection of slot machines that cluttered the Barkley house and thought that Harold's room looked pretty swell with all of those machines.

Barkley's mother had sent a "Bullet-Proof, Good Luck Bible". It was a small Testament sporting a brass plate for a cover. Accompanying it was an advertisement in which a soldier assured the reader that it actually saves lives in battle. Supposedly, the thin brass cover would deflect any bullets. "I want you to be sure and carry that Bible in your left shirt pocket always," she wrote, "and read it, too."

He learned that his father was back to work at Dayton-Dowd, but had had a cold for three weeks. When his mother read that Harold was sending home some of his pay, she complained that she and

Harry had been notified by the government that they would receive $10.00 a month, but never received it.

His mother was still hoping that her boy would be granted a 14-day furlough. She said that she was trying to fatten her chickens so that they could have a nice chicken dinner when Harold got home. "I think they are too smart to get fat", she lamented, "still I have 9 and the two hens, they won't lay either, 'slackers' laid 3 and quit."

She was worried sick about her son: "I sure hope this awful war comes to a quick end before you or any more of the boys have to go over."

Camp Wolters, February, 1944 -- In silent black and white the soldiers advanced. One was struck in the face by a bullet or a piece of shrapnel and had fallen, writhing and kicking with a horrific silent scream. The only sound, however, was the clacking of the motion picture projector as it cast its flickering images on the screen. The trainees sat mesmerized by the terrifying scene before them.

As the film continued, it centered on the wounded man in gory detail. His lower jaw had been ripped away and his mouth was a great bloody mass. Splinters of shattered bone protruded near his nose, augmented by splattered teeth. Stretcher bearers rushed forward under fire to take the poor wretch away. His comrades moved on.

Barkley surmised that these films were intended to toughen up the boys mentally for what lay ahead.

The film resumed, displaying dead and wounded soldiers. The camera peeked inside a destroyed tank and revealed what happens to fragile human beings when a shell from an anti-tank gun scores. It wasn't pretty. *That will be my work*, Barkley thought.

The images stuck in his mind. Speaking of wounds, he wrote home: "When I get mine, I hope it knocks me out when it hits so I can't see what it did to me."

It was late February and the training was all but finished. There was nothing left to learn except by actual experience -- the True Teacher. Anxiety ruled. Soon, very soon, each man would have his orders. Barkley cautioned his folks not to send anything other than letters, as he'd be shipping out before long.

IN DEATH'S DARK SHADOW

He discovered that his platoon would be broken up after they left Camp Wolters with some of his barrack room buddies bound for different locations. His friend Ackel, for example, was not shipping out with him; he had orders for another destination. They exchanged addresses and vowed they'd keep in touch.

Harold Barkley's nineteenth birthday passed without fanfare on March 1st -- it seemed insignificant in light of the war. He and his comrades were getting restless waiting on their furloughs. They had been informed that they would be sent immediately overseas following their seven-day furloughs. A number of recruits didn't believe they'd go over that soon. To squelch their hopes about staying stateside, they were told that some of the guys who shipped out at the same time their company was formed four months earlier had already been killed.

This sobering news left each to ponder his own tentative future. The stark reality that they, too, may soon be faced with mutilation or death evoked a wealth of emotions ranging from disbelief to surrendering to fate ("Well, this is it") to various degrees of cowardice and self-doubt. Barkley was angered when he discovered that a few shirkers in his company immediately sought duty in other branches of the Army to avoid being sent to combat. He vented his anger in a letter home:

"I know how those guys get those easy jobs. It is just like a half dozzen guys we got here. Whatever the Plattoon sergant says they aggree and laugh at all his jokes and tell him what a swell guy he is so they can get to be a squad leader or a office job or as a corporal of supply so they won't have to go across. The biggest suckass we have here was 1-A untill they talked of shipping us right out and some they would keep here that were not 1-A so he developed a weak heart or something and now they are going to keep him here.

"They think they are better than us and because they were made squad leaders or Plattoon acting Sergants they bossed us around for 17 weeks.

"Now a lot of the guys that gave out the orders and wouldn't do a thing that the Sergant wouldn't like are going to combat and I will say one thing -- they will be lucky if they come back for they will go across with the same guys they trained with and they hate them."

22

Each day the men checked the bulletin board. Barkley became agitated when he discovered that a different group of soldiers was being released before his company. However, he was certain that he would be heading home by the next Saturday or Monday, and was positive that he'd be home by the following Wednesday, March 8th, at the latest. "Don't write," he warned his parents, "as I will leave before I get letter probably."

Ultimately the time came and the appropriate furloughs were issued. Surprisingly, Barkley's orders commanded him to report to an east coast post at the end of his sojourn at home, not one on the west coast. It seemed that he would be fighting the Germans, not the Japanese when he went overseas.

CHAPTER 2

HOME

March 10, 1944, Quincy, Illinois -- Dormant now, the train spilled its passengers onto the platform where a flock of citizens waited anxiously, hallooing and waving to gain the attention of their respective parties. A sprinkling of soldiers and sailors wended among the crowd but drew scant notice, for it was the third year of the war and soldiers and sailors were a common sight in these troubling times. Hugs and kisses greeted some while others departed unattended. A cool breeze chased the remaining passengers into the street and soon the station was all but empty.

Private Barkley hoisted his barracks bag and stepped away from the station. Badges dangled from his breast pocket, boasting marksmanship and proficiency with the rifle, machine gun, anti-tank gun, tank weapons and the bayonet. With his load balanced on one shoulder he began the short trek home. As he passed the rows of dwellings in Quincy's south end he was probably looked upon as just another soldier home on leave. But when he turned east off of 8th Street and climbed the steep steps to his house on Monroe he wasn't just another soldier -- he was Harry's and Nettie's son. He was, to them, the most important soldier in the world.

It was a delightful reunion. He received a lingering embrace from his mother and a firm grip from his dad. A scratching at the door signaled a desire for entry and soon Tippie and Spotty came galloping across the floor, sniffing and wagging with unbridled joy, while Kit's the cat remained aloof, as cats are prone to do, and scarcely raised an eye in recognition.

And then there was Pig, Spotty's pup. Harold had only read about Pig. A white mongrel with black spots like his mother, Pig had inherited short hair from whomever his mother had enamored in some canine impropriety. He wore an old sock for a collar, was short-legged and full of energy. Harold wrestled him to the floor while his parents looked on with glee.

Weeks ago, Harold's mother had promised him a chicken dinner upon his return, so busied about the kitchen in preparation of supper. As she rattled pans and sifted flour, Harold sat at the kitchen table and detailed his life at Camp Wolters. Now and then a story sparked a memory in his father who interjected with a similar story from his own Army days some twenty-six years previous and both reveled in the joy of experiences shared.

In time, Harold excused himself and slipped upstairs to marvel at his newly acquired slot machines. They were heavy contraptions and he recalled his parent's complaint of how cumbersome they were to drag upstairs. He pulled the arm of the nearest one, testing the action, feeling a tremor of excitement as the reels spun, then locked in place. Satisfied he moved to the next. He'd have some fun with these whenever the war was over.

"Harold Gene!" his mother's voice carried up the staircase, "Supper!"

Three plates graced the table. His mother bowed her head and gave thanks for the return of her son and prayed for a swift end of the war. That said, the chicken was served, even if it was a scrawny bird.

After supper, Harold visited with several neighbors, especially those who had written him at camp. But of even greater interest was a reunion with his friends. Although some were still in school, they managed to get out and have some fun in the evenings and on the weekend as well, providing Harold with welcome relief from weeks of Army discipline.

He ran around with several of his old pals: Ernie Hemmings, Ted Fritzmeier, Bill Nichols, and Loren Belker. He fielded questions about Army life and in turn asked about recent events in Quincy. He discovered that many of the seniors at Quincy High School were enlisting right and left into the service, ready to go after graduation. Most preferred the romance of the Navy's air arm and a few the Marines; some had already received draft notices.

Barkley's buddies, Loyd Boden, Russell Gordon and Merle Lamb, were already in the Army. Loren Belker confided that he wanted to go into the service as soon as he was out of school. Harold advised him to wait awhile and give it some thought.

Later, Belker, Nichols and Barkley went to the movies where they saw the thriller, "King of the Zombies".

Barkley spent a lot of time at the Belker's house on North 12th Street where he became acquainted with Loren's sister, Marilyn. Although she never went out with the guys during Harold's furlough, she thought that Harold was a pretty swell fellow and enjoyed his company immensely.

The few days at home passed quickly and suddenly it was time to report back for duty. He had told his parents that he would be going overseas very soon. He didn't know exactly how long it would be before he went, but they could rest assured that he would not be staying on this side of the ocean for very long.

His mother braced for the final day of her son's leave -- he was going to war. She and Harry were very proud of their son but she was filled with anguish at the vision of her boy being horribly wounded or, God forbid, something worse.

When the time came, Harold re-packed his bag and dragged it downstairs and through the kitchen where his parents quietly waited. There, at the door leading to the porch, they said their good-byes. Shouldering his bag, Harold turned and marched down the brick walkway that led to the street below. As his parents looked on from the porch he disappeared in the direction of the train station.

CHAPTER 3

OVER THERE

March, 1944, Fort Meade, Maryland -- Although Spring was fast approaching, snow still blanketed the earth and capped the boughs of the surrounding pines and frost still nipped the air.

Private Barkley had been at this post for only a couple of weeks but now, under orders, he was packing away his excess uniforms for transportation overseas. Barkley had already sent a box of personal things home, including his camera, which was forbidden anyway. A train was to take the troops to New York City where a ship awaited them.

As he folded his uniforms he reflected on the events of the past few weeks. When the month began he and his pals were still at Camp Wolters in Texas. Then came the whirlwind furlough at home which was over far too soon -- he actually cut his leave short one day to ensure that he would not be AWOL. Next he was aboard another train that snaked across the country through Terre Haute, Indiana; Columbus, Ohio; and Pittsburgh, Pennsylvania, passing a number of coal mining towns before reaching Maryland. It was a nice trip, he recalled, but it would be a nicer one if he could come back that way some day.

Arriving at Fort Meade in mid-March, he was re-united with many of his comrades from Camp Wolters. They assigned to the Army Ground Forces Replacement Depot -- a temporary assignment as the men posted here were simply in transit for overseas duty.

Barkley marveled at the immense concentration of military might assembled here. He had never seen so many men, tanks, tank destroyers, anti-aircraft guns and artillery pieces in one place before. There was even a mounted cavalry troop! The post bustled with activity, bugle calls and crisp salutes.

Although only at Fort Meade a short time, Barkley did receive some mail. His friend, Loren Belker, wrote saying how much fun he had the few days Barkley was home and hoped that he would get another furlough before going over. Loren felt optimistic about Barkley staying stateside. He wrote: "...somehow, Bark, I don't think you'll go over for awhile." Barkley received this letter the day before he was ordered to pack up and prepare for movement overseas.

Loren's sister, Marilyn, also wrote and expressed how much she enjoyed the brief time Harold spent at home. She wanted to keep in touch with him by exchanging letters while he was overseas. Harold consented. It was kind of nice to have a girl back home to write to.

The Army began the process of weeding out the men who didn't seem capable of coping with overseas service. Soldiers lined up before a desk and one by one stepped forward for evaluation. A doctor, presumably a psychiatrist, asked each man the same question: "Can you think of any reason why you shouldn't be sent overseas?" A good number came forward with alarming maladies, diseases and hardships as reasons for avoiding combat: "I've been getting terrible headaches lately -- every day..."; "I have a wife and two kids. One's sick..."; "... injured my back in training and I don't think that I..."

and so it went, one lame excuse after another. All of the men with complaints were sent to a line on the left.

Others answered: "No. No, can't think of anything," and were sent to a line on the right. When Barkley's turn came he said, "No, sir. That's what we trained for. I'm ready." He could have mentioned that he was an only child and therefore qualified for exemption from combat and be transferred to a non-combat unit, but that was not his nature. In fact, he was eager to get overseas -- to him it was a big adventure!

Despite their grievances, Barkley noted that most of the complainers were sent over anyway.

He wrote his parents and informed them that he would be in a combat zone by April and had been ordered to make out his will. He was also having another $20.00 taken from his pay to send home as he didn't think he'd need much money where he was going. He felt certain that he'd be in some of the major battles of the war and believed he was bound for Italy, the only active combat front in Europe. With youthful bravado, he brashly promised his father that he'd send him a souvenir from a dead German.

On March 30th, Barkley and his buddies were issued official change of address cards on which they notified family and friends that their new "home" would be Company P, Infantry, APO 15186, c/o Postmaster, New York, New York. They were shipping out.

Within days they boarded a troop train which steamed from Fort Meade to New York City. Once in the city they were ushered to the docks where an ocean liner, the *Ile de France*, awaited them.

After ascending the gangplank, the enlisted men were steered to their berths in the lower decks. Before the deckhands had cast off the moorings the good ship boasted a cargo of 1,000 officers and nurses and 10,000 enlisted men.

As befit their class, the officers and nurses were quartered in the state cabins of the upper deck and enjoyed all the luxuries of first class passage. The multitude of enlisted men, however, was crammed into every conceivable space from the next lower deck all the way down to "E" deck. Antonelli, Balchunas, Barkley, Bartas, Bell and their new acquaintances of Company P had the misfortune of drawing

"E" deck, deep in the bowels of the great ship. Supposedly it was illegal to house people below the waterline, but due to the urgency of mass troop movement, "D" and "E" decks were utilized and loaded beyond the safety limits.

Tug boats muscled the leviathan away from the docks as black clouds billowed from its trio of smokestacks. Then, under its own power, the ship navigated through New York Harbor and cleared the Statue of Liberty with considerable blasting of horns and whistles. It was April 7, 1944.

The crowded liner struck out across the cold and turbulent North Atlantic. In the ensuing days the miserable troops, cramped among tiers of bunks in the lower holds, succumbed to the nausea of sea-sickness. The sight of pale-faced soldiers sitting or laying very still was common. Being several decks removed from fresh air, the stench of vomit and the sweat of thousands of men permeated the hold. Within a couple of days, however, Barkley adjusted to the motion of the ship and managed to survive the passage in reasonably good health.

Although allowed topside each day for a few precious minutes of fresh air, many soldiers never overcame the rocking sensation and remained sick the entire voyage. When assembled in the galley for mess call, the vessel would shift direction, roll and pitch, causing the food trays to slide along the tables. Invariably there would be at least one guy who had just puked his chow onto his own tray. Soon the ship would toss again and the putrid tray would slip a few places until it rested before some other soldier. Generally this fellow's stomach would turn and he, too, would retch, then spew his lunch across the table, often initiating a chain reaction.

"For christsake!" the cry would arise, "Hold on to you goddam mess kit!"

While at sea it was believed that the *Ile de France* was being tracked by a German U-Boat. As a precaution the great liner zig-zagged in evasive action patterns, and to the relief of all, no torpedoes were fired. Apparently the ship was too fast or too difficult to target.

The episode ingrained a thread of fear in Barkley. He didn't want to drown in the lower decks as men scrambled for the ladders, trapped like proverbial rats. He resolved that in the event of torpedoing, he'd find one of the many portholes that lined the upper decks, open it, and slip out and over the side. It never occurred to him that the porthole might be under water at the time. But at least he was thinking, and thinking of action, and action was better than doing nothing at times of crisis. This would be proved time and again in the months to come.

After a week at sea they were in sight of the British Isles. On the eighth day, April 14, the *Ile de France* slipped into the safety of the Firth of Clyde and docked at Glasgow Harbor in Scotland. They made it. They had arrived.

Excitement gripped the men as they trod down the gangplank. The effect was amplified as the shrill wail of bagpipes pierced the air and the rattle and boom of drums competed with the Yanks' pounding hearts. Kilted pipers formed up quayside, striking up a skirling martial air while the drummers, draped with leopard skin aprons, twirled their drumsticks with great flair. It was a stirring sight. To Barkley it was a scene straight from "Gunga Din" or "The Charge of the Light Brigade", the movies that had so enthralled him as a boy. His buddy, Balchunas, held a more cynical view of the Highlanders. He thought they appeared as "a bunch of fruits!"

The men were not given much opportunity to adjust to terra firma before embarking on the next leg of their journey. Again they were stuffed into trains, the peculiar ones with the outward facing doors, and steamed southward.

Arriving "somewhere in England", the troops tumbled from the coaches as sergeants barked orders to form into columns. The men shouldered their bags and marched off the platform, gawking at the quaint English homes and their inhabitants. Soon they were unpacking their gear at one of the numerous U.S. Army camps that infested southern England.

"Here I am in another place and this time it is England," Barkley wrote matter-of-factly. He wished he could tell of the voyage over but said that he knew he couldn't.

Earlier, the troops had been informed of the strict censorship of their correspondence home. Whatever they wrote would be reviewed by censoring officers who would determine whether to blot or cut out pertinent phrases that could be detrimental to the war effort.

Entire letters might be returned to the writer for re-submission. Barkley's first experience with censorship accompanied his first letter home when he wrote: "The people here are very friendly, especially when we XXXXX XXX XX XXXX." The censor's blotter expunged the jeopardizing words.

"Write V-Mail," he suggested[*]. "Be sure and write in large print so I can read it." Regular air mail would reach a soldier just as quick, or quicker, than V-Mail, but was more costly.

Barkley felt fortunate to have been sent overseas with a number of his buddies from training days, but he also met new friends. One of these was a muscular, dark haired fellow from Philadelphia, Pennsylvania -- Ralph Barrella. Barrella was a hot blooded Italian boy whose eyes flashed with passion as he recalled life in the big city with girls and dances and all the rest. Barkley listened attentively, but kept silent for he had little personal experience with girls. He viewed young Barrella as a modern day Casanova. Like most of them, Barrella was young with an endearing air and was readily accepted into the ring of Camp Wolters boys. He and Barkley quickly bonded.

After settling into six-man tents, their training resumed. Each day began with the regimen of daily exercise, followed by the drudgery of close order drill. After stomping around the parade ground they were often marched to the rifle range to hone their shooting skills and occasionally they'd tackle a field problem. But all in all, it was nothing compared to the strenuous training experienced at Camp Wolters.

They were now receiving British money for their pay. The peculiar denominations were puzzling to Barkley -- he was having difficulty ascertaining the values of crowns, shillings, and pence. Fortunately each GI was issued a booklet to facilitate his knowledge of the English monetary system.

---

[*] V-Mails were written on regular 8 ½ X 11 inch stationery which was then photographed onto reels of micro-film for ease of transportation. Upon arrival in the States, the film was developed onto reduced 4 ½ X 5 ¼ inch photo pages. This process greatly aided the movement of untold numbers of letters crossing the Atlantic when space was limited to war materials and personnel.

Once paid, everyone seemed anxious to get into town and spend it. Many had visions of blowing their pay on booze and women. By late April their dreams came true. Men lined up for passes, then rushed the gate on their way to town. They were in for a dose of culture shock.

They soon discovered that the English spoke English, which was different from "American". The English language possibly became more confusing than their strange money. Barkley noted: "The British people certainly talk funny and it is hard to understand what they are saying." New words were springing into the GI vocabulary. They learned that a lorry was a truck; a flat was an apartment; a bonnet was the hood of an automobile; that the word "bloody" was a swear word, and if they called someone a bum, they had just referred him to someone's backside. If a soldier had too much to drink someone would comment that he was "pissed", even though he remained in good humor. English was a perplexing language with its distinctive accent, but the Yanks caught on quickly enough and found the English people and customs charming.

Barkley also discovered that common luxuries were rare -- everything seemed rationed: not only were wartime essentials such as gasoline limited ("petrol" to the British), but also every day items such as soap and even clothing. He'd give almost anything for a bottle of milk, but he didn't have ration stamps to buy any, even though he had two shillings in his pocket.

His sweet tooth craved satisfaction, but like everything else, candy was rationed as well. The soldiers were allowed only two bars each week. "I got my ration of two candy bars and ate them in about 10 seconds flat," Barkley lamented in a letter home. He asked his parents to send him more.

While in town Barkley got a haircut for six pence, fairly cheap, he thought. He had it clipped "GI", down to about one-half inch. Then he and his new buddy, Barrella, teamed up to take in a movie, the "cinema", and were surprised to discover that there wasn't a reduced rate for servicemen. The cost was three shillings, six pence -- the equivalent of about seventy cents. They sat in the "circle", what is called the balcony in America. The seats of the gallery below were referred to as "the stalls" by the British.

Before the picture began, the strains of *"My Country 'Tis Of Thee"* poured from the band box and everyone rose to their feet. Flattered and amused, Barkley and Barrella joined them. The other patrons stood rigidly and sang with enthusiasm. The lyrics, however, were foreign to the two Yanks. Then the words sank in and Barkley nudged Barrella, "Oh... It's the English National Anthem!" The melody of *"My Country 'Tis Of Thee"* was the same as that for *"God Save The King!"*

After the show they stopped by the American Red Cross station for donuts and coffee before returning to camp. That completed their big night on the town. Barkley didn't have much money anyway, especially since he authorized the additional allotment to be taken from his pay.

In early May the men were ordered to pack up and prepare to move out -- their destination unknown. Assembled by companies, they loaded into waiting trucks that soon merged with others to form a long column that rolled along winding roads, passing picturesque farmsteads and meadows dotted with dairy cattle. They slowed to negotiate the cobbled streets of charming hamlets and towns, then sped again until they arrived at their new camp in Somerset County, west of Yeovil. It was called Wind Whistle Hill. Located on an impressive estate entitled Cricket St. Thomas, the camp had a view of Chard, a town perhaps two miles farther to the west.

Barkley assessed his new surroundings and was pleased by what he saw. The camp overlooked rolling fields that stretched for miles around. A cool breeze shunted across the meadows below, rippling the lush grasses like waters of an emerald sea, and adrift on the sea floated tiny white cottages that rose starkly above the beckoning waves. The occasional village sprouted here and there, displaying tired gray roofs and a sprinkling of thatch that appeared so graceful and elegant and unbothered by war. It was a scene ripped from the pages of a Victorian novel. Barkley dropped his gear inside a six-man tent. This was his new home.

The training escalated. The troops were given pep talks to fire them up for the coming ordeal. Long marches became common. As usual, rotund "Major" Bartas petered out on the more grueling hikes, shaking his head woefully as he fell out and waved his buddies on. Antonelli grinned broadly as he passed his blown companion. "See ya back at camp!" he crowed over his shoulder as the column tramped on. "Awright, El-l-mer," Bartas wheezed in reply. He and Antonelli had become fast friends in the course of their training.

On other days different types of weapons were fired and the men were allowed to whet their combat skills on field problems. They practiced fire and movement maneuvers. Rehearsals were conducted where men went on patrols and crept and crawled through farmer's fields in simulated battle scenarios.

During one such exercise the men were told to dig foxholes. Barkley and Frank Balchunas began to chop and scoop at the soft earth when suddenly Frank yelped. "Bark!"

Barkley turned to his friend. "What's the matter?"

"My God... Look! Potatoes!" Frank began to dig in another location and reaped more tubers, causing him to laugh out loud. He was digging up someone's potato patch.

Each night they collapsed in their cots, exhausted, and each night the bone-chilling English weather seeped into their muscles and joints, rendering them stiff and sore by morning. But they were accepting it as routine, for they knew it would be much rougher when they got into combat.

One morning, in the gray half-light that precedes the dawn, Frank Balchunas peeked precariously from his blanket and shivered. An icy breeze snapped wildly at the canvas of the squad tent, daring any and all to venture forth and brave its insidious wrath. Barkley, in the next cot, was also awake, biding his time until reveille called. Nearby, Barrella snored with abandon while the others slept like the dead.

Balchunas, cocooned tightly within his blanket, pulled his wrap over his head until it shaded his brow like the hood of a monk's habit. He stared bleakly into his buddy's face. Puffs of vapor jetted from his mantle. The vapor spawned words: "Bark, I gotta go to the latrine." He shivered again. "But I'm too cold."

Barkley peered at his friend; he looked miserable. "Well just do like I do and hold it 'til it warms up."

"H-how can you do that?" Balchunas' teeth chattered, "It... it's so damn cold! I can't wait that long." But he remained wrapped in his blanket, shivering.

Barkley studied his friend's features. From beneath his shroud, Frank's eyes glared red from fatigue. His face sprouted whiskers that jutted at every conceivable angle, giving him a wild, bizarre appearance.

"My God," Barkley chuckled, "You look like a barracuda."

Barracuda, thought Barkley -- the name sure did fit his friend's uncomely features at that moment. Although they didn't know it at the time, from that day on Frank Balchunas *was* "The Barracuda".

Throughout their stay at Wind Whistle Hill the men of Company P were impressed by one officer in particular, Lieutenant Robert O. English. Confident and competent, he seemed to possess the right knack for handling men, earning their universal respect and admiration. The men followed his instructions willingly.

A brutish scar marked the lieutenant's left cheek. Scuttlebutt had it that the lieutenant was no greenhorn -- that he had seen action against the Japanese and the scar was a souvenir of that encounter.

The rumor was true. Robert English had participated in the Battle of Attu when the Army's 7th Division retook the Aleutian Islands from the Japanese in May of 1943. He had been hit in the face by small arms fire, thus the scar.

What the men didn't know was that Robert English had previously been an enlisted man -- a draftee like many of them. He had applied for Officer Candidate School after recovering from his wound and graduated as a "ninety-day-wonder". He never forgot his humble beginning as a private and that knowledge helped temper his actions toward enlisted men. He was soft spoken yet firm when it came to performance of military duties and the men never failed him. He was a good officer and all spoke well of him.

The training was strenuous, tough by necessity. Yet there was also a time for recreation. Baseball games and athletic competitions were arranged for the sports minded soldiers. Others leaned toward more seedy forms of entertainment and initiated maverick poker games or rattled dice in a red-hot game of craps. When permitted, the men went into town to soak up the warm English ale, while others attended dances.

Barkley didn't follow sports and didn't know enough about the various games of chance to gamble his pay, so opted for a pass into town. Frank Balchunas and young Barrella joined him. The streets were packed with GIs and the occasional Tommy[*], but it was the Americans who ruled the streets. The Americans had money, and plenty of it by British Army standards. The Tommies didn't stand a chance when the Yanks were in town and the Yanks walked like kings.

They rolled from street to street, seeking their pleasures when The Barracuda decided he'd duck into a pub to enjoy the heady flavor of the dark English ale. Barkley and Barrella, who didn't care to drink, moved on.

The sound of music dragged the pair farther down the street until they came upon a dance hall that throbbed with the pulsing rhythms of horns and the banging of a trap drum set. A swing band blared from deep inside, carrying the sound of merriment and shuffling feet as Yanks danced with the young English maidens and hoped for encounters that would lead to more amorous conclusions before the night was through.

"C'mon," cried Barrella as he tugged on Barkley's sleeve, "Let's go. There'll be girls!" He snapped his fingers to the primal beat and grinned lasciviously. Barrella always fashioned himself a ladies man and was anxious to make the rounds.

"Aw, we went to a dance the last time," Barkley protested. He never learned to dance and always felt self-conscious about it. And besides, he was shy around girls. "Let's go to a movie," he countered.

On another trip into town, Barkley enjoyed a soda pop, or "minerals" as the British say, and traded anecdotes with several Englishmen. He spoke of life in the Midwest and they in turn countered with tales and folklore of their own. When Barkley

[*] Slang for British Soldier

revealed that he had been a spelunker, his hosts declared that there was a grotto nearby that was a favorite haunt of local cave explorers. It piqued Barkley's interest, but he never found time to go.

Barkley yearned for news from home -- the mail was excruciatingly slow. Perhaps due to their frequent movements the mail was having difficulty keeping up with the men of Company P. Barkley had been in England for better than a month, but except for a couple of letters from Marilyn and her brother, Loren, he hadn't received any mail since May 3rd, save a postcard from his parents postmarked the 4th of April. He was certainly writing every chance he got and didn't understand what the hold up was with the incoming mail.

His anxiety was relieved the third week of May when he received a fat bundle of letters all at once. A few days later, May 23rd, seven more letters were at hand. Barkley's morale soared.

His old pals, Hemmings, Fritzmeier, and Nichols kept him abreast of local events. Loren Belker mentioned that he was joining the Merchant Marine. Marilyn wrote often and sent a nice photograph of herself which Barkley proudly showed the others. She also had the address of another girl who wished to write a soldier and she thought of Harold. Harold Barkley, however, was having enough time keeping up correspondence with his family and friends, so he offered the girl's address to his buddy, Frank Balchunas. The Barracuda didn't have a girl to write to and jumped at the chance. In time they corresponded regularly and Frank even promised to visit her after the war was over -- he didn't mention the possibility of not surviving.

In answer to an earlier request for candy, Barkley's mother informed him that they were not allowed to send chocolates overseas. Reading this, Barkley blew up! He didn't know who told her that, he answered, but "they are full of XXXX!" The censorship was his own. ("I can't use any cuss words," he offered as means of explanation for the X's). He immediately scribbled a request for candy which his parents were to show at the Post Office and have stamped, thereby verifying a written request from a soldier.

He also received a letter from the War Department commending him on his invention for the Tank Corps which he had drawn up back at Camp Wolters. However, they replied, they were working on a better idea. Nonetheless, they thanked him for his suggestion and initiative and enclosed a letter of recognition to be given to his company commander. Barkley proudly stashed the letter among his few personal items.

The howl of air raid sirens wailed into the night. Barkley, Balchunas and the others scrambled from their tents and were met by sergeants and officers who screamed at them to take cover in prepared foxholes located on the hillside. Not knowing where or how soon the bombs would be dropping, the men raced for the holes and dove in.

Ears strained to separate the squalling sirens from the sound of hostile activity. A faint droning of aircraft was heard -- then muffled explosions. The western darkness pulsed with flashing light. The deep thumping of massive detonations wafted up the hill as bombs plummeted to their targets, but no explosions wracked the encampment on Wind Whistle Hill. It soon became obvious that the Nazi bombs weren't intended for the men entrenched on the heights, but fell on the nearby town of Chard, two miles distance. Rumor had it that a British Defense plant was located there.

Barkley peeked above the rim of his hole to see what all the commotion was about. Sensing no immediate danger, he pulled himself to the surface and sat with his feet dangling in the foxhole. Many of his comrades remained in the safety of their shelters. Barkley attempted to coax Balchunas out to have a look, but he refused -- the Barracuda was fine just where he was.

"Get down here!" urged the Barracuda, concerned for his young friend's safety.

"No. I want to see this."

From his vantage point atop of the hill, Barkley was treated to a ringside view of a bombing raid on an English town. He marveled at the bizarre beauty of the whole affair: The flash of exploding bombs. The fleeting glimpses of the darkened town as each bomb struck and all the while muffled blasts of concussion rolled up the hill in successive waves. A myriad of English searchlights swept to and fro in search of their antagonists, and sometimes one would spot a bomber and hold it fast in its blinding beam. Then, one by one, other beacons locked onto the lone plane and clung tenaciously to their target. The German aircraft swerved and swayed in vain attempts to escape the condemning shafts of light which only invited death from below. Anti-aircraft guns opened fire. Bright tracer bullets floated upward and criss-crossed the night sky in hopes of riddling the invaders with large caliber projectiles. Larger batteries came to life, splintering the night with fire. Shrapnel burst all around the desperate bomber, the black puffs of exploding shells clearly visible in the spotlights' glare. Yet, not one plane was hit as far as Barkley could tell and that seemed impossible considering the amount of ordnance being sent skyward.

Although it was a life-and-death struggle between the airmen and the beleaguered defenders of Chard, it was an amazing spectacle, a thrilling show for the GIs on Wind Whistle Hill.

"We are going to move tonight." So wrote Private Barkley on May 28th. It was a sunny Sunday and he and Barrella were lying in the grass on their GI blankets, writing letters.

As with many rumors in the Army, the move never developed -- at least not that night. But the men were ready. Although their training was over, they were kept in a near continuous state of alert for the inevitable move to a port of embarkation. The forthcoming invasion of mainland Europe was eminent. Everyone knew it was coming, probably sooner than later.

The weather turned inclement and a heavy rain fell. The troops were restricted to camp -- it was forbidden to go into town. They grew fidgety in the confines of their tents and boredom set in. The men gambled or gathered in bull sessions to pass the time. Barkley wished he had a copy of "Billboard" magazine so he'd have an idea of what was going on in the entertainment world -- anything to while away the time.

The tension built. Everyone sensed it as more preparations were made for the invasion. Weapons were cleaned, inspected, and cleaned again. On June 1st Barkley wrote his parents: "I will send this letter while I have the time. I am pretty busy but I figured I had better send this letter while I can tell you not to worry if you don't hear from me for awhile... I'll write again when I can. Your Son -- Harold Gene Barkley." It was the first time he had signed his full name. Perhaps he perceived he was about to take part in something bigger than life itself, and that he was only one minuscule mortal in the grand scheme, that *maybe* he might not fare so well in the near future.

The great move still hadn't taken place by June 3rd. The men sat idly on Wind Whistle Hill. "Well, I'm still here," Barkley announced in another letter home. The waiting gave the fellows a lot of time to think. On June 4th he wrote again, saying, "Remember, I am getting partial pay and if anything goes wrong the Government still owes me some money so collect it." He had no way of knowing it, but that was his last letter home for quite a long time.

Tuesday, June 6, 1944 -- *"Under the command of General Eisenhower, Allied naval forces, supported by strong air forces, began landing Allied armies this morning on the northern coast of France."*

Thus the landings on the beaches of Normandy were announced by this simple, terse phrase. Now the gears of the great Allied war machine were turning and all of the pieces, so carefully planned, were falling into place -- a battalion; a tank; an airplane; crates of rations or even a single typewriter. Each piece was allotted a precise time slot for its role in this grand undertaking, and the pawns of Company P were about to fulfill their obligation.

Company P, like its brother companies, was not an integral part of any particular infantry or armored division. It was a replacement unit. Although they trained like all the other combat soldiers, they would not go into battle as a cohesive unit. Instead they would be parceled out individually or in small groups to divisions on the front line that needed to fill their ranks depleted by casualties. The system worked alphabetically. If one's name began with the letters "A" or "B" he would be among the first to be tossed into the "meat grinder". If one's last name started with an "S" or "T", for example, he would have a slight reprieve before he went to the front. However, in those early days of the Normandy Campaign, all of the replacements were used up very fast.

On D-Day, Wind Whistle Hill was a flurry of activity. The news of the landings electrified the camp. Every company was alerted for movement. The men's personal gear was stored away and they knew that their time was coming. But when?

On the 7th of June, D+1, the troops were ordered into big army trucks for transportation to a port of embarkation. The convoy motored through the lush English countryside, moist and green from the recent rains. Exuding blatant bravado, the GIs boldly waved and cheered from tailgates as they passed civilians standing by the roadside.

Later that day they arrived at the seaport of Southampton and bailed out of the trucks, then marched to a camp where they spent the night. Barkley was filled with excitement, anticipating high adventure!

The next morning the entire battalion fell in, donned in full marching order. Each man carried complete battle equipment, rifle and a full load of ammunition. They were combat ready! Once assembled, they were marched en masse by companies to the docks where the various companies were assigned ships to board. Everything was going like clock-work. Company P waddled up the gangplank of a British destroyer. This was it! Next stop would be the Normandy beaches.

CHAPTER 4

COMBAT

June 9, 1944, off the coast of Normandy, France -- Through the night and into the following morning the warship weaved through the congestion of ships riding the choppy seas of the English Channel. It had been several days since the beach assaults took place, yet the Channel was still clogged with ships coming and going between England and the beachheads. Each bound for the beaches was crowded with men or war materials; those passing in the opposite direction were returning for another load, and some of these carried back the wounded and dead from the battles raging a short distance inland.

As the British destroyer approached the French coast the infantrymen were alerted to prepare to board assault landing craft. Topside, Barkley and his friends clutched their rifles and waited, swaying on the pitching deck under the weight of their cumbersome field packs. Men peered nervously toward the shore as waves of Allied aircraft roared overhead. Before them stretched Omaha Beach.

The ship's horn blared a warning and the men were ordered over the side. Climbing down cargo nets, the soldiers warily eased themselves into one of the LCVP's bobbing haphazardly below[*].

When the last man was aboard, the coxswain gunned his engine and his boat steered for shore, leaping and bounding as it plowed through the choppy waters with its cargo of 32 infantrymen. As they neared land the boat suddenly crunched to a halt, bottoming out in the shallows about one-hundred yards from the beach.

The forward ramp slapped down and the men leaped into the surf with rifles held high as they struggled against the swelling waters to gain the shore. Some men fell into deep holes created by artillery during the beach battle and disappeared beneath the waves, weighed down by their heavy equipment. They resurfaced, wide-eyed and sputtering salt water, requiring assistance from nearby buddies who dragged them to shore.

Soaked from the waist down, Private Harold Barkley splashed ashore -- he had arrived in France. As the rest of his company emerged from the sea they were promptly greeted by a Beachmaster who directed them toward the bluffs overlooking Omaha Beach.

As Company P marched off the beach they got a good look at the carnage left by the fierce struggle that took place some days previous. Swamped landing craft wallowed in the surf -- some had been destroyed by gunfire. Wreckage was strewn everywhere: burned-out vehicles, tangles of barbed wire and discarded battle equipment littered the beach. Shell holes from artillery pocked the earth. And bobbing like saturated flotsam in the surf line was the occasional corpse not yet recovered from the D-Day assault.

Hundreds of soldiers in column snaked inland. Barkley and his friends were now one segment of this serpentine file as it meandered its way up the bluffs. While they trod on, they passed

---

[*] LCVP -- Landing Craft, Personnel and Vehicle. A small assault boat designed to carry a platoon of soldiers or a light vehicle from ship to shore. Its bow doubled as a ramp that would be dropped to disgorge its load when the boat beached.

engineer battalions that labored with bulldozers to clear additional routes off the beach. Warning signs had been posted, alerting soldiers to stay clear of areas still infested with land mines. Heaps of supplies were being stockpiled on the beach where trucks lined up to carry them to the front.

Now and then, artillery shells exploded randomly upon the congested beachhead as German gunners attempted to disrupt the Allied build-up, but none fell very close to Barkley's group. In retaliation, unseen batteries of American guns boomed a defiant response.

Company P crested the hill and was ordered to occupy the many foxholes abandoned by previous inhabitants. The faint, unsettling sounds of a battle in progress wafted from some distance inland, the volume of gunfire rising and falling as the struggle varied in intensity. Several boys stared towards the sound with furrowed brow as they unslung their packs.

Once settled in, the men tore open boxes of K rations and wolfed them down -- their first meal on French soil. While eating they were treated to a panoramic view of the beach below and the mighty armada reaching to the far horizon. As far as the eye could see the waters were crowded with boats and ships of every size and description. Blimp balloons hovered diligently over the fleet, straining at their moorings, and above them soared flights of Allied aircraft sweeping inland to strike enemy positions. Impressed, Frank Balchunas pulled out a camera and began to snap photographs like a holiday tourist. Cameras were strictly prohibited, but Frank had smuggled one into his equipment. To Barkley it was all very exciting. He was part of it now -- or would be very soon.

Suddenly a German plane roared overhead. The sky exploded with streams of tracers as anti-aircraft batteries opened fire. Glowing bullets chased the plane but none struck their target and the plane was gone as quickly as it had arrived. The newcomers on the bluff were thrilled as they gazed up from their foxholes and again photographer Balchunas attempted to record it on film. Barkley was fascinated by the air show. He assumed the plane must have been on a reconnaissance mission, for it never strafed or dropped any bombs on the opulent targets below.

COMBAT

As twilight passed into darkness the inland horizon shimmered with the flashes of distant artillery and more anti-aircraft fire splashed into the void. For all its deadly intent, the scene reminded Barkley of one hell of a Fourth of July celebration.

Later that night, as the men sought comfort in their holes, they were welcomed to the war by a barrage from the German artillery. Shells exploded all around and the earth quaked as the men cowered deep within their foxholes.

The following morning, June 10th, broke clear and cool. The men were assembled then taken by groups of squads on a short hike down a sunken road that cut through the Norman countryside. Their view was restricted by the earthen banks and tangles of vegetation that rose on either side of them, yet all the while the foreboding sound of rifle and machine gun fire kept up a faint but constant din from the direction in which they marched. After a spell they halted in the protection of the sunken road as sporadic artillery fire burst to either side.

Before long, a haggard looking officer and a sergeant appeared and singled out the replacements' officer. After a hasty conversation, this officer and his sergeant commenced to take eight or ten men at a time to deliver them to various outfits. From this point in time, Company P ceased to exist. It had served its purpose.

Eventually it was Barkley's turn. "What's your classification?" the officer asked.

"Anti-tank gunner, first class."

Not acknowledging his answer, the officer moved on and talked briefly to some of the other replacements. Satisfied, he ordered, "You men come with me," and he turned and started down the sunken lane.

Antonelli, Bartas, Barkley, Balchunas, Barrella, Bell, and some others followed him, passing between the foliage covered banks that sheltered the road. The sound of gunfire increased at every step -- they had to be almost on the very front line.

After awhile they approached a line of soldiers hunkered at the base of a hedgerow and joined them. Just ahead lay a town which resonated with the clatter of gunfire and explosions. The town was Trevieres.

Private Barkley didn't know what to expect. Here he was, at the front but not yet a participant in the fighting, even though the sounds of battle raged a few hundred yards away. Taking his cue from the others, he scraped a hole in the ground and dug in for the night.

The other soldiers were a tough looking lot who had little to say to the newcomers. Sitting in his foxhole, Barkley took his first real look at the front. He was surrounded by devastation. The field was pocked with ugly holes where artillery had turned the earth inside out. Every tree seemed scarred by shrapnel, and many had been reduced to splintered trunks, twisted and ripped by the uncompromising power of high explosives. It was evident that terrible things had happened here.

Night fell. As before, the horizon pulsed with flickering light as artillery rumbled in the distance, a thunderous serenade without beginning or end. The occasional flare arched skyward, sizzling bright against the pitch black sky, then burst, washing the landscape with eerie luminescence as it swayed slowly to the earth. The shattered branches, silhouetted against the shimmering light, appeared as spindly arms that reached to the heavens for salvation. But if Heaven existed in some lofty place above, then this scene on earth was surely straight from Hell. The landscape reminded Barkley of photographs he had seen of the battlefields of World War I.

Rolling over, he closed his eyes and attempted to sleep, wondering what tomorrow would bring. *I'm in it now*, he thought as he squirmed to get more comfortable.

Trevieres was captured that day by the Second and Third Battalions of the 38th Infantry. It had been a two day battle. The 38th was one of three infantry regiments of the 2nd (Indianhead) Infantry Division which had landed on Omaha Beach on June 7, D-Day plus One. The other regiments were the 9th and the 23rd Infantries.

Trevieres was a welcome prize for the Americans. Not only did it serve as the site of a German headquarters, but also commanded the road net running to, from and parallel to Omaha Beach. It had been stubbornly defended. Its capture broke the backbone of German resistance in that sector and opened the way for a general advance by the U. S. V Corps. The two battalions of the 38th Infantry were awarded Certificates of Commendation for that action.

June 11, 1944 -- The sun rose, bold as brass, and shoved the night away. Long, grotesque shadows reached from the bushy rim of the nearest hedgerow and touched each soldier as he performed his morning routine. The new men, not sure what to do, clustered in small knots and engaged in nervous conversation until ordered to disperse, for snipers were still a threat. While the replacements kept to themselves, the veterans remained aloof, occasionally shooting them sidelong glances, as if they didn't fully trust these interlopers who had stumbled into their midst.

Barkley crouched in the safety of his foxhole. His bowels rumbled and churned and he knew that he had to take a crap but he sure as hell didn't want to dirty his own foxhole, that was for certain. He had to go nonetheless.

He and some of the others decided to utilize the many shell holes created by artillery barrages as open air toilets. But they had a problem, and it was a major one. They were now in a combat zone. They had already been warned of the possibility of German snipers and no one wanted to get caught, literally, with his pants down. A basic chore such as taking a dump could prove fatal.

Grabbing some GI toilet paper from his pack, Barkley tensed in preparation for the trip. He pictured the site of the nearest shell hole in his mind, calculated the distance and his chances of making it before a sniper's bullet stuck him down. It didn't seem too far away, but still... He took a deep breath, then sprung from his hole and sprinted towards the target crater and tumbled inside. A smile played across his face. *I beat him!* he thought, *I beat the sniper!*

His business done, he psyched himself for the return trip. If a sniper was out there, he reasoned, he'd probably seen the first leg of the journey; he'd be waiting for the return pass and have a much greater chance of scoring a hit. Springing over the crater's lip, he raced back, zigging and zagging, and dropped into is own foxhole. *Ha! I made it!* He was almost giddy with delight. It was like a game.

Later, an officer appeared with a roster and began to call out the names of the replacements: "Antonelli!... Bartas!..." and so on. As each man answered he was assigned to one of the front line units, and thus Elmer Antonelli and Anthony Bartas were spirited away from their friends and comrades of training days. Those remaining watched solemnly as wide-eyed Antonelli and his rotund pal, The Major, trailed off to their new outfit, and Barkley was reminded of Antonelli's distraught cry of, "What are we going to do?" and his own answer of, "Whatever we have to."

Then the officer bellowed, "Balchunas!... Barkley!... Barrella!... Bell!..." as the squad of replacements dwindled to nothing.

They marched through the cover of a dusty sunken road that led towards Trevieres. As they advanced they came upon two dead German soldiers, one behind the other, lying on one side of the road. Both were completely coated with gray-white dust. Apparently they had been caught by a bursting shell and each soldier's jacket was swept back as if still running to escape the deadly blast. One's head was twisted so that its chalky face stared at the approaching GIs, accusing each with dull lifeless eyes. Each soldier uneasily stared back as they passed in Death's review.

The corpse's comrade lay close behind him. One hand still clutched his rifle, as if duty compelled him to do so -- the faithful soldier to the end.

Barkley's eyes met the unyielding gaze of the dead man and he contemplated the corpses with fascination. They were his enemies. Each was so rigid and dust covered that it appeared as if they were sculpted from limestone. The morbid impression was chiseled forever into his memory. They were the first dead Germans he had seen. He would see many more in the weeks to follow.

They entered Trevieres and paused beside a shell torn building. As they waited, Barkley assessed the battle damage. Houses and businesses were roofless and many thick walls had crumbled under the heavy bombardments, leaving rubble strewn throughout the streets. Bullet holes perforated the homes and some ruins smoldered from recent fires. The odd civilian or two peeked from doorways or windows and stared blankly at the Americans, aware that their coming had brought the destruction of their home town. They, too, had paid a price for liberation.

The column began to move again. "Be careful," they were cautioned, "There's still snipers in the town." Instinctively, men scanned the roofs and upper levels, not certain exactly what they were looking for, but searched all the same, hoping their efforts were all in vain. They passed street after street of utter devastation and all the while the coarse rasping of artillery shells soughed high overhead, bearing evidence that the struggle continued somewhere up ahead.

After passing through town they resumed their cross-country hike, keeping cadence to the continuous rumble of artillery. They stayed close to the cover of the wall-like hedgerows, following a heavily trodden path as they approached the front, now only a short hike away. As before, every tree seemed stripped of leaf and limb, and were reduced to naked, ravaged trunks.

Filing through a hedgerow gate, their eyes were drawn to a fire that blazed in a meadow to their left. An American plane, a P-47, stood on its nose and burned wildly in the middle of the field. Its tail thrust up at a jaunty angle as flames licked maliciously at the charred fuselage, releasing rolls of thick, black smoke. Awed by the sight, the column moved on. Not far ahead, a curious object rose from the grass that bordered the trail. As the column drew closer it was readily recognizable -- an airman's boot, standing upright, jettisoned from the crash. As Barkley neared he was shocked to see that the foot was still inside with the bloody shank jutting above the grass. Aghast, his eyes were riveted to the apparition. It was obvious that the pilot had failed to bail out before his plane plunged to earth. The burning aircraft had become his funeral pyre -- a Viking's funeral. Sickened, the column marched silently to the next hedgerow.

In time they arrived at a battalion area near another battered village. What remained of the Camp Wolters boys was then further split up and farmed out to the different companies. Barkley's buddy, Ralph Barrella, went one way and Frank Balchunas, the venerable Barracuda, went another. Barkley and several others were corralled and taken to a smaller group of soldiers entrenched along a hedgerow near some farm buildings. These dirty, worn looking creatures were men of Headquarters section of Company G, an integral part of the 38th Infantry's Second Battalion. Their battalion had landed on

Omaha Beach on D+1, enduring harassing artillery and machine gun fire. The battle for Trevieres had been their first major action. Company G, a rifle company, was commanded by Captain Lauren A. Raymond.

The string of replacements collapsed along a hedge bank and talked quietly among themselves. As Barkley absorbed the scene a couple of soldiers approached with deliberation. One was an officer who stopped before him. "Where's your weapon?" he demanded. Barkley presented his M-1 rifle and the other soldier, a sergeant, stepped up and took it from him. He then thrust a Thompson sub-machine gun into Barkley's hands and passed him several boxes of .45 caliber ammunition and a fistful of extra magazines.

"You're now a second scout, 38th Infantry," the officer declared matter-of-factly. "You know how to use it?" he asked, nodding at the Thompson.

"Yes, but I'm an anti-tank gunner, sir," Barkley protested, thinking that the officer had made a mistake.

The officer studied Barkley a moment, then stated bluntly, "You are now an Army scout!"

The filtering of Replacement Company P was complete.

The struggle for Normandy resumed that day. While the Second and Third Battalions of the 38th Infantry were held as Divisional Reserve, the remainder of the 2nd Infantry Division pushed onward, passing through part of the Cerisy Forest. The advance, while swift at first, was slowed by ever stiffening resistance as gunfire emanated from patches of woods and from behind man-high, bush covered hedgerows.

The hedgerows were *the* unique terrain feature of Normandy. A hedgerow was a solid earthen wall, about four to six feet high and just as thick at its base, sometimes taller, sometimes shorter. Foliage of every description sprouted from base to crest which was capped by a dense tangle of shrubs, hedges, and trees which elevated the wall several more feet, making it impossible to see into the next field.

These hedgerows bordered the small Norman fields, which were usually rectangular or trapezoidal in shape, measuring 100 to 200 yards long and 50 to 100 yards wide -- again, each field was unique to itself and varied in size and configuration. Within these boxed parcels might be found fields of grain, apple orchards, or more commonly, just plain pasture.

Twisting roads, flanked by hedgerows, meandered throughout the entire region, connecting the tiny hamlets and individual farm houses that dotted the countryside. The roads wound so aimlessly that they confused and disoriented those who tried to follow them. It was easy to get lost, even in daylight. Sometimes these lanes were shrouded by trees whose heavy branches blotted out the sunlight, creating dark, green tunnels, perfect for ambushes.

Each hedgerow made a formidable barrier and the Germans utilized these natural forts to maximize their defenses and had ample time to perfect them. By digging dugouts and trenches into the base of these sturdy mounds, they were easily defended by integrating murderous cross-firing machine guns with riflemen and a generous sprinkling of Burp guns. Narrow, low-level firing slits were excavated through the side of the hedgerow facing the Americans and were concealed by expert camouflage, rendering them nearly invisible to advancing enemies. Once pinned down in the field before them, pre-registered mortars or artillery blanketed the designated killing field, mulching men into the ground. Land mines were sown throughout the gullies and fields so that each step of an advancing soldier was an experiment in terror.

Tanks could not penetrate the thick walls and were forced to creep along the narrow roads -- easy prey for anti-tank weapons. Or, if encountering a low hedge wall, a tank's treads would grind up the bank, placing it at such an angle that its lightly armored underbelly was exposed -- a very inviting target for alert German gunners.

In the end, the hedgerows had to be taken one at a time by brutal infantry assaults. Each field was a potential battleground. Sometimes a full day of exhausting combat yielded only one small field, or maybe no gain was made at all. The entire countryside was one vast quilt of hedgerows. The hedgerow country stretched for miles and miles.

The Second Battalion rested for a day, absorbed its replacements then moved back into the lines on June 13th. Barkley, now a member of a rifle platoon, marched to battle in the company of strangers.

Second scout Barkley prepared for his first action. His platoon squatted behind a hedgerow, ready to rush the next embankment only one short field away. Overhead out-going artillery grated noxiously across the sky, then slammed hard onto the German lines somewhere to the front. The earth trembled at every blow.

Barkley's heart pounded wildly as another salvo ravaged the enemy positions. Trees leaped from beyond the far hedgerow, tumbled awkwardly through the air, then crashed heavily amidst clouds of smoke and dust. Explosions flashed brightly as another volley struck, and then another, seemingly more wicked than the last.

Deafened by the din, Barkley concentrated on what his sergeant had told him. His orders were simple. He was to follow the first scout over the hedge bank when the attack began and accompany him across the field -- he was to keep his eyes open for enemy activity -- push on quickly to the next hedgerow -- simple as that -- easy. He only had to go about one hundred yards to cross the field.

The other scout had coached him on how best to get through the tangled growth that crowned the hedgerow above them -- to try to find a less foliaged place and wriggle through as fast as he could, then move swiftly to the next hedgerow. It was imperative to clear the hedgerow as quickly as possible, for a soldier presented a luscious target as he struggled through the bushes.

Barkley glanced at his tutor a few feet away. Like himself, the first scout carried a Thompson sub-machine gun. His jaw worked nervously, as if chewing gum or tobacco, grinding rapidly, absently, a nervous reaction to a tense situation. Looking left and right, Barkley evaluated the others. They waited tensely, crouching low as they sweated the coming attack.

Again a banshee cry howled overhead and the earth lurched as if possessed. A wave of concussion fluttered the leaves.

Barkley swallowed hard as he readjusted his grip on his tommy gun. The stock and forearm were slippery with sweat, the same sweat that seeped from beneath his helmet to smear his face with pungent odors. His heart hammered furiously. His mouth was dry. His temples throbbed, painfully aware of the thunderous drumming that pressed upon his ears.

Another salvo screamed overhead and the earth quivered from shock. And then the world was filled with ominous silence.

From down the line a voice rose: "LET'S GO!... SCOUTS OUT!" The order shot through the ranks like a jolt of electricity. The first scout scrambled up the hedge bank and was gone. Barkley sprung after him and wriggled desperately through the brush, then dropped heavily onto the other side. The lead scout was already trotting rapidly through thigh-high grass and Barkley raced to catch up, following like a well-trained dog.

As they reached mid-field the platoon commenced pouring over the hedgerow and spread out in a wide skirmish line behind them... and as if that was a signal, all hell broke loose. A terrifying sound erupted from the far hedgerow. For all the world it sounded as if someone was tearing a gigantic piece of canvas -- *Rrrrrrp!* Bullets cut through the ranks at 1200 rounds per minute -- German machine guns were firing from concealment on either flank. Everyone hit the dirt. And then all was still.

Not a soul lifted his head. Again the machine guns spoke, traversing the field as if hosing a lawn. Grass toppled like wheat before a scythe.

By now both scouts were burrowed deep in the tall grass half-way across the field. Barkley panted, bewildered. *What the hell do we do now?* he wondered as sweat gushed from every pore. Then a voice from the rear shouted with authority: "Come on! Let's go!" Barkley heard the unmistakable sound of men getting to their feet -- racing forward.

Closeby, the lead scout jumped up. "C'mon!" he hollered without even looking to see if Barkley complied. Without a second thought, Barkley clambered to his feet and stumbled after his tutor.

Again the machine guns fired. A man grunted and spun to earth.

"Go! Go!" the voice shouted as bullets swept the field, "Keep Going!" Now everyone rushed forward, desperate to reach the far hedgerow before being cut down themselves. Several fired their rifles as they ran. The first scout sprayed the opposing hedgerow with his Thompson, then tumbled to the ground and rolled. Barkley followed his lead, releasing a cursory burst as he dove to the ground, then rolled once or twice before rising to charge again.

He had only taken a few more steps before the sky seemed to collapse around him. Great black eruptions sprouted left, right and all around as mortar shells pummeled the length and breadth of the field. "Jesus Christ!" Barkley cried as shards of white-hot steel shot past him.

"Keep going! Move!"

The earth quaked as more shells fell. Barkley hunched his shoulders against the storm and bowed his head as another hail of shrapnel hissed past him. "Jesus Christ!" he exclaimed again as he glanced quickly over his shoulder to ensure that the others were still coming. Bullets popped madly past his cheeks.

Again he fired a short, rattling burst before plunging to earth. Behind him, the platoon quickened its pace. Some fell heavily and disappeared in the tall grass while others were lifted by blinding explosions that whipped them through the air like rag dolls. Like madmen, the survivors advanced, dropping and rising at their own discretion, desperate to reach the German occupied hedgerow before being cut down themselves. Again Barkley rose to join the headlong dash into Hell.

As the scouts crashed against the enemy's hedgerow the lead scout quickly sprayed the hedge top with a long, sweeping burst. Following his lead, Barkley stepped back and did the same, and as he did the thin line behind him slammed into the hedge wall with the force of surf breaking upon a rocky shore. Immediately, a desperate, close quarter fight broke out. Grenades sailed awkwardly over the hedge top -- exploded. Rifles barked all along the line. Cursing, yelling. The Germans stood their ground as killing went on at arms length. Only the earthen embankment separated the quarrelling forces as they slaughtered each other at point blank range. More grenades flew blindly over the hedgerow, hoping to score additional hits. More explosions and cries of agony. Smoke and dust rose above the foliage.

A couple GIs gained the brushy parapet and fired rapidly upon the other side. Another squad rushed up and crossed over the hedgerow but was met with withering fire and driven back. By now most of the enemy had pulled out, leaving a handful of die-hards to cover their flight, but soon these, too, bolted for the safety of the next hedgerow, a hundred or so yards away. Several soldiers mounted the hedge top and tried to kill them with rifles as they ran across the open ground, but were quickly discouraged as machine gun bullets swept the crest and drove them from their perches. Men quickly slid down the lee side of the embankment as bullets clipped branches from the brushy mane. To raise one's head above the hedge wall now was all but suicidal.

Subsequent attempts to take the next hedgerow proved futile as mortars churned the field and in the end the attacks were called off. Panting GIs pulled shovels from their scabbards as they hugged the near embankment and hacked desperately at the soil. Barkley wondered, *What the hell are they doing that for when it seems evident that we may be moving again at any moment?* As if in answer, mortar shells began falling all around. Terrified, Barkley flung himself to the bottom of the ditch that ran the length of the hedgerow and pressed his body hard against the earth. Each shattering explosion seemed to punch him in the gut as the earth convulsed and all the while shrapnel sang overhead and slapped heavily into the hedgerow wall above him. After what seemed an interminably long time, the barrage ceased and all again was quite.

Before long, a sergeant moved down the line. "Dig in, boys," he exhorted, "Dig in. We're staying here for the night." And so it was that the attack had run its course.

By now Barkley, too, had shovel in hand. He chopped furiously at the base of the hedgerow, aping those around him as they deepened their pits. He was amazed at what had just happened -- his first action -- and realized it was going to be a brutal, savage war. A good number of men had fallen, dead or wounded he didn't know, but for all the blood spilled they had gained only one small field. It seemed incomprehensible. He later learned that some of his fellow replacements had not survived their first day of combat.

As he mulled over the day's events, word was passed to be prepared to repel German counterattacks. Up and down the line men stood watch, but as daylight waned it became apparent that nothing would happen. The battle was over.

As the threat of counterattack eased, the men of Company G began to consolidate their new position. Officers selected fields of fire for the automatic weapons. Riflemen constantly strove to improve their hastily dug foxholes. The deeper each man got into earth the better, for incoming mortars and artillery could do horrible things to flesh and bone.

As darkness fell, pairs of men were sent forward to man listening posts in no-man's-land to circumvent German prowlings or attacks. American night patrols climbed stealthily over the hedgerows to reconnoiter the enemy lines. It was to be a long, nervous night filled with bursting flares, explosions and the rattle of guns.

The following morning, Barkley again evaluated the events of the previous day. The whole affair seemed unbelievable and he couldn't see how anybody survived that mad race from one hedgerow to the next. Yet they did -- *he did!* He began to ponder the possibility of surviving another such attack and in due course was moved to jot down a few lines on a scrap of paper. It was his first poem from the front lines:

THE SOLDIER'S PRAYER

O God protect me thru the fight
And give me courage
That I might
Be calm and strong
Throughout the storm
O Lord God, keep me
Safe from harm.

But should I stagger
And I fall,
To You alone
I then shall call,
To You -- my Faith
My Hope -- my Friend,
To You alone,
My God,
Amen.

HGB

A crosscut view showing the approximate height and depth of a Normandy hedgerow. A hedgerow was a solid earthen wall, about four to six feet high and just as thick at its base, sometimes taller, sometimes shorter. Foliage of every description sprouted from base to crest which was capped by a dense tangle of shrubs, hedges, and trees which elevated the wall several more feet, making it impossible to see into the next field. Most had drainage ditches along their base.

CHAPTER 5

BATTLES IN THE HEDGEROWS

Normandy, France, June 1944 -- The GIs in France experienced long hours of daylight and short nights throughout the Norman summer. Since the U.S. Army utilized English double summer time, the sun rose at about 5:00 AM and didn't set until roughly 10:00. Offensive combat operations often continued until nearly 11:00 when full darkness deemed them all but impractical. But even then, the hazardous duty continued. Perilous night patrols were organized to creep up to the German lines in search of weak points or discover other valuable information. Some patrols prowled deep behind the enemy positions in their quest for intelligence.

While those unfortunates probed the enemy lines, other men were selected to crawl into the blackness of no-man's-land* where pairs of soldiers occupied isolated observation posts to give warning

---

* No-man's-land: Any terrain that lies between opposing forces and not controlled by either army.

of approaching German patrols or attacks. With security out front, the remainder of the company collapsed in their damp foxholes and slipped into drooling, fitful sleep. Yet sleep only came in bits and pieces. American artillery howled overhead to disrupt the Germans' rest while enemy mortars and artillery did the same to the Americans. Although the enemy shelling caused only minimal casualties since the men were sheltered by their foxholes, the terrifying explosions robbed them of the few precious hours rest available, and all too soon the deadly cycle of long days and short nights resumed anew.

Men were roused from their holes, red-eyed and weary, resembling ghoulish apparitions ascending from desecrated graves. More often than not it would be raining, or at least misting, and mud became the order of the day. It would become routine.

June 14, 1944 -- Other than a few minor skirmishes, the Second Battalion's attack was held in check while the division launched limited attacks in other sectors to adjust its curvy line. Only marginal gains were made against ever stiffening resistance and as a result the offensive was temporarily suspended. As a consequence, operations were reduced to probing enemy positions with reconnaissance patrols or countering German incursions that prodded the American lines. Although the action had quieted, clusters of mortar and artillery shells continued to fall all along the line and men were reluctant to stray from their foxholes.

During this lull, Barkley had the opportunity to take note of the men he'd been fighting alongside. One would have hardly guessed that they had been in combat only a matter of days longer than he. They appeared as if born for battle -- a hard, mean looking lot, dirty and unshaven. In short order, Barkley, too, would undergo a radical metamorphosis and be transformed into the same maligned state and be indistinguishable from the rough veterans that now surrounded him.

Being an enlisted man, he never socialized with his officers, and as a member of a rifle squad on the line, didn't have much chance to get acquainted with the men of other squads of his platoon, leave alone the remainder of Company G which was lost from view in the checkered maze of hedgerows. His fellow replacements, his friends, had been scattered to the wind, being assigned to other squads or companies and he had no further contact with them. He didn't know if they were alive or dead. He believed The Barracuda and Barrella were also in Company G, but he wasn't sure. God only knows where Antonelli and The Major had been taken. Bell was still with him, but everyone else was a stranger.

Company G's first sergeant, Percy Imbody, was a hefty, sandy haired twenty-four year old from Pennsylvania. As top kick he was charged with the administrative functions of the company and kept the morning reports up to date -- not an easy job considering the ever rising number of casualties. During large attacks he was put to task trying to account for all his men and sometimes it took several days before he'd tally a final tabulation of casualties -- a heartbreaking job considering the fact that he personally knew all of the old hands -- their habits, their quirks, and even their families in some instances. Whereas some first sergeants worked from somewhere safely behind the front lines, Percy stayed with his company as part of the company command group.

Technical Sergeant Norman Blackmore was Barkley's platoon sergeant. He was a dark-haired, muscular man, perhaps six-feet tall whose speech was liberally laced with profanity in the heat of battle. Barkley soon discovered that Blackmore was brave almost to the point of recklessness. He was virtually fearless in combat and proved to be holy terror to the Nazis. What Barkley didn't know was that Blackmore was motivated by a personal vendetta -- his brother had been killed by the Germans earlier in the war and he had vowed to avenge his death. He was a very capable combat leader and was about as close to an officer as Barkley would get, socially speaking.

Barkley's squad leader was Staff Sergeant Fretwell, a stocky Easterner in his mid- to late-twenties[*]. Although Fretwell generally performed his duties adequately, Barkley quickly discovered that he often avoided taking personal risks in favor of delegating the more dangerous details to others of the squad while he remained in a relatively safe position.

Another sergeant was Wayne Parker, a tall, trim, athletic looking Texan. A courageous, soft-spoken man, Sergeant Parker led by example, inspiring all who saw him.

---

[*] Following my father's wishes, I have changed this man's name.

The balance of the squad resembled the novelist's conception of the All-American rifle squad. His fellow scout was Smitty, a young, agile fellow who didn't talk much.[*] The BAR[**] man, a large fellow, sat and methodically dismantled his weapon for cleaning. Being the squad's sole source of heavy firepower, he drew much attention in battle from the enemy and his life expectancy in combat wasn't much longer than that of the lead scouts' -- which was said to be only a matter of days.

Barkley's buddy, Bell, from Camp Wolters, was already being called "Shorty" by the men. He had been assigned as the assistant to the BAR gunner and now wore a suspended ammunition belt designed to carry extra BAR magazines. The added weight of the BAR ammo plus his own kit and rifle was almost too much for him. A bigger man should have been selected for the tiring job but it went to the replacement.

The others were typical, dirty-faced riflemen, young and healthy. They had lived and trained together since before the 2nd Infantry Division was sent to Britain in October of 1943 and had formed strong bonds. They had spent D-Day on board a troop transport in the English Channel and had landed amidst sporadic artillery and sniper fire on Omaha Beach the following day. They had been under fire ever since. Among these were two Mexican-Americans, Joe Benavidez and Joe Guajardo, who would, in time, become good friends of Barkley.

But for now, Barkley was a new guy, a pariah, a greenhorn yet to prove his worth and earn his place in the squad. He settled uncomfortably among his new family -- the adopted child.

The entire squad was heavily armed. Drab-clad men carried M-1 rifles and packed additional ammunition in cloth bandoliers slung over their shoulders to supplement the standard load in their ammunition belts. Hand grenades bobbed in derring-do fashion from

---

[*] I will use the name "Smitty", for unfortunately Dad can no longer recall the original First Scout's name.

[**] BAR: Browning Automatic Rifle, and pronounced as if spelling the letters. The BAR was the squad automatic weapon that fired .30 caliber bullets from detachable twenty-round magazines.

pack straps, resembling malignant lemons waiting to be plucked and force fed to defiant Nazis. Steel helmets crowned every head.

One man bore the responsibility of lugging the squad's BAR. The weapon weighed nearly twenty pounds -- twice as heavy as the M-1. Add to that a web belt containing as many as twelve twenty-round magazines and one realized it took a sturdy man to tote the monster. Shorty Bell, as mentioned earlier, was assigned as the gunner's ammunition bearer and assistant. Barkley judged the BAR as an over-rated piece left over from the First World War. He acknowledged that it had long range, but it was too heavy and the gunner could only fire twenty rounds before having to change magazines. Barkley believed that it would have been better if the BAR was replaced with a light machine gun. He noticed that the Germans sure seemed to have plenty of machine guns and therefore dominated the battlefield.

Barkley felt as if he was "loaded for bear". He carried the Thompson sub-machine gun which fired the heavy .45 caliber bullet. When fired at full automatic, the vicious recoil caused the muzzle to rise so abruptly that it was difficult to hold the weapon onto its mark when aiming at long range targets. To counter this, Barkley learned to bear down on the fore-grip when firing. But it was an ideal weapon for the close-in fighting of the Norman Bocage where the enemy was often less than 100 yards away. Frequently the distance between combatants was much less than that, and an erratic spraying of bullets was generally more effective for a scout than the aiming and triggering of an M-1.

Later, Barkley learned to carry plenty of ammunition when going into battle -- he didn't want to exhaust his supply in the middle of a hot fire fight. He generally kept a 30-round magazine[*] inserted in the weapon. He carried five or six extra magazines of either twenty or thirty rounds each, tucking several into each cargo pocket that billowed from the legs of his fatigue trousers. In his pack he stored a reserve of two or three boxes of additional bullets. Attached to his pack was a trench knife which replaced the traditional rifle bayonet. Initially, he also accepted hand grenades when issued, but later shunned them after learning that one or two other fellows had

---

[*] Magazine: A metal receptacle for holding bullets, erroneously, but commonly called a "clip".

snagged the safety rings in the brambles while passing through hedgerows and had inadvertently blown themselves up. He didn't trust the safety pin while clawing his way through such heavy foliage.

Generally, company officers were armed with Colt .45 automatic pistols as well as .30 caliber carbines. At about six pounds, the carbine was much lighter than the standard M-1, but it lacked the punch of the latter and some officers opted to carry they heavier piece in battle.

HILL 192

The town of St. Lo, lodged on an elbow of the Vire River, was a prime objective for the First U.S. Army. It's military significance lay in the fact that St. Lo was a hub for a radiating network of highways and railroads leading to all parts of Normandy and the interior of France. The Germans could easily counter Allied threats by shifting their forces by means of these connecting roads. Once St. Lo was captured, the Allies would in effect split the German Seventh Army's line of communication, thereby disrupting their means of supply and reinforcement. The taking of St. Lo was essential to First Army's success.

However, before St. Lo could be taken, a mound of high ground a couple of miles to its east had to be conquered. This high ground, designated Hill 192, rose gently to a height of 192 meters above sea level (thus its name). Although it was only about fifty meters higher than the surrounding countryside, it dominated all the approaches to and from St. Lo. From its summit the Germans had clear view of the entire countryside for miles to either flank and as far back as the Normandy beaches. German observers could easily detect all activity in the American V Corps sector and part of the newly formed XIX Corps which now bore down on St. Lo from the north. As long as German forces occupied Hill 192, St. Lo could not be taken.

The task of taking the hill fell to the 2nd Infantry Division, as it lay in that organization's line of advance. Once taken, the soldiers of the 2nd Division were to continue down the reverse slope and cross the St. Lo-Berigny Highway which girdled the base of the hill's southern bank, thereby severing one of the Germans' East-West supply routes in addition to denying them the use of a strategic observation post.

For the First U.S. Army the hill had to be captured, despite the cost. St. Lo was the lock that held the U.S. forces penned in their beachhead positions and Hill 192 was the key.

Opposing the 2nd Division was the crack 3rd Fallschirmjaeger (Parachute) Division. This unit was classified among the very best of the German forces and the young volunteers that comprised it were eager for action. They were extremely tough, motivated soldiers, highly trained in infantry tactics. Imbued with fanatic Nazi doctrine, they maintained a high level of esprit-de-corps. As paratroopers, they even dressed differently than the regular German foot soldier, wearing camouflaged smocks and special rounded parachutists helmets that lacked the flared rim at the back of the neck that so typified the headgear of the regular German soldier.

As a ground combat unit, the 3rd FJ Division was noticeably larger in manpower than the standard German infantry division and comparable in size to the U.S. infantry division. The major difference came in fire power, especially automatic weapons. Trained for the assault, the paratroopers had nearly twice as many machine guns as the regular German division and *eleven times* more than their American opponents. While roughly equal to the Americans in manpower at the company level, the parachutists' company boasted twenty machine guns and forty-three sub-machine guns, whereas the U.S. rifle company was equipped with only two light machine guns and nine BARs. It is clearly evident how a German company could be stretched over a wide front yet still maintain a cohesive defense against a numerically superior foe.

A fundamental aspect of the German defense was their use of 81mm mortars. Mortar sections operated from the trench-like protection of the many sunken roads which allowed easy movement from one firing position to the next before the Americans could place counter-battery fire on them. Firing rapidly from seclusion, the mortars played hell with the attacking Americans.

The young Fallschirmjaegers were very capable adversaries for the men of the 2nd Infantry Division. Elements of this division were perched atop Hill 192 while the remainder of its battalions were deployed to defend the lateral slopes and fields on either flank. Well entrenched and deployed in depth, they were determined not to give an inch and calmly awaited the approach of the Americans. For the Americans there would be the Devil to pay.

Previous attempts to take Hill 192 had failed. The 23rd and 38th Infantry Regiments had battled to the foot of the hill and suffered accordingly as the Germans looked straight down their throats and threw everything they had at them. Casualties had been heavy. Still, orders had been issued to try again on June 16th.

The assault units selected for the attack were the Second and Third Battalions of the 38th Infantry. The Second Battalion was to advance over the hill's right shoulder while the Third attacked directly towards the summit. The Regiment's First Battalion, temporarily attached to the neighboring 23rd Infantry, would give support on the far left. Company G, Barkley's company, was one of the assault companies for the Second Battalion. Isolated from the rest of the battalion, Company G was to conduct a flanking maneuver, utilizing a draw that knifed towards the hill from the right.

June 16, 1944 -- The assault was preceded by the usual fanfare of artillery with shells screaming overhead by the hundreds to pummel the German positions. Explosions crashed in a continuous chain, giving rise to great clouds of smoke so thick and sinister that they rivaled the wrath of Vesuvius on the eve of Pompeii's destruction. The din was deafening.

Up front, the infantry huddled in their holes and sweated the cannonade. They knew that when it ceased, they would be the ones who would go "over the top" and charge into the mouths of enemy machine guns. They would be the ones who would be ripped and torn by shot and shell. They would be the ones who would bleed and die.

Barkley hunkered deep in his hole and attempted to disengage his mind from what was about to happen. He didn't want to think about the coming attack or who would survive -- or if he would survive himself. He recalled his first attack and how the field was literally raked by bullets and shrapnel. He didn't want to ponder the consequences, and besides, it didn't do any good to worry anyway -- he was here and that was that. No getting out of it. For now, he only wanted to numb his senses and blot out all the sounds that assailed his being. When the time came to attack, he knew that somehow he'd do his duty. It was just the waiting that got to him.

The clamor continued. Salvo after salvo pounded the German lines. Tremors radiated from the battered slopes until the earth's trembling matched the intestinal quiverings that flourished in each man's gut and filled each heart with trepidation.

Somewhere some artillery officer's watch ticked on schedule and the barrage shifted a notch to rain destruction on the next line of enemy works. Taking their cue, the dogfaces emerged from their burrows and squatted beneath their hedgerow walls and waited for the word they feared the most.

A figure knelt beside Barkley's foxhole, casting a dark shadow which compelled Barkley to look up and stare into anxious, fret-filled eyes. It was Smitty, the first scout. "Let's go," was all he said. *My God!* Barkley thought as he crawled from his hole, *This is it!* His heart thundered as he searched the hedgerow for easy passage, then crouched and waited for the inevitable order -- the command that would place him squarely in harm's way. His pulse quickened. Others, too, poised beneath the dense vegetation, gripping weapons with sweaty palms.

Outgoing artillery continued to ravage the distant fields. Looking up, Barkley could see a heavy pall of smoke and dust rising beyond the hedgerow's brim, a thick, gritty wall that seemed to veil not only the front, but the unknown dangers that lay beyond. Nervous eyes darted about, stealing furtive glances from one another as they steeled their nerves for the coming ordeal. No one spoke. Wads of saliva lumped thickly in throats already constricted with fear. Some closed their eyes and moved their lips in silent prayer while a chorus of devilish explosions thundered across the front. A team of machine gunners cursed as they propped their weapon on the hedgerow's crest and pushed its nose through the briery crown. The gunner fed a belt of cartridges through the feeding block, double-jacked the bolt handle and waited.

Adrenaline pumped fiercely through Barkley's veins. *This is it!* The simply phrase kept running through his head. How many times had one said that? Well, this *is* it! Smitty crouched a short distance away, appearing highly disconcerted and edgy. Barkley caught his eye and nodded absently, then hefted his Thompson and tapped its magazine with the heel of his hand to ensure the clip was secure. He squatted and waited, a tight wound spring tensed for the moment of release.

Mortars coughed from behind, followed by a breathless pause until the nearest hedgerow shuddered from the impact of plunging shells. Other shells fell in rapid succession while one or two more plopped ungraciously in the intervening field and gave rise to clouds of veiling smoke.

Then a distant voice rose taut and shrill: "Let's go. Scouts out!"

Up and down the line scouts clambered over their sheltering walls to lead their squads to battle. Soon, the clatter of small arms fire greeted the bold advance, followed by more gunfire and machine guns and the terrible sound of mortars. The covering American gunners answered with long, rattling bursts. The battle had begun.

On the Second Battalion's front, Companies E and F moved directly against the western slope of Hill 192 while Company G set off on its circuitous route, guided by the draw that hooked in from the right. Initially, the assault squads knocked off the enemy screening forces with relative ease, then moved on for a field or two until the leading platoons blundered into a veritable web of destruction.

No sooner had Barkley and Smitty reached the midway point of a unkempt field than the entire hedgerow before them erupted with uncompromising noise. Tracers flashed brightly in crisscross patterns while rifles and burp guns fired directly into the attacker's faces. It seemed to have been precisely timed for shock effect and it worked -- the platoon reeled as if struck by a gale force wind. Then mortars began to fall and the attack was knocked to a standstill.

Barkley lay in the grass and cringed as the world disintegrated around him. Each explosion seemed to knock the earth deep into his chest, as if kicked by a mule. Metal fragments whined overhead while a flurry of bullets snapped in a continuous stream. It seemed suicidal to rise up to return the deadly fire and most simply lay there, pinned down by the murderous storm. The noise was overwhelming.

From behind, the staccato hammering of the covering American machine guns rattled across the field only to be answered by the bold, buzz-saw rip of the faster firing German guns. Mortar shells fell in a near continuous chain, or so it seemed, and men cowered, dreading every burst. Men were hit, howling their agonies which only aggravated their comrade's fears. Sergeants hollered and screamed and cajoled men to move. To remain in place was to invite death. A resolute few responded and leaped up to follow their leaders.

Heeding their words, Barkley stumbled to his feet and plunged forward, bent double in a full tilt charge. Anything was better than staying where he was. Bullets snapped and popped as they whizzed past his cheeks, drawing oaths and curses from between clenched teeth. "Go, go, go," someone shouted, and the ragged line surged forward.

A scream caused Barkley to glance over his shoulder. In that brief moment he was treated to a vista of the drama unfolding behind him. A dozen or more GIs struggled to clear the hedge top while murderous machine gun fire raked its crest. Some men were hit and dropped back to the other side while the others toppled over the dike and charged and some of these seemed to stumble and sink in the tall grass like men drowning at sea. Earth and fire leaped from the ground as mortar shells exploded all around. It was a frightening and surreal vignette.

Still out front and miraculously untouched, Barkley gained momentum. His training automatically kicked in, as if Sergeant McKay of Camp Wolters was hollering into his ear: *"Dodge, drop, get up, run! Fire! Drop! Roll, get up…"* and he'd do so, dropping at the run, rolling, then popping up to touch off a burst as he sprinted forward only to repeat the action. His knees were impervious to the sharp stabs of rocks and twigs as he crashed to the ground. Rocks and twigs were the least of his worries! It seemed impossible that anybody could survive this macabre race across such a ghastly, bullet swept arena. It was identical to his first action, reminiscent of the phenomenon called deja vu, the intense sensation of having been somewhere before.

After what seemed an eternity, Barkley slammed into the enemy's hedgerow. Gasping, he crouched low and hugged the earthen bank. *Now what?*

The Germans were just on the other side and still firing madly at the soldiers in the field. Time for action. Smitty whipped a grenade over the hedgerow wall. Kneeling, Barkley aimed his Thompson at the hedge top and raked it with a long burst, then sprung to his tip-toes with his weapon held high overhead as he sprayed a wild stream over the hedgerow wall, hoping to pin down any Germans on the opposite side.

Smitty, too, stepped back and swept the hedge top with short, deliberate bursts. Down the line, Sergeant Blackmore scrambled above the hedgerow and screamed epithets as he gunned down startled Germans who scurried for cover below him. A shower of leaves and twigs exploded all about him as he fired, clipped neatly by bullets intent on killing him, but the sergeant never so much as flinched. Barkley gawked with disbelief. *My God!* he thought, *He's crazy!* He could hardly do less than admire Blackmore -- the man was fearless.

Others arrived and joined the fray and a wild melee broke out. Rifles of both sides banged away. Grenades arched back and forth over the hedgerow, exploding at random. Men cursed and screamed. The stutter of German burp guns ripped the air. Barkley answered with showers of .45 caliber bullets, emptying another magazine into a tangle of briers and branches. With a sweep of an arm he ejected the empty and jammed home a fresh one.

The gunfire slackened as the Germans abandoned their position and bolted for the rear. Several GIs sprung to the hedge top and emptied their rifles at several stragglers who dashed across the field in a desperate bid to gain the safety of next hedgerow a short distance away. The fleeing enemies' fate was sealed as another squad gained a flanking hedgerow and mowed them down as they ran.

From up ahead more gunfire sounded as some other platoon engaged the enemy.

Not wanting to loose momentum, Barkley's platoon was ordered to continue the attack. Sergeant Fretwell came up behind Barkley and roughly shoved him. "Go, go," he hounded, "Get yer ass over that goddam hedgerow." Barkley had paused for a moment to catch his breath, but was already on the move by the time his sergeant spoke. He scowled at his squad leader as he struggled up the obstacle's face. He noticed that Fretwell wasn't making any effort to join him, but stalked up and down the line to push others into the attack. Maybe that was his job. Who knew? But it seemed to Barkley that a sergeant ought to be with his squad when attacking, not hanging back. A leader should lead! *The dirty bastard!* he thought as he pulled hard on a fistful of shrubbery as he scaled the steep wall, *let others do your fighting for you, will you?*

As Barkley cleared the hedgerow he noted the carnage of battle strewn along its base. A number of Germans lay twisted and tangled in the crazy posture reserved solely for the dead. Smears of bright blood slicked the grass around them. More Germans were scattered along the hedgerow, half in and half out of the bordering ditch. Some of these were clearly out of the picture, more dead than alive, convulsing with spasmodic twitches as Death pulled the last vestiges of life from them. A few sat with backs propped against the bank, bearing numb, dazed expressions while the less severely wounded assumed postures of submission with hands clasped upon their heads. They glared spitefully at every GI who passed them, and some were so audacious as to offer encouragement to their stricken comrades by giving stiff-armed salutes and yelping, "Heil Hitler! Heil Hitler!" and other unintelligible slogans. They were tough nuts. Fanatics. GIs warily guarded them as the remainder of the squad came sliding down the hedge bank.

"Hey! There's someone down here."

Eyes turned towards a soldier who pointed deep into a cavernous dugout. The occupant, or occupants, refused demands to surrender. Another entreaty fell on deaf ears. Someone hollered into the hole, "Kommen Sie heraus!" A burp gun answered from the depths. Enough of that. The soldier pried the pin from a grenade and pitched it into the hole, and that was that.

Meanwhile, the squad prepared to move out. As they set off across the field, one of the sitting wounded suddenly pulled a grenade from beneath him and flung it at the passing Americans. *BOOM!* A soldier bowled over. Startled GIs spun in their tracks and riddled the fanatic die-hard with a fusillade of gunfire. In a fit of rage, a solider mowed down the remaining prisoners. Such treachery from supposedly surrendered enemies was met with swift, vindictive reactions. Many of the young, zealous paratroopers were devoted to the twisted Nazi ideology, having been brainwashed in its doctrine since childhood, and were more than willing to sacrifice their lives for Fuhrer and Fatherland.

Barkley was rattled by the incident. It left an indelible mark on him and underscored yet another hard lesson of war: *If you want to live, don't trust any by-passed enemy wounded or surrendering soldiers, for they, too, can kill you.* As the lead elements of his squad tumbled over other hedgerows in the heat and fury of battle, they learned to quickly scan the overrun position for survivors. Any Germans who weren't reaching for the sky were killed on sight. It was survival, pure and simple. One could not afford to take chances in this deadly game, for enemy soldiers, whether wounded or not, could be other fanatic Nazis, eager to kill Americans when their backs were turned. It was a chilling, cold-blooded business. In war you had to survive by whatever means necessary.

The attack pressed on. Again the scouts took the lead as one platoon leapfrogged the other. Apparently the Germans had anticipated Company G's maneuver along the draw and hammered them incessantly with torrents of mortar and artillery shells. Machine guns seemed to cover every field they attempted to cross, pinning down attacking squads and setting them up for the next round of high explosives.

The sounds of battle rose to new heights. There was so much racket and noise that the din blended to form one continuous roar. Men would move along and suddenly the next man's head exploded, splattering brains and blood and slippery bone chips all over the grass and onto those nearest him. Or one spun abruptly in his tracks for seemingly no reason as a bullet slammed home, leaving a look of complete and total surprise upon his face as his brain struggled to evaluate what had just happened. Or a man was catapulted skyward as a pillar of fire and smoke launched his body in undignified flight.

Bloody bodies and body parts were common sights. Dead and wounded lay everywhere and blood soaked the soil.

In the open fields it all boiled down to chance. One might stumble and avoid a fatal wound while the same stumble may just as easily have pitched him directly into a bullet's path. An entire burst of machine gun fire may be directed at one man and miss while a ricochet from the same burst might drill another's head.

Mortar and artillery shells fell nearly continuously. Terrified by the mayhem, men swallowed hard and moved forward only to drop again as the next cluster of shells exploded. Much to the officer's and sergeant's chagrin, men quickly pulled their entrenching tools whenever they stopped and chopped frantically at the earth. Each explosion generated waves of uncontrollable terror, causing twinges of fear to race up and down the spine until muscles knotted tightly and knees grew weak. To rise seemed virtually impossible. A quick calculation verified that the odds of survival were clearly stacked against them. A fatalistic attitude governed the battlefield and one could trick himself into believing that the very next shell was aimed specifically at him, that it would land squarely on his back and blow him to kingdom come. Some men simply fell apart and balled up like fetuses and sobbed like babies. At times like this, with swarms of bullets pop-pop-popping overhead and shrapnel screaming about by the bucketsful, the months and months of training seemed to account for little and everything did, indeed, boil down to chance. Only the actions of natural leaders such as Sergeants Blackmore and Parker could offer a wild card chance to defeat the odds and tilt the scales of Fate in favor of the attackers, and men responded to their selfless acts and moved forward. In battle one gambled against Fate and took his chances, though the Devil seemed to hold all the cards.

The fighting grew increasingly bitter. Progress had been slow at best and by mid-morning, after continuous assaults, the company had cleared only a handful of hedgerows. Yet still, advances were made. Whenever overwhelmed, the enemy fell back a field or two to set up their next trap. The leading platoons shook off their losses and cautiously entered fields now ominously silent, expecting the worse.

Hours later Barkley's squad was again overlooking a grassy field -- a shell-pocked pasture cluttered with a sprinkling of dead cattle. Although fierce combats raged to either flank, not a sound broke the foreboding silence before them. Sergeant Fretwell, suspicious of the silence, sent out his scouts. Barkley and Smitty tread cautiously as they entered the field, ever conscious of the hedgerows that surrounded them, for they knew that the enemy could be entrenched behind any one of them and all hell could break loose at any moment. Neither scout was in a hurry to trigger that event. Death would come soon enough.

As Barkley proceeded, he noted the dead cattle that littered the field. Some were bloated tight as balloons with legs thrust stiffly in the air -- casualties of war, some farmer's loss. Un-nerved by the silence, the scouts moved swiftly through the field.

As the scouts reached mid-field, the rest of the squad came tumbling over the hedgerow. And then the expected happened.

Barkley's skin nearly leaped from his flesh as a maddening burst ripped from the left. Everyone dove to earth. One or two men cried out that they'd been hit. Again all was silent. Barkley, who had been in the lead, had crashed headlong into the grass and scrambled for the dubious shelter of a dead cow. Another gust of bullets scythed the field and thudded savagely into the carcass. Barkley cringed. *My God! Where's he at?* Although he had searched intently while advancing, he hadn't seen anything that betrayed the enemy's presence. As often was the case, one never knew where the enemy was until he opened fire -- they always seemed to have the advantage.

Men lay where they dropped, eyes bulging, sweat popping, lungs heaving dry as leather. A wounded soldier writhed and disturbed the grass which provoked another burst and he was still.

Fortunately, most of the squad had not ventured too far into the field and played their chances as each saw fit. One by one, men stole back between erratic bursts to reach the safety of the hedgerow behind them.

Barkley, shielded by his cow, was in a hell of a predicament. He and Smitty had advanced pretty far and it was a long way back to where his comrades now safely lay. Every time he moved, machine gun bullets ripped the earth around him and drove him back to his bovine shelter. More bullets splattered into the beast and he quickly gave up on any notion of returning to his comrades. He was pinned down, stranded in the middle of a wide open field.

Before long, a voice called hoarsely from the rear, trying to determine who remained in the field. Barkley hollered that he was alright but couldn't move due to the machine gun. Another voice rose from the pasture saying that he was okay, too. It was Smitty. Apparently the Germans had caught the platoon with flanking fires from a ridge on the left that covered the draw. It seemed as if they had concentrated their fire on the main body as they entered the field, thereby missing both scouts. The bullets must have either been directed behind them or had passed safely overhead. Whatever the reason, both scouts were now trapped in the field.

It was obvious that the stranded men would not be able to make it back, so were ordered to stay put while others tried to devise a plan to rescue them. It was either that or wait until they could steal away under cover of darkness, and it was a long way from dusk. It was going to be a long day. Again a voice bellowed from behind the hedgerow: "Hang low, men. Hang low." It was Sergeant Blackmore.

Barkley lay with his face near the belly of the dead cow. Its abdomen was split open, exposing a mass of lacerated guts which stewed beneath a mid-day sun. Apparently the beast had been killed days earlier by shrapnel or machine gun fire. Now maggots writhed in the putrid mess. The odor was nauseating. *Well this is a helluva fix,* he thought as his nostrils filled with the stench of decaying flesh.

Sweat flowed from beneath his helmet. Flies buzzed in and out of the rotting carcass and danced lightly across the steaming entrails strewn before his face. A careless movement caught the eye of a Nazi gunner. *Rrrrrp!* Flesh flew from the carcass. Barkley shrunk behind his cow. They knew he was there, alright. Perhaps they were amused at his dilemma and were only toying with him. No matter, he couldn't move. He lay low and waited, not knowing when, or even *if* he'd ever get out of this one.

Apparently anxiety conceives strange notions, and for Barkley this was certainly an anxious time. He remembered that he had a tin of cheese in his pocket, so despite the stench of rotting entrails, he decided to eat it. He didn't know why; he certainly wasn't hungry. It was something to do, to while the time away.

Keeping low he pulled the can from his pocket and opened it. Nervously, he peeled away the paper liner, but before he could bring it to his mouth he fumbled the cheese onto a smear of cow dung. "Dammit!" he swore. Nonetheless, he yearned to eat it. He gingerly brushed off the affected areas, then began to nibble on his treat. It was a rather unsavory picnic, but what else was there to do?

Time dragged. The day grew warmer. Small arms fire crackled from the confines of distant hedgerows, accompanied by muffled explosions, bearing testimony to other hard fought contests as the battle ebbed and flowed in other fields. The sonorous rumbling of artillery provided a perpetual undertone to the struggle.

Still no reaction from Barkley's company. He could only guess how long he had been in the field. He polished off his cheese and still he waited. At least the Germans hadn't fired on him.

Then, quite suddenly, artillery pounded the suspected German position. Mortars dropped smoke shells on closer hedgerows and soon the platoon swarmed into the field and Barkley and Smitty were compelled to rise and join them and another field was taken.

It was tedious, perilous work. It took time... and sweat... and patience, not to mention a considerable amount of skill. Barkley and Smitty had just survived a close call and didn't want to risk another. But they knew as long as they had the squad and leaders such as Sergeant Blackmore to back them up, they'd hopefully get out of any other tight scrapes. By utilizing the doctrine of fire and movement, so tirelessly drilled into them during countless training maneuvers, the squad worked as a team, supporting one another as they closed on their enemies, forcing them to abandon their positions or pay with their lives. Undisputed trust and confidence in comrades welded the squad into a family, so to speak, a brotherhood of warriors where young soldiers such as Barkley literally trusted men like Blackmore with their lives.

Company G strove to drive the enemy from the fields skirting the right side of the draw but was stopped cold by a curtain of steel as German artillery found the range. Heavy mortar concentrations stalled further attacks and each subsequent assault across barren fields or through shattered orchards was met by withering machine gun fire that poured from hedgerows on the ridgeline to their left. More gunfire emanated from a grove of trees at the head of the draw. The company had been lured into a trap.

The situation became extremely fluid. Troops lost their bearings and became disoriented in the jumbled maze of hedgerows - - *Who's on the left? Is the right flank keeping pace, or are they behind? Or are* we *behind?* If a squad or platoon had advanced faster than those in the neighboring fields they were prime candidates for massacre as Germans closed in from the flanking hedgerows and destroyed them with machine guns. Sometimes enemy fire came from the rear as well as either flank. It was like shooting fish in a barrel.

To add to the confusion, German 88's exploded in rapid succession, spraying shrapnel upon horrified soldiers and a few more men went down. The German 88mm artillery was a terror. Whereas other artillery shells gave a tell-tale whistle or whoosh to warn of their approach, the 88 came at such high velocity that it actually exploded *before* the men could react to the sharp delayed crack of its flight. When presented with targets, German gunners could throw shells at an alarmingly rapid rate. How they hated the 88's! Under such relentless bombardments it became impossible to advance any farther. Squads became isolated and vulnerable to selective counterattacks as machine guns fixed their positions and prevented further movement. Again the dreaded mortars began to fall, eating away at brave men's resolve. A disaster was brewing.

The enemy mortars did not let up. It became apparent that if they remained in place any longer, no one would be left to continue the attack. Finally a voice carried above the din: "Fall back. Fall back. Every man for himself." Instinctively, desperate men began to scramble for the relative safety of the last hedgerow taken. Ponderous eruptions spouted from all points of the compass and again men were down on their bellies. Shards of jagged steel knifed the air. Again machine guns burred. It seemed painfully slow crawling beneath the deadly storm, but one by one, men began to gain the shelter of their coveted hedgerow wall. Barkley, like the others, scurried on hands, knees and elbows until he, too, scuttled up its brambly wall and tumbled over the other side. Panting, he watched awestruck as others came clambering over the hedge top. But rest was not to come.

No sooner had the survivors assembled on the lee side of the hedgerow than mortar shells commenced their deadly promenade. Each shell fell precisely behind the earthen bank at measured intervals to reap a bloody harvest. Men did the only thing they could and pressed their bodies flat against the earth while fire and steel shot all about them.

And then all was still. But not for long.

In the interim, while the GIs fell back and cowered beneath the mortars' hell, the enemy moved up in counterattack and now raked the entire line with flanking machine gun fires. Panic ensued and again soldiers bolted for the rear with bullets flashing all about.

Falling back to the next hedgerow they fell into the laps of the reserve platoon which promptly mounted the hedge wall and provided covering fire. U.S. mortars were called and soon German boys were feeling the sting of American steel. And again all was quiet.

Barkley's heart nearly burst from the exertion. *Jesus Christ*, he thought, *How the hell did I not get hit?* He was not alone in his thoughts. Others of the platoon stared in wild-eyed wonder, stunned by what they had just experienced. Hands trembled as canteens splashed hot water down parched throats. Already, U.S. artillery was softening up the enemy line and before long the reserve platoon went over the top and the next hedgerow was taken and then the next. But here again the attack stalled in the face of withering fire.

So it went. Each field taken was paid for by rivers of blood and gallons of sweat. They were hard fought contests where the enemy only gave way grudgingly, and then fell back only far enough to spring their next trap. Casualties soared. Filthy men stumbled painfully to the rear, bearing sopping red bandages that stanched the flow of life giving blood. Others, those so badly injured that they were incapable of returning on their own, were born away by sweating stretcher bearers who strained to remove their wretched burdens from the field of battle. And the dead lay where they had fallen, individually or in disgusting heaps -- red meat spilled from the butcher block of war. The living bucked up their courage and stared bleakly at the next hedgerow. They were far from reaching their objective and the attack pushed on at an excruciatingly slow pace.

Fierce see-saw battles raged for possession of the tiny fields. Once again Barkley's platoon had been driven back a field or two before they managed to rally. Everybody looked distraught. Men were on edge and didn't know what to expect. Perhaps they'd be ordered once more into the jaws of Death, or maybe they'd fall back another field. It seemed as if they were loosing control of the battle. Confusion reigned.

Only one field separated the antagonists and the battle disintegrated into a savage exchange of small arms fire. German bullets pounded the hedgerow's crest to dust. Branches spiraled through the air while leaves fluttered like confetti onto soldiers wincing below. Every bush and tree bore vivid white scars where shrapnel and bullets had marred them.

Barkley's heart thumped wildly. He had barely made it back to their present position after the attack broke up and fell apart. The constant fighting and climbing up and over each hedgerow was taking its toll and he was exhausted. They had been going at it all day without rest. Death hovered over him like an entity, something real and tangible, a thing he did not want to know. Casualties had been heavy, yet there was no sign of relief. Water was low. Ammo was low. Morale was low. They were far from achieving any success but still they were expected to fight. Although he hadn't a watch, he believed it had to be sometime in the afternoon by now. It seemed an eternity.

He hardly flinched as a bevy of bullets rustled the foliage above his head. Elsewhere, soldiers continued to shoot back, hoping to discourage further counterattacks, but it seemed obvious that the enemy had gained the upper hand. Rifles were no match for the deadly German machine guns, and the measured crack of M-1's seemed highly inadequate compared to the rapid firing German weapons.

Infuriated, Sergeant Blackmore stalked up and down the line. "Keep up the fire," he implored, "Keep it up, goddamit! Pour it on 'em." His face was contorted and black from battle. But all the cajoling was for naught, and before long the American's return fire slackened, then tapered to almost nothing. Blackmore launched into a litany of curses. Many men were nearly out of bullets and held their fire until a sure target presented itself. Barkley, too, chose to conserve his dwindling ammunition supply. He had used up most of his reserve ammo in the course of the fierce struggle and was concerned about running out before the fight was settled. He knew his Thompson was a close range weapon and saved it for a German attack. He'd be ready to mow them down if necessary.

Another gust of bullets swept the hedge top and a man suddenly let loose his rifle and slumped against the hedgerow wall. He looked dazed, bewildered. A dark stain spread across his chest. His trembling hand clawed at a shirt pocket and groped for a cigarette. Instinctively he placed it in his mouth, then left it dangling from chapped, split lips.

Several men moved to his side and eased him to the ground. The wounded man gurgled, then coughed and sprayed his buddies with a crimson mist as the cigarette spilled to his bloody chest.

"Aid man! Aid man!" one fellow cried as another round of gunfire exploded down the line.

The stricken soldier looked up at the buddy who held him and took a ragged breath, then grimaced and suppressed a moan. "At last," he rasped, "I'm going home." His friend winced at the words, then looked away with quivering chin. The wounded man's breathing became labored and heavy. His face took on an ashen pallor as blood dribbled steadily from tight clamped lips.

"Aid man! Where's the goddam aid man?"

Another cluster of mortar shells pasted a neighboring field, giving rise to a cloud of smoke that drifted over the hedge top like Death's dark shadow.

The wounded man gurgled again, then rolled his eyes as he sucked his final breath and all the while his buddy hugged him close and wept, unable to release the corpse that had been his friend. Barkley monitored the scene from a distance and was chilled by the spectacle, and he knew sure as hell that Death would be his constant companion from here on out.

A gruff voice broke the spell: "Let's get some fire out there." It was Blackmore. Barkley forgot the dead and commenced worrying about the living and aimed his weapon over the hedgerow wall.

Finally the word came: "We're pulling out." Machine guns had been placed at the hedgerow behind them to provide covering fire as the men disengaged from the enemy.

The covering guns opened up, a deep throated *chugg-chugg-chugg* as bullets flashed overhead. Some men crawled while others crouched and ran for the rear, then bellied over the hedgerow's wall. Once everyone was safely over, the process was repeated again and again until they came to the last open field before the draw. Across the draw was the remainder of the Second Battalion whose lines stretched to the east, away from the murderous draw. Across the draw was sanctuary.

Individually, or by small groups, men plunged down the slope, then dashed across the open space that separated Hell from safe haven. Staggering up the opposite slope they tumbled over the nearest hedgerow. They were safe. They had completed their exodus from their personal Valley of Death.

The men of Company G trickled back to the battalion area where the other companies had fared somewhat better than they, making perhaps five-hundred yards at the end of their attacks. Company G rallied and was ordered to prepare to repel expected counterattacks. Exhausted men dug in on the battalion's right, echeloned to face their deadly draw while the remainder of the battalion occupied hedgerows fronting the hill that stretched obliquely to their left.

Many a corpse had been left behind… and wounded men, too -- some would not be accounted for, for days to come. The attack had been a failure. The steady pounding from German mortars and artillery in conjunction with the heavy concentration of machine guns at the far end of the draw had proved fatal. Company G had taken a beating and had been bled white. But there was no time for self-pity. The probability of a counterattack was all too real.

CHAPTER 6

STALEMATE

June 16, 1944, late afternoon -- The survivors of Company G were bushed. They knew they had been whipped. A simple head count could attest to that. Friends were gone. Squads had been decimated. The fight for the west side of the draw had been a fiasco, a tragedy of catastrophic proportions. They didn't want to do it again.

But for now there would be no more assaults and orders came to dig in. As others dug, Barkley threw off his pack and rummaged for his last box of bullets. The threat of counterattack seemed imminent and he wanted to be prepared. Nearby, Smitty chopped diligently at the hedgerow's base then paused momentarily to wipe a hand across his blackened face. "We made it," he wheezed. Barkley did not answer but concentrated on cramming bullets into his empty magazines.

Meanwhile bone weary men continued to improve their foxholes, hacking purposefully at the tangled roots that weaved through the hedgerow's base. A few enterprising soldiers scrounged planks from nearby farm buildings and leaned them over their holes as roofs while others dragged felled logs for protection from incoming mortars.

By now the sun had all but set. Satisfied with their defensive positions, the men were now at liberty to eat their rations. Young men looked old and worn far beyond their years as they pried open their meat cans and lethargically spooned the contents to their lips. They were too tired to taste -- too tired to care. Nothing really mattered except that they had survived another day.

As twilight neared, a distant growl heralded the approach of vehicles from the rear. It grew increasingly louder. It wasn't tanks. It was trucks. Soon a big army six-by-six, a two and one-half ton truck, appeared and rumbled into the field behind the GIs. The truck rolled to a halt and men leaped from the cab. Even from where the riflemen sat, they could tell that they were from Graves Registration. They would come up to the front lines when able, or just behind them, to clear the dead. It was a grisly task that generally fell to black soldiers.

Barkley watched with disgust as they fanned out and beat a swath through the field in efforts to locate the corpses.

"Here's one," one would call out, and another Graves man would come over to help remove the body.

"Ugh! Gawd! Look at dat!"

"Gimme a hand."

They'd each grab a foot and drag the cadaver to the rear of their truck where one would grasp it by its wrists or shoulders while his partner grabbed the ankles. Chanting, "One... Two...Thu-REE!" they'd swing the corpse and pitch it over the tailgate. The rag-doll body would flail through the air and tumble limply onto a bloody pile of its brothers in death, American and German alike, before settling between the high plank sideboards.

Barkley turned his face away. He wondered how many mothers, after receiving the dreaded telegram, had been led to believe that their darling sons had been removed from the battlefield with dignity by solemn stretcher bearers. *U.S. ARMY FIELD MANUAL 21-100; Chapter 16; paragraph 295 -- Burial Expenses: The*

Government provides the burial expenses for a soldier who dies while in active service.

The Graves Registration men resumed their search for more carcasses and duly towed the mutilated bodies to their truck. As soon as the pasture was cleared of the dead, the truck rumbled away, piled high with War's grisly offal, bequeathing the field to those who were about to die.

One more day's work done, one or two more hedgerows cleared. The hedgerows stretched on forever...

The sky crackled and men flattened. Massive explosions shook the earth. Once again the German artillery had found them. The GIs cowered deep in their foxholes while the barrage continued unabated. And with the artillery came darkness.

It seemed as if Barkley had been asleep for only a moment when he was jarred awake by another soldier. "C'mon, let's go. We're moving out." Barkley blinked groggily. It was daylight. He felt numb, fuzzy. His head swam with fatigue. He blinked again and stared blankly at the cool morning light.

Up and down the line men squatted in their foxholes, absorbed with their individual priorities. Some shoveled the last spoonfuls of cold chow into their jaws while others chatted quietly with a friend while still others solemnly checked their weapons in preparation for the work reserved for infantry.

The battalion had orders to resume the offensive. During the night jeeps had drawn up as close to the front as they dared to off-load supplies. Carrying parties distributed bandoliers of bullets and hand grenades along with cartons of rations. Barkley accepted several fresh boxes of .45 caliber bullets. Canteens were filled from five-gallon jerry cans. Now all that remained was to hear the word that everybody dreaded -- the word to attack.

Before long the sky shuddered as another out-going barrage passed overhead. The red-eyed doughboys braced for another day of combat. Tense, dirty, dog-tired and scared, they knew what lay ahead.

Due to the beating taken on June 16th, the action of the following day was limited to a series of minor probing attacks. Groups of men crossed into no-man's-land to feel out the enemy's defenses only to be forced back by machine gun and mortar fire. Excited men breathlessly reported their misadventures to those who remained behind.

The attack on Hill 192 had ended disastrously -- casualties had been heavy. By the time the casualty list was completed (and it took several days to locate some of the bodies) Company G alone had lost nearly sixty men on June 16th, mostly from artillery and heavy machine gun fire that emanated from a series of strong points that commanded the draw now known as "Dead Man's Gulch". The strongest of these, located in the fields at the head of the draw, was a labyrinth of mutually supporting positions that not only covered the draw, but also the approach routes used by the other companies of the battalion as they assaulted the hill. It was such a veritable hornet nest that the GIs quickly dubbed it "Kraut Corner". It was the cornerstone of enemy defenses covering the western slope of Hill 192 and would remain a point of contention for many weeks to come.

After two days of hard combat, the 38th Infantry had gained little ground, only succeeding in attaining a toehold at the foot of the hill. The two-day cost to the 2nd Infantry Division: 1,253 men.

Offensive operations were suspended. The men of Company G had been thoroughly shaken by the ordeal of "Dead Man's Gulch" and morale dropped to rock bottom. As a consequence, the company was designated battalion reserve and deployed a field or two behind the other two rifle companies. In theory, the reserve company would support the two assault companies during attacks to exploit any successes, or be committed whenever either of the leading companies became bogged down by heavy resistance. But in the ensuing static situation that followed the abortive attacks on Hill 192, the reserve company took on a defensive role. Their purpose now was to counter any enemy breakthroughs and also to provide personnel for battalion reconnaissance patrols. Although "in the rear", so to speak, they were still only a couple of hundred yards from the actual front line and were still subject to mortar and sniper fire. In some ways, due to the dangers encountered while patrolling, the role of reserve was more hazardous than that of holding the foxholes farther forward.

By now Barkley had survived several days of intense combat and his initiation to the brutal war of the hedgerows proved to be nothing short of organized murder. He began to assume the same rough features that so marked the company's men when he first joined them less than a week earlier -- he was fast becoming a seasoned combat veteran. The cruelties of combat forced hard lessons upon him -- lessons he had to learn fast or pay the consequences.

He had acquired a highly developed sense of hearing that sifted through the battle sounds and sorted threatening noises from non-threatening ones. He could now discern the difference between the sounds of incoming or outgoing artillery, and whether the shells were passing safely overhead, falling short, or dropping right on top of them. A drawn out rasping sound, like the rustling of dry leaves, indicated that a shell was passing safely overhead. But if it gave a curt *"ZHOOSH!"* it was falling close, real close, and one had about one-half of a heartbeat to hit the dirt. Lightning reflexes became instinctive and essential to longevity -- one had to instantly take cover whenever particular sounds warranted.

Each army's small arms fire made distinctive sounds, too. Barkley could now easily distinguish the horrifying rip of a German machine gun from the rapid clatter of a BAR or the jolting rhythm of the U.S. machine gun.

As time wore on and days evolved into weeks, his eyesight seemed to grow exceptionally keen. He could detect the slightest movement at distances he previously would have thought impossible. Any unusual movement or vague rustling of branches could bring instant death and would send him pitching headlong to the ground, scrambling for cover until its cause was determined. He was an Army Scout, the eyes of his squad. The lives of his comrades, and his own, depended on his staying alert. His every sense was tuned to battle.

After nearly two weeks of intense combat, the assault battalions had been whittled down to a core of hard, battle savvy veterans. By some quirk of fate they had survived. There may have been men who were better trained, or better marksmen, or even more intelligent than they, but Death had plucked them from the field and now fewer and fewer of the original men remained. Those still on the line had somehow endured the trials of battle and every hour of every day spent in combat made them wiser in the ways of survival. They were quicker to react to every menacing sound. They invented tactics to meet unusual circumstances and now were alive simply because of a strong desire to remain that way... and a great deal of luck. But that kind of luck doesn't hold forever. The odds against them coming through the war unscathed were stacked high against them.

Nor were the casualties the exclusive burden of the enlisted men. Although the common soldier suffered the bulk of the deaths and wounds, officers took their hits, too. Leadership in the savage hedgerow battles was essential for success and leaders had to rise above their own fears to encourage the men to move forward. Many key sergeants and company officers had been killed or wounded. Captain Raymond received a serious wound during the battle for the draw and command of Company G passed temporarily to Lieutenant "Lucky" Lawson of the Second Platoon until Lieutenant Bertrand Warner arrived from Regimental Headquarters to assume command.[*] A platoon leader had fallen during the same attack and another was evacuated with combat exhaustion.

In the coming weeks fresh lieutenants came and went so fast that at times the men didn't know who their platoon leader was. Barkley recalled how one replacement lieutenant was killed very shortly after arriving at the front, laying in a sea of mud when hit. He had no idea who he was. Another fresh face showed up to take his place. All positions in a rifle company were temporary -- it was just a matter of time before one was hit. In time one came to expect it.

Although one's life was daring by necessity, no one cared to tempt Fate. In an effort to reduce the risk of becoming a casualty, the original members of the company had learned early in the campaign

---

[*] Years later, Barkley's old First Sergeant, Percy Imbody, told him that Captain Raymond finally succumbed to his injuries, weighing only seventy pounds when he died.

to cut the distinctive divisional shoulder patch from their jackets. The black shield's bright white star that bore the Indian head was too inviting a target for German snipers. Those that had the emblem painted on the front of their helmets before the invasion scratched them off with rocks or bayonets or obliterated them with mud. Officers removed bars of rank from their uniforms and saluting at the front was prohibited. Officers were prize targets.

Periodically, additional replacements were brought up and used up almost as fast as they arrived. The ratio of casualties to replacements never seemed to balance, so companies, platoons and squads were constantly fighting at reduced strength.

These new men arrived in confused groups, nervously clutching their rifles as they were doled out to the depleted rifle squads. Most appeared to be young kids not long out of high school, scared out of their wits. The veterans could look at some of them and just *knew* that they'd never make it -- and many didn't, being killed or wounded on their first day or two at the front.

The strain and sudden shock of combat was too much for others and they quickly succumbed to combat exhaustion. Some became so un-nerved at the prospect of going into battle that they simply fell to pieces, bawling and trembling uncontrollably until taken to the rear. Percy Imbody, Company G's First Sergeant, noted that a few malcontents would show up at the command post with obviously self-inflicted wounds to a hand or foot, claiming it was an accident or battle injury. But Imbody knew what really happened. He noted that the hand wounds were never sustained by the dominant extremity. Still, no matter how it occurred, the wound had to be treated at a field hospital and those who bore them reasoned that a mangled hand or foot was preferable to what they felt was certain death in battle. Some simply couldn't cope with combat.

However, others adapted quickly to this strange, bizarre lifestyle and lived to be veterans of many days or weeks or even months before getting hit. The burden of combat fell to those resolute stout-hearts who could take it.

June 18, 1944 -- The weather roughened. By evening the sky took on an evil, menacing cast as brisk winds pushed heavy black clouds across a slate gray sky. Rumbling thunder and sharp cracks of lightning mimicked the roar and crash of artillery.

Disgruntled soldiers rolled their eyes to the turbulent heavens and cursed. There was no shelter save the sparse cover some had achieved by placing scavenged boards or logs over their holes as protection from a more lethal steel rain. Their chances of keeping dry were bleak. Despairing soldiers wrapped their jackets about them and huddled in their foxholes and waited for the storm to arrive.

The first heavy drops splattered hesitantly onto the leaves of the hedgerows, as if testing their targets for resistance. Then the clouds ripped open, releasing bullets of rain that plummeted in a leaden deluge.

Thousands of miles away, Nettie Barkley fretted while Harry puffed on his pipe and tuned in the radio for war news. Daily they'd scan the headlines of the Quincy Herald-Whig and poured over the paragraphs with disquieting alarm, hoping to glean any information that might hint at their son's location. The last they knew was that he was in England. But that was before the exhilarating announcement of the D-Day landings on June 6th.

"INVASION ROLLS INLAND", blared the headline that day and tongues wagged with excitement across backyard fences and over telephones as the news spread like wildfire across town.

"BATTLE FOR FRANCE GROWS", declared the June 7th headline.

"ALLIES ADVANCE SWIFTLY," the banner line boasted on June 12th, but it didn't mention that it was a short lived advance, bogging down among the bloody hedgerows.

Searing battle stories filled the pages and regarded every action as an unequivocal Allied victory. Harry Barkley knew his son was in the infantry, and that the infantry did the lion's share of the fighting… and dying. But he didn't disclose that information to his wife -- she was already worried sick over her son, having read daily reports of local boys being wounded, killed or listed as missing in action. She watched with dread every time a Western Union courier appeared on the street, searching for an address. Telegrams only brought bad news, notification that someone's son or husband had become a casualty.

The last letter they had received from Harold was dated in May when he was still in England. Nettie sincerely hoped that he was still there. But she knew her son could be anywhere by now. Each new day brought a torturous fear of the unknown.

June 19, 1944, Normandy -- The vicious storm intensified. Gale force winds whipped the English Channel into a churning sea of destruction. For several days colossal waves battered the artificial Mulberry harbors constructed off the Normandy beaches to serve as an ersatz port and beat them to pieces. The damage to Mulberry was irreparable and the flow of men and materiel was reduced to a trickle, hampering the Allied build-up for the breakout from the beachhead.

The storm created a logistical setback that stalled the Allied offensive and postponed the projected thrust into the hinterland of France. The majority of supplies that did reach the beaches were forwarded to the divisions of the VII Corps which were forcing their way up the Contentin Peninsula to capture the coveted port of Cherbourg. On the V Corps front the 2nd Infantry Division had been reined in at the foot of Hill 192 east of St. Lo and went on the defensive with neighboring divisions. Under constant bombardment, they waited for orders to push on.

The rains did not stop the war, but only slowed it down. The company dispatched patrols all day long the 19th of June. Small groups of men crept through alternating drizzle and downpour to prowl the maze of enemy hedgerow by day and night in quest of the elusive flaw in the enemy's lines. But the Germans were masters of defense and flaws were not to be found. There were more skirmishes and several tense encounters with snipers. What little knowledge garnered was passed on to the intelligence staff at Headquarters. Meanwhile, the mortars fell regularly and snipers continued to deal death with solitary shots. Only rarely did anyone venture from their holes. And the rain continued to pour.

Although it was summer, it rained nearly every day and cold mud became the infantry's constant companion. Ill-prepared foxholes became quagmires. Just walking in the mud wore them out. At times one's foot sank ankle deep or deeper into the muck, requiring a concentrated effort to pluck it from the mire just to take the next step -- a terrifying experience if under fire. Mud oozed into the working parts of their weapons, requiring frequent disassembly for cleaning.

Nobody liked the rain. Everybody hated the mud. The only good thing about them was that they were neutral.

No longer attacking, Private Barkley was contentedly bored. He knew he owed his parents a letter but he just hadn't had the time to write, or if he did, he surely didn't have the energy to do so. But now there existed a period of inactivity and despite the uncomfortable rainy night and the periodic crash of harassing mortar fire, he was relatively rested.

Borrowing a sheet of paper and an envelope from a fellow soldier, he began his first letter from a combat zone: "June 20 -- Somewhere in France," it began; it was forbidden to disclose a more precise location. "I am sorry I haven't wrote and I know you are worrying about me and you may XXX" (the censor blotted out a small segment) "when I tell you I am in France but am O.K., so don't worry about me…" Later he added: "… I will be able to write only now and then for there aren't stores at every corner to buy writing paper in. HA-HA." He still retained a wry sense of humor, but another sentence spoke in cloaked tones of the horrors he had seen: "When I get back to Quincy I'll never move from there again. I was scared when I first got here but I feel swell now. Don't worry about me." He knew if he told them anything more they'd worry unnecessarily and there was no point in that. There was nothing that he or they could do about it. That said, he signed his name.

On the morning of June 21st, the entire company was ordered to conduct a large combat patrol. Platoon leaders had been briefed on the mission and extra ammunition had been issued -- apparently the company was looking for a fight, and there was little doubt that they'd find one.

As usual, a bone chilling rain fell as the platoons assembled behind the hedgerows' shelter. The prospect of meeting the enemy again generated little enthusiasm among the ranks and no one was anxious to go. Some spoke softly among themselves, uttering expressions of disgust with the entire situation and it was universally agreed that it was another wet and miserable day in Normandy.

Then the order came to move out. Soldiers bowed their heads against the rain and splashed toward their jump-off point a few fields away. Arriving at the line of departure, the platoons hunkered in the mud and waited for the order to pass through the lines.

The men who held the frontline stared at the men of Company G and did not envy them. Although they, themselves, held the most advanced positions and were closest to the enemy, it was these wet and miserable sad sacks of Company G who were going forth to meet the enemy on his own turf. There was bound to be a firefight and no guarantee that everyone would return safely.

Then the order came: Move out.

A pair of scouts mounted the slippery hedgerow, then slid down the opposite side. The lead platoon followed, and then the others. They had just entered no-man's-land. After traversing several hedgerows and fields without incident, the lead scouts came upon a cluster of farm buildings and signaled a halt. Allegedly, an enemy command post occupied these buildings. But where were the defenders? Not a shot had been fired during the company's approach. It was very suspicious. After a cautious investigation, the buildings proved to be abandoned and the company moved in to secure the farmyard, while the lead platoon set out for the next objective.

No sooner had the leading squads crossed a nearby road than a storm of gunfire erupted from all points of their front. Startled soldiers dropped and scrambled for roadside ditches. More machine gun fire swept the road. Men reeled from the vicious assault and fell back to the farmyard where the remainder of the company had deployed. No sooner had they arrived than the entire yard exploded from the impact of mortar shells. Another crushing salvo fell, followed by another and another. Chaos ensued. Men crumpled and lay motionless in muddy pools now tainted with their own blood.

Others scrambled between bursts for the shelter of the nearest buildings as shrapnel whirred all about. Apparently the Germans had been watching them all along, had anticipated their movement and had pre-selected the farmyard as their killing zone.

Another round of gunfire ripped from the road where elements of the lead platoon tried to disengage from the enemy. More explosions rocked the buildings. Shovels chopped frantically at the mud. Remnants of the lead platoon trickled back, hounded by intense machine gun fire. More mortars fell. Panic and confusion prevailed. *What to do?*

Company G was in a hot spot, deep in enemy territory. The farmyard was being destroyed by a continuous storm of mortar shells and for all the GIs knew, the Germans may be closing in from all sides to finish the job with machine guns. It seemed suicidal to remain. Images of Dead Man's Gulch leaped to the fore, visions of being cut off, surrounded and annihilated. At times such as these discretion is the better part of valor and word was passed to pull back. Cries of "Fall back! Every man for himself!" rose above the din. Men chose their own time to cut and run and dashed between explosions, slipping and sliding in the mud, desperate to gain the safety of hedgerows to the rear as shrapnel hissed all around. Demoralized men evacuated the killing zone and made their way back to the American lines.

The combat patrol had proved to be another catastrophe as far as the men of Company G were concerned. Stragglers and wounded men trickled in all day, finding their way back as best they could. A number of men had been killed. Lieutenant Warner reported to Battalion and gave his account of the action, but what it proved was anybody's guess. The enlisted men only knew that they got their butts kicked -- again. The officers and intelligence staff probably gleaned some sort of valuable information from it, such as American attacks would be met by stiff resistance, or that the Germans had plenty of machine guns and mortars at such-and-such co-ordinates to defend their positions. But the newest private on the line could have saved them time, and lives, and told them that.

Nonetheless, another patrol was concocted and again Company G was called upon to carry it out. It was to take place the following day. Lieutenant Daniel Pray's platoon was to provide the personnel. Platoon Sergeant Blackmore moved among his squads, picking the men he wanted to go. Barkley was chosen to act as lead scout.

June 22, 1944 -- A tepid breeze ushered the dawn and gently rustled the leaves that glistened above the hedgerows that sheltered the men of Company G. The grimy mudmen peered up from the depths of their burrows and blinked, awestruck by an unfamiliar sight -- blue skies. The weather had cleared. The violent storm of the past few days had abated and once again the sun sparkled with dazzling brilliance, warming the men huddled in their filthy holes.

The foliage was fresh and green as ever, shining with vitality from the abundant rains. At first glance, the lush greens, warm skies and golden sun composed a picturesque landscape. But further scrutiny revealed a less idyllic scene. Clumps of clay coagulated on the rims of foxholes already littered with an assortment of military equipment, empty cans and discarded ration boxes. Scores of ugly shell holes marred the verdant fields like huge ruptured boils that festered with stagnant water. Trees and bushes had been ravaged by shot and shell. Splintered trunks stood starkly against the azure sky and mourned dismembered branches that had been hauled away by soldiers for protection from shrapnel and other deadly missiles.

If one had lost his sense of smell, he might be compelled to believe that the air was pure and sweet. But "pure" hardly described the putrid odors of sweat, mold, urine and feces that assailed the human nostril. And "sweet" could only be the sickening stench of decaying flesh that emanated from mangled livestock that rotted in the fields. The repulsive odors permeated the air and soaked the earth. The stink impregnated men's clothing and seeped into their skin. It was the perfume of Death.

Yet the sun was out and it was warm, and that was enough in itself.

Sunlight glinted off of the bright brass of the .45 caliber cartridges as Private Barkley inspected a clip of ammunition, then jammed it purposefully into the receiver of his Thompson sub-machine gun. The weight of extra clips, fully loaded, tugged assuredly in his trouser pockets. Satisfied with his preparations, he leaned back in his foxhole and waited beneath the hedgerow's brushy mane.

Nearby, others, too, conducted their own personal rituals, examining weapons and ammunition, making certain that they were free of mud and in good working condition. Not much talking, just grim, determined motions as they hefted their firearms and adjusted straps and belts. Lieutenant Pray was about to take them on patrol.

It was a fairly large patrol, ten or eleven men, being sufficient in size to extract themselves in event of trouble. In fact, they *were* looking for trouble. The previous day's action had established the German's main line of resistance. Armed with this knowledge, Lieutenant Pray was determined to glean more information as to the enemy's disposition. He knew that when they found it, his men would have a fight on their hands. The lieutenant would then attempt to chart their positions, note types of weapons employed and approximate enemy strength. Once detected, however, they were to return as rapidly as possible to the American lines before the Germans could envelop them and wipe them out. It would be a tricky operation.

Why only a handful of men were going when the entire company had failed the day before Barkley didn't understand. Maybe ten men would be less conspicuous, he reasoned, but it mattered not -- for he was ordered to go.

Barkley slipped over the hedgerow and proceeded down the right arm of a narrow country lane that paralleled the battalion front. Tree-topped hedgerows pressed tightly from either side, creating a closed green corridor, a verdant tunnel where dense shadows cloaked potential dangers. Gripping his sub-machine gun, Barkley eyed the flanking hedgerows with suspicion and set a cautious pace. He was the scout, the eyes and ears of the patrol.

Some distance behind him tramped a stranger who filled the role of second scout, followed by Lieutenant Pray and the reliable Sergeant Parker. Then came the others, weapons held at high port, ready to respond to any trouble encountered by the scouts. The squad's heavy fire power was provided by a two man BAR team whose heights contrasted so sharply that they reminded Barkley of the "Mutt and Jeff" comic strip characters. The gunner was a tall, sturdy fellow whose slothful inclinations hinted that he was clumsy or perhaps even a bit dim-witted -- but Barkley had seen him in action and knew he was quick to react in battle, skillfully laying down accurate covering fire for endangered buddies. Slow men didn't last in combat; this man had lasted. His ammunition bearer was none other than Shorty Bell, Barkley's buddy from training days. Shorty sagged from the weight of the heavy BAR ammo belt that girdled his waist as well as his own rifle and bandolier. His bugged-eyes peered spookily from beneath the rim of a seemingly too-large helmet that comically off-set his long lantern jaw. A radio man accompanied the patrol, hunched forward beneath the burden of the awkward radio set strapped to his back. He stuck close to the lieutenant to give him immediate contact with the battalion in case they needed mortars to cover a withdrawal or to bring up supporting troops.

As Barkley advanced he'd stop periodically to study his designated route. It was perfect ambush country. The enemy could be anywhere. He squinted to penetrate the layered foliage, for every shadow had the potential of releasing sudden death. If the road twisted or turned, he'd warily peek around the bend before moving on. If suspicion arose, he'd freeze and raise a hand, signaling the next man to halt, who in turn silently relayed the message to the patrol, and the world quit spinning until Barkley's eyes dissected the terrain inch by inch. If not certain what action to take, he'd signal the second scout to send up the lieutenant. The lieutenant and Sergeant Parker would work their way up to Barkley's position and together they'd plan their route of approach. In this manner, the patrol crept down the lane, warily scanning the flanking hedgerows as they went.

Before long, Barkley was ordered to abandon the road and cross over the left hand hedgerow to scout the adjacent field. Dropping into tall grass, he crouched and surveyed the terrain before him. All was quiet. He moved deeper into the field. The patrol followed. Barkley knew the Germans were masters at camouflage, that machine guns, or even a solitary sniper might be concealed in the tangled growth of the surrounding hedgerows. Usually one wasn't aware of them until they opened fire, and then it was too late. Death could come as sudden as the next heartbeat.

Another hedgerow was crossed and yet another and still nothing. Barkley knew that the Germans had to be near -- they sure as hell hadn't packed up and pulled out.

The lieutenant ordered a breather. While the men rested, the lieutenant and Parker consulted their map and plotted their next route of approach. So far their luck had held. The lieutenant decided they'd push on to the next hedgerow. He cautioned his scouts to remain alert, as contact seemed imminent. Tense, edgy, the patrol pushed on.

Barkley gingerly parted the branches. Before him lay another neglected pasture, and at the far end, perhaps eighty or so yards away, stretched a peculiar hedgerow -- peculiar because it seemed to be nearly barren of the dense vegetation that so characterized the typical Norman hedgerow. It looked suspicious.

"Let's go, Barkley. Scouts out."

Up and over, Barkley set out again. The blunt snout of his Thompson swayed above the knee-high grass, as if sniffing for unseen enemies. As he neared the next hedgerow he noted it was indeed sparsely foliaged compared to others in the region and stood about shoulder high. Keeping low, he and the other scout edged up and discovered it, too, was clear of danger. Again the patrol moved up.

Immediately, the lieutenant ordered his scouts to cut straight across the next field.

Barkley rolled over the embankment, followed by the other scout. On all fours, they scanned the field before them. It, too, was tall pasture -- no trees, just a broad level plain extending to the next hedgerow. Barkley's heart pounded. Again his eyes swept the field. Still nothing. He didn't detect any suspicious movement or disturbed terrain indicating the enemy's presence. Yet, he sensed something was wrong. This could be it. An entire company might be sighting in on him for all he knew, entrenched in the next hedgerow, waiting for the kill. *How many times can you roll the dice and come up a winner?*

Turning to the other scout, he said, "C'mon, let's go."

Barkley swallowed his fear as he eased to his feet and pushed on, a solitary figure adrift in a soft green sea. Soon the other scout pulled abreast of him and tramped thirty or so feet to his right as they cut parallel lanes across the center of the field. Sweat flooded Barkley's brow. Each step seemed to be amplified by the silence as he moved through the dense grass. His eyes were glued to the next hedgerow -- a shaggy hedgerow -- a foreboding hedgerow blossomed in full glory.

As the scouts advanced, the patrol dropped one by one over the hedgerow behind them and formed a skirmish line. *RRRRP!!* Just like that, the blood chilling ratchet of a machine gun shattered the silence. As one, the patrol hit the dirt. Only one quick burst, and that was it. Stark, sinister silence followed. No one moved. Rivers of sweat stung Barkley's eyes and dripped from his nose. He hugged the soil, panting, praying, wondering what would come next. The tall grasses isolated each from the other and he wondered if anyone had been hit. Time was suspended in one prolonged, breath-held moment of panic. Perhaps they had surprised the Germans and a startled gunner let loose a hasty burst. *How many are out there? What should we do?* Hearts pounded wildly as they waited on word from the lieutenant.

Then the moment of silence exploded as the whole length of the forward hedgerow erupted in raucous bedlam. Bullets swept the grass in broad arcs, maliciously clipping the blades as they sought the intruders. The GIs reacted instinctively, directing their return fire at the menacing hedgerow. Barkley sprayed a stream of bullets along its crest as riflemen fired at invisible targets, but their gunfire quickly petered out, suppressed by the heavy volume of machine gun, rifle and burp gun fire that poured from the far hedge. Somewhere off to the right the BAR team, alone, hammered a sharp, defiant response but was beaten down by a torrent of bullets and soon only the sound of German weapons could be heard.

Then again all was still. The Americans cowered in the tall grass. They were caught, feeling naked and exposed in the open field. The Germans must have been watching them all along, waiting in ambush. Apparently a nervous gunner had triggered the first brief burst, prematurely springing the trap. Now the patrol wasn't sure what to do or which way to go. Every rustle of grass drew the attention of German gunners and invited a deluge of bullets.

Then things worsened. Blood drained from their faces as mortar shells began dropping in measured bursts. The earth convulsed as if attempting to dislodge them from their hiding places, shake them loose and toss them up as sacrificial offerings to the bloodthirsty machine guns. Shards of shrapnel hissed overhead. Another series struck, followed by another as the devilish shells walked the field, intent on destroying everything and everyone trapped within the hedgerows' bounds. Then the machine guns resumed their deadly combing. That was the last straw. The boxed-in field had become a slaughter pen; to remain meant certain death.

"Barkley... Barkley!" a frantic voice called from the left.

"What?" he answered, keeping his face pressed hard to the earth.

"Pass the word. Make your way back as best you can. Every man for himself. Got it? Every man for himself! Pass it on."

Barkley understood. It was a drill they'd performed on numerous occasions before. Each man was to find his own way back as quickly as possible and regroup behind the last hedgerow crossed. Individually the men commenced creeping towards the safety of the hedgerow behind them. No one dared to slip off to either flanking hedgerow for fear that more Germans might be laying in wait. Only the hedgerow behind them was known to be clear. It was their only chance.

Bullets popped maliciously as men wormed through the grass. Mortar shells dropped in a continuous chain, exploding in black death clouds as their gunners worked the field. White-hot steel flew in every direction. As each soldier neared the hedgerow, he'd search for the best location to cross over. The sparsely foliaged crest that had aided the enemy in monitoring their approach now teased each man with a glimmer of hope. Devoid of the usual vegetation, it would be much easier to cross over than the traditional tangle of brush and briers previously encountered. Desperate men calculated their chances, then sprang up by ones and twos to dash for their goal, hitting it at a run before scrambling frantically over its crest. Machine gun bullets traced every step. Another round of mortar shells wracked the field. Once again the BAR team came to life. The heavy

Browning churned the far hedgerow with rattling bursts as the crew bravely provided covering fire whenever a comrade bolted for the hedgerow.

One or two GIs vanished over the hedge top as bullets thudded into the embankment and ripped the surrounding leaves. Somewhere to the right the sharp cracking of the lieutenant's carbine sounded above the din. Again the BAR spoke as another soldier rose and made his lunge for the hedgerow, tumbling breathlessly onto the other side.

Barkley had been farthest into the field when the ambush was sprung and after a painstaking effort, had managed to crawl to the base of the hedgerow. He had witnessed most of his comrades go over, or try to anyway. Now it was his turn. It seemed miraculous that he had made it this far. It was time. He knew he couldn't remain in the field any longer. Another burst of machine gun fire swept the grass. Again mortar shells jolted the earth as shrapnel smacked heavily into the hedge bank above him.

Hidden by the tall grass, Barkley lay on his back and looked up. The hedgerow loomed above him -- it seemed incredibly tall. No time to waste. With one motion he heaved his sub-machine gun over the hedge wall, then sprung after it, desperately clawing the bank as machine gun bullets pulverized the earth around him. He was over in a heartbeat and dropped roughly onto the other side as bullets spattered the leaves above him. He could hardly believe he could move so fast. Still panting, he retrieved his weapon.

A couple of soldiers leaned into the hedge bank and returned fire as a knot of survivors assembled at the backside of the hedgerow. Someone said that the lieutenant was still out there, that he had been hit in the buttocks early in the engagement and was unable to move. Despite his wound, he had given the order for his men to get out. Another fellow was also known to be down in the field. No one knew if he was dead or wounded but they knew that he, like the lieutenant, would have to be left behind.

Meanwhile, the radioman crouched beneath the hedgerow and worked frantically at the dials of his set. Something was wrong. Sergeant Parker hovered over him, imploring him to get through to the company -- they needed help -- fast! The radioman looked up and grimly shook his head. It was no use. Apparently the radio had taken a hit. Parker made a snap decision -- they had to clear out -- now! The Germans would be on them at any moment.

"They're coming!" a lookout warned.

That was it. "Let's go," Parker ordered, "Move."

The survivors bolted in the direction of the American lines. They knew their wounded would have to rely on the mercy of their enemies. There was nothing else they could do.

Their route paralleled the hedgerow wall. They raced one against the other, lungs heaving, feet pounding, legs driven by unspeakable fears. Barkley followed Parker. Next came the BAR gunner with Shorty Bell riding his tail. Bell, weighed down by the heavy BAR ammunition, struggled to keep pace with the long, swift strides of the gunner. Two or three others brought up the rear.

Reaching the corner of the field, they shot off to their right, tracing the wall of another hedgerow until they chanced upon a deep, grass filled gully. Hoping to lose their pursuers , they plunged into the ditch, then proceeded steadily but cautiously down its narrow chute, not knowing who or what lay on either side. Suddenly Barkley skidded to a halt. "Oh, Jesus," he cried, "Wires! Wires! We're in a mine field."

Everyone froze in place. Frantically, Barkley's eyes swept the ground. More wires, red and blue, crisscrossed in every direction. The entire gully appeared to be mined.

"Watch your step," someone cautioned. Desperate men carefully selected each footing, gingerly planting one foot at a time in an effort to gain the near bank. A sense of urgency gripped them as the Germans could be upon them at any moment. If caught in the ditch, a massacre would ensue.

Almost immediately a terrorized voice cried out, "Oh my God. I… I think I'm on one… Something clicked!" The riflemen stood still as stone. He was certain that he was standing on a Bouncing Bettie.[*]

---

[*] Bouncing Bettie -- A German anti-personnel land mine; officially designated the S-Mine. It was a can shaped device with several short antennae-like wires flaring from a central stem on the top of the cylinder. When the wires were disturbed, there would be a slight delay before a preliminary charge launched the mine to a height of about three to four feet where it exploded a split second later, hurling several hundred steel ball bearings and pieces of mine casing over a radius of about

"For God's sake stay put!" came a frenzied plea. Everyone feared that if he lifted his foot, the mine would spring up and explode at waist level, flinging hundreds of deadly ball bearings in every direction.

Sweat poured from the doomed man. His wild eyes pleaded, *What shall I do?*

"Look, you're gonna have to stay there until we get outa here," came the grim request. The words fell like a death sentence.

Rivers of sweat streamed down the trapped man's face. His eyes rolled hysterically. He knew the instant he lifted his foot the can would burst from the soil and explode, probably all but cutting him in half.

It all happened so fast. There was no time to think of a solution for the poor man's plight. He was a dead man and he knew it. They had to leave him. The condemned man faithfully surrendered to his fate, standing rigid as a statue while his comrades concentrated on working their way out of the gully. They could only look at him in fleeting glances. Guilt gnawed at them for having to leave him so, but what else could they do? Time was ticking against their own bid for survival.

By now Sergeant Parker was carefully prodding the left-hand slope with his bayonet, probing for more mines while the remaining five or six men followed his path. Soon they emerged from the ditch only to cross another hedgerow that bordered a narrow lane. They paused for a moment to gain their bearings, then chose the direction they believed would lead them to the American lines and raced off to their right.

They sprinted down the road, gasping, lungs aching. Barkley raced alongside the tall BAR gunner. Shorty Bell, still laden with the heavy BAR ammo belt, struggled to keep pace. His cheeks puffed like bellows as he staggered beneath his cumbersome load, feet plopping heavily upon the road. Shorty began to lag behind. "Bark," he wheezed, "I can't..." a labored gulp, "I can't go anymore... I'm done!" His resolve to go on dissipated as he surrendered to exhaustion and Shorty dropped out of the race.

---

150 feet -- thus the nickname, "Bouncing Bettie". Sometimes they would be interconnected by trip wires, or detonated electronically.

Just then, several Germans leaned over a hedgerow behind them and cut loose with burp guns. *BRRP-BRRRP!!* A gust of bullets whizzed over the fleeing Americans' heads. Instantly, worn-out Shorty flashed past Barkley and the gunner with wide, terrorized eyes nearly popping from their sockets. He clenched his ammo belt with both hands, lifting it high above his waist as he sprinted down the road with mercurial speed, easily leaving the others behind. Shorty had found inspiration. A fresh burst of adrenaline surged through the others, too, and they chased after Shorty, bolting down the road before plunging over another hedgerow to continue their frantic flight.

The exhausted remnants of the patrol dragged into the American lines, and in breathless phrases, told of their ordeal. Thoroughly shaken and physically drained, they were in no condition to return to the scene of the ambush. Another, stronger, combat patrol was assembled and set out with a medic to retrieve the wounded.

Later, the rescue patrol returned. They had discovered a wounded GI who told them how he had hidden in bushes while the Germans searched the field. He had kept his cool and despite his pain, avoided making any sounds until the Germans gave up in favor of pursuing the others. He had pointed out the location of Lieutenant Pray who was secluded in another clump of brush. The lieutenant was dead. Litter bearers carried the wounded man and the body of the lieutenant back to the American lines. Nothing was learned of the man left stranded in the gully.

Barkley quizzed the returning medic -- he could hardly believe the lieutenant was dead. "He was only shot in the ass!" he exclaimed in consternation, "How the hell can you die from being shot in the ass?"

"You'd be surprised how much blood you can loose from a wound like that," came the answer.

The ambush survivors silently returned to their holes, shaking their heads in bewilderment. *What the hell did* ***that*** *accomplish*, they wondered, *other than get two men killed and a couple others wounded?* Sergeant Parker, the man who was instrumental in extracting the ambushed patrol from destruction, was among the stricken, receiving shrapnel wounds from a grenade.

Although the patrol seemed a dismal failure to the men who conducted it, it did accomplish something. In light of "The Big Picture", it determined the approximate location of the German lines in that sector. It revealed that machine guns and mortars were abundant in that area and that the line was well manned, strong enough to have launched a squad to pursue the patrol in an effort to kill them as they stole away with such valuable information. The patrol returned with their report and thus the mission was deemed a success.

Intelligence officers would compare the patrol's story to other bits of knowledge gleaned from other patrols and piece together a sort of jig-saw puzzle on their map overlays. Each piece pinpointed key enemy positions and types of weapons that future attacks would likely encounter. Approximate troop strengths were noted.

All of these pieces of information, bought with blood and sweat, ensured that the planners at S-2 (Intelligence) would have a clearer, more precise picture of what laid ahead and plan future offensive operations accordingly -- hopefully leading to success with a minimum of casualties.

Yet for Barkley and the others it was still considered a failure -- an ill-planned blunder. Their opinions, of course, were of no consequence and they resumed their life of misery on the front, living in earthen holes, destined to go on more patrols. The memory of their narrow escape would never leave them, conjuring up nightmarish images that would haunt them on every subsequent patrol.[*]

Postscript: Although crippled by his wound, Lieutenant Daniel Pray had retained the presence of mind to order his men out of the killing zone of that dreadful field, even though he knew that he would not be able to escape himself. Though bleeding profusely, he managed to provide covering fire for his men as they moved out of harm's way. In effect, by his leadership and cool conduct, he

---

[*] Company G Morning Report for June 22, 1944, lists Lt. Daniel W. Pray and Private Raymond J. Simcik as KIA; S/Sgt Wayne Parker and Private Junior Rollings as WIA.

probably saved the lives of most of his patrol. Whatever else took place in that horrible field Barkley never knew, but years later discovered that the lieutenant was awarded the Silver Star Medal for his actions that day -- posthumously.

June 23 - 26, 1944 -- The harsh routine of the front dragged on. No longer attacking, the infantrymen squatted in the squalor of their damp, fetid foxholes, bored by the drudgery of life on a static front. Outposts remained forward, alert for enemy activity. Occasionally small arms fire rippled from hedgerows only a short distance to the front, resulting in brisk firefights until the perpetrators were driven away. From time to time, single bullets spat through the overhead foliage as snipers played their game, and all the while frightened men hunkered in their holes, for enemy mortar or artillery attacks could come at any given moment.

Patrols continued around the clock, feeding coveted bits of knowledge to satiate the ravenous appetites of information-starved intelligence officers. Larger probes or feint attacks often culminating in sharp encounters with German strong points or patrols. Enemy machine guns seemed to cover every avenue of approach. At times the scouts came across four or five dead GIs all in a row where enemy guns had dropped them. All the gunner had to do was aim down the hedgerow's length and pull the trigger, dropping one soldier after the other. As always, it was best to spread out and move directly across the center of a field, even though it provided little cover.

At night patrols of three or four men stalked through no man's land in pitch darkness. They'd slither silently along the foot of German held hedgerows in order to observe enemy activity. The slightest noise compelled them to stop, and they'd wait with hearts lodged firmly in their throats until the source of the sound was ascertained.

Sometimes enemy mortars coughed from seclusion and they'd attempted to locate the position by sound, or by sight if close enough. They'd listen for troops on the move and estimate their strength and direction of march, and all the while they strove to remain undetected.

A constant order stood to bring back a prisoner if possible -- a risky proposition at best. Such events were rare and seldom succeeded. However, on one occasion several raiders returned from the darkness with a reluctant captive in tow. Punchy Nolan, who had custody of their prize, pressed his knife so firmly to the prisoner's neck that Bill Dudas, another member of the patrol, thought for certain Punchy would cut his throat before they managed to regain the American lines.

While the unfortunate few risked life and limb on patrols, enemy artillery and mortar fire continued to pound the front on a daily basis. Shells large and small fell among the foxholes with unpredictable regularity. At such times Barkley remained squirreled in his hole as monstrous explosions pummeled the earth with sledgehammer blows. Some struck so close that it seemed as if the concussion would surely suck eyeballs from sockets and air from lungs and he wondered if this is what it was like in the Great War. Time lost all meaning. Each second stretched into an eternal minute, and every minute into a nerve shattering trial too long to endure and he wondered if the next round would be a direct hit that would blow him to bits, or maybe bury him alive.

And then all was quiet.

The inevitable cry of: "Medic! We need a medic over here!" broke the stillness. Sometimes soldiers dragged dead men from their foxholes-turned-graves and laid them out in the field with a blanket or raincoat spread over them to conceal them from living eyes. It was always an uneasy sensation to have corpses lying about and officers quickly got on field phones to call for someone to come up and remove the bodies. And sometimes a soldier staggered from his foxhole, staring blankly as if his eyes had seen the future and he'd been stunned by the revelation. There wasn't a scratch on him, yet he trembled violently and babbled incoherently as he wandered aimlessly along the hedgerow until restrained by comrades. He had met his limit and had cracked under the strain -- another combat exhaustion case.

It was just another day on the battlefront in Europe, in 1944.

June 26, 1944 -- It had been twenty days since D-Day. Operation Overlord's time table called for First U.S. Army to be more than fifty miles deep into France by this date, but it was still engaged in heavy fighting in the Norman bocage. It's V Corps had only penetrated roughly fifteen or so miles inland, and was cramped in its precarious beachhead positions; its main drive held in check by Hill 192. The hill had become a painful thorn in the side of the First Army; the 2nd Infantry Division was still expected to extract it.

CHAPTER 7

RELIEF

Evening, June 26, 1944 -- Word was passed from foxhole to foxhole: We're coming off the line. The entire battalion was to be relieved by soldiers of the Third Battalion. The Third Battalion, which had suffered heavily while holding an exposed point at the foot of Hill 192 just to the Second's left, had been relieved by the First Battalion five days earlier. Now rested, they were being returned to the front. The Second Battalion, which had been in combat for nineteen consecutive days, had also suffered greatly and was more than ready for a much needed rest.

Under cover of darkness, squads and platoons of the relieving command filtered up to replace those of the Second Battalion. It was a slow process with each squad of the relieving force exchanging places with those on the front, man for man. Silence was imperative, for any unwarranted noise was apt to draw a storm of shells. But there was no shelling. There had been no casualties. The relief was a success.

By morning the men found themselves encamped in a rest area several hundred yards behind the front where they were designated regimental reserve. Although off the line, they were still within sight of German artillery observers who kept a constant vigil from their posts atop Hill 192. Danger from bombardment was rarer in the rear areas, but the occasional harassment shelling from larger caliber German guns or even their big 120mm mortars was not unheard of, so foxholes continued to serve as their primary accommodations. But at least they no longer occupied the actual firing line and life, comparatively, was good.

The company cooks had set up their kitchens in the rest area to await their reunion with their comrades. For weeks the dogfaces had subsisted on tasteless K rations and now produced their mess kits in anticipation of a hot meal. As the cooks served their food, they readily noticed that this was not the same company that they had fed in Wales before the division embarked for the invasion. Plenty of new faces now claimed membership in Company G. Many of the "old hands" were conspicuously absent, mute testimony to the hard times at the front.

Farther back, an engineer unit had erected field showers. Until now, baths, if one could call them that, had been taken from an upturned helmet filled with water dipped from a flooded shell hole[*], or chanced during a quiet spell from some nearby pond. Now scrubbed men exited the showers and walked away as new men.

The only thing missing now was sleep. Sleep! Above all else the men craved precious sleep. While at the front they benefited little from sleep. The Germans had shelled them day and night, wearing on their nerves and denying them rest. But that could hardly be called quality rest. The grueling all-day attacks, constant patrolling and stints on outpost duty robbed them of more sleep and ensured that they would remain physically drained. Sleep at the front was a luxury

---

[*] American soldiers jokingly referred to these as "French Baths", or "Whore's Baths".

none could afford. But now, in the rear, sleep would be plentiful; plenty enough to rejuvenate sagging bodies and bolster lagging spirits. It was heavenly! They were off the line. They were receiving hot chow. They were getting sleep. Morale soared.

Clean, with full bellies and adequate sleep, the men pondered what to do now that they were "in the rear". They soon discovered that there really wasn't much else to do but rest. Rear area villages were off limits. There wasn't much fraternizing with the local citizens either, as civilians were scarce. In fact, Barkley never saw any and wondered where they were. He supposed they had been evacuated due to the heavy fighting -- refugees in their own country.

Bored GIs were prone to wander off when the opportunity arose to reconnoiter abandoned farmhouses. Chickens and eggs were rare finds. Amateur poachers nabbed squawking hens and collected eggs into helmets to supplement GI diets.

Some fellows infiltrated nearby villages to ply the time-honored soldier practice of scrounging. The vacated villages proved to be a source of ill-gotten goods. Although entry was forbidden, men rummaged through the houses, outbuildings and cellars, scouting for prized relics and war souvenirs -- mementoes to be cherished after the war.

Others, bent on getting drunk, broke into houses and cellars in their quest for booze. Bottles of wine and hard cider were "liberated" in the name of the Allies and heartily consumed. The local specialty was an evil concoction called Calvados, an apple brandy that carried a mule's kick. The drink helped anesthetize the pain of war and numbed the brain, erasing the horrors of the battlefield, if only temporarily.

Initially, Barkley refused to partake in the pilferage and didn't care for liquor anyway. For the most part he remained in his platoon area, content with the opportunity to rest. However, in time he, too, fell under the spell of soldiery plundering and ventured into a nearby hamlet to search for items of interest. One of his new-found buddies, Joe Guajardo, accompanied him.

The town was a wreck. Every building bore gouges and scars from previous battles and bombardments and a few had collapsed altogether. The two scroungers had just entered a house when several mortar shells crashed nearby. Apparently German observers on the heights had spotted them as they lurked among the ruins and called down the hell that now erupted around them. In the process of diving for cover Barkley bumped heavily against a stout bed, jarring loose two bundles of papers that clumped to the floor. Curious, he pulled them closer. One seemed to be a stack of war bonds, but the other piqued his interest. It appeared to be a sheaf of old papers. Evidently they had been stashed there for safekeeping. He pulled a paper from the older bundle and scanned it. It was old -- *very old*. It was some kind of document, hand-written on yellowed parchment, bearing an official red wax seal at the bottom. It was dated 1696. Even under mortar attack, the "collector" surfaced in Barkley. He grabbed another paper... *Good God!* It was graced with the signature of Napoleon! He scooped up more of the documents. Although he couldn't read French, they appeared to be old land grants. Perhaps this was the home of the village priest, or maybe a town elder who had been keeping important papers for the townspeople. Why else would so many old documents and war bonds be hidden in one place?

Excited about his discovery, Barkley eagerly sorted through the treasure. He discarded the war bonds as he supposed they were now worthless, but the old documents were another matter. He stuffed them into his battle jacket -- spoils of war.

When the shelling stopped, Barkley and Joe ducked out of the house and scampering back to the comparative safety of the company area. Secluded in his foxhole, Barkley examined his loot and wondered what other gems awaited discovery.

The following day he convinced Joe to return to the village to search for more treasure, but both came up empty handed. Disappointed, they chose to return to the company area via a sunken road flanked by hedgerows. They hadn't gone too far when the unmistakable whistling of incoming artillery pierced the air. By now, Barkley and Joe had enough battle experience to know that the shells weren't intended for them and neither bothered to take cover. The barrage struck a group of men bivouacked some distance before them. The two scroungers could tell that it was far enough away not to be an immediate threat to them, so continued their journey while monitoring the action with detached interest.

But then one of those small noises that portends danger pricked Barkley's ear. A faint, fluttering sound was rushing towards him. *Whirr-whiRR-Whirr-WHIRR.* In an instant he noted a long piece of shrapnel cart-wheeling through the air, whirling straight down the road and directly at him. Although he saw it, he could not react. For some reason it did not fully register in his mind, so he just stood there, mesmerized by the apparition.

Joe saw it too, and made a last moment's dodge to escape the twirling jag of steel. But for Barkley it was too late. "Oof!" he grunted as dust puffed from his jacket. He just stood there, stunned.

Immediately, Joe leaped up and rushed to his buddy's aid. "How bad are you hit?" he asked, thoroughly distressed, "How bad is it?"

Shaken, Barkley examined himself. There was no pain, no blood. The piece of shrapnel lay in the dust at his feet. Apparently it had spent its energy in the long flight from the bombardment area and didn't have sufficient velocity to do any damage. It had hit Barkley flatly on his left side, then plopped harmlessly to the ground.

Astonished, Barkley answered, "I'm not hurt at all!"

That was the last time Barkley and Joe prowled that village.

Back in the rest area, mail was brought up and distributed, but there was no mail for Barkley. Some kind of foul-up, he supposed. Typical. He assumed the Army was probably having difficulty forwarding his mail since his arrival in France. Maybe next time. He sulked away empty handed, alone with his thoughts.

While others read of home and loved ones, Barkley reflected on the past few weeks. Life on the front had been rough. Combat was pure hell. It was nothing like the movies where Douglas Fairbanks, Jr., or Errol Flynn charged fearlessly into masses of enemies, wielding bayonets or swinging swords with swashbuckling flair. Errol and Doug never suffered anything more than superficial wounds, if any, and continued their heroics in the face of tremendous adversity. Even the dead in the movies were clinically clean, clutching bloodless wounds as they tumbled to the ground on comparatively pristine battlefields. No mud. No rain. But that was the movies.[*]

---

[*] In all fairness, it must be mentioned here that Fairbanks did, indeed, serve his

But here... here it was so very different. Men were scared all of the time. No one felt heroic, yet still they performed their duty, doing their best to stay alive from one day to the next until they themselves became casualties. Many a brave deed went unnoticed and unsung. And the casualties! Men were shot through and through. Others were literally ripped apart by high explosives, having limbs torn from torsos, exposing pink bone fragments that jutted from mangled flesh; some were disemboweled with their guts strewn to hell and gone. Bodies were flung through the air like rag dolls. Skulls split open like pumpkins, splattering their contents against hedge walls, or into the mud... or onto buddies. It was a crash course in human anatomy. Barkley believed he had witnessed every type of wound and suffering imaginable. Horrific wounds! Only a supreme sadist could even try to compete with war. It was small wonder some fellows couldn't cope with combat and broke under the strain.

Combat proved to be physically taxing, too. Barkley possessed the incredible stamina afforded those who were young and in excellent health. Yet at the end of each day he was totally exhausted, sapped of strength as well as lucid thought. How the "older" men kept up he never clearly understood. It must be exceptionally rough on them. And that brought to mind his good friend, Frank Balchunas -- the Barracuda.

The Barracuda, he thought, *I wonder how the Barracuda is making it.* His thoughts drifted to the clutch of men with whom he trained and came overseas with him. Up to this point, Barkley had had little or no contact with them. Bell was in his platoon, but he had never been as close to him as with some of the others. Now he wondered if they were faring any better or worse than he. *How many are still alive?*

He wasn't sure, but he believed that Barrella and the Barracuda were with his company somewhere, but he sure as hell hadn't seen them and he feared the worst.[**] A friend had told him that they had been assigned to the medics and Barkley wondered where they were now and if they were alright.

---

country, being a decorated U.S. Naval officer who conducted commando raids in the Mediterranean Theater.
[**] In truth, Ralph Barrella had been sent to Company F of the same battalion.

God only knows where Antonelli and The Major were. He hadn't seen them since they were all split up way back at Trevieres when they came up from Omaha Beach. That seemed a lifetime ago. For some it was a lifetime.

Separated from his old friends, Barkley now formed new friendships with the men who made up his squad. He was one of them now, a combat veteran. While in the rest area he enjoyed the camaraderie of men bonded by the mutual experience of war, joking around with them or just taking it easy while they had the chance. They knew that all too soon they would be back at the front, so they made the best of their time in the rear.

He chummed with Joe Guajardo and Joe Benavidez, two affable young Mexican-Americans who were original members of Company G. Just as Barkley had been separated from friends after his arrival in France, these two had also lost buddies to combat. He and Guajardo especially liked each other, having shared their adventure in the abandoned village.

There were other new men in the squad, too, men who had come up as replacements some time or another after Barkley's arrival. Among these were Earl Hoernke and a Southern boy named Leroy Hinson, as well as a fellow named Adair. Barkley became acquainted with a few men from other squads, too, men like Walt Popham, a lanky, red-haired soldier from Kentucky, and a fellow named McDonner, who were also scouts, like Barkley. McDonner, it turned out, had also arrived in the company via Wind Whistle Hill.

Sergeant Fretwell, their squad leader, pretty much kept to himself while in the rest area, and that was fine with Barkley, for he did not like him much, anyway. Barkley assumed Fretwell spent much of his time crawling out of a bottle.

As they sat beneath the hedgerow's shade, each told stories of home. Barkley fantasized about the slot machines that awaited him and how much fun he'd have playing them after his return. He planned on getting a vendor's license and placing the machines about town -- a sure money maker with virtually no work involved, save for making the rounds to collect the coins.

Benevidez and Guajardo countered with stories of their own, talking just as enthusiastically of events back home, or of how the entire division had been transported from warm Texas to the frozen lands of Wisconsin for winter maneuvers before being shipped overseas. They recalled their stay in Northern Ireland and spoke fondly of pubs and fish and chips and the pretty Irish girls. And one added that girls of Wales were just as friendly when the division was transported to that rugged land before the invasion. Hinson offered his tales of life in the South while Hoernke or one of the others interjected now and then with their two-cents worth, completing the round of conversation.

Sometimes several of the fellows broke out a deck of cards and played everything from rummy to poker. But other than that, there was little to do.

About this time Barkley was treated to a remarkable sight -- he could hardly believe his eyes. From a distance he watched as a cluster of fresh replacement officers were being herded through an assembly area. Although he couldn't make out their features, he noticed one displayed a certain, all-too-familiar, brashness to his step. Barkley was sure that he had known him somewhere before but just couldn't place him. As the officers drew nearer, Barkley's eyes nearly popped from their sockets. The officer he had been scrutinizing strutted with an arrogant swagger, *slapping his leg with a ridding crop.* Barkley's jaw dropped in astonishment. *My God!* he thought, *it's Lieutenant Quirt of Camp Wolters. Well, he'd better damned well get rid of that quirt! It'll do him no good here.* The officers sauntered off to wherever they were going and that was the last time Barkley ever saw Lieutenant Quirt.

Far to the rear, the planning staff at Division had a problem. They noted with much dissatisfaction that the infantry assaults on Hill 192 had been stymied by the Germans' ability to utilize the defensive network of hedgerows to maximum effect. Company after company had been chewed up and spit out every time a battalion advanced up the slope. The thick hedgerows were proving to be disastrous to all U.S. units embroiled in the tangled maze of the Bocage. What the foot soldier needed was adequate tank support. However, as proven earlier, the Bocage was not tank country -- the tanks simply could not maneuver effectively among the hedgerows and survive.

To remedy this, new tactics were developed where infantry assault teams would work in concert with combat engineers and tanks. The engineers would excavate a section of each forward hedgerow at the line of departure just wide enough to accommodate the width of a tank. To screen their intention, they'd leave a thin shell of hedge wall facing the enemy, which, in effect, would mask its location. When the attack began a tank could easily smash through the thin veneer aided by a new device -- an array of saw-toothed blades welded across its forward hull. These blades acted as both scythe and bulldozer and greatly enhanced a tanks chance at penetrating the thick hedge walls.

Initially, one tank, one infantry squad, and four engineers would be assigned to each field. Under covering fire from automatic weapons and the tank's cannon, the infantry would rush the next hedgerow. Upon arrival, they'd signal the tank and engineers forward. The tank would easily punch through the earthen shell before it and move up. The engineers would then confer with the infantry squad leader to determine the best location to place their explosives for the next penetration. After removing satchel charges from a rack welded to the tank's rear deck, the engineers would blow another gap as the infantry rushed forward and again the tank would punch through, and on and on until the hill was taken.

In effect it was a team effort. The tanks kept the enemy machine gunners off the infantry's back; the infantry kept any Germans armed with Panzerfausts[*] off the tank's back; and the engineers provided the means for the tank to advance through the hedgerows without exposing its vulnerable underbelly. It was a brilliant concept.

Another problem solved was the lack of communication between infantry and tank commanders. Previously, armor and infantry forces worked virtually independent of each other, resulting in unnecessary casualties for both. To facilitate infantry-armor

---

[*] Panzerfaust – a tube-shaped, disposable rocket launcher that was fired by one man, hurling a bulbous, flower-pot-shaped warhead at its target. It was easy to use and very, very effective.

communications, field phones would be installed at the rear of each tank to enable the infantry to coordinate each phase of the assault.

Once again the 38th Infantry's Second Battalion had been selected as one of the assault elements. Being in reserve, the battalion commenced a regimen of intensive training. Companies E and F were to lead the battalion's attack and received in-depth instruction, conducting actual mock assaults on rear area hedgerows employing the new tactics. Company G, which had suffered heavy casualties in earlier attacks, was not stable enough to lead another full scale assault and would be held in close reserve during the coming fight. It would trail the assault companies until needed. As usual, Company H, the weapons company, would farm out its machine gunners and mortar teams to the three rifle companies as required.

Although given the role of battalion reserve, it was still necessary for Company G to understand the principals of the new tactics. Barkley listened intently as an officer briefed them. He recognized the advantage that would be gained by the tank's tremendous fire support and felt confident about the new tactics. It seemed destined for success and would be a great boost to morale... if it worked.

One blustery day the company was assembled in a hedgerow-boxed field where a colonel or lieutenant-colonel awaited them. The officer launched a grand but brief speech that, in the end, called for a volunteer to accompany a lieutenant on a special mission.

The veterans were not impressed. They had seen plenty of patrols and knew there was no glory or glamour in them -- only a good chance to get killed. They fully endorsed the old Army adage of "never-volunteer-for-anything" and not one stepped forward.

But then a commotion arose from the rear as a boy sprung up, ardently waving his hand -- a volunteer. The boy had just arrived in France and knew absolutely nothing about combat. Yet there he stood, all bright-eyed with face beaming, anxious to become a hero. He wore a T-shirt emblazoned with the name of his high school back home and looked for all the world as if he was excited about the prospect of going on a dream date with the queen of the junior prom. The colonel beckoned and men parted like the Red Sea as the volunteer stepped forward. Dark clouds churned overhead as the lieutenant and his young protégé departed for their precarious mission -- and then it began to rain.

Some days later Barkley asked another fellow what ever happened to the kid and the lieutenant. The other soldier slowly shook his head and answered, "Never made it back."

June 29, 1944 -- It had been sometime since Barkley had been able to write a letter. But now that he had experienced a couple days away from the front he was rested, so sat down to write his second letter since arriving in France.

"Somewhere in France," it began. They all began that way -- censorship dictated it be so. "June 29 '44. Dear Mother and Dad: If I find an envelope I can send this out today while I can. I am allright and so far have been lucky enough. I hope my luck holds out until after we…" a section was torn out, censored. In relating his experiences he declared: "I never knew I could run so fast on my hands and knees before but the other day we had a race between us and German bullets and we won…" (another section censored) "…is a experience that nobody wants to go through again."

Another paragraph lamented how it wasn't easy being in combat. Still, he realized that the job had to be done: "If I wasn't here though someone else would have to be and I am no better to fight than anyone else so I don't mind doing my share."

He complained about not having received any mail since D-Day and wondered where a promised box of candy might be. He then urged his parents to say hello to his friends back home for him since paper and envelopes were scarce. After enclosing some souvenir French money he signed off, then went scrounging for an envelope.

Quincy, Illinois -- Just as Harold Barkley was not getting any mail, his parents, too, suffered from the communications breakdown. They were still receiving letters written by their son when he was in England and Nettie could only hope that her boy was still there, safe from harm. Nearly three weeks had passed since D-Day and she worried herself sick over his whereabouts. The last letter they had received was dated June 4 -- two days before the invasion. God only knows where Harold was now.

Meanwhile, back at the home front, Harry was in better health and continued to work at Dayton-Dowd Company. His take home pay was still only about $13.00 a week -- not very much for two people to live on. Nettie continued to brood over her hens, hoping to bring in a little extra cash from the sale of the eggs. The pup was growing up. By now the cat had adjusted to the young upstart and begrudgingly accepted the hound's presence.

Across the Mississippi River, in Canton, Missouri, Barkley's grandmother had also acquired a blue star service flag and displayed it in her window in honor of her only grandchild and prayed daily for his deliverance.

June 30, 1944 -- Orders came to prepare to move out. The rest period was over. Men strapped on packs and cartridge belts and slung their weapons and fell in, grumbling as only soldiers can, for they knew where they were going -- and it wasn't pretty. By the end of the day they were in a forward area near the village of Saint-Georges-d'Elle.

Situated on the northeastern fringe of Hill 192, Saint-Georges-d'Elle was a hot spot, the scene of bitter fighting throughout the course of the struggle for Hill 192. Elements of the division's 23rd Infantry had been tossed out of town time and again. But the dogfaces of the 23rd weren't about to say "uncle" and had attacked once more. They owned it now, or at least most of it, although Germans still clung tenaciously to the southern outskirts, manning a number of strong points that played hell with the 23rd's patrols and probes.

While the 23rd maintained its precarious hold on Saint-Georges-d'Elle, Company G and the rest of the 38th Infantry's Second Battalion dodged the occasional mortar shell as they occupied foxholes in their reserve positions behind the village. Then, in the wee hours of July 3rd they moved again, marching 2,000 or so yards to the west to relieve their own regiment's Third Battalion. Before them lay the northwestern slope of Hill 192 -- they were basically occupying the very same positions they held before their own relief seven days earlier.

They quickly discovered that little had changed. Mortars and artillery still clobbered the foxhole line in varying degrees of intensity. The dreaded snipers continued to peck away at careless soldiers. And as if in retaliation, U.S. artillery pounded the German occupied hill with occasional concentrations that thundered by day or night. For the battalion, it was as if they had never left. Private Barkley had returned to the scene of his worst nightmare.

It was during this period that Barkley and several other scouts of the company were ordered to report to the command post a short distance to the rear. Upon arrival, they were greeted by an officer who ordered each scout to surrender his weapon in exchange for a new type of sub-machine gun.[*] They were told that it was an experimental model and that they were to use them for only one day, then return them and report on how well they had functioned.

Barkley studied the weapon with misgiving. It appeared to be crudely manufactured of stamped metal. Although it had the familiar pistol grip like his Thompson, it sported a cheap sliding wire shoulder stock instead of the sturdy wood he was accustomed to. Bullets were fed into the receiver by magazines similar to his Thompson's. After receiving brief instruction on its operation, the scouts were allowed to test fire the weapons. *Well*, thought Barkley, *It's something new. I'll give it a go. Maybe it'll be pretty good.* He was optimistic as he returned to his outfit and showed off his new toy.

Meanwhile, the company was preparing to make a local attack.

The attack, like so many others, jumped off with scouts leading the way. After clearing one hedgerow, Barkley's squad pressed on to the next. Although he had only fired a few bursts, Barkley's new sub-machine gun had performed well and his concerns and doubts began to fade. He had almost reached the next hedgerow when a German suddenly popped from its crest and aimed his rifle point blank at him. Instinctively, Barkley's weapon snapped up and he pulled the trigger. Nothing happened -- the new sub-machine gun

---

[*] Years later, Barkley believed the weapon was a Reising sub-machine gun. Although its description resembled the M-3 "Grease Gun", other veterans have described a similar weapon during this period and also claimed it to be a Reising.

RELIEF

had jammed! But fortunately, Barkley's reaction netted results. Upon seeing the muzzle of Barkley's weapon in his face, the German quickly dropped behind the hedgerow and at the same moment, Barkley dove into a drainage ditch that skirted its base.

"Shoot!" he cried as other Germans took aim and fired, "Shoot the sonovabitch!" Bullets cut the grass inches from his face. *"SHOOT, GODDAMMIT!"* Sweat poured by the quart. A fusillade of American bullets lacerated the hedge top as Barkley cringed in the ditch below it, clutching his impotent weapon.

The Germans were quickly driven off and soon Blackmore and the others came up to where Barkley lay. Barkley was clearly rattled. His uniform was drenched with sweat. His Thompson had never jammed on him. This damned, cheap piece of crap almost cost him his life!

As the squad secured the hedgerow, Barkley drew back the bolt of his weapon and inspected the receiver. A bullet was stuck in the chamber. He attempted to pry it out with his trench knife, but it was wedged in too tightly. Apparently the hot brass casing had fused to the metal of the barrel. It was no use, the bullet would not budge and Barkley was forced to sling the useless weapon and complete the action with a rifle taken from a dead Kraut -- and he only had three or four bullets for it at that! It was a hell of a fix to be a scout and denied your own weapon. Fortunately, he made it through the remainder of the day without incident.

When he and the others were called back to report on how the new guns had performed, Barkley retorted, "Give me back my Thompson. This is a piece of shit!"

Throughout the week more patrols departed the lines only to come limping back with harrowing tales of narrow escapes. Machine guns and mortars met every incursion. As always, snipers were a terror to all who encountered them. Barkley never knew the men of Company G to have mercy on snipers. Snipers always lay in wait, more than willing to kill unsuspecting GIs who came across their sights. But whenever surrounded and cut off from their own men, these cold-hearted killers often tried to surrender when there was no way out. No dice. Snipers killed without mercy and were shown none in return. Snipers were seldom taken prisoner.

As noted, one of the toughest enemy positions on Hill 192 was the cluster of fields known as Kraut Corner. A fortress unto itself, Kraut Corner sat at the head of Dead Man's Gulch, replete with deep dugouts and inter-connecting entrenchments where one hedgerow position covered the next. Webs of interlocking fields of fire guarded the northwest approach to Hill 192, denying access to any and all who tried. Machine guns and mortars ensured the entire area remained a death trap for anyone who dared enter it. Kraut Corner remained a formidable obstacle that had to be dealt with, if not actually eliminated.

One night one hell of a commotion erupted from beyond the front. Explosions flashed brightly while machine gun and rifle fire resonated from the far darkness. It sounded as if a full-scale attack was taking place. Later it was discovered that Company E had carried out a daring combat patrol that night that knocked the hell out of Kraut Corner. That was encouraging news, yet the patrol was only a raiding party that had no intention of occupying the position. The men assumed the Germans would recover and reinforce the site, perhaps making it even stronger than before. It would still be waiting for them, more daunting than ever. They knew the order to attack was soon coming. But when?

Back at Regimental Headquarters, intelligence officers collected the patrol information, pieced it together and put it into some semblance of order, then delivered it to Operations. The operations officers set to work devising their plan of attack based on the data provided by intelligence. In the end it was decided that any assault would be preceded by a massive bombardment from all of the Division's artillery, plus four batteries from adjacent divisions augmented by heavier guns from corps artillery. Thousands upon thousands of shells would converge on the hill, crushing it like a giant's heel smashes an anthill. There was even provisions for tactical air strikes, weather permitting. By implementing the new tank-engineer-infantry tactics, the planners were confident of success. The day for the attack was set for Tuesday, the 11th of July.

The Germans were waiting and well prepared. They knew the attack would come and had had weeks, if not months, to lay out their defenses, carefully sighting every machine gun, every mortar, every artillery piece, rocket launcher and tank to cover every conceivable approach. They were well entrenched. Some of their dugouts were as deep as ten or twelve feet underground, reinforced by heavy logs.

They knew the terrain, had studied it. They arranged their defenses in depth in such a manner that one position covered the next, designed to gradually slow the attackers, then stop them cold to be destroyed by heavy weapons. The troops were still the confident, young paratroopers of the 3rd Fallschirmjaeger Division -- tough customers. Superbly trained and well armed, they were determined to hold the hill against any and all comers. Supported by artillery, combined with the skillful use of their own deadly mortars and preponderance of machine guns, they selected pre-designated killing fields where the slaughter would take place.

Although the Germans were unaware of the new American tank tactics, they would be well prepared to counter any armored thrust. Anti-tank guns covered the narrow roads. Individual paratroopers armed with hand held anti-tank weapons such as the Ofenrohr* and Panzerfaust were a particular threat in the Bocage country. Solitary soldiers were able to hide in the dense foliage of the hedgerows, then pop out and fire these weapons at near point blank range, all but guaranteeing a kill.

Disturbing signs of the coming offensive appeared all along the American front. Every rifleman was given a cloth bandolier of additional ammunition as well as several hand grenades apiece. Barkley received several boxes of .45 caliber bullets for his Thompson. The weapons platoon stockpiled mortar shells and belts of .30 caliber bullets for their machine guns. Each man was handed a supplemental allotment of K-Rations and D-Bars and was ordered to wear his pack when the attack order came, for they were expected to be far from their present location when the battle was over and would need sustenance. But the most telling sign of all came with the arrival

---

* The Ofenrohr was similar to the American bazooka, and could be used multiple times. The one-shot Panzerfaust had been described earlier.

of a hot meal. For the infantrymen, a hot meal served at the front was the ultimate bad omen. There was no doubt that a major attack was in the offing.

The Germans were well prepared and waiting. The American infantry knew only too well the monumental task set before them.

CHAPTER 8

BATTLE OF HILL 192

July 11, 1944, 0500 Hours -- Barkley jolted awake, startled by a whisper as Sergeant Fretwell called softly into his foxhole. It was time to go. Barkley shook the cobwebs from his head. Groggily he gathered his equipment and weapon, then crawled from his burrow to join others of his platoon who milled restlessly behind their hedgerow wall in anticipation of the coming attack. Helmets glistened dully as men stood hunched against a fine mist that blurred their shadowy features. Each man was heavily laden with his own personal array of weaponry and a full load of ammunition. Most had additional bandoliers slung across their chests; cargo pockets sagged from the solid steel weight of hand grenades. Barkley cradled his tommy gun and re-adjusted the extra clips that protruded from his pants leg pockets, then simply stood and waited. Save for a whisper here or a muffled cough there, not a sound was heard.

Once assembled, the company marched to the rear as precaution against any short rounds of the coming barrage falling on the assault elements. Sergeants growled muted curses at those who spoke or carelessly banged a rifle against a helmet, for the withdrawal had to be made without the enemy's knowledge.

Before long, they arrived at their destination and halted within the confines of a broken apple orchard. Fractured limbs jutted from a vaporous sea, guarded by rank upon rank of dark, splintered trunks. Crooked, spindly twigs thrust from the murky haze, reaching out like so many cadaverous fingers straining to touch each soldier and mark him for his fate. Some men shuddered as the mist brushed their cheeks with its cool, wispy breath. Others shivered involuntarily, touched by something more foreboding and sinister than damp climate and stifled haunting premonitions and the sickening realization of their own fragile existence. They felt extremely vulnerable, mortal, incapable of repelling the nagging fears that possessed them. *This is it -- the big attack.* A full scale battle was in the making.

The occasional shell continued to crackle overhead, en route to harass the occupants on the hill. Muted thuds followed. Then silence. The mist continued to fall.

Suddenly, the earth trembled. Dull red flashes shimmered like sheet lightning across the distant horizon, followed by a disturbing, deep-voiced rumbling that sounded from far to the rear. It sounded unfathomably ominous, as if emanating from the bowels of the earth itself. Soon, raucous, hoarse moans scraped the sky, then accelerated in volume as a hundred shells passed overhead to slam into the face of the German held hill. More high explosives followed, shaking loose knee-buckling tremors that rippled down the slopes. The vibrations triggered the release of a thousand butterflies trapped in each man's stomach and everyone knew that the show had begun. The big shells poured in by the hundreds. Thousands more would follow.

Within half an hour daylight strained to penetrate the morning sky, and as if that was a signal, all the mortars of the infantry weapons companies contributed to the din as their bombs coughed from steel tubes to blast the lower slopes of Hill 192.

Company G received a cautionary order: stand by to move forward at a moments notice. Barkley's platoon was stretched out in column alongside a hedgerow that hemmed the apple orchard. His squad was first in line. A field or two to their front Company E waited patiently, primed for the assault. Deployed somewhere to the east was Company F which constituted the battalion's left wing. Company G, as the reserve company, would follow in bounds behind Company E, ready to respond to any difficulties encountered by either of the battalion's attacking companies. It was the classic infantry formation: two up and one back.

It was now daylight. Watch hands swept past 0600 hours. On cue, the bombardment promptly shifted to devastate the supporting lines of German entrenchments and the next moment Company E rose as one and rushed forward. Company G remained in place, tensed for action. Up front, toothy-bladed Sherman tanks revved their engines, geared down and lurched forward to ram the thin veneer of hedge walls excavated by the engineers, then roared into the fields beyond with all guns blazing. The rattle of their machine guns pierced the air while the deep booming of their cannon resonated through the misty veil. The attack had begun.

An electric shock raced up Barkley's spine. *This is it!* Things would be happening quickly now. His stomach knotted. He looked down the line of soldiers kneeling behind him. Bleak, solemn expressions were chiseled onto every face. Cigarettes flickered up and down the line, glowing softly within cupped hands. Barkley, too, fumbled for a cigarette. His hand trembled as he placed it between his lips. *Damn these nerves*, he thought as he drew hard on the damp tobacco. He was always high strung before an attack, wound tight as a spring. He knew full well that Death leered at him and delighted in his misery and the opportunity to once again play his evil games. *Let's go*, he said to himself, anxious to get the show on the road, to start moving. The waiting was always torturous -- the fear of the unknown played heavily upon him. Once the order was given to advance he knew he'd react instantly and go forward. That was his job. Only then would his nerves be soothed -- he'd be too busy to notice them, then. *Let's go*, he silently pleaded, *Let's go, let's go*...He fidgeted and took another hard pull on his cigarette as he sweated the inevitable.

It seemed that no sooner had Company E vanished beyond their hedgerow than the first crisp stammering of German burp guns announced that the infantry battle had begun. Other weapons joined in and within moments German artillery came down with a vengeance. The explosions were clearly visible from where Company G waited. Nonetheless, Company E, aided by the tanks, reached the next hedgerow with relative ease. Yet the experienced soldiers knew that they had only overpowered a screening force. They knew that things would get tougher as they ascended the hill -- the German's main line of resistance still lay ahead.

Back in reserve, Company G's officers and sergeants stirred. Barkley's eyes darted about, alert for any indication that they were moving up. A relentless crackle of small arms fire flowed from the battlefront. Artillery continued to pummel the distant slopes with devastating concentrations, causing the earth to roll underfoot in one continuous undulation. Barkley took one last drag on the stub of his cigarette, then flicked the butt to the mud.

Lieutenant Welch came up, hunched over as he trotted along the line. His face seemed as grim and gray as the sky above. "Okay," he announced as he darted past Barkley, "Let's go. Follow me."

Barkley sprung up, driven by pure adrenaline, and chased after his leader, dragging the rest of the platoon in tow. From up ahead, a flurry of gunfire, punctuated by the wicked crump of mortars told of rough going for Company E. More gunfire wafted from the left where Company F was making a similar assault. Things were heating up. The lieutenant steered for a broad gap ripped through a hedgerow and the platoon surged through as if drawn irresistibly by the vortex of Hell. Blinded by the surrounding hedgerows, Barkley could only guess what was happening a field or two before him, but could judge the ferocity of the fight by its sounds. Apparently the heavy bombardment hadn't affected the Germans very much. They must have patiently waited out the barrage in their sturdy bunkers with practiced discipline. Now they had come out of their bomb proofs full of spite and malice.

The company had barely begun its displacement forward when a torrent of artillery shells ripped through the ranks. Men dove for cover. Several more shells screamed in, then all was still. As the smoke began to clear, it was evident that there had been casualties and Barkley knew then and there that even as the reserve element, Company G's day would be fraught with danger.

No time to loose, the men were urged forward -- but not for long. Up ahead, the gunfire rose to a crescendo and the company was ordered to hold up. The men hugged the cover of the nearest hedgerow as stray bullets popped and whined overhead. Immediately everybody pulled out their entrenching tools and furiously scraped at the muddy soil. No one wanted to get caught again by enemy artillery.

As Barkley dug, he nervously listened to the brutal stutter and rip of German automatic weapons several fields to the front. The sharp crack of M-1's and the rapid chatter of BAR's responded defiantly, bearing testimony that Company E was meeting stiff resistance.

Artillery shells howled overhead in droves, forcing men to shout to be heard above the din. Another sharp blast sounded from the front, followed by a flurry of small arms fire. Barkley, still blinded to the action, wondered how the fight was going. Sergeant Blackmore stalked up and down the line, muttering curses beneath his breath. Then, as if he couldn't stand it any more, he clambered up the hedgerow and thrust his head above the hedge bank, anxious to gain some insight to the battle. Bullets spat through the foliage. Blackmore ignored them and stood his ground as if he was born bullet proof -- Achilles at the siege of Troy.

The sickening crump of mortars was heard but not seen, increasing the anxiety of the men strung out along the hedgerow. The enormity of it all was reflected upon faces now drawn and blanched a sickly white.

From the rear a squad of grim-faced litter bearers emerged from the waning mist. Their helmets bobbed precariously upon their heads as they loped towards the front, desperately clutching their collapsed stretchers as they ran. One had a Red Cross flag tucked beneath his arm. They were brave men. Red crosses on white armbands offered scant protection from bullets and flying shrapnel. They trotted past the dormant file and disappeared beyond the next hedgerow, drawn to the sound of battle.

Crump! Crump-ca-rump! More mortars. Another intense round of automatic fire. *Jesus!* thought Barkley, *there's hell to pay up there.* He listened intently as several hollow thuds reverberated from somewhere beyond the hedgerow -- *Grenades... they're up close now.* Black smoke rose maliciously from distant fields. More small arms fire followed, enhanced by machine guns and still more mortars. Then an outburst of erratic rifle fire preceded a long, tense, silence. The deep thunder of artillery rumbled farther to the front where smoke rolled incessantly higher.

The lieutenant, who had been on his radio, turned to his men. "Let's go!" he cried, "We're moving up."

The platoon funneled through a massive gap ripped through a hedgerow, then streaked down the edge of the next field. Craters, large and small pocked the earth. Several bloodied bodies lay about, and felled trees, too. Artillery had done all this. The men pressed on, passing through another hedge bank to enter another field.

As they trotted forward, several men were startled by the sudden rustling of the foliage that capped the flanking hedgerow. Weapons snapped up, then lowered in relief as a GI emerged. Red Cross armbands girdled each arm. He tumbled over, then reached up to tug on one end of a stretcher. The stretcher cleared, followed by other litter bearers who slid down the embankment to claim their share of the load. Grim-faced, they trudged heavily towards the rear, their breath raspy and labored as they passed the advancing line. The litter sagged from the weight of a shredded life form. The head was swathed in blood-soaked bandages. The bandages groaned. A gut wrenching moan. Several of the company winced at the sight. Barkley had seen it many times before, but the new men were visibly shaken. One retched and another puked, but few noticed for their attention was arrested by the mounting battle sounds that swelled from the front. Company G moved steadily towards that ominous roar.

Again the company was ordered to halt. Harried men collapsed against the hedge bank to take a breather. Just ahead, several GIs stood guard over a cluster of German prisoners.

Barkley wedged another cigarette between his lips and numbly monitored this latest development. The prisoners sulked under the watchful eye of their guards. There were about a dozen of them -- German paratroopers -- tough, haughty young men, even in captivity. The guards were lining up their sullen charges in preparation for movement to the rear. Barkley noticed that some of the prisoners were wounded and remained sitting or laying on the ground. The guards kept their rifles leveled and warily watched them, for fanaticism ran rampant through the enemy ranks. It was not unknown for some young Nazis to have concealed weapons: a pistol, grenade, or even a knife, so the guards maintained their vigilance until each could be thoroughly searched.

One of the guards, a sergeant, insisted that all of the prisoners stand, including the wounded. "Hande hoch! Hande hoch!" he bellowed as he made jerking motions with his arms, indicating that he wanted hands placed on top of heads. He was furious and seemed to vent his wrath on the prisoners left in his charge. His exhortations were met with searing, hate-filled glares. A couple of the more severely wounded remained on the ground. The sergeant strode over to them. "Get up!" he snarled as he booted one in the ass, "Get up, goddamn you!" They got the message and staggered to their feet, faces contorted in pain as they attempted to obey the sergeant's command.

Barkley regarded the prisoners with indifference. God only knows how many GIs they had killed before being pressured into surrendering. He had little sympathy for them. But then his eye was drawn to one young German in particular. He appeared to be about seventeen years old. The youth stood hunched over, his face racked with pain. Intestines seeped from a ragged belly wound and he struggled to hold them in place by cradling them in both hands. His uniform was sopping wet with blood. Barkley studied his tormented face. It seemed certain that this young fellow was going to die.

The sergeant noticed that all of the prisoners had their fingers locked on top of their heads except this pitiful creature. Angrily, he stomped over to where he stood and roughly smacked the boy's head and barked, "Hande hoch! Hande Hoch!" and gestured for him to raise his hands over his head. The boy meekly protested, indicating the severity of his wound. He sobbed unintelligible words. It seemed that he was saying that he was Czech, not German. Unmoved, the sergeant insisted that he stand like the others. "Czech my ass!" he mocked, "Yer all f___ing Czech or Polish when you give up."

The boy regarded the sergeant with furrowed brow, then shakily removed his blood-glazed hands from his belly and tried to clasp them over is head. The upward motion put additional pressure from within his abdomen, forcing a perceptible grimace as his guts oozed a little farther from their cavity, glistening slick and obscene in the morning light. What little color remained drained from his face, yet somehow he managed to comply with the sergeant's cruel demand. Satisfied, the sergeant stalked off.

The whole scene was just too much for Barkley. Sure, he had suffered through combat and had lost buddies at the hands of the Nazis, but this cruel act was not justified. He rose to his feet and walked over to where the suffering youth stood half-stooped, and indicated that it would be alright for him to lower his hands. Fearfully, the lad's eyes glanced about in effort to locate the sadistic sergeant, but Barkley assured him that it would be okay.

Accepting Barkley's word, the wretch lowered his arms and again clutched his bowels. "Ich bin Czech," he sobbed as if in explanation or apology, "Ich bin Czech". He then stood very still with eyes clenched tight, his trembling hands wrapped about his exposed intestines. Again he sobbed.

"Let's go, Barkley!" a voice boomed. It was Sergeant Fretwell. "We're movin' out." Fretwell glared hatefully as Barkley returned to the platoon and soon the company was on the march again, leaving the prisoners and guards behind as they passed into the next field.

As they advanced, they passed the clutter of abandoned equipment and other junk that littered the hedgerow's base. A series of mud streaked boards propped against the hedgerow failed to shield the filth of several German corpses. They were the result of all the previous gun firing. Apparently the Krauts had tried to hold the line here and failed. The dead paratroopers underscored the tenacity of their stand and their willingness to fight to the death. Closeby lay other bodies, some writhing and twitching in their agonies as life struggled to escape -- the mortally wounded. There would be no time to give them medical attention and the column moved on. Barkley noted that there were drab-clad bodies, too.

By now the mist had long burned off, yet clouds continued to cloak the sun, ensuring a morning haze. Up ahead, the battle inched up the hill. So far, Barkley's company had not been required to assist either of the assault companies. Still, the perpetual clatter and thump of machine guns and mortar fire assured him that the battle was far from over, the murderous struggle still raged in the fields and meadows before him.

SSOOOSH! As one, the men dove flat. The earth heaved violently. Hot steel sliced the air as soil rained down in pelting clods. More shells ripped the field. Bodies pressed hard against the earth, oblivious of the mud as shrapnel slapped heavily into the hedge bank above them. Again the earth thumped savagely. Ribs ached as the ground knocked hard against them. Someone screamed. Barkley, like the others, cringed at every blast and then suddenly all was still.

Slowly, men pried themselves from the ground and surveyed the damage. Smoke swirled above fresh, raw craters and snaked along the ground to bite men's nostrils with its acrid scent. Several boys remained down, moaning pitifully, whimpering. Calls of "Medic! Over here!" rang out as soldiers knelt attentively over stricken comrades. Officers and sergeants quickly re-organized the men and got them moving again and soon the shelling was only another bad memory.

The company advanced over ground so beaten that every field seemed a haven for massive craters. The trees and shrubbery of each field and bordering hedgerow had been blasted to splinters and pitched in the mud to join the dead that now were common.

Company G advanced in bounds, hot on the tail of Company E. Artillery seemed to badger their every move, claiming one man here and another there. Another violent encounter erupted to the fore and in short order, the company was again compelled to hold up. Company E had run into another nest of resistance.

The column sank to ground and waited in the shadow of a hedgerow that angled towards the front. Again shovels broke the soil.

Barkley's squad was still in the lead, near the corner of the field where two hedgerows intersected. To his right, a fallow pasture stretched a hundred yards or so to the next hedgerow. Although his company had not yet been committed to battle, Barkley was exhausted. The entire route from the reserve position to their present one had been plagued by artillery fire and there had been casualties. All of the running, digging, dodging and diving for cover was wearing him down.

He listened to the sounds of battle as he dug, occasionally stopping to stare at the drab clad soldiers strung out behind him. Some faces were familiar, but there were so many new ones! Over the past weeks casualties had mounted day by day -- on bad days they came wholesale. This day held all the promise of a bad day. The thought prompted him to wonder how many more chances he would have to cheat Fate.

As he mulled over the odds, his thoughts were interrupted by the noxious clatter of an American light tank that lumbered noisily into the pasture to his right. He watched its approach and waited for others to appear but none did. *What the hell is it doing here all alone?* he wondered. No other tanks seemed to be anywhere near. It moved deeper across the far side of the field.

Suddenly it jolted to a halt twenty or thirty yards from the facing hedgerow and perhaps a hundred yards from where Barkley knelt. It just sat there, motor idling, motionless and unsupported -- a solitary tank at the far end of the field. *It must be lost,* Barkley mused. The lone tank became a focal point for Barkley, something to take his mind off of the coming fight.

By now it was nearing mid-day. Small arms fire crackled continuously all along the front where artillery rumbled in never ending spasms. Up and down the line eyes peered spookily from beneath helmet brims as ears strained to decipher the distant battle sounds. Several heads rocked back as men lifted canteens to their lips, taking measured swigs to appease burning throats. The disconcerted few toiled faithfully with their shovels in their latest attempts to get underground. Another round of heavy gunfire exploded from somewhere up ahead, drawing dread expressions from grave, brooding faces.

Barkley was still gazing at the tank when a slight rustling of leaves in the hedgerow that angled to his right front caught his eye. A thousand needles pricked his spine. *What was that?* His vision sharpened as he focused on the point. It was about midway between him and the tank. Suddenly the torso of a German soldier leaned from the foliage and aimed a Panzerfaust at the unsuspecting tank. *POOM!* Awestruck, Barkley watched as the bulbous warhead soared through the air, then bounced roughly on the ground somewhere short of its mark. He gawked incredulously. *It missed! It missed!* Then he realized that it did not explode. It must have been a dud. Meanwhile, the cagey German had slipped back into the cover of the hedgerow.

It had all happened in a matter of seconds. Initially, Barkley had been too stunned to react. Now the deadly missile lay somewhere in the grass before the tank. Without giving a second thought, Barkley launched into a full-tilt sprint towards the tank. He felt that *someone* had to warn the tankers lest they move forward and crush the bomb with their heavy treads. The dud would surely explode then, destroying the tank and injuring or killing the crew. He charged on, tommy gun ready as he scanned the suspect hedgerow for any more Germans. God only knows how many more might be hidden on the other side.

The telephone, he thought as he ran, remembering their pre-battle briefing, *I'll have to use the field phone attached to the back of the tank.* As he neared, he saw that the warhead had landed directly in front of one tread. He trotted behind the tank and jammed the phone's handset beneath his helmet. "Hey in there," he panted, "For God's sake don't move! A Kraut just fired an anti-tank rocket at you. It's right in front of your tread. Now listen, I'm going to run out and get it. Tell your bow gunner to cover me. But be careful! It'll be me out front." He added these last words as an afterthought -- he didn't want a nervous machine gunner to be alarmed by the sudden appearance of a figure looming before his sights and start shooting.

That said, Barkley bolted to the front of the tank and nimbly scooped up the warhead with one arm, then darted to the forward hedgerow and pitched it onto the other side. Never once did it occur to him that the damn thing might explode at any time, literally blowing him to bits. And all the while, he kept a sharp eye for any more Germans, but none showed and his deed was done.

Not stopping to catch his breath, he raced back to where his platoon still squatted alongside their hedgerow. They had watched his mad dash and were bewildered by his seemingly unexplainable action. Gasping, he arrived at his squad area and sank to the ground, panting. Sergeant Fretwell was furious. "Dammit! What the hell are you doing?" he growled.

Barkley glared incredulously. "Didn't you see that? A German damn near blew up that tank with an anti-tank rocket. I ran over there to warn them."

"Dammit, you belong *here*! We're about to attack. You don't worry about that goddam tank. We've got enough problems of our own. Leave the tanks to theirs!"

Having been thoroughly chastised, Barkley glowered at the sergeant as he struggled to catch his breath. *You worthless sonovabitch*, he thought as he sized up Fretwell, *You never put your ass on the line for anybody!*

Overhead, a faint buzzing grew to a roar as American dive bombers knifed through the clouds and lunged at the hill. Bombs tumbled from their bellies and plunged towards the gentle slope. Massive explosions shattered the air and the earth's foundation shook. Black clouds rolled skyward. The bombs fell awfully close -- too close it seemed. Another strike transformed the hill into a convulsing volcano. Tracer bullets slashed the sky as German anti-aircraft guns hammered away at the planes, attempting to knock them down like so many annoying insects. The war birds screamed defiantly as they swerved and danced among the bright tracers, then swooped skyward and punched through the clouds and vanished as quickly as they had appeared.

Meanwhile, Company G was again on the move. As Barkley ran all the blood drained from his face as a veritable wall of high explosives sprouted in the near distance and drew closer by bounds. It was a rolling barrage, a tidal wave of fire and steel intent on intercepting them as they moved forward. The collision was inevitable.

Terrified, Barkley watched helplessly as the barrage neared. And then Hell was upon them. *WHOOSH!* It was as if a freight train was hurtling through the sky. The veterans dove to the earth. *SCHUHH-WHAMM!!! SCHUHH-WHAMM!! SCH-WHAMM!!* Shrapnel cut like scythes. Several replacements who were too petrified to react were hit and butchered horribly while another was launched skyward, dumbstruck by the absurdity of what was happening to him as he defied gravity and sailed away. His body struck the earth like a sack of grain and bounced once or twice, followed by its pack and a severed arm, and then lay still. Blood pooled beneath the corpse.

The barrage swept over them, trampling them like a stampeding herd, and then was gone.

The lieutenant sprang up. "Let's go! Let's go!" he bellowed as he sprinted towards the next hedgerow, anxious to maintain contact with the assault elements before the next series struck. "Follow me!" A blood soaked soldier attempted to rise but faltered, not realizing his intestines were strewn to hell and gone, then tumbled to the ground. A comrade struggled to hold him down with blood slicked fingers. "*Medic! Medic!*" he cried as the disemboweled soldier shrieked in horror. "Leave him," a sergeant bawled, anxious to get his men out of harms way, "Leave him for the medics." Pale faced, Barkley ups and rises from a haze of smoke and dust and chased after a mob of figures galloping behind their lieutenant. An ashen faced aid man trundled up to the wounded man to stuff the soiled and lacerated entrails back into the gutted man's cavity, knowing that his patient will surely die.

More shells struck in measured bursts. *Schuh-Whamm! Schuh-WHAMM!* Flat trajectory stuff. Barkley raced between explosions that erupt left, right and behind, goading him to greater speed. Another shell screams close, but he is already down as the earth quakes and shrapnel hisses. "Go! Go!" Up and moving again, he follows the mob that surges through a gap and into the next field. Others straggle in as the platoon pushes on, desperate to escape the field of endemic death.

Panting, the squads assemble. "First squad, over here," a sergeant calls. "Third squad," another hollers, "Third squad, on me!" The platoon reforms and moves to the next hedgerow and crouches low. Second Scout Barkley took a cursory headcount and realized that First Scout Smitty was no longer with them. Barkley had just received a radical battlefield promotion.

139

Several fields to the front, Company E continued to engage the enemy in savage firefights. Stray bullets snapped and whined overhead, prompting the soldiers of Company G to cower behind their shelter. Then single bullets began to smack at odd intervals into their own hedgerow from behind. That meant only one thing -- a sniper was behind them! Everybody was down now. Barkley, like others, began to scan the terrain behind him, hoping to spot their nemesis. Another bullet slapped savagely near someone's head. "Jesus!" Another miss. *The bastard must be firing from some distance,* Barkley thought as he focused on a church steeple far to one flank. Judging the frequency of misses and the fact that no other terrain feature seemed likely, he deduced that the steeple was the most logical vantage point for a sharpshooter. He raced down the line to report to the lieutenant.

"Can't do anything about that now," the lieutenant snapped, "We're about to move out."

"Well you could at least call on someone to check it out!" Barkley retorted. Disgusted, he high tailed it back to his squad while bullets continued to torment his prostrate comrades.

Eventually, Company E pushed the battle through a cluster of houses and beyond, following a curtain of fire and steel as artillery paved their way. The radios of Company G crackled, then the lieutenant announced, "Let's go," and again they are up and moving, grateful to escape the sniper's domain. They passed ripped up hedgerows littered with scores of dead and dying soldiers, then skirted several shattered houses surrounded by heavily cratered fields. A couple of German tanks burned in a road, testimony to the bitter nature of the struggle.

Another fierce exchange of arms roared from the front, and again the advance ground to a halt. Throughout the battle, the assault elements had pushed hard on the enemy, endeavoring to keep him off balance whenever penetration was achieved. At times, the attacking squads were ordered to press the attack, thereby by-passing a few stubborn Germans to be dealt with by follow-up troops. As a consequence, the men of Company G were compelled to range up and down the length of the captured hedgerows, cautiously peeking into enemy fighting holes and dugouts. While one fellow investigated a hole, several other stood by, covering him with rifles leveled at the dark, gaping cavern. Sometimes movement could be heard within a bunker and excited calls of "Raus! Raus!" were shouted into the entrance by nervous GIs. Riflemen crouched or stood outside the entrance, ready to fire a volley into the abyss at the first inkling of treachery. They knew that many of these German paratroopers would rather die fighting for their Fuhrer than surrender.

A muffled snarl might be heard from within a dark bunker, as if some hideous monster resided there, and, in a way, one did. The GIs took no chances. They were all aware of the vicious, cornered-rat psyche of many of these Nazis. Sometimes the calls for surrender were answered by a potato-masher grenade flipped out of the entrance, or maybe desperate bursts from a burp gun. In reply, American rifles and BARs pulverized the interior of the dugout in hopes of riddling the occupant with bullets. Sometimes such actions evolved into a tense stand-off between GIs and a lone German. The hunters and the hunted -- pack hounds baying at the badger hole. A grenade would often be the answer to reluctant Germans.

A low moaning flowed from deep within one such dugout. Several Yanks stood near the mouth, peering apprehensively into its depths. The bunker was a sturdy one, deep, with a reinforced roof of logs and earth. A tangle of brush and bushes veiled the entrance.

"There's one in here," a GI called excitedly.

The moaning continued.

Barkley was nearby. He could hear it -- a pitiful groaning.

One fellow tried out his German: "Kommen Sie heraus!"

Another soldier approached rapidly. "What do you got here?" he demanded. It was Sergeant Parker.

"A Kraut's in there. He won't come out."

The sergeant cocked his head and listened. The moaning persisted. "I'm going in after him," Parker declared arbitrarily as he threw down his helmet and slipped off his pack. "I'm going to pull him out."

"You're crazy," exclaimed the others, "You're nuts!" The GIs were aware that the man in the hole might be lurking with a burp gun, or a knife, or even a grenade, prepared to send them both to Hell. Their solution would have been to toss in a couple of grenades themselves and end the matter, period.

"I'm going in there," Parker repeated, then dove into the dark chamber. The other soldiers gawked incredulously and waited tensely for something to happen.

A muted scuffling and cursing sifted from the dugout, followed by a scraping, dragging sound. Before long the backside of Sergeant Parker emerged, tugging on the collar of a startled wounded German as he was towed from his refuge.

His audience looked on in amazement, shaking their heads in disbelief. They'd be damned if they'd have gone into that hole to drag out an enemy. They still contended that a grenade would have been much simpler -- and safer. But Sergeant Parker was that kind of guy, the type of fellow who wouldn't ask his men to do anything he wouldn't do himself. He performed similar acts of courage time and again, never faltering in his resolve.

The position cleared of enemy, the company again moved up a field or two. The battlefield was now one continuous roar. Artillery crashed from seemingly every point of the compass -- and then the sky exploded with cataclysmic effect. "Jesus Christ!" Barkley cried as shrapnel rained all around. Incredulously he was untouched, but others were not so lucky and lay torn and bloody upon the ground, quivering in agony while another remained still as stone. An overworked medic sprung into action.

By mid-day the assault elements crested the hill, then pushed on towards the St. Lo highway that skirted its base. Maintaining its interval, Company G descended the slope, then peeled to the right of Company E and passed through a shattered orchard which fronted a hard paved road that fed into the St. Lo highway. Suspicious of the road, the lieutenant called a halt. Soldiers spread out behind the bordering hedgerows and gazed apprehensively at the fields beyond. Barkley knew that there was nothing on the other side that bore any love for him.

In time, Sergeant Fretwell sauntered up to Barkley. "The lieutenant wants you to get out there an' walk up an' down that road to see if you can draw their fire." *Holy shit!* thought Barkley, *that's suicide*, and his face must have reflected his thoughts for Fretwell responded, "We'll cover you from here."

Barkley glanced once more over the hedgerow. Although vicious artillery and reams of gunfire sounded from every direction, nothing stirred to his immediate front. Before him lay the typical Norman countryside -- a tangle of hedgerows and shrubbery and small clusters of trees. The enemy could, and would, be anywhere. *This is truly suicide*, he reiterated. He quickly examined his Thompson, ensuring it was operable, then slung himself over the hedgerow and stepped warily onto the road.

His heart pounded savagely as he paced slowly up and down the pavement. He walked as if stepping on eggshells, ready to drop at the slightest provocation. His ears were attuned to every noise, his eyes drawn to every movement. More than once intuition caused him to fling himself down, heart in his throat as blood raced through his veins. He fully expected a deluge of bullets to sweep him from the road, but nothing happened. No gunfire. Nothing. His imagination must have been playing tricks on him. Or was it? Sweat poured from every pore. If the Germans were over there, he reasoned, they were wise to his ploy. They'd surely wait until they could catch an entire squad or platoon. After a long pause, he gingerly rose and resumed his nervous promenade, expecting death at any moment.

Although he paraded up and down the road for quite some time, the enemy never took the bait. In time the lieutenant must have decided that it was clear, but as a precaution he began sending men over by ones and twos. In that manner they would not present such lucrative targets for enemy machine gunners. Once a couple of squads had safely crossed, Barkley was relieved of his precarious duty and he and the balance of the platoon infiltrated over the road and deployed among the hedgerows on the opposite side.

"Dig in, boys. Dig in," came the order as a gentle rain began to fall. They were warned that enemy tanks had been reported in the vicinity -- Company E had knocked out one or two only a few hundred yards to the company's left rear. Everyone expected a counter-attack. Surprisingly none came.

Daylight waned. A fine mist continued to fall and the day ended as it had begun, with a delicate spray soaking the earth with its soft, velvety touch. Companies E and F had now secured the far side of the St. Lo highway and were reined in -- the Second Battalion had reached the village of la Calvaire, its battlefield objective. The village itself was now the property of E Company. Barkley's Company G was echeloned to E's right flank while Company F held hedgerows across the St. Lo highway to the left. Although the men didn't know it, their battalion was the only unit of the Division to achieve its goal. Still, the other battalions had made spectacular gains against fierce opposition and had a firm hold on the hill.

Hill 192, the thorn in First Army's side and key to the capture of St. Lo had at last been taken after weeks of bloody stalemate. It had been achieved by an unprecedented one-day assault. The innovative tank-engineer-infantry tactics proved invaluable. St. Lo finally lay at the American's feet and they could now plan with immeasurably more confidence their breakout from Normandy. The cost, however, had not been cheap. In previous attempts to take the hill in June, the 2nd Infantry Division had sustained more than 1,200 casualties over a three day period. In the interim period the daily routine of shelling, snipers, probes and patrols had whittled away more strength.

The successful assault of July 11 also had its price. The First Battalion of the 38th Infantry lost 97 men; Barkley's Second Battalion suffered 179 casualties, including ten officers. And elements of the 23rd Infantry that went over the eastern slope suffered comparable losses -- a platoon from its Company A got caught in a gully called "Purple Heart Draw" and was nearly annihilated by mortars, artillery and machine guns. The supporting armor of the 741st Tank Battalion fell victim to German anti-tank weapons as Panzerfausts and 88's left a number of tanks blazing on the hillside.

Although not committed to the main attack, Company G had followed closely behind Company E and tallied 25 casualties[*] when the counting was done, most of them from the artillery and mortar fire that constantly plagued their route of advance. Two men were killed

---

[*] Initially, Company G listed 17 casualties for July 11, but over the next few days it was discovered that more men had been wounded than reported at the end of the day-long battle.

outright and another died of his wounds a few days later. The attack had scarcely begun when their company commander, Lieutenant Warner, was wounded, and before his second-in-command, Lieutenant "Lucky" Lawson, could take over, he, too, fell victim to enemy artillery. Command of the company then fell to Second Lieutenant William Harmon, the third commanding officer of the company after only one month of combat.

The Germans, too, suffered. One cannot discount the effects of the preliminary bombardment or the barrages that preceded each phase of the assault. All in all, American artillerymen sent 20,000 shells onto the German positions. Although it required a direct hit to knock out the well constructed dugouts, the heavy volume of fire kept the enemy in their holes until the attacking elements were closing in for the kill. The bombardment was demoralizing. A letter retrieved days later from the body of a dead paratrooper spoke of the horrors of enduring the tremendous shelling before the attack. Yet still, the Germans emerged to man their posts and fought tenaciously. During the fight for Kraut Corner, several paratroopers refused to surrender and subsequently were buried alive by a tank dozer. And the German paratroopers' fanaticism can be attested by a 2nd Division medic who attempted to aid a horribly wounded German. But the German held him at bay with a pistol, cursing the Americans and shouting "Heil Hitler" until he eventually bled to death. What price glory? The Fuhrer would have been proud.

Units of the German 5th and 9th Parachute Regiments bore the brunt of the attack and were decimated -- losses that could scarcely be replaced. It was reported that the commander of the 9th Parachute Regiment wept when he learned of his loses -- his regiment was nearly wiped out. During the course of the battle these battalions were reinforced by the 12th Parachute Gun Brigade and the 3rd Parachute Reconnaissance Company. As a last resort, the 3rd Parachute Engineer Battalion was tossed in, but to no avail. A number of supporting tanks had been knocked out by the Americans, including two destroyed by American armor during Company E's fight for the village of Cloville. Company E claimed another late in the day on the St. Lo highway.

But the greatest loss of all for the Germans was Hill 192, their lofty observation post that had given them a bird's eye view of the entire V Corps area of operation. Its loss would prove crucial in the days to come. Now men of the 2nd Infantry Division covered the heights and could look back the fifteen bloody miles to Omaha Beach.

Every regiment of the division had sustained grievous losses in the grueling hedgerow warfare. Since coming ashore at Omaha Beach on June 7, the 38th Infantry alone counted a loss of 1,052 men. The other two rifle regiments logged similar numbers. More hedgerows lay ahead of them. And Berlin was still a long way off.

CHAPTER 9

STATIC DEFENSE

Evening, July 11, 1944 -- Dusk had fallen. The shelling had stopped and, save for the muted rumblings of distant artillery, it was relatively quiet in the company area. Exhausted soldiers continued the never ending task of improving and deepening their foxholes. Each man worked as if the Devil himself was watching over his shoulder, for snipers remained a constant concern and fear was everlasting.

Another band of crimson flashed across a fading horizon. Barkley paused in his labor to monitor the distant barrage. The sound quavered and rolled, reminiscent of a violent prairie thunderstorm that had vented its anger, then moved on to die in the next county.

Nearby, Leroy Hinson, the youngster from the South, toiled at his own hole and ignored the cannonade. With Smitty gone, Hinson had received the dubious honor of being appointed Second Scout.

Oblivious to the distinction, he chopped diligently at the soil. Dog tired, Barkley pitched his shovel aside to take a breather and Hinson quickly joined him. Both teetered on the brink of exhaustion and words were few and far between.

Before long, a figure shambled towards them, stooped double as if the weight of the world rested upon his shoulders. The figure stopped and knelt beside their holes. It was Sergeant Fretwell. After a dry salutation he got to the point of his visit: "When it's dark, I wants you two t'crawl out to the center of that field there," he nodded towards the front. "Find a shell hole or somethin' and stay there until I send someone t'get you."

Barkley was irritated. "What the hell for?" he railed.

"The lieutenant wants an advance warnin' in case the Krauts try a night attack. If they come, you can engage 'em long enough t'give us a few seconds so's we can wake up and repel the attack."

Barkley said nothing. The sergeant returned to his own hole. *Well*, thought Barkley, *he sure as hell didn't mention what would happen to* us *if an attack came. No way we can get back. The Germans will run right over us. We'll be dead meat.*

He and Hinson were, in Army parlance, "expendable", and they knew it.

When it was dark, Fretwell returned and said it was time. As the two scouts climbed from their holes, Fretwell passed a wrist watch to Barkley so he and Hinson could mark time as each man took his turn as lookout while the other slept. Fretwell was going to accompany them so he'd know the location of their outpost for their relief before daybreak.

All three slipped over the hedgerow and dropped into misty blackness. Down on their bellies, they slithered through no man's land, each movement a measured effort to remain undetected. Wet grass sopped their clothing. Slowly, silently, they inched into the unknown.

A muffled, metallic cough broke the silence and a hissing incandescent line threaded skyward. The three GIs froze as the flare rose higher and pressed their bodies hard into the soil, hoping to blend into the landscape and remain undetected. The flare reached its peak and burst with a pop. Stark shimmering light illuminated all below. Each man cringed and lay motionless, heart pounding, praying and hoping that the Germans didn't see them.

The flare sizzled and floated to earth then sputtered as it burned out beyond some hedgerow wall. Dark again, the trio resumed their prowl. Before long another flare streaked and burst and the whole episode was repeated.

About halfway across the field the men bellied into a deep shell hole. A shattered log lay across its rim, affording additional cover. It was as good a place as any for their mission. The sergeant took a mental note of its location, then tapped Barkley on his foot and whispered, "Good luck. I'll be back before daylight," then slithered from the hole and was gone. Barkley and Hinson were on their own.

Both men were dead tired. Barkley, now the First Scout, felt obligated to take the first watch and allowed Hinson to doze off. Checking his timepiece, he marked the commencement of the first two-hour shift.

Barkley crawled to the fallen log and laid his Thompson before him, then nestled into the muddy soil. It was spooky. Visions of Nazi infiltrators sneaking up to cut his throat induced him to draw his trench knife and thrust it into the ground beside his weapon -- just in case. Peeking around the log he strained to hear any threatening noise, anything at all. He was on edge. His nerves were wired.

Faint sounds played across the field. He listened intently as hushed words floated towards him -- German words! The guttural gibberish came from behind the far hedgerow. Then an engine growled, accompanied by nerve-grating squealing and clanking sounds. *Tanks! That was a tank! Oh, Christ, tanks!* An electric shock raced up his spine. It was maneuvering somewhere behind the German lines. Or was there more than one? Surely the fellows heard that!

Flashes of light danced on the horizon as artillery thundered and thumped farther down the line where some obscure activity must have disturbed the monster of war. Elsewhere, a muted machine gun hammered a sharp challenge.

Despite the voices and the tank and the threat of knife-wielding infiltrators, Barkley was absolutely drained, sapped by the rigors of a full day's battle. His eyes burned. Every time he blinked his lids felt as abrasive as sandpaper. He was so tired! His eyelids drooped. He struggled to keep them open, making a conscious effort to stay awake.

More voices gobbled in German. Barkley's eyes sprung open. They still seemed to be on their side of the next hedgerow. *Oh, Jesus! Are they going to come now?* His finger tensed on the pistol grip of his weapon. *"Engage 'em long enough to give us a few seconds warning..."* that's what Fretwell said. *Should I wake Hinson? No. No, wait and see... We'll be dead meat. We'll be dead meat.* Sweat surged from every pore.

Several shells screamed overhead, then slammed hard onto the hedgerows behind him. They seemed to have landed squarely where his platoon was dug in. *I wonder if anyone got hit?* Again silence claimed the darkness.

Another flare popped and swayed in its descent, slashing the field with bizarre shadows. Inanimate objects appeared to take life and move. Mounds of earth were transformed into crouching figures. Dark hollows appeared as crawling men closing in with the knife. Barkley stifled panic as his eyes darted from one shadow to the next, trying to determine what each actually was. Then the flare died and it was dark. Blinded by the sudden blackness, Barkley was alone with his fears and pounding heart. Again a solitary machine gun spat a sharp, rapid burst, then all was quiet.

Finally, two hours elapsed. It was Hinson's turn. Barkley gently nudged his partner. Hinson stirred vaguely, but didn't respond. Again Barkley tried but didn't succeed. He knew that Hinson was bushed, too, so decided to give him another hour, then wake him.

Back at the crater's rim, Barkley stared bug-eyed into the void. *Damn, it's dark!* Again his lids sagged. His head dropped heavily, then snapped upright. *Was I asleep?... No... No, only for a second.* He squinted at the luminous dial of the watch. Only a few minutes had passed since his decision to stand another watch. The second hand advanced sluggishly, fighting the progression of time as if immersed in molasses.

His eyes strained to pierce the gloom. Time and again his eyelids drooped, then sprung wide open. *Stay Awake!* he told himself as he struggled to keep alert. Again his head fell and jerked upright. *STAY A-WAKE!!*

150

STATIC DEFENSE

A series of rifle shots rang in the distance, barking like startled dogs in the night. Various colored flares sizzled brightly as they arched and fell. *What did that mean? A barrage? Maybe it's the signal for the attack? My God, this is it.* His heart leaped to his throat as he stared desperately, anticipating the worst. *"Engage 'em long enough..."* We'll be dead meat. *Nothing you can do about it... got to stay awake.* Then a solitary red flare sputtered up, then down. Again Barkley searched the darkness for suspicious movement.

He glanced at the watch. Less than ten minutes had passed since he had tried to rouse Hinson. It seemed like hours. He pulled a D-bar from a pants pocket and nibbled on it, hoping that the thick, sweet chocolate would give him energy and keep him awake. He prayed that no moon would come out -- he sure as hell didn't want to get caught in the middle of no man's land beneath a full moon. *There ain't no stars*, he thought, *it must be cloudy. It'll probably rain again.* The very thought seemed to generate thunder as another barrage shimmered in the distance and rolled across the heavens.

Another peek at the watch revealed the retarded movement of the second hand. Sounds, if any, appeared to be distant, fuzzy -- the faint drumming of artillery -- an abrupt, electrifying rip of a machine gun a field or two away -- then numbing silence. Time and again Barkley's head dropped and recoiled. His eyes burned and felt gritty. *Jesus*, he thought, *I'll never make it.* He crawled to where Hinson lay huddled at the bottom of the hole, oblivious to the terrors surrounding him. "Hinson!" Barkley hissed, his voice barely audible, more breath than vocalization. "Hinson! Wake up!"

Hinson teetered on the brink of consciousness. "Can't," he mumbled, "Too tired..." He lay still, already lost in slumber.

"Hinson!" *Aw, shit! This is hopeless.* Barkley returned to his post. His eyelids seemed heavy as lead. His entire body ached and cried for rest. His ears were no long capable of picking up sound. *Hell*, he reasoned, *if they come tonight we are dead anyway... I've done all I can do... I can't stay awake any longer. I can't...* His head plopped into the dirt.

Another flare burst. The immobile forms of two GIs lay prostrate in a shell hole somewhere in no man's land. Fatigue crowed victorious as Barkley surrendered to drooling sleep. His Thompson sub-machine gun lay by his side, his trench knife planted firmly in the ground nearby.

Barkley snapped awake. Alert! Very alert! Some sixth sense had tipped him off -- something was moving behind them. It was still dark. His senses were incredibly keen now. He gripped his tommy gun and waited. The grass rustled. Something *was* out there! His pulse quickened as blood throbbed in his ears.

Again the grass moved. Someone was creeping towards them, slowly, deliberately from the rear. *They've found us! My God, they've found us!* His heart pounded wildly, thumping like a jackhammer. *Too late to warn Hinson.* His finger brushed the trigger of his weapon, ready to release an entire clip if necessary as he stared into the darkness. The grass parted. The Thompson snapped up. It was Sergeant Fretwell. Barkley released a long-held breath and lowered his weapon. Fretwell stuck his ugly head over the lip of the crater, "C'mon in," he said, "It'll be light soon."

Barkley slid down the crater and clamped his hand over Hinson's mouth to stifle any cry and gently shook him, "We're going back," he whispered.

Barkley was extremely relieved to get back to the American lines. He plodded to his foxhole, dropped in and instantly fell asleep for another hour or so.

Mid-morning, July 12, 1944 -- Barkley's shovel arched high, then plunged heavily into the soil as he toiled to enlarge the shallow foxhole he had dug the previous evening. No sooner had the blade sunk to its limit than it was pulled free and stabbed forcefully again into the earth, as if each stroke was violent retribution for some personal grievance, payback for a long-held grudge.

Panting, he paused to wipe a forearm across his brow as he took a breather and listened to the rough scrapings of other shovels as his squad labored at their own excavations. The company had dug temporary entrenchments the night before after they had been halted somewhere beyond the far side of the highway. Now they all struggled to improve their shelters since they only offered minimal protection from mortars and artillery.

Barkley gazed down the length of the hedgerow and surveyed his fellow diggers. Shovel blades rose and fell in irregular sweeping motions as if governed by the rotating cams of a great engine's crankshaft, rising and falling tirelessly, lethargically, in a never ending rhythm of muscle, sweat and steel. It seemed to Barkley that he spent half of his life digging holes anymore, either scooping out new foxholes or improving existing ones. But he realized that it was an integral part of survival on the battlefield, an absolute necessity -- there was no viable alternative. It was a staple of life now, as essential as bread and water and the air he breathed. He adjusted his grip, took a deep breath and resumed his laborious toil.

As always everyone was exhausted, having passed a harrowing night waiting in alarm, sweating out the counterattack that never came. Trigger happy replacements saw monsters in the dark. Isolated shots rang out. Shimmering flares altered the landscape from night to day and back to night while the clatter of machine guns broke the silence with intermittent bursts. As with Barkley in his outpost hole, it had been a long night for the men of Company G.

But now daylight had come. The men continued to deepen their holes while others scoured the countryside and outlaying farmsteads for anything stout enough to angle above their holes to act as shields against deadly shrapnel and thwart the incessant rains. A few opted for less elaborate cover and simply leaned heavy branches over their holes.

Periodically, German mortars interrupted their work, forcing them to dive for the bottoms of their imperfect burrows. When the shelling ceased, they cautiously re-emerged, like rabbits venturing from their warrens, and resumed their excavations, a sluggish, tedious, muscle aching chore. It seemed as if they had always lived in filthy holes. They had degenerated into mud dwellers -- cavemen -- troglodytes.

Meanwhile, off to the right, the 29th Division continued its drive on St. Lo itself, finally free from enemy observation now that the 2nd Division had evicted the Germans from Hill 192. To the left, the 38th Infantry's First Battalion resumed its attack in effort to cross their section of the St. Lo-Berigny Highway. The sounds of artillery and machine guns reached the men of Company G, but had little effect on them -- that was someone else's war. By noon the First Battalion was also across the road and commenced to dig in.

Mid-July, 1944 -- Although the 38th Infantry had been instructed to hold up its advance, it didn't mean that the front was inactive. As before, constant patrolling was the order of the day. Small groups of GIs slipped from their lines by day or night and slithered across a narrow strip of no-man's-land to reconnoiter the new enemy lines, often only one short field away. Barkley was frequently called upon to participate on such patrols. Being reconnaissance patrols they were small in number, usually comprising a sergeant and two or three privates -- sometimes an officer would accompany them. Their mission was to gain knowledge of what lay ahead. They crept along hedgerows, crossed fields, and snaked through grassy ravines. They trod softly as they traversed the many sunken lanes to peer warily over the bounding hedgerows, determined to glean information about the German defenses. Eyes narrowed as they searched hedge tops and fields for signs of enemy activity. They noted likely locations of strong points, then moved in as close as they dared to determine if, indeed, they were occupied.

Other patrols conducted terrain studies, recording the composition and condition of the varied roads and lanes that cross-hatched the land. Roadblocks were discovered on the routes leading south from the St. Lo highway. Soldiers tested the depths of creeks and streams. The heights and thickness of intervening hedgerows were noted. Although all of this would prove valuable in the coming days, no one took unnecessary chances. They were recon patrols, not combat patrols. Each expedition was under orders to avoid contact with the enemy. If detected, they were to fall back as swiftly as possible. Any other action only invited death -- and dead men cannot report what they had seen.

By now Barkley's scouting skills were highly developed. Still, he was very much aware that the Germans usually spotted him before he saw them. Once discovered, a patrol had to hightail it back to their own lines, usually hastened by a flurry of bullets or a few mortar rounds. They had to act quickly and decisively. Any hesitation could lead to death or capture. Barkley only too well remembered the ill-fated patrol when Lieutenant Pray and the others were killed or wounded. He was keen not to let that happen again. Stealth was the name of the game.

From past experience, he now dreaded going on patrols led by Sergeant Fretwell. He simply could not rely on him in tough situations as he did sergeants Blackmore and Parker. As Platoon Sergeant, Blackmore had proved his worth time and again. His courage was legendary. Although his actions bordered on recklessness, Barkley knew that Blackmore would always be there to back him up, if not actually accompany him on a perilous foray. The same went for Parker. It was Parker who had quickly assessed a deteriorating situation when Lieutenant Pray had been killed, and safely got his men out of a very hot spot. And it was Parker who acted selflessly when he pulled those German prisoners from their dugouts on the hill. That took guts. He had proved himself a natural leader and Barkley was proud to know him.

But his squad leader was another story. As the weeks wore on, Barkley feared that the incompetent Fretwell would eventually send him to his death. He recalled how Fretwell always seemed to hold back during an attack while pushing his squad out before him. And whenever things got rough, it was Sergeant Fretwell who always layed low while others risked their lives. Barkley recalled a time when one of Fretwell's patrols had just entered a field of tall pasture when a solitary shot rang out. Everyone hit the dirt. Barkley had been on point and was farthest into the field. Somewhere behind him lay Fretwell.

"Where'd that come from?" the sergeant demanded.

Cautiously, Barkley peeked above the tall grass to search for their nemesis.

K-Pow! Another bullet cracked overhead. Barkley dropped hard. *Sonovabitch!*

"Where's he at?" Fretwell asked.

"I don't know."

"Goddammit, somebody find the sonovabitch!" Fretwell cried.

Irritated, Barkley glanced over his shoulder and was disgusted by what he saw. Fretwell lay with his face buried in the dirt, paralyzed with fear. He was making no effort whatsoever to help locate the sniper.

Fretwell's eyes rolled up to meet Barkley's. "Barkley! Get out there and find him." The sergeant's face remained pressed to the earth as he spoke. He appeared to be trembling.

The hell with you, Barkley thought, *You want everyone else to risk his neck while you just lay there and do nothing?* He knew the sniper was aware of his location and that if he raised his head again, it would be bad for *him*! And if he took it upon himself to advance on the sniper, he did not feel confident that Fretwell would be able to provide adequate backup. Instead of proceeding, the patrol wriggled back through the grass and away from harm.

The incident only exacerbated Barkley's aversion for his squad leader. He never felt as confident when Fretwell was in charge of a particular mission and believed the day was coming when the sergeant would leave him hanging out to dry. He felt certain it was only a matter of time before he met his fate.

Meanwhile, back at the foxhole line, the routine of war continued. The threat of mortar or artillery attacks kept men cloistered in their holes. At times German patrols worked in so close that contact was imminent. When detected, such incursions were driven off by a few well-placed mortar rounds or the rapid response from riflemen manning the line. Occasionally, a few rounds of incoming sniper fire clipped the overhanging branches, causing much alarm throughout the line. A careless man was an easy target. A solitary shot created a neat hole in a helmet. Death lurked everywhere. Men remained in or near their holes.

Yet despite the daily dangers, there were also periods when the front was cloaked in uneasy stillness and life was reduced to a monotonous bore. As always, there was absolutely nothing to do. Men hoped for relief or dreamed of days gone by in a faraway place called home. A common question, asked nearly daily, was: "How far did the Russians get today?" It was asked not so much in jest than as a serious inquiry -- for the more ground the Russians took the sooner the war would be over. But obviously the war was far from over.

During one such lull, Barkley had time to reflect on incidents that had occurred before the fall of Hill 192. On one occasion the company had been held up as they were now, entrenched behind a hedgerow. It was one of those rare days when the sun actually made its appearance, radiating warmth and the illusion of hope. It was quiet. No gun firing. No mortars. No rain. A mild breeze played across the soft green pastures, compelling the blades to sway in rhythmic pulses. Everything seemed so peaceful.

Lulled into a false sense of security, one fellow rose from his foxhole and leaned back against the hedgerow wall to absorb the sun's warming rays. He smiled wistfully as he peeled back the wrapper of a chocolate bar in anticipation of his treat. Just then a dry crack sounded and a bullet punched a neat hole through the soldier's head. The chocolate bar slipped from dead fingers as the youth slumped over, then fell. A sniper had scored another hit. Other than that, it had been a bright blue summer's day.

How he hated the snipers! They all hated them -- the cold-hearted killers who lay in waiting, steely eyes focused as they centered their sights on an unsuspecting soul. Their fingers tightened on triggers until the firing pin snapped forward and his weapon barked, sending another boy to an early grave.

He had chilling encounters with them himself. He remembered an incident that occurred during the recent attack when his platoon had been held up by the vicious fighting ahead of them. They were compelled to seek cover behind a very low hedgerow. Fearing the barrages that had menaced their every step, Barkley immediately put his shovel to work. He had hardly broken the surface when a bullet ricocheted off the low hedgerow before him. Believing it was a stray round from the battle raging to his front, he shrugged it off and continued digging. *Whing-g-g!* Another bullet struck at nearly the same spot and burned past his face. *Sonovabitch!* That was no stray! A sniper was zeroing in on him. This was personal. Immediately, he dropped flat and continued digging from the prone position. He was not going to give the bastard a third shot.

Barkley shook off that sobering image. When able, he kept to his foxhole, not venturing out unless necessary -- no sense taking any undue chances. One fellow, however, could be seen bounding from foxhole to foxhole, squatting above the lip of each, flailing his arms in great animated gestures. When he neared Barkley's area, Barkley could hear what he was saying. He was exhorting the men to prepare for the Day of Reckoning. In time he hovered above Barkley's hole.

"Have you made your peace with God, my friend?" he implored.

"You'd better get back to your hole before you get hit," Barkley cautioned.

The disciple thrust a finger skyward and declared: "The Lord will protect me! The Lord will protect me!"

"Maybe so. But you'd still better take cover."

The man continued his preaching, despite the others' urgings to return to his foxhole. When he was satisfied with his sermon he would move on to the next man's position where again he would be told, "Get down, you fool!" As before, he declared his trust in Providence: "The Lord will protect me!" But not for long. One day a shell burst and laid him open, leaving a hole in his chest large enough to shove your fist through.

Such was life on the battlefront of Normandy. In the hedgerows, danger filled each waking hour and every minute of the night.

CHAPTER 10

SECOND RELIEF

July, 1944, Quincy, Illinois -- By now, Harry and Nettie Barkley had finally received the long-anticipated letter, a letter that verified their worst fears -- their son was in France. The news threw his mother into a chronic state of worry and she prayed fervently for his salvation. Harry noted the date on the letter and knew that his boy had been among the invasion forces -- perhaps he'd even been among those who landed on D-Day... at any rate, his son was no longer in England as his last letter reported. Harry listened to the radio and read the papers with immeasurably more interest, fighting back conflicting emotions of exhilaration and despair. Although filled with deep concern for his son, he also boasted proudly to neighbors and co-workers: Harold Barkley was in the fight. Nettie silently wept mother's tears and began to pen a letter: *Dearest son...*

Normandy, France -- After fifteen days on the battle line, which included the full scale assault on Hill 192 and the subsequent dangers of holding a defensive position, the Second Battalion was relieved by the First on the night of July 18. Once again Company G was coming out of the line. The battalion conducted a midnight march over the battlefield of two weeks earlier until they arrived at the reverse slope of Hill 192. Finally safe from enemy observation, the men settled into a string of abandoned dugouts and foxholes that lay beneath the myriad hedgerows that scored the hill.

German artillery still dropped randomly on the back side of the hill, but their gunners now fired blindly. Any GI worth his salt could easily avoid the rare shell or two that disturbed his daily routine and the shelling became more nuisance than threat, and as a result, the soldiers' life became more tolerable. Although still denied the pleasantries of civilization, the men were content to be where they were, away from the front and the killing. Once again they could relax and enjoy the simple pleasure of a hot meal. Once again they could sleep. Once again they could dream.

Meanwhile, as the veterans adjusted to their new environs, another herd of replacements had been driven from the beachhead to the hill where they were greedily absorbed into the battalions. At each battalion they were split up again and doled out to the depleted rifle companies where the final cut was made as new kids were torn from buddies and assimilated into the ranks of the battle hardened veterans. Barkley didn't care to get to know them. They remained nameless faces. Why bother when they'll only wind up killed or wounded like all the others. The thought nourished a fatalistic attitude and plunged Barkley into a burgeoning state of depression.

July 19, 1944, Reverse slope of Hill 192 -- Artillery drummed in the distance as Barkley dipped his mess kit into a vat of steaming water, then shook it dry. Another rumble of big guns echoed from afar, yet he showed no concern, for the shells were falling elsewhere on the far side of the hill, not on him. That was someone else's war.

It was warm and he was content, having just gorged himself on a fried chicken dinner. *I wonder what the other fellows are up to,* he mused as he surveyed a bank of dark clouds that menaced the horizon. As if annoyed by his observation, a peal of thunder rolled from the turbulent heavens. That seemed about right. It hadn't rained for a while and he felt they were long overdue for another storm. It seemed it always rained in France.

He sauntered in the direction of his squad mates as he monitored the coming storm. Upon arrival, he saw that his buddies were engaged in a lively bull session. Barkley plunked his helmet down and sank to ease his back against the hedgerow.

The squad continued its conversation. Now and then a remark drew a chorus of robust guffaws or rude exclamations of doubt expressed at some fellow's tall tale. Barkley listened as the stories unfolded, waiting patiently for an opportunity to join in. The two Joe's, Benavidez and Guajardo, were present as well as Earl Hoernke, one of the earlier replacements who had managed to avoid death long enough to become a veteran. A couple of other GIs lounged in the grass and eavesdropped on the conversation, occasionally tossing in their own two cents worth. Guajardo and Benavidez were swapping stories of Texas and life in the Southwest. Hinson was present, too, and contributed a yarn of his own hometown antics.

A new kid sat on the fringe of the group and listened attentively. He was a timid boy with dark hair and blue eyes. They knew him simply as "Willie"[*]. One would have been hard pressed to have guessed his age at any more than eighteen years. Shy and reserved, he seemed awed by his present company and did not contribute much to the conversation at hand.

In time the conversation lagged, providing Barkley an opening to speak his piece. He reminisced, as he had done before, about some of his own adventures before entering the Army. His mind drifted to his days with the carnivals -- happy times when he ran the Hoopla concession... *"Hey-hey-hey! Come and play! Bring your friend, your girlfriend. One dime! A tenth of a dollar! A prize every time! Hey-hey-hey!"* His memory took him back to the excitement of the fairway.... the crowds... the rides and gaudy lights... the blaring music and sideshow freaks. He could almost smell the sawdust.

---

[*] I will use the name "Willie" in place of his real name.

He launched into the story of when a chimpanzee broke free from his keeper while in Hannibal, Missouri. They were in an armory building and the ceiling was quiet high. The chimp, delighted to be free, scampered up to the girded rafters and swung from one beam to the next, chattering madly as the keeper tried vainly to snag the nimble creature. Ladders reached to the steel beams as others tried to assist in the capture. Barkley recalled how he had laughed as its keeper managed to get close enough to grab at the beast just as the animal skittered away, howling defiantly. The keeper grew angrier as the evening wore on and became more frustrated at every aborted attempt at capture. Eventually the chimp was snared and taken to his cage. But not before receiving a supreme beating. Barkley hated that. He always had a soft spot for animals.

In time, the subject changed to women. Of course there were no women to be seen for miles, but some of the fellows felt obliged to regale the others with ribald stories of personal triumphs, whether real or apocryphal. After awhile, one of the Joe's dug out a photo of his girl back home and passed it around to the good-natured whistles and cat calls of his buddies. Soon other photos were produced and for a moment everyone fell silent, absorbed in dreams of home. Home -- it must be light years away.

The silence was broken as one fellow blurted out a gambling story. Barkley lit a cigarette, then chimed in, describing his pin ball and slot machines waiting for him back home. He spoke of his plans to place the machines about town where they'd provide a source of easy money.

"Now there's an idea!" someone agreed, "A man who is able to lay back and let a machine make the money, and all he'd have to do is make the daily rounds to scoop out the loot. A fellow could spend the rest of his time sleeping!" Everybody laughed.

Barkley surrendered the floor and leaned back in wistful reminiscence while Hoernke spoke up and carried the conversation in his slow, deliberate manner. Everyone had a story. They spoke of jobs, sports, women, even incidents back at training camps. There were no bounds. Only one subject was conspicuously absent: war. No one spoke of combat -- they were trying to forget.

"I'm looking for Barkley." The demand came from somewhere down the length of the hedgerow.

"Yes, sir. Over there."

Barkley looked up as two soldiers approached and was speechless. The familiar figure of his old buddy, Frank Balchunas, the Barracuda, was shuffling toward him, accompanied by none other than Lieutenant English, one of their officers back in England. Barkley was flabbergasted. The surprise was complete for he hadn't expected to see the Barracuda anytime soon, if ever again. After a brief salutation, Lieutenant English bade them farewell -- he had duties to attend to elsewhere. Fortunately, Balchunas had run into the lieutenant earlier and inquired about his young friend. Although English was assigned to the First Battalion, he had made it his personal concern to reunite two of his former men.

After the initial joy of reunion, each began to catch up on how the other had fared, so far. "I heard you and Barrella had been made medics," Barkley began.

"Yeah," Balchunas answered dolefully, "I was a litter bearer in the last attack. I tell you, Bark, it was god awful...all those guys torn up or killed..." He averted his eyes and slowly shook his head. "It was awful," he repeated. He had come to understand a different meaning for the words "litter bearer": a litter bearer bore off the litter of war.

When Barkley told his friend that he had been made a scout for his squad, Balchunas' jaw dropped. "My God, Bark," he exclaimed, "you take too many chances!"

"I can take care of myself."

"You be careful," his buddy admonished. He was deeply concerned for his young friend's well being.

A brief silence ensued, then they began to discuss the whereabouts of their former comrades of training days.

"I guess you heard about Antonelli and Bartas," Balchunas continued. The tone of his voice hinted that something was wrong.

"No, what?" Barkley answered apprehensively, fearing the worst.

"Dead."

"No!"

"Yeah..."

"Oh, Jesus!"

"Mortars got 'em," Balchunas went on, "I heard they went out to bring in some wounded GI when they got caught in the open." He paused. "Really messed them up, I guess."

"Jesus."

Again awkward silence.*

"Have you seen Barrella?" Barkley finally blurted, hoping his burly friend was alright.

"No. I think he's in some other platoon or even another company."

"Oh."

Silence again. Then Barkley continued. "Bell was with me for a while..." He suddenly paused, "Hell, I don't know what the hell happened to him. He was with me in our squad, but one day he was gone. I really don't know what happened to him." And with that an expression of puzzlement fell upon his face. *Just what the hell did happen to Bell?*

Both men remained wordless as they remembered the faces and personalities of their old comrades, and recalled some of their antics during training days. Then the reunion continued on more pleasant thoughts. No one wanted to dwell on war.

In time, Frank Balchunas rose to return to his own platoon and the two friends regretfully parted company.

Alone again, Barkley brooded over the loss of his friends. He could still picture the worried look on Antonelli's face as he and Bartas were culled from their dwindling replacement package back at the beachhead. "What are we going to do?" Antonelli would ask with

---

* At the time, Barkley and Balchunas believed that both of their buddies were dead. In reality, only Antonelli had been killed, but still, Frank Balchunas had most of the story correct. Antonelli and Bartas did, indeed go out to bring in a wounded GI when mortars began falling all around them. Both were hit. Antonelli was very seriously wounded and died of his wounds. The first round tore off Bartas' arm. In shock, he tried to rise, not realizing his arm was gone, and stumbled to his feet just as another round ripped out a lung and a couple of ribs. The wounds definitely looked fatal. But miraculously, he survived and was returned to the States to recover. After much time in hospitals, he was released and returned to his wife in Chicago. He worked for a company that manufactured prosthetic limbs. Fifty years passed before Barkley and Balchunas learned the truth -- but their old buddy had died in the 1990's and both lamented that they never knew he had survived.

big, imploring eyes. "Whatever we have to," Barkley always replied. *"Whatever we have to…"* the words echoed in Barkley's head. *Well, Antonelli, you did what you had to do… The Major, too.* He recalled how they gave the heavy set Bartas the nickname, "The Major", way back at Camp Wolters. *Way back? It had only been a few months ago. The Major had a wife…. Alice…. She came down to camp during our training so she could be with her husband for a week or two…And then there's Bell… Why can't I remember what happened to him? He always had those spooky eyes peering from beneath his helmet…Now there's only The Barracuda… maybe Barrella… and me. How much longer will we last?*

As he pondered his fate, a cool breeze swept the fields. The tall grasses rippled and bowed in submission as a deep rumbling reverberated from high above -- thunder this time, not cannons. The dark clouds that had menaced the horizon now sealed off the sky and churned with powerful, malignant surges. Another storm was brewing. The weight of darkness pressed heavily as a strong gust chased men to the foxholes that infested the hedgerows like the catacombs of old -- the dwellings of the dead.

Lightning crackled.

Branches and leaves strained against the wind, whipping wildly as if trying to take flight. Soon, torrential rains pounded the hillside and poured like a million mothers' tears as each mourned their children sacrificed on the altar of Freedom. The heavens wept for Elmer Antonelli and Anthony Bartas, for Captain Raymond, for Lieutenant Pray and Ray Simcik and all the others. It would continue for days.

July 22, 1944 -- Rain drummed steadily upon the boards angled over Barkley's foxhole. When the deluge began several days before, everyone had raced for the shelter of his own foxhole. Now, sitting in the clammy dankness of his earthen refuge, Barkley was bored -- there was really nothing to do, nothing at all. His knuckles drew the collar of his battle jacket tight against his throat in efforts to ward off the inherent chill.

Raindrops plunged to the mud and burst in tiny geysers that mimicked the eruptions of exploding shells.

Barkley thought of the poor Joes up at the front. It had been raining heavily for days. They must be up to their armpits in cold mud and scummy water by now. Well, he'd been through it, too. *I guess it evens out*, he reasoned, *They were probably in reserve when we were drowning in mud.*

He lit a cigarette, for there was nothing else to do.

The rain poured throughout the nights and into the following days, filling foxholes and flooding low areas until roads were rendered into near impassable quagmires. For six days and nights the heavens had opened and dumped its contents onto the miserable mortals mired in the mud and blood and battered ruins below. Then on the 25th of July, the seventh day, the morning dawned bright and clear. A brilliant sun swathed the saturated countryside with warming rays. Moist, vibrant foliage glistened beneath resplendent light and seemed to reach up in attempts to touch the sun and shake off the last glistening drops of rain. Water swirled in deep ruts and crevices of mud-clogged roads where trucks and jeeps sank to their axles and geared down, and growled, and strained to pull away from the sucking muck. The meadows and fields, pocked with water-filled shell holes, resembled a land of a thousand shimmering lakes. The sun ruled all below it. Finally, with clear skies, air support could be given to the Allied forces. The war could now go on.

July 25, 1944 -- Barkley lounged on the high ground of Hill 192 and basked in the sunlight. The warm rays embraced his face and pressed softly on his chest and shoulders -- it was good to feel the sun again. Others, too, enjoyed the simple beauty of its golden light and devoured its delicious warmth.

From his vantage point atop the hill, Barkley could look out over miles of verdant scenery that stretched to the far horizon. Green fields and orchards checkered the rolling countryside, interrupted now and then by dark patches of forest or the occasional farmstead or village that sprouted at the junctions of a web of sunken roads. Everything was clearly visible from the heights. The Germans sure had a good view when they held this ground.

His gaze swept to the west towards St. Lo, the unclaimed prize of the campaign, now only two or three miles away. It was a dead city now, crumbling beneath the blows of countless shells and bombs. Although it was still within the German lines, Barkley knew that someday his company may be ordered to assault the town and there would be hell to pay; but for now he only wished to enjoy the glorious sunlight and allow it to draw out the aches that dwelled in tight-knotted muscles.

A faint murmur arrested the attention of those with the sharpest hearing and one barked a word of caution, then cocked his head and listened. Others, too, strained to hear the noise. For a moment only the booming of distant artillery could be heard, but then, by ones and twos, others began to hear it, too. It was the sound of aircraft -- lots of them. Hands shaded eyes as soldiers scanned the horizon for the source of the incessant thrumming.

"There!" someone shouted at last, "There they are!" He leaped and pointed deeply into the sky. Others tracked the azimuth of his finger and caught sight of them, and then the rest. Hundreds of planes thundered closer from the direction of the English skies. Excitement swept the hill. "Look at 'em! Look at 'em!!" A thousand planes, all big bombers, surged ever closer, propellers beating a sonorous rhythm on the bright blue sky.

The men were ecstatic as they whooped and shouted encouragement to the airmen flying thousands of feet above them. Soon the sky was filled with bombers, echeloned in formations of twelve, and each group of twelve was flanked by other groups and these were followed by wave upon wave of others that swept from the far horizon. They flew in such tight formations that their wingtips seemed to touch. It was a gigantic exhibition of Air Force might. Wherever they were going, it didn't bode well for the Nazis.

The vast entourage pushed steadily southward and passed over St. Lo, casting evil shadows that danced like vultures among the carcasses of gutted buildings and homes of the once prosperous city. Then a deep, sinister thudding sounded from afar as the leading bombers released their loads just beyond the town. Concussion waves rippled along the earth's surface as the sound rolled up the hill where men had gathered in curious groups and squinted to see the show. A thick cloud of smoke and dust rose from beyond the ruins of the battered city. Overhead the mighty armada droned tirelessly towards its target.

German anti-aircraft batteries opened up, dotting the skies with irregular black blotches, and occasionally a bomber would burst into a ball of flame and cartwheel willy-nilly toward the earth. Its sister ships held their formation as black puffs of flak burst all about them.

Barkley sat on the hillside and tilted his face skyward, mesmerized by the spectacle. He could hardly believe that so many huge planes could be in the sky at one time. It was a grand sight. For certain the Germans had nothing to compare to this -- it was a show of invincible force. It was a harbinger of things to come -- of victory.

The parade of bombers kept coming and seemed to stretch in an infinite loop that reached from one end of the world to the other. Tons of bombs cascaded to the earth and exploded in one continuous chain that sent shock waves pulsing across its surface and Barkley thanked God that he was not on the receiving end.

Barkley didn't realize it, but he was witnessing one of the great carpet bombings of the war -- the 2,000 bomber raid. Five thousand tons of explosives were to saturate a compact target only 7,000 yards wide and 2,500 yards deep. The massive bombing was designed to destroy German resistance to the west of St. Lo where the Americans planned to break out of the hedgerows.

Once First Army had pierced the German lines, armored spearheads would exploit the breach and thrust deep into enemy territory, setting the stage for a broad advance all along the American front. This was the day the Allied commanders had been waiting for -- the end of the Normandy stalemate. It was code named Operation Cobra.

Unfortunately the plan was off to a bad start. Initially the bombing was to have taken place the previous day but had been called off due to poor weather conditions. However, some of the bombers never got the word and, not being able to see through the clouds, inadvertently dropped their loads onto the American lines, causing a number of casualties. The ground commanders were furious.

On the following morning the skies were clear, the raid was on -- but thick clouds of smoke from the first wave of bombing drifted and obscured the front lines and once again bombs fell on both German and American soldiers. Army commanders seethed -- the error was unpardonable. Nearly 900 U.S. soldiers had been killed or wounded during the two mishaps; some had been buried alive.

Word of this swept like wildfire through the American lines, creating a strong distrust by the infantrymen for the usually excellent air support given by the Army Air Force. Barkley later learned that after the bombing, stunned soldiers from both armies wandered aimlessly across a lunar landscape, dazed, like zombies whose bodies only responded to the most basic motor skills.

Nonetheless, the offensive was on. Units of the VII Corps, still rattled by the bombing, launched their attacks on schedule and shouldered their way through the German defenses. Soon, the attack dog of the U.S. Army, Lieutenant-General George "Blood-and-Guts" Patton, Jr., and his newly arrived Third Army, would be unleashed to rip through the countryside in a scathing assault that would strike deep into the heartland of France.

Meanwhile, V Corps, of which Barkley's unit belonged, remained in the wings to the east of St. Lo and waited for orders to attack in support of the operation. The attack order came on the second day of the offensive -- July 26.

Once again the brief rest for Company G was over.

CHAPTER 11

BREAKOUT FROM ST. LO

July 26, 1944, 0540 hours -- Far to the rear the big guns rumbled and the earth trembled as if anticipating the visitation of the promised apocalypse. Soon, untold flights of high explosives screamed overhead, howling their war cry as they fell as one to herald the dawn in an earth shattering revelation of hell to come. The entire front quaked for twenty minutes. Fire and steel and wanton destruction ravaged the German lines while the earth convulsed, as if rapt in its own death throes, suffering unbearable agonies as it resisted Death's cold solicitations.

At 0600 hours tank-dozers lurched forward to breach the first few tiers of hedgerows, protected by a mantle of time-fused shells that exploded not on the ground but overhead to keep enemy soldiers sequestered within their shelters. A shower of earth and brush and uprooted trees spewed forth as the great blades plowed through each successive hedge bank. Mission accomplished, the tank-dozers withdrew to await their next assignment. Then the infantry advanced.

Using the St. Lo highway as a springboard, the 38th Infantry welled from the hedgerows on the division's right, surging through the fresh-plowed gaps with the power of something unstoppable, a tidal wave of olive-drab invested with rifles, machine guns and mortars. Sherman tanks joined the fray and hammered the first hedgerows with point blank fire to suppress the waiting enemy now tumbling from their earthen bunkers and bent on revenge. German paratroopers set up their machine guns with optimum fields of fire or leveled Panzerfausts to greet the marauding tanks. Mortar crews poised shells at the mouths of their tubes to destroy the attacking infantry. It was 0630 hours. The big push was on.

The Third Battalion attacked on the left while the First advanced on the right and the Third made good progress, overpowering what resistance it met and crossed many fields and orchards and bypassed farmsteads and sidestepped nests of enemy to be dealt with by follow-up troops and, by the end of the day, came to rest upon a road that crossed their line of advance some 1,000 yards beyond the Line of Departure.

The story of the First Battalion was different. The First jumped off on schedule and crossed the St. Lo road and walked over light opposition in the first couple fields, then got caught, bald-faced, in open fields and was hit hard by mortars and artillery that wounded many and killed others and sent assault companies into disarray and confusion. The supporting tanks flew apart in the face of galling anti-tank fire and blazed fiercely in the fields, prompting the remainder to withdraw, leaving the infantry to their own devices. Then murderous machine gun fires took the infantry from the right flank, totally demoralizing those that survived and killed many more and the entire battalion fell back almost to the St. Lo road and was hammered by more mortars and artillery and its participation in the assault was ruined. Those officers that remained attempted to rally their troops and succeeded and led them forward only to fall in droves and defeated men fell back again to the shelter of the hedgerows at the St. Lo road. They could not move, and shortly after noon the regimental commander called Norris of the Second Battalion and ordered him to get his battalion moving to fill the substantial gap that now existed between the Third Battalion, by then hundreds of yards to the front, and the First Battalion which was shot up, demoralized and stalled at the point of departure.

The Second Battalion filed down Hill 192, utilizing a sunken road that fed into the St. Lo highway where its companies would fan out in preparation for their assault. Enemy shells fell steadily to either side as they descended the hill and made much noise, debauching shrapnel with great regularity which caused much alarm. But mercifully, the sunken road, screened by thick-walled hedgerows, doubled as a trench and the men proceeded unmolested.

It was midday now and a blistering sun bore down as the column slowly closed the void that separated them from Hell on Earth. Sweat darkened the seams of uniforms and saturated cloth wherever belts and straps girdled bodies and sorely chafed men's skin. They grew hotter and became more sullen as they descended the hill and each was preoccupied with his own doubts and personal misgivings, underscored now by the storm of battle that drew them in like moths to the flame.

Another salvo bracketed the road. Shrapnel thudded savagely into the flanking hedge banks or hissed evilly overhead, causing veterans to cringe instinctively and greenhorns to gawk in wide-eyed wonder. Only too soon would the replacements be baptized in fire and blood, and then they, too, would cringe at every unwarranted noise -- if they survived.

More shrapnel screamed overhead and men cursed, then cursed some more as a massive detonation shook the earth around them. And then, as if additional omens were required, a jeep came tearing up the road with a Red Cross flag snapping madly as it neared. Strapped to its hood was a stretcher laden with a gray-faced casualty. Another stretcher straddled the cargo bay, heavy with butchered meat wrapped in rags that fluttered like guidons as the jeep raced past -- rags that once clothed unblemished flesh. A grim-faced medic hovered over the bloody soldier, holding a plasma bottle high as the jeep churned up the hill, desperate to reach the battalion aid station before his patients died. Soldiers stared with ashen faces as they passed. Disturbed by the sight, the men resumed their march, sickened by the realization that they may well be the next to take that wild ride.

A chain of distant explosions reclaimed the dogfaces' undivided attention as the battlefront erupted with renewed vigor. Thunderous detonations rippled across the front, rolling from one end to the other then back, giving rise to great clouds of smoke that seeped from the earth like volcanic gasses. The veterans knew that somewhere beneath that heavy pall men suffered and died. Dry-mouthed, the column pressed on, ever conscious of the tumultuous storm that magnified at every step and blended to form one voice, a mesmeric incantation that conjured up all the demons of Hell.

Suddenly the column halted. Just ahead, perhaps a hundred yards' distant, the lane spilled into the St. Lo Highway and beyond that, somewhere, the battlefront. Individual rifle shots could be heard now. The stubborn stutter of an American machine gun rattled defiantly somewhere to the right, prompting faltering hands to readjust equipment that now seemed awkward and ill-fitting. Packs and rifles, helmets, grenades and extra ammunition seemed a cruel burden to bear when one must be quick or be dead.

Battle sounds swept over them in undulating waves. Several replacements looked to the veterans for tokens of reassurance, and receiving none, resorted to consoling themselves, looking like frightened puppies amidst a pack of feral hounds. Their days of innocence had come to an end. Transfixed, they listened helplessly, unable to shake the demons that danced wickedly within fluttering hearts, prodding and goading their inner fears until tears welled in some and many shivered uncontrollably.

Nor were the veterans immune from the specter of the unknown. Although some made crude attempts at gallows humor during the march down the hill, no one spoke now. The combination of heat and dust and mounting fear all but strangled them. Trembling fingers unscrewed canteen caps and quavered as leathery throats gulped wantonly at metallic tasting fluid.

Again the battlefront demanded their attention as another cluster of shells ravaged a distant field, followed by a truncated burst of machine gun fire. Hearts plunged to the pits of churning stomachs. *This is it! This is it! Oh, God help me.* Catholic lips feverishly mumbled acts of contrition while others struggled with the Twenty-third Psalm, leaving the less pious to simply stare blankly, as if gazing beyond their physical world and into the realm of the future -- and the future for all was grim.

Like many old hands, Barkley had seen plenty. He had witnessed unspeakable horrors and had done things that many would not understand. As he dwelled on these things his throat tightened and he swallowed hard. He knew that beyond the highway lay the Gates of Hell. He and others had patrolled it extensively over the past weeks, knew it intimately, or at least parts of it, and it wasn't pretty. Those hedgerows bristled with mutually supporting machine guns that would cut them down with devastating cross-fires. Mortars would chew them up at every field entered where land mines waited patiently for the errant foot to release their wrath. Artillery barrages could easily lay out an entire platoon, and a single sniper could snuff out all the hopes and dreams of a young man with a solitary shot. Soon, too soon, they would earn their pay. Ten dollars a month extra for combat, wasn't it? And a much better chance for their beneficiaries to collect their GI life insurance, too.

Artillery bantered and screamed overhead and a wayward shell dropped unexpectedly close, exploding with a deafening roar and all dropped as one as shrapnel whirled overhead. Clods and debris rained all around. *Jesus Christ!* Barkley's heart raced madly as his eyes met Hinson's. Hinson stared back, appearing just as pale and terrified as everyone else. The Southerner's Adams apple bobbed erratically, as if trying to erase a thick lump lodged in his throat, and as a consequence looked as if he was choking. It only served to remind Barkley of his own incredible thirst and he unscrewed the cap of his canteen and allowed himself a dram or two to appease the demands of a tortured throat.

Then sergeants moved along the line. "Off and on! Off and on!" they exhorted. "Off yer asses and on yer feet. Let's go! Let's go!" The waiting was over. *This is it!*

They raced across the St. Lo road, turned left and skirted a hedgerow, then dashed through a gap created earlier in the day by a tank dozer before settling uneasily alongside the closest hedgerow. The field they occupied had been trampled to chaff by a hundred boots and was blemished with a score of smoldering craters. At the far end a tank blazed wildly, sizzling and popping and blackened by fire, a flaming tribute to its crew that no doubt perished within. *Tankers. Who wants to be a tanker? Who wants to rumble around the hedgerows in an iron coffin, blinded on all sides save for what one can see through a narrow slit? They are easy prey to an array of German anti-tank weapons. And they go up in flames so easily and men roast to death in their crippled oven -- or are rendered into hamburger, literally, as an armor piercing shell enters, explodes, then bounces its fragments throughout the interior, ricocheting off of every surface until everything and everyone is completely riddled by splinters of red-hot steel. Barkley knew this for a fact. He had seen it once, but only once, out of morbid curiosity when he peeked inside a knocked out tank after a battle and it turned his stomach. Bloody sacks of cloth and splintered bone. Who wants to be a tanker?* Smoke rolled thickly from the battered hulk, marking the demise of proud American steel.

Corpses littered the field, too -- the dead of the First Battalion -- the men who tried valiantly, yet vainly, to breach the enemy's defenses for six long hours -- the men who were slaughtered time and again within a stone's throw of their starting point. In places the bodies lay in heaps. It was a ghastly sight for those about to enter the fray and men swallowed hard as they viewed the scene, for now it was their turn.

Fortunately, the men of the Second Battalion had little time to reflect on the fate of those who preceded them. Once in position, things began to happen fast. The leading company sprang up and rushed through the next gap. A chorus of machine guns greeted them -- the rapid clatter of MG 42's, Hitler's Saws. The machine guns were soon joined by the sickening crump of mortar shells and then the heavier artillery began to fall. Sinister black smoke rose from the field. Company F had hit a hornet's nest.

Company G remained tensed behind its hedgerow shelter. The hair raised on the nape of Barkley's neck as he listened to the slaughter. He knew his company would be the next to go. Blood pulsed through his temples, driven by a racing heart. His mouth seemed dry as cotton. Hot air lacerated heaving lungs. Eyes and throat burned red and raw. *This is it!* My God, how many times had he said that? Although it was extreme in its redundancy, they all thought it, repeatedly, *This is it -This is it -This is it!* And how they meant it! How many would meet their fate in the next few minutes? How many would still be standing at the end of the day? *And will I survive?* That was the question, now, wasn't it? How much longer can one dodge the odds? And deep down each knew the answer was closer than he cared to admit.

Suddenly Sergeant Blackmore was up and moving, trotting at a half-crouch as he bounded down the line. "We're moving out. Get ready. We're moving up soon." And that was that. Barkley gripped his Thompson and swallowed hard. He was the scout. He would be the first to enter the cauldron.... he and Hinson. Blood pumped fiercely through his veins. *Yea, though I walk through the valley of the shadow of death, I will fear no evil*...Barkley looked at Hinson, and then Blackmore... *for thou art with me.* They, too, examined their weapons... *Thy rod and thy staff they comfort me...*

"LET'S GO-O-O!" Blackmore waved an arm and an all too familiar shiver shot up Barkley's spine as he lunged forward and followed the sergeant. Explosions crashed in other fields and a storm of gunfire sounded from somewhere to the right, but no bullets struck closeby and the platoon moved on to the next hedgerow without incident. Barkley assumed that the other platoons of the company were leading the assault -- he would be spared -- for now.

The squad halted and squatted in column alongside another hedgerow. Barkley was up front, ready to lead off when so ordered. Just behind him panted Hinson, then Sergeant Fretwell. Small arms fire continued to rattle all along the front. Dull, sickening thumps announced the employment of mortars. Black smoke shot skyward beyond the hedgerow walls, marking the spot where other GIs suffered and the air fairly howled with flying steel.

"Alright, let's move." The lieutenant led off, followed by the others and the platoon raced across a smoke-hazed field. Popping sounds snapped the air. Bullets! Someone was shooting at them. A squad to the right gained the hedgerow and immediately opened fire. Men shouted. Others darted along the hedgerow's base. More gunfire. Shouts. Machine guns tore through the ranks and men fell. Then mortars walked the length of the hedgerow and suddenly the right flank broke and ran, compelling the others to follow suit.

"Fall back! Fall back!" someone shouted.

Barkley's squad turned to retrace their steps and soon were back where they had started. Many men pulled out their shovels and began hacking at the earth.

"Get ready," Blackmore raged as he steadied his men, "They'll be coming soon."

Barkley gripped his Thompson with white-knuckled desperation as he chanced a glimpse over the hedgerow's crest. Save for wisps of swirling smoke, the field remained empty. Nearby, young Willie looked up with watery eyes. "H-How will we know when they come?" he stammered. His fingers looked frail upon the stock of his rifle. Barkley regarded the boy. "Oh, you'll know it alright. Just hold your fire until they get into that field. When they start coming, open fire and keep firing." The pale-faced boy swallowed hard as he listened, then staggered down the line where he sank to his knees and trembled like a new-born fawn.

A machine gun opened up from somewhere unseen. Bullets snapped through the overhead foliage at an accelerated rate, ripping leaves from quivering branches. Several mortar shells crashed closeby, but still no counterattack. Another explosion tossed earth and debris over the hedgerow wall. Clods and branches clattered all around. Fearing the mortars, battle-savvy GIs resumed their eternal digging, but before anyone got too far underground, orders came to move once again. From down the line a commotion erupted. Several soldiers hovered over a shallow foxhole, making strong gestures with their arms. At their feet cowered young Willie.

"Let's go, we're movin' up."

"Get up, goddamn you!" bellowed Fretwell.

Willie remained in his hole, shivering uncontrollably. Others continued to make impassioned pleas for the boy to rise and join the attack, but he simply blubbered and cried unabashedly, a quivering wreck huddled in his hole. Barkley, too, joined in the exhortations. "C'mon, Willie, you gotta get up. Were movin' out." But it was no use, Willie was not budging.

"…Goddamn coward," Fretwell muttered.

Sergeant Blackmore arrived and made a quick decision and beckoned the platoon medic. With the aid man's assistance, young Willie was pried from his shelter and ushered to the rear. Barkley looked on as the boy stumbled away. *Poor Willie*, he thought, *He's just a kid...Hell, we're all kids, I guess, but he doesn't belong here. He's never been away from home before. He's just homesick and scared.*

Willie was never seen again.

The platoon moved up amidst sporadic mortar and machine gun fire, then halted again beneath a hedgerow's wall. Barkley noted that there were no more gaps cut through the thick hedge walls as before. The tank assault had not made it this far. They were on their own.

Meanwhile, the world erupted in pandemonium as incoming shells ripped the fields in an orgy of groaning, blasting, tearing and flashing. Machine guns rattled incessantly from one flank. Elsewhere, rifle fire popped sharply, barely audible above the battle's roar.

"Barkley!" Fretwell shouted above the din. "Get ready. This is it. We're goin' to take the next hedgerow." Barkley's gut knotted. His worst fears were realized. The moment had come -- the platoon was pushing the attack forward.

Again Barkley glanced at Hinson. Hinson looked pale. Who wouldn't? Explosions flashed continuously from fields to the front. He had no idea where the other squads or platoons were positioned. All he knew was that the enemy lay before him, and their only desire was to keep him from crossing the next field -- they would do everything in their power to kill him.

The shelling stopped and then the order came: "Let's go-o-o!"

The platoon crested the hedgerow and charged headlong across the field. Bullets cut through them like wind-driven sleet. Round after round of flat trajectory artillery fire swooped in from the right -- and then the mortars began to fall. The volume of enemy gunfire was staggering and the attack unraveled and again men fell back, leaving shredded comrades moaning in the field as defeated soldiers scrambled back to the safety of their starting point.

Barkley lay behind the hedgerow, panting, terror-stricken by the unrelenting savagery of the enemy's response. As before, he couldn't believe he was still in one piece.

After a pause, orders came to try again, and again they failed, and in time word came that tanks were on their way. Tanks, with their hedge-breaking attachments, would save the day.

Again Barkley waited, and like the others, quickly put his shovel to work.

It was late afternoon by the time the roar of engines was heard and two Sherman tanks lumbered into the field. One was fitted with a bulldozer blade; the other with a row of toothy hedge cutters. As officers conferred with the tankers, the men were cautioned to be ready to resume the attack.

Before long, artillery began its preparatory barrage. Other concentrations worked over the troubling fields of the right flank that had so menaced the advance. Meanwhile, the two tanks positioned themselves at opposite ends of the field, then lunged against the hedgerow wall. Barkley watched in fascination as the full-bladed dozer burst through the massive dike as if punching through paper, then roared into the field with cannon booming and machine guns blazing. The other tank had more difficulty and was compelled to back up and charge again before breaking through to join its fellow monster on their destructive foray.

"Let's go-o-o!"

Soldiers rose and poured through the gaps and fanned out to accompany the tanks as they rolled into battle. The tanks continued to hammer the enemy positions, keeping machine gunners at bay. Once again mortars began to fall, but the infantry, aided by the suppressive fires of the tanks, advanced more boldly and rapidly closed the gap between them and their hedgerow goal.

Whenever a German chanced to rise above the hedgerow wall, Barkley released a spray of automatic fire to pin him down. Others did the same, providing covering fire for the tankers whose vision was restricted within the confines of their massive war machines. The foot soldiers knew that a lone German with a Panzerfaust could easily render a 33-ton fighting machine into a flaming hulk in a matter of seconds. Sharp-eyed infantrymen remained alert to gun down any German so audacious as to try. It was a mutually supporting team and it worked well. Enemy resistance melted before the awesome firepower of the tanks and the opposing hedgerow was soon secured. Again the tanks deployed to breach the wall before them.

Barkley noted what a big difference the tanks were making and was glad to have them along. Previously, the dogfaces had been compelled to claw their way over the thick brushy hedgerows before charging near bare-assed naked into the mouths of enemy machine guns and mortars. They had always been easy targets. But now, with the aid of the hedgerow breaking tanks, things were different and attacking soldiers entered each field with relative ease. As a consequence, the Germans resisted at their own peril. Now enemy corpses littered the fields.

Each platoon took its turn in leading the attack. One field was cleaned up, then another, and after a stiff fight another grudgingly gave way and in time a large clump of trees loomed in the distance -- a shaggy island isolated by fields of yellow and green. It looked suspicious. Any number of Germans could be secluded in the tree line, waiting in ambush, and again the attack ground to a halt.

While Battalion pondered what to do about the impeding forest, the assault companies held up and waited for orders. Meanwhile, carrying parties brought up a fresh supply of ammunition. Re-supplied, Barkley's platoon settled behind a hedgerow overlooking the forest perhaps a couple hundred yards distant. Although closing in on evening, there would still be several hours of good daylight remaining. Again shovels broke the soil.

As the men dug in, the tanks that had accompanied them veered off to the left towards Company F and were gone. Company G was alone, facing the right half of the woods. It had been a long day. Everyone was dead tired.

Barkley looked to his left and right. Faces stared back… glum faces… grim faces… faces molded waxen white, appearing cold as death… frightened faces. Not as many faces as there was some hours before. Sweat trickled down his cheeks to his chin where it congregated, quivered, then dropped heavily onto the stock of his Thompson. His heart hammered like a war drum. Blood pulsed through his temples and pushed another bead of perspiration from beneath his helmet's sweatband… to the jaw… to the chin.

As he waited, he lit his umpteenth cigarette and allowed it to dangle from his lips as he listened to the storm of battle. Farther down the line he watched Sergeant Blackmore and the lieutenant perform a pantomime of tragic proportions. Sergeant Blackmore knelt beside the lieutenant who alternated between pointing forcefully at his map and sweeping his arm toward the front as he spoke. As if in answer to some pertinent question, Blackmore scrambled up the hedge bank and peered over its crest, neck craning as a machine gun chattered in the distance, then leaped down to report his findings. Now Blackmore's arm thrust vaguely in directions that indicated likely enemy positions. They exchanged several more sentences, then the lieutenant beckoned his radio man as squad leaders gathered around him.

Before long the huddle broke and Sergeant Fretwell approached his squad. "Okay, listen up. We're going over. We're going over now. Get ready. When the word comes, we lead off." And that was that -- Barkley's squad was to be the first offering on the latest sacrificial altar.

Barkley's heart thundered anew. His mouth seemed dry as talc as he inhaled deeply from his cigarette. Those dreaded words, *Scouts out*, were imminent now. Fretwell had already cautioned him, had pointed out the intended route of approach and their immediate goal. They would advance straight across the open field and into the woods. Barkley stole another peek over the hedgerow's crest and his heart sank. The field was devoid of cover, a barren plain overgrown by tall grasses. *How long can one's luck hold out?* he wondered. Not very long. *Maybe this is it. Maybe I won't make it through this one.*

Another peal of artillery thundered from afar. Fear gnawed his gut and goaded his imagination to new heights of despair. *How far did the Russians get today? That was the standing joke, wasn't it?* Well, Pfc. Barkley was hoping to make it one more field, and then one more, and it was a hell of a long way to Berlin. The hopelessness of ever surviving the war overwhelmed him and he surrendered to his fate. *Come on. Let's get it over with. Let's go...* Every second dragged into infinity as his nerves stretched to the point of breaking.

A torrent of mortar shells ravaged the fields to his left. Perhaps another platoon was catching hell. Who could say? The impenetrable screen of hedgerows completely isolated one unit from the other and often men didn't know if the adjacent fields were vacant or occupied. And in the crazy, tangled maze the prevailing question was: occupied by whom? Again the specter of Dead Man's Gulch raised its ugly head -- the dreaded draw that was the scene of

Company G's slaughter back in June. Were they once again being lured into a trap?

Barkley drew on the stub of his cigarette, savoring the last drag, then pitched the butt to the ground as he exhaled a vaporous stream. The craving for nicotine was habit now, something to placate threadbare nerves. He was as ready as he'd ever be, but still word didn't come. "What are they waiting for?" he muttered beneath his breath as his heel drummed nervously against the soil.

The harsh smoke of his cigarette seemed to irritate a throat already parched by tension and fear. His fingers fumbled with the snaps of his canteen pouch. *This could be my last drink on earth for all I know. A man shouldn't go to Hell thirsty*, he chuckled blackly as he hoisted his canteen and allowed a sip or two.

Meanwhile, heavy cannon fire sounded from the far left as the tanks let loose with everything they had. Fireballs blossomed in the forest, giving rise to a cauldron of dust and smoke. *They're going to soften them up for us*, Barkley thought.

Down the line the lieutenant pushed the earpiece of his radio beneath his helmet and spoke loudly into the mouthpiece while pressing a finger hard against the opposite ear.

Again the tanks thundered. Another salvo splintered the woods. Tree tops took flight, riding fountains of smoke and dust as they performed ungainly summersaults before tumbling from the sky. The lieutenant hunched his shoulders against the din and spoke even louder, "Roger that. On our way. Out." Returning the set to his radio man, he spoke to Blackmore who promptly rose and trotted along the ranks.

"Let's go!" he shouted, "Scouts out!"

Fretwell motioned to Barkley, and with that, Barkley scrambled up the hedge bank and was gone. The attack against the woods was on.

Barkley and Hinson closed rapidly on the tree line while the tanks knocked hell out of the forest to their left. Both scouts expected bullets or mortar shells to strike them down at every step, but none did, and before long they burst through the tree line and were in the forest. The squad was right behind them.

Barkley's eyes widened as they adjusted to the sudden darkness. Black, shattered limbs lay entwined with tangled underbrush upon the forest floor. To his left the forest continued to quake and glow with thunderous explosions. He had hardly commenced his movement forward when suddenly a group of soldiers in camouflaged smocks burst from the smoldering foliage. Rounded helmets topped their heads. Barkley's eyes lock on those of the first one he saw. "Germans! Germans!" he hollered as he pointed their direction. He hit the dirt and rolled, knowing that the leading paratrooper had seen him. The Kraut was quite a bit ahead of the others and it seemed to Barkley that he must have been a scout, like himself, leading his unit in a counterattack. Or were they simply running from the maelstrom that drove them like rabbits escaping a forest fire? At any rate, the leading German had seen him go down, and now, in the dim forest light, Barkley's war had narrowed to a one-on-one confrontation between him and his German counterpart.

The others were very close, secluded somewhere in the underbrush. Burp guns emitted their signature stammer. Rifles barked in reply. Barkley listened and tried to determine which way his opponent had gone. Hazy shafts of light slanted through the leafy canopy, washing everything with its eerie, greenish cast, creating a tension all its own. It seemed as if the gods themselves leaned from the edges of their thrones and awaited Barkley's next move. After a pause, he slithered closer towards his enemy. Sweat slicked the grip of his tommy gun as he inched forward. More shots rang out as several of the company engaged the other Germans in a sniping contest. Curses and oaths echoed through the forest. Again a burp gun sputtered.

Suddenly a subtle movement caught Barkley's eye and at the same moment, the German saw him. Both ducked for cover. Barkley rolled and clutched his weapon. His heart thumped wildly. Sweat burst from every pore. *Had he seen me? Yes*, came the immediate answer, *yes, I know he did.* Barkley reacted swiftly, moving rapidly to prevent his enemy from gaining a fix on his location. He plunged behind some bushes and lay still, pressing his face close to the earth. Slowly he raised his head. He held his breath and listened intently, examining every bush, every tree, every depression that might conceal his enemy. And then he saw him. Or rather, was conscious of a faint rustling of branches and it appeared as if his foe was not falling back as he had hoped, but was moving forward, as if searching. Barkley was being stalked.

He ignored the sounds of other gunshots and shouts as he concentrated on his immediate plight. Now the rules had changed, became crystal clear: Only one of them was going to leave the woods. Barkley knew, just as certain as anything he had ever understood before, that he had to kill his brazen counterpart. A rush of blood surged through him at the very thought of it and he felt weakened for a moment, unequal to the task. Then, just as suddenly, he resolved to see it through. As if the deed was already done, he acted deliberately, instinctively, and began to hunt his nemesis.

He decided to flank him and dodged from tree to ditch to bush, hoping to outmaneuver his prey and take him by surprise. Somewhere, his foe was doing the same. It had become a deadly game of hide-and-seek.

Barkley continued to jockey for position and eventually hid behind a fallen log where he waited for the German to make the next move. A slight rustling of leaves prompted him to chance a look. There was his adversary, unsuspecting of his position and close enough for a clear shot. Barkley popped up and leveled his weapon. *Budda-da-dup!* The forest rang with the harsh stutter of his tommy gun and it was over before the echo faded, absorbed by the lush, succulent foliage. The only witness was the forest itself whose towering trees stood like solemn, silent judges who judiciously declared a victor.

Barkley dropped and shuddered as he released a long-held breath. Regaining his composure, he joined the others of his platoon who moved steadily against the enemy and in short order the company swept what Germans remained from the fringe of the forest.

The forest secured, the squads quickly swung outward to cross a field to protect the battalion's right flank. No sooner had they emerged from the tree line than the nearest hedge top fairly disintegrated as 20mm cannon fire ripped along its crest in rapid succession. Men hit the dirt. The large caliber tracers flashed brightly from the distance and seemed to originate from a field several hundred yards to their right front.

Then heavier artillery began to fall. Officers and sergeants pushed their men onward to the protection of the devastated hedgerow. More shells screamed in from another direction. Then small arms fire erupted from their left and men flung themselves down only to be hit by another round of flat trajectory artillery. Shovels hacked desperately at the earth. Meanwhile, officers and sergeants rose amidst the confusion to determine from whence the deadly fires came. Once detected, Captain Skaggs radioed battalion and called for supporting fires.

In time the comforting sound of outgoing artillery was heard and fields to the front, left, and right disappeared amidst smoke and fire. The artillery poured it on, releasing salvo after salvo on the menacing fields, forcing the enemy guns to cease and no more shells struck the company area.

The squads remained prostrate behind the hedgerows while cries of "Medic! Medic!" filled the air. Snipers continued to plague the ranks and, save for the aid man, no one dared to rise. Barkley lay panting, dreading the next leg of the assault. He was totally drained from the exertion. Sweat trickled from beneath his helmet and saturated his uniform. His throat seemed dry as old leather.

Another shot whined off the hedgerow's crest, causing Barkley to nestle closer to its base. Before long, a voice rose from behind him. "Barkley, got any water? I'm out and need a drink." It was Sergeant Fretwell.

Annoyed, Barkley pulled his canteen from its pouch and sloshed the contents. Not much remained. After hesitating, he answered, "Alright. But I ain't got much, so take it easy, okay?"

"Yeah, sure. Toss it back."

With a flick, Barkley pitched his canteen back to where Fretwell lay. After a few minutes, the canteen came sailing back. Retrieving it, Barkley noticed it was light -- very light. *Sonovabitch!* he swore as he shook it, *The bastard drank it all!* For the remainder of the day, Barkley fought without water. How he hated Fretwell!

"Let's go! Move out!" One platoon remained to provide covering fire while the others rose and trotted along the hedgerow to their left. Before long they came upon a sunken road that emerged from the corner of the forest to their left. Several squads pushed on to occupy the fields across the road while Barkley's platoon filed left down the dusty lane and sank in its trough-like track with the forest to their backs. More gunfire sounded from the front where the others had gone, but for now, Barkley's platoon remained in place, hunkered in the road.

The sun hovered on the horizon, a fiery ball suspended in a cloud of thick battle haze. Although twilight was nigh, there was no telling when, or if they'd be moving again. No matter, no one wished to remain above ground and again shovels scraped the earth with desperate excavations. Exhausted, Barkley chopped at the roadside bank. Behind him the forest remained a dark, sinister place filled with cold black shadows -- a place now haunted with dead men's souls. Somewhere to his front was the enemy still dedicated to killing him and all his friends.

As soldiers dug, artillery rumbled from distant quarters and small arms fire clattered from several fields to the front, but for now all was quiet in the immediate area. The day was almost done.

Barkley had hardly begun digging when his work was interrupted by a commotion behind him -- sharp voices and scuffling. He turned to see two GIs herding a sullen German paratrooper at gunpoint from the woods. They prodded him to where the lieutenant was and announced that they had a prisoner. The German scowled with Prussian arrogance. He was a hard case, no doubt a fanatic, a dangerous man. The lieutenant told the Kraut's captors to escort their prize to the rear and turn him over to the MPs. One of the GIs, a sergeant, gave the German a rough shove in the direction he wanted him to go. The young paratrooper spun in his tracks and glared at his guard. The sergeant was in no mood to take any crap from the arrogant Nazi and thumped him harshly on the shoulder to get him moving. "Raus!" he growled as he pointed the way. His captive rebounded with an icy stare and swore a blue streak in German, then punctuated his curse by spitting a glob of saliva into the GI's face. The American was shocked by the audacity. An unmistakable expression of revulsion swept across his face. Slowly, deliberately, he wiped the slime away. *"Get moving, you sonovabitch!"* he bellowed and jerked his ward around and gave him a mighty shove. The prisoner complied and they disappeared through the trees.

Buddy, thought Barkley as he monitored the scene, *you just made a **big** mistake!*

Before too long, the sound of gunshots rang from the rear and shortly after that the sergeant emerged from the woods -- alone. His jaw was set so firmly that his face seemed as if chiseled from stone, twisted into a mask of darkest hatred. His features could have been etched by a dagger. The lieutenant looked up, startled. "What happened?" he asked. The sergeant smirked maliciously. "Aw, lieutenant, you know how them sonsabitches are. The bastard tried to make a run for it." And that was all he said. The lieutenant didn't say anything more and the sergeant returned to his squad. But everyone knew what had really happened.

As darkness closed, Sergeant Fretwell ordered each of his men to take a turn standing a one-hour watch while the others slept. Barkley was to be first. Taking Fretwell's wristwatch, Barkley noted the time and commenced his term. He was barely able to stay awake himself, but managed to fight the weight of fatigue and after sixty minutes, slithered to Hinson's hole and shook him awake.

He settled into the damp soil of his own hole and closed his eyes.

"Barkley!" a voice hissed softly, "Barkley!"

Confused, Barkley jolted awake. His hand reached for his weapon. *Wh-what's happening?* he thought... *An attack?*

"Barkley, it's your turn."

Confused, Barkley realized it was the voice of one of the other squad members.

"No... can't be," he murmured. His head swam. It seemed as if he had just fallen asleep. Where were the other members of the squad? It couldn't be his turn again.

"Get up! It's your turn," the voice repeated, and then as if to prove his point, the soldier pointed to the luminous dial of the watch. Sure enough, it was several hours later.

Groggily, Barkley pulled himself up and accepted the wristwatch. The other soldier quickly disappeared in the dark.

Bleary-eyed, Barkley stared into the early morning darkness. His body felt as if it were made of cement. After twenty or thirty minutes passed, he couldn't understand why it was still dark. According to the hands of the watch, it should have been getting light by now. Then a stunning revelation struck him: The dirty sonovabitch who stood watch before him had advanced the watch hands, making it appear as if he had already stood his turn. The dirty bastard!

Outraged, Barkley finished his second turn of guard duty.

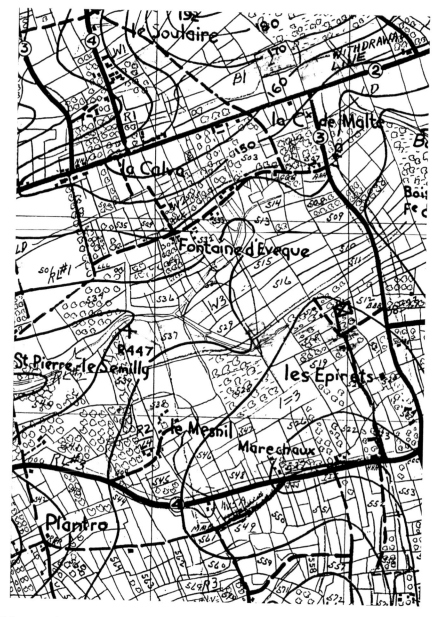

This map shows the patchwork maze of the hedgerows. Hill 192 is located at the top, center. On July 26, 1944, the Second Battalion followed the sunken road (dotted line) from le Soulaire to field 503 across the St. Lo Highway (dark diagonal line running across the upper portion). The small woods where Barkley encountered the enemy scout is numbered 528 and is located between le Mesnil and Le Espirets. (Detail from map at National Archives)

CHAPTER 12

PURPLE HEART

Daybreak, July 27, 1944 -- The sun rose like a blood red god of war and christened the dawning of a new day. Pfc. Barkley awoke, still groggy from a fitful, restless night. Sleep, a twitching, fidgety, teeth grinding affair, had become a relative term and bore little resemblance to its civilian namesake. As a result, Pfc. Barkley slumped in his shallow hole, consumed by chronic fatigue. He was dead dog tired.

Ammunition had come up during the night, and water and rations as well and once again Barkley had plenty of ammo and a full canteen. He felt weary, as if he were drugged, but managed to pry open a ration can to fill a hollow stomach. As he stirred its tasteless contents, he looked around and noted that the squad numbered less than it had the day before. Young Willie was no longer with them, nor was Joe Benavidez. A number of others had fallen as well, and that left the seed of doubt in his mind as to his own survival. A queer, uneasy sensation gripped him as he attempted to choke down his meal. No matter what he set his mind to, he just couldn't shake the gnawing notion that something was not right, and as a consequence he had no appetite. He simply sat there, numbed by a persistent foreboding.

Then a voice broke the trance. "Let's go. We're moving out." Sergeant Blackmore was assembling what remained of the platoon. Exhausted, Barkley rose from his hole and joined his squad as they stepped off in a staggered column.

Artillery was already hammering the next objective. They had only moved a short distance down a sunken lane when orders came to halt. Twin files collapsed on either side of the road. The right hand column rested beneath the shelter of a shaggy hedgerow. The left file, which included Barkley, sank shoulder deep against an embankment with an open field to their backs. The disturbing rattle of machine guns clattered from the not too distant front, followed by the ominous thumping of mortars. Hell was brewing anew.

The battle sounds sank into the sump of the road and did not go un-noticed. Again Barkley counted heads. Hinson squatted just to his right, appearing lost in troubled thought. His good friend, Joe Guajardo, held his place farther down the line with others strung out behind him. To Barkley's left, towards their direction of march, knelt Sergeant Fretwell, and beyond him was the lieutenant and Sergeant Blackmore. Their faces were tense, acutely aware of what lay ahead. Only minutes separated them from the promise of death or mutilation. Their demeanor only reinforced his earlier premonition of impending doom and his blood ran cold. His gaze drifted across the road to study his comrades resting beneath the hedgerow's mane. Some slumped against the verdant bank while others simply sat in the dirt with rifles and BARs poking above their heads at odd angles, giving the surreal image of a ragged picket fence. Weary faces, worn grim and taut by the previous day's combat, stared back from beneath heavy helmets.

As he scanned their features, his eyes locked onto one -- a worried, broad face with wild whiskers sprouting from a rugged chin. Eye glasses glinted from beneath the helmet's rim. *My God! It's the Barracuda!* It was Frank Balchunas. He was sitting several men's distance, opposite Barkley's left, crouching beneath the hedgerow's shade. Barkley rose to join him.

As he came abreast of his old friend, Barkley noted that Balchunas wore some sort of harness festooned with bazooka rockets. A bazooka man sat closeby. Obviously Frank was no longer a litter bearer. Barkley turned and sat on the low bank that hemmed the road. "Hello, Frank."

The Barracuda's face lit up. "My God... Barkley!"

They were delighted to see each other, grateful that neither had been hurt, so far. Balchunas, still hunkered in the road, became concerned about his young friend sitting upright on the opposite embankment. "For Christ's sake, Bark, get down. You're gonna get hit!"

Barkley looked casually left and right and remarked that there was no shelling in the immediate vicinity, therefore no immediate danger, and much to his buddy's chagrin, remained perched upon the ledge.

As they spoke, the din of battle rose sharply, causing Balchunas to flinch. Barkley noted that his buddy appeared grimmer than ever, and that launched another bout with his own nagging premonition. "I don't feel too good about this one," he confessed, "If, uh... If anything should happen to me, you'll write my folks, won't you? Tell 'em what happened."

Distant battle sounds accompanied his request.

The Barracuda stared at Barkley with spooky eyes. "Yeah. Yeah, sure, Bark, I'll tell 'em." Then his brow wrinkled as he revealed his own misgivings. "To tell you the truth, I don't feel so good about this one myself. I'm not sure if I'm gonna make it either! If something happens to *me*, you be sure and write *my* mother, will you?" Both men sat with grave expressions etched upon their faces. An ominous mood loomed over them like an evil harbinger.

Just then Lieutenant Welch came loping down the road. "Third platoon! Let's go. Hubba hubba!" The row of soldiers lining the left side of the road rose and tramped away, sweeping Barkley with them. Frank Balchunas remained seated and watched dolefully as his buddy disappeared toward the unholy racket of the Devil's playground. Hell was fast a-coming and retribution was in the offing.

The company attacked all morning with one platoon supporting the next. Machine guns and mortars met every advance. Within hours the battle degenerated into a series of isolated combats, with the Germans resisting with the ingrained stubbornness that so characterized the Teutonic warrior. But as the day progressed, the attackers noted a perceptible change. Now and then, a squad here, and another there had managed to cross a field or two with little or no opposition. *Hallelujah!* A revelation! The German line was beginning to crack!

The attacking forces capitalized on this unexpected development and by mid-day assault squads were racing across fields all but uncontested. Upon reaching one hedgerow, Barkley's squad was surprised to see a flock of enemy soldiers fleeing across an open field. Rounded helmets bobbed rhythmically above the grass as the paratroopers struggled to gain the next hedgerow. They ran slowly, as if weary from the weeks of bombardment and ensuing battles.

Sergeant Blackmore leaned into the hedge bank and centered his sights on a German's back. *K-pow! K-pow!* His target toppled. "Kill 'em! Kill 'em!" he roared, as he fired again and again. The entire squad came up on line and gunned down men who ran like frightened animals. They ran with their backs to their tormentors and were easy marks. One by one, German soldiers tumbled in the tall grass. One was a machine gunner whose weapon balanced like an iron post upon one shoulder as he plodded beneath its ponderous weight. Another soldier ran beside him, burdened with ammo belts and both keeled over -- one, two -- as bullets found them, and in the end only a couple paratroopers managed to escape the vicious fusillade.

Blackmore was down in the field even before the enemy had vanished over the next hedgerow. "C'mon, goddammit, let's go!" he cried. He knew the enemy was on the run and wanted to keep up the pressure before they regrouped to build a new defensive line. Barkley, the ever devoted follower, slid down the hedgerow bank and joined his mentor as he raced across the field.

Arriving at the next hedgerow, they clambered up its side just in time to discover the remnants of the fleeing foe struggling over the far embankment. Again Blackmore fired, but missed, and the enemy disappeared through the shaggy green wall.

"C'mon! C'mon!" he goaded. His eyes burned like coals.

The squad charged again. Barkley was elated. The Germans were actually on the run! A feeling of invincibility swept over him. They were finally breaking through the hated hedgerows, one after another. He realized that the more ground taken today, the less they'd have to take tomorrow. Though exhausted, he ran all-out.

Another field entered and no enemy. Blackmore paused to catch his breath. Although he wanted to press their advantage, he realized that their mini-blitz had far outdistanced the other squads. His small group was now several fields ahead of the rest of the platoon. As a precaution, he returned to tried and true practices. He ordered an attack formation. Scouts would precede the next leg of the advance.

Excited by their whirlwind assault, First Scout Barkley reclaimed the lead. He pushed on at a rapid pace with Hinson tramping off to one side. The balance of the squad spread out behind them in a classic skirmish line.

Upon reaching the next hedgerow, Barkley paused to peer over its crest. Before him lay a broad field of over-ripe wheat, boxed in by the usual hedgerows. Nothing stirred before him. Blackmore came up and urged him on. "Go, dammit! Go!"

Taking a breath, Barkley scrambled over the hedgerow wall. The others came pouring after him and just then the expected happened.

Rrrrrrrp!

Bullets cut through the ranks like an electric shock and everyone went down. *Oh, Jesus! Machine gun!*

Barkley lay flat, heart pounding.

Another burst scythed the wheat and Barkley's foot kicked hard as a bullet tore the heel from his shoe while another clanged loudly off his helmet. Elsewhere someone moaned.

"Keep low, men! Keep low!" Blackmore bellowed.

No sooner had the sergeant spoken than the deep throated growl of a massive engine reverberated across the field, and at that moment a tank lurched from the hedgerow wall to their right. Blood drained from Barkley's face. *Oh, Christ!* he thought as he lay beneath cusps of golden grain, *What the hell do we do now?* Frantic, he searched the brittle stalks for Blackmore, seeking guidance. The sergeant lay a short distance behind him and again Barkley's heart stopped cold. Bright blood sopped the sergeant's pants legs. Blackmore moaned softly, grimacing in pain. It looked as if both knees had been blown out. *No! No! Not Blackmore!* How many others had been hit he couldn't tell.

Blackmore's eyes narrowed as they met Barkley's. "Keep down!" he snapped.

Another burst ripped the wheat. The earth trembled as the tank churned closer. It seemed to be traversing back and forth as if attempting to crush anyone laying in concealment, or maybe flush out the intruders to sate the blood lust of its wicked machine guns.

Barkley lay in the field, terrified. He blamed himself for getting the squad into such a predicament. He was the scout, after all. Although the tank had been well camouflaged, he believed he should have seen it as he crossed the field. He felt as if he had failed his buddies.

Accepting responsibility, he decided it was up to him to rectify the situation. His mind raced. There weren't many options. He quickly concluded he had to draw the tank's attention so the survivors could make their escape.

Taking a deep breath, he sprung up to face the iron monster. As he did, he swung his Thompson forward and squeezed its trigger and at the same instant the tank's hull twinkled with fire. *Rrrrp!* A sledgehammer blow spun Barkley to the ground.

He hit the ground hard. Dumbfounded, he tried to evaluate what had happened. *My God!* came the grim realization, *I'm hit!* A dull, throbbing sensation pulsed from his right shoulder. Then his shoulder was consumed by a white-hot burning that seared his flesh with mounting intensity. *My God, how it burned!* It was as if his shoulder had been pierced by a red-hot poker. His jaw clenched in teeth-gnashing agony as he thrashed in the wheat. Crimson blood smeared golden straw. The burning intensified and he realized that it must have been a tracer bullet that knocked him down and now the phosphorus tipped bullet remained lodged somewhere within his flesh where it burned and burned and burned. In short order his right arm was reduced to a useless appendage. It seemed as if made of lead.

He knew he couldn't rise lest he'd be shot again, so he absorbed the pain. In agony, he clawed at the earth. His fingers found a rock and he splintered his nails upon its surface in anguished desperation. But nothing eased his suffering. The pain became unbearable -- he could take it no more so decided he had to dig the bullet out himself. His trench knife was over his left shoulder, attached to his pack. By now his right arm was completely useless, so he attempted to draw the knife with his left hand but was unable to reach it.

The tracer burned like molten glass.

Then he recalled that Sergeant Blackmore lay closeby. Barkley called over his left shoulder, "Blackmore! Blackmore! Can you hand me my knife?"

The sergeant refused. "Lay still," he hissed. Blood soaked the earth around him.

Barkley lay in excruciating pain, blinded by ranks of yellow stalks as the tank continued to thrash through the wheat. Now and then its machine guns rattled, but Barkley knew not if it had found one if his buddies, or was simply firing blind.

Suddenly, the earth shook as a tremendous explosion wracked the field. Or maybe there were two, and then the sound of gunfire followed by the pounding of many feet. A dark shadow raced past, followed by another as the balance of the platoon pushed on to take the next hedgerow. The stench of burning diesel filled the air.

Before long, a medic loomed over Barkley. Kneeling beside him, the medic punched a morphine syrette into Barkley's skin, then cut away his jacket and shirt. He was still wearing long-john underwear and the cloth was sopping wet with blood. Snipping away the remnants, the medic bound the wound. A filthy hand slipped sulfa pills between Barkley's teeth, then pressed a canteen to his lips and forced him to swallow a gulp or two. Other medical men arrived to evacuate the wounded, carefully lifting the worse cases onto stretchers, then carried them off, away from the front.

Barkley was helped to his feet. Already the morphine was taking effect. The tank sat dormant in the middle of the field, trailing a plume of black, oily smoke. Somehow, someone had knocked it out -- probably a bazooka -- but whatever the cause, it was no longer a threat to Barkley and his squad. But it was too late for some of them.

It seemed as if half of the squad had been hit by the tank's machine gun fire. Some were dead. Again guilt racked Barkley. They had started the attack the day before with eleven men in the squad. Now it was almost wiped out. He was starkly aware that those terrifying minutes in the wheat field had cost the squad five or six men killed or wounded. Add to that the others who had fallen the day before and one quickly gained insight to the harsh reality of war. It was a disturbing thought.

Meanwhile, Blackmore's legs had been bandaged and now, with the assistance of two others, he hobbled to a jeep that had been driven into the field. He was helped into the back, sharing space with a mounted .30 caliber machine gun. Barkley was ushered to the same vehicle and numbly joined his platoon sergeant, taking a seat near a long, brassy strand of bullets that dangled from the machine gun's breach. Then a man on a stretcher was lashed to the jeep's hood and they were ready to depart.

The driver was extremely nervous. The battle still raged a short distance to the front and he wanted to get out of there fast. He was aware that snipers and by-passed pockets of enemy soldiers might be encountered on the way to the rear, so offered a proposal to the two casualties sitting behind him. He wanted them to man the jeep's machine gun for their defense. Blackmore, with bad legs but two good arms, said he would operate the weapon. Barkley, with only one good arm, offered to assist his sergeant by feeding the belt of bullets into the powerful gun.

Before they departed, the two invalids had time to reflect on their ordeal. "Blackmore," Barkley addressed his friend, "Why didn't you hand me my knife when I asked you to?"

"You just wanted to cut out the bullet."

"Yeah… Yeah, I wanted to…"

The driver ground his gears and the jeep lurched forward to begin the painful, jouncing journey to the battalion aid station. Two bloodied defenders were perched in the rear, clutching a machine gun and holding on for dear life.

Barkley and Blackmore were processed through the various medical detachments, traveling farther and farther from the front until they were finally dumped off at a field hospital. It was a large tented complex, bustling with activity. Medical personnel scurried hither and yon in pursuit of their errands. Jeeps and ambulances stirred up clouds of dust as they deposited their loads of injured men, then roared off to the front for more. Medics and nurses knelt over stretchers laden with wounded soldiers and determined the severity of their injuries. Those which required immediate attention were rushed into tented operating rooms where bloodied surgeons fished in their guts to pluck out shrapnel, or probed punctured skulls in search of bullets, or amputated shattered limbs that were beyond salvation. Sometimes there wasn't an arm or leg. The doctors worked round the clock when a big attack was underway.

Those with less severe wounds remained outside, lying on stretchers lined up in neat rows to await their turn. Barkley was one of these. He and Blackmore lay near each other and Barkley rose up on his good elbow and surveyed the scene around him. Wounded soldiers were everywhere, swathed in bloody field dressings. Some moaned or cried out sharply, racked in agony. A few whimpered softly, absorbed in self-pity while others remained stone silent and stared blankly at the sky. Each casualty had a paper tag attached to him on which a field medic had written basic information concerning their wounds and treatment given.

Barkley gazed curiously at the writhing mass of humanity. In time his eyes fell upon a disturbing sight. "Well I'll be a sonovabitch!" he exclaimed, "Look at that." Interspersed among the GIs were wounded Germans, dressed in field gray or the distinctive camouflaged smocks of the paratroopers. They talked among themselves, jabbering in their guttural language. Several of the younger ones shouted encouragement to one another and some of the more audacious even barked, "Heil Hitler! Heil Hitler!" much to the astonishment of the wounded Americans. Even in captivity, their devotion to their Fuhrer remained untarnished. Barkley was offended to be laid among the very men who only a few hours before were trying to kill him and his friends.

Later, several of these same Germans chattered excitedly when hospital orderlies brought them food. They were given the same generous portions that the American wounded received. Nearby was a GI who spoke German and he laughed as he explained that the Krauts were astonished to see food in such abundance. Apparently they had been told that the American supply system was on the verge of collapse and food was in short supply.

In time, Barkley was taken to a steamy tent where an X-ray was made of his wound. Afterwards Red Cross personnel came through passing out writing materials to the slightly wounded men. Accepting an envelope and a letterhead, Barkley wrote a quick note home, left handed, to ensure that his parents would know that he was hurt, but would surely survive. In very shaky writing he penciled:

> *July 27 France*
> *Dear Mother and Dad*
> *Here I am waiting my time to be pached up. I had a X ray and no bones or anything like that was broke. It's just a shoulder wound. They are very nice to us here and the wounded get the best of care. We have nice nurses, Doctors, and anyone connected with this place is very nice to us. As you can see my writing isn't any too good but in a few days I will be as good as new again. I know you would be worrying if I wrote like this and said nothing was wrong so I tell you the truth, its just a slight wound.*
> your son,
> H. Barkley

Shortly after, a medic came along and gave him another injection of morphine and he drifted into a semi-conscious state. Everything seemed as if in a dream, thick, and in slow motion. It was an odd sensation. He lay back and gazed at the sky, lulled into a stupor by the pain-killing drug. Medics hovered over him. They said something, garbled words, then bent down and gripped the stretcher. Grimy, bearded faces gaped at Barkley as he levitated above them and floated away. He was in a tent... bright lights and distant, fuzzy voices... Soon a surgically masked face was poised above his own. It was a woman's face. He was puzzled by a woman's presence. "Who are you?" he asked.

A soft voice flowed from the mask, "I'm your doctor."

His vision swirled, then caught sight of something in her hand -- a set of long forceps. Mellowed by morphine, he was only mildly alarmed. "Wh... what are you going to do with that?" he asked groggily.

"I'm going to take out the bullet in your shoulder." Barkley's eyes locked on hers -- eyes of compassion -- angel eyes.

"Oh," he answered meekly as he succumbed to the effects of anesthesia.

Barkley regained consciousness. He was in another tent, a makeshift recovery ward. His right shoulder ached terribly. As the drugs wore off, he became aware of another sensation -- his hand felt different. Looking down, he saw that something was taped to its back. A distinct lump rose from beneath the tape. Puzzled, he studied it, then recognized it for what it was. It was a bullet. It was the very bullet that had been extracted from his wound. In time he discovered that indeed it was a phosphorus-tipped tracer bullet. That's why it burned so badly during his wounding. The bullet's nose was actually bent from when it glanced off his shoulder bone before boring deep into his chest cavity to lodge beneath his collar bone. Or maybe it had ricocheted before it struck him, but anyway, the bullet's nose was definitely bent and Barkley found that amusing. It was a very personal souvenir. He realized Blackmore's wisdom when the sergeant denied him the use of his knife when he wanted to dig the bullet out himself. He would have surely mangled his flesh in the process and cause more damage than he already had suffered. He would have never reached the bullet.

Still groggy from drugs, he slipped back into dreamland where nightmares lay in ambush.

After spending a day or two at the field hospital, Pfc. Barkley was transferred by plane from Normandy to a convalescent hospital in England. The plane touched down at Heathrow Airport, London.

CHAPTER 13

LONDON

Summer, 1944, France -- With St. Lo and the hedgerows behind them, the American armies moved swiftly across the face of Europe. Although ferocious combats still occurred, gains were now measured in miles instead of yards. At the Battle for the Falaise Gap, converging forces squeezed the 2nd Infantry Division out of the line on August 16, near the town of Tinchebray. It was their first break since coming ashore on June 7, ending seventy-one days of continuous combat operations. After a brief rest, the entire division was trucked west to the Brittany Peninsula where the VIII Corps was inching forward against stiff opposition at the port city of Brest. Attached to this corps, the 2nd Division resumed its offensive on August 21. While the VIII Corps tightened the noose around Brest, the First and Third Armies rolled eastward to the German frontier where they were halted not so much by enemy resistance than by an acute shortage of fuel.

By now the line companies of the 2nd Infantry Division had suffered a casualty rate of more than 100 per cent. The earlier groups of replacements were now considered "old hands" among the fighting squads and many of these had fallen. More and more replacements came up to fill the ranks.

Meanwhile, Pfc. Barkley recuperated from his wounds.

August, 1944, U.S. Army hospital, London -- Barkley jolted awake, startled by a horrifying dream. Electric lights shined brightly, causing his heart to jump. *Don't they know light will attract enemy fire?* For a moment he was disoriented, but after a blink or two everything began to fall into place. He remembered that he was in a hospital ward in England, safe from harm. There would be no incoming mortars. There would be no sniper fire.

A vague murmuring haunted the room. One man whimpered. Another moaned softly, his mind lost in the numbing effects of morphine. It was all so very strange, so quiet, such an alien atmosphere after weeks and weeks of living in a mud hole on the battlefront, dodging bullets and shells and God knows what. It was... strange.

A dull pain throbbed through his right shoulder and knifed into his chest. His shoulder was swathed in bandages that hid an ugly blue bruise that discolored his entire shoulder. Beneath the bandage the wound itself was encrusted by an ugly scab. Laying back, he stared at the ceiling while visions of wheat and bullets and a tank flashed through his head -- recollections of terror and pain and again he tried to figure out what had gone wrong in that fateful field.

Hazy sunlight filtered through window panes and bathed the ward with soft, warm rays. Hospital life was great for the most part. Barkley could sleep as long as he liked -- and he had a lot of sleep to catch up on. It was heavenly to lay between the crisp, clean linen that graced his bed. The sheets smelled wonderful, almost sterile. He now received three meals a day -- hot meals, not tasteless K-rations. He was indoors, comfortable and warm with a roof over his head. He had no duties other than to rest and recover.

Homefront, Quincy, Illinois -- The mail had arrived and Harry and Nettie Barkley read their son's letter with alarm. Although they were relieved to know that he was alive, they were still concerned about his wound and if he was suffering. Soon after, a telegram arrived from the War Department officially stating that Pfc. Harold G. Barkley had indeed been wounded in action in France, and that his wound was of a slight nature. They didn't know that the War Department always said a wound was of a slight nature unless one's limbs had been blown off, or internal organs destroyed, or one had suffered a head wound that left him as witty as a vegetable -- then one was granted seriously wounded status. The next grade would be killed in action. Nettie submitted the information to the local newspaper which ran a blurb among others in the "Our Boys In Service" column.

She and Harry continued to receive letters written by their son while he was still in combat. At first it was strange, because they knew he was in a hospital in England. The V-Mail system was reliable, but slow. In time, however, his hospital mail began to arrive. He told them how he hoped to return to the States when his wound healed and maybe be allowed to instruct troops at a training center. He believed his combat experience would prove invaluable to the Army. He wanted to send home his coveted Combat Infantryman's Badge, but lamented that in his outfit, in order to receive the $10.00 a month extra combat pay, he had to actually possess the blue and silver badge.

When evening came, Nettie sat at the kitchen table to write her son. She expressed her hopes and prayers for his safe keeping. She and Harry were very proud of him, but she believed that he had done his share and now wanted him safe from harm. She hoped that he could get some other job in a rear echelon outfit, far from the fighting.

U.S. Army hospital, London -- Again Barkley jolted awake, shaking and cold with sweat. *The tank was right **there**!* The recurring

203

nightmare plagued his nights and haunted his days. He tried to place the events of that terrifying day into perspective. He still believed he was responsible for getting his squad into such a predicament and the guilt only mounted as he recalled the incident. He was the scout. *The scout!* He should have seen that damned tank.

Other thoughts also crossed his mind. He recalled how after the first burst of machine gun fire he almost rolled into a slight depression off to one side. Why he didn't, he didn't know, but in retrospect he concluded that if he *had*, he would have been inches lower than he was when he rose to confront the tank. It would most likely have been his head instead of his shoulder that took the bullet. Although it was one of those variable quirks of combat, it remained a puzzle to him.

Third week of August, 1944 -- Hard soled shoes tapped a steady rhythm upon tiled floors, echoing louder and louder until a nurse halted at the foot of Barkley's bed. A pleasant face regarded him. A female face. After jotting a few entries onto his chart, she asked, "Are you ready for your therapy?"

His therapy. Doctors had prescribed a regimen of exercises to strengthen his shoulder and increase its mobility. Barkley swung his legs to the floor, and with the help of the nurse struggled into his robe.

His wound was healing fast. By now the scab had fallen off to expose an ugly purple indentation puckered shut by taught sutures. His shoulder still ached, but was not near as painful, and the arm that once was feeble was now regaining some of its former strength. Daily exercise was the order of the day. As he practiced his routine, Barkley was amused by the way the wound would suck in, then pop out every time he flexed his arm. A distinct absence of tissue created a film of discolored skin that stretched across the wound like a diaphragm spanning a void. He could trace a finger over the pectoral muscles of his right breast and feel a definite groove where muscle should have been. The bullet had done a good job.

Now that he was on the mend, Barkley applied for, and received, a number of passes. As long as he showed up for his exercises he was granted nearly unlimited freedom to come and go as he pleased. The only requirement was that he had to be back in time for bed check.

The hospital was near the center of London and Barkley intended to see as much of the historic city as possible. He became familiar with the bus schedule and various subway routes. Having a yen for history, he visited the best museums in the world. He toured the British Museum, the Victoria and Albert Museum, and others. He marveled at rank upon rank of suits of armor that guarded the halls, each equipped with any combination of swords, lances, halberds and shields. There were uniforms and weapons of every type since the dawn of recorded history. There were artifacts of every facet of not only British life throughout the ages, but of virtually every civilization and culture known to man. It was all there and Barkley absorbed it and wallowed in the richness of past glories. It nourished a fertile seed long since planted, and he dreamed of someday acquiring collections of his own.

He also found time to feed another of his passions -- motion pictures. He prowled the cinemas and finally settled on a thriller entitled "Bermuda Mystery". Another time he attended a live performance given in a theater for American servicemen. A gentleman took center stage and began to recite passages from the works of William Shakespeare. He waxed eloquent with flowery speech, but his recital was not what the GIs had expected, and before long a chorus of boos and jeers erupted from the gallery. Two or three soldiers got up and left. Their departure prompted others to do the same, and in time the theater was all but half empty. The ever diminishing audience culled a look of distress from the thespian's face, yet he persevered, valiantly struggling to complete his lines. Barkley felt sorry for the man -- he was doing the best he could. Not knowing much about Shakespeare, Barkley supposed he was even doing a great job. Out of simple courtesy, he remained seated for the duration of the performance.

When the final word echoed off the walls, the crestfallen fellow stepped from the stage and filed past the few remaining GIs. As he passed, Barkley rose and tried to comfort the dejected actor.

"It's alright," he offered, "They didn't leave because you were doing a bad job. It's just that Americans don't go much for Shakespeare."

Back at the hospital, Barkley reaped pleasure from another benefit offered convalescing soldiers. Each patient received a ration of two packs of cigarettes per week. Although Barkley smoked in combat, he had more of a sweet tooth than a craving for nicotine and eagerly swapped his cigarettes for the smokers' candy rations. He relished the delicious seven-in-one English candies -- each chocolate segment hid a different flavored creamy center. Some fellows were heavy smokers and consumed as much as two packs of cigarettes a day and were easy marks for barter.

In time, Barkley's personal effects caught up with him. They had been left behind, stored in his barracks bag somewhere at regimental or divisional level. Among them were various souvenirs acquired while in France, including the documents he had confiscated from the French house when he and Joe Guajardo had dodged the mortar shells. He discovered that there was a market for the parchments among the hospital orderlies and he was soon charging them one British pound per document -- a handsome sum. Still, he held back several of the finer ones for himself and chose to send them home.

As before, Barkley's mail was all screwed up. It seemed that no sooner had he gotten it straightened out from when he joined the 2nd Division in France than he was wounded. Now his new address was Detachment of Patients at an APO in England. Once again, it took several weeks before the jam was broken, but in time his mail arrived regularly. Marilyn wrote nearly every day. His pals back in Quincy wrote as well, but not as often has he would have liked. The oddest of all was a package of candy sent by his mother shortly after he had left the States for England. It was postmarked April of 1944 -- four months old. Barkley opened it, expecting the worst and it was. The confectionaries were too stale for even his sweet tooth so he threw them all away.

One letter from his mother set his blood boiling. She wrote how glad she was that he was in the infantry instead of an anti-tank unit. It called for an immediate reply. "Were you kidding when you said you were glad I wasn't in the Anti-Tank for it's more dangerous than what I was in?" he asked sardonically. "I hope I get in the Anti-Tank. Ask Mr. Nixon what a 1st scout does," he retorted, "or ask Mr. Bissel and see what they say." Both neighbors had served in the First World War. Young Barkley seethed at the notion.

By late August his wound had healed sufficiently enough that it would only be a matter of time before the stitches would be removed. While waiting, he learned of a mean-spirited joke that had been played on another soldier. He was a black man who also had been wounded. Through the course of his stay in the hospital it became common knowledge that this Negro soldier was terrified of needles, and this fact became the nucleus of a cruel joke.

Two orderlies decided to pull a prank on the needle-phobic soldier by attaching a long, phony needle to a small fire extinguisher. At first glance it appeared to be some kind of monstrous hypodermic syringe with a needle nearly twelve inches long. Wielding their weapon, the orderlies marched through the ward and halted by the Negro's bed. The ebony face gawked in horror at the sword-like projection.

"It's time to remove your stitches," declared one of the orderlies, "But first we'll have to give you this shot. I'm afraid it's gonna hurt quite a bit."

The black soldier leaped from his bed, eyes bulging with terror as he backed against a wall. "You're not gonna stick me with *that!*" he shrieked. The two orderlies leered maliciously at their victim, delighted at their prank.

When Barkley heard of this he sympathized with the black man. He wasn't overly fond of needles himself.

It was early September and Barkley's stitches had been removed. His exercises were becoming more arduous and demanding. By now he had gained almost complete mobility of his shoulder. He could swing it sideways with ease, but it was still rather stiff whenever he attempted to raise his arm. He was afraid that any abrupt movement would break open the wound. Nonetheless, he knew it would only be a matter of time before he would be re-assigned for duty.

During the first week of the month he was reviewed by his doctor who told him that he was recommending that he be returned to his unit at the front. Barkley's heart plummeted. He knew what was expected of him in combat and protested.

"Sir," he began, "I don't think my arm is strong enough yet. I'm going to have to dig a lot of foxholes when I get back."

"Oh, it's fine," replied the doctor, "It'll get stronger as the days go on."

Easy for you to say, thought Barkley, *I'm the one whose life will be on the line!*

Depressed, Barkley returned to his ward. He felt numb. *I'd better write my folks*, he thought. For some time he had planned to send home his medals and ribbons he had already earned, so placed them in a small packet and sent them airmail. Among them was his latest award -- the Purple Heart Medal for wounds received in action. He had been presented the gold and purple medal during a brief ceremony held in his ward a couple of weeks earlier. After addressing the box, he penned a quick letter. "Today is the last day at this address" was the solemn opening. He closed his message with:

...Expect to hear from me probably anywhere at anytime. It may be a long time before I to get to write again. Will write when possible. Guess where I'm going? HA.

Your Son, H. Barkley

It was September 9, 1944. It had only been little more than a month since he had been wounded. He was, as he had written previously, "going back for seconds."

By September 11th he was gone.

CHAPTER 14

PARIS

Mid-September, 1944 -- Once again Harold Barkley found himself on Omaha Beach. But this time was different. This time there was no sense of urgency with troops wading ashore amidst the residue of battle. No carnage littered the beach. Nor was there the random shelling that greeted him and his friends some three months earlier. This time the beachhead was simply a site for the unloading of men and war materials bound for the front, now hundreds of miles away.

Off shore lay the scuttled ruins of the artificial Mulberry harbors that had been destroyed during the violent storms of June. But even that setback did little to hamper the Allied build-up of men and equipment. Landing craft of every size and description lined the shore to disgorge their cargoes directly onto the coast of France. Even without docks, the beach possessed all the qualities of a bustling seaside port.

Barkley sat on his barracks bag as he waited with a host of others to be transported to a replacement depot somewhere farther inland. Before long, a soldier approached and stopped. "Do you remember me?" he asked.

Barkley studied his features. "Yeah, I remember you." The man had been the sergeant who supervised his barracks back at Fort Meade before he and his buddies were shipped overseas. His sergeant's stripes were conspicuously absent.

The man continued: "So, you're just getting here, too, huh?"

"No," Barkley answered. Then, as if to add weight to his statement he proceeded to unbutton his shirt to expose the ugly purple scar that marred his shoulder. "I'm coming back for seconds." The ex-sergeant paled at the sight.

"What are you doing here?" Barkley inquired as he re-buttoned his shirt. He knew that the man had a cushy job back in the States.

"Oh, I screwed up and went AWOL," he sighed, "They busted me to private and sent me over as an infantry replacement."

"You'll regret that!" Barkley snorted.

The replacement package that Barkley belonged to was loaded onto trucks and driven to a replacement depot located at Etampes, not far from Paris. The "Repple Depple", as the replacement depot was derisively called, was a depressing place where new troops and returning veterans like Barkley were held until they could be posted to their units. To the American soldier it was the Army's cruel version of limbo. There was little to do and life was reduced to pure drudgery and boredom.

However, there were a number of incidents that broke up the monotony. One day, while returning from the mess hall, Barkley noticed a group of about thirty or forty soldiers running in formation at double-time under the supervision of two Military Police sergeants armed with Thompson sub-machine guns. Each of the men in the formation had a large letter "P" stenciled onto the back of his fatigues. They were prisoners, U.S. soldiers that had been court-martialed for committing some heinous act and sentenced for their offenses. They looked miserable.

One of the armed sergeants barked, "Halt!" and as one, the miscreants stomped to a standstill and came rigidly to attention. Not one face veered left or right. All eyes were focused intently to the front.

Barkley reviewed the wretches, aloofly scanning their faces until one caught his eye. He looked vaguely familiar. He could have been mistaken, but the prisoner sure bore a striking resemblance to one of the fellows he had served with in Normandy. He wondered what foul deed these men had committed to wind up serving time in this God forsaken unit. Every man seemed terrified of the guards. No doubt they were all condemned to hard times at hard labor.

As luck would have it, Barkley was fortunate enough to have been at Etampes when a USO troupe passed through. The featured entertainer was none other than the sultry movie star, Marlene Dietrich. Hundreds of soldiers crowded the theater to catch what may well be a once in a lifetime experience.

After a few preliminary acts, Miss Dietrich made her appearance, accompanied by a whirlwind of catcalls and whistles from the rambunctious mob. Barkley had a prime seat, being only four rows from the stage. The music began and Marlene slinked around a piano to center stage where she propped one foot upon a chair to expose a length of black nylon stocking. The audience exploded with lusty roars. Then her husky, sensuous voice swept over them like silk and held them spellbound as she crooned her wartime staple, "Lili Marlene". After her performance, the crowd burst into a hearty cheer which seemed to continue unabated for the duration of her act.

Another diversion from the Repple Depple was a bar situated just across the street from the main gate. Rumor had it that it was operated by the U.S. Army. The joint was always teeming with rowdy GIs who kept a constant flow surging to and fro between the depot's entrance and that of the bar. A broad balcony overshadowed the honky-tonk's doorway. Below it was a mad jumble of jubilant soldiers who elbowed their way to the bar or shared tables with a buddy or two. Raucous, profane language filled the air.

A team of waitresses served the men. Some were not so pretty, but at least they were young and that was more than enough for men who had been deprived of feminine companionship for longer than they cared to admit. It was a boisterous place whose bawdy atmosphere was punctuated by hard language and the stench of spilled liquor.

Although not totally innocent to the taste of alcohol, Barkley didn't care to join them. He simply was not much of a drinker. He recalled how once as a youth he had gotten deathly ill after consuming a bottle of wine while with the carnival. The following morning provided a long, hard lesson, replete with vomiting, headache and the ensuing dry-heaves. He didn't care for an encore. However, he was decidedly bored at the replacement depot and eventually caved in to another soldier's cajoling. They decided to give the place a visit.

They crossed the street and claimed a sidewalk table located below the balcony. After ordering their drinks, they took in the view. Drunken soldiers slouched in corners of the dingy room with their arms draped around the shoulders of plump young ladies who flirted unabashedly with all who cared to notice.

Barkley's companion sipped his cognac then gave him a nudge. "Say, look at that."

Soldiers were queued up in a long line that extended completely out of the door. At first its origin wasn't clear. But then it became all too apparent -- the bar doubled as a brothel. The line of troops stretched into the bar and up a staircase where the men's sexual mores were satisfied in dark, dingy rooms.

"Well I'll be damned!" came Barkley's reply. He was amazed that so many men could willfully seek relief from overworked prostitutes who had been practicing their trade all day long. It sure didn't stir any romantic notions in him. In fact, he found it rather disgusting.

Then a commotion erupted from the balcony. A woman leaned over the railing with impish eyes, giggling as she viewed her audience below. The men looked up, laughing in wonder at her surprised expression. She held her fingers only inches apart and chortled, "Petite! Petite!" and she laughed again. The men below exploded with uproarious howls of delight. By the nature of the men's conversation it became clear that the subject of her amusement was the manhood of a rather fat soldier, one of their buddies.

The robust prostitute rattled off a stream of French, triggering another round of jocularity before slipping back to her sultry den. Delighted men grinned lasciviously and chucked each other in the ribs before shouting up words of encouragement to their corpulent comrade, evoking a fresh wave of guffaws from the bystanders. Barkley and his new friend couldn't help but laugh. What the hell.

But the thought of the fat soldier jostled Barkley's memory, and a vision of Anthony Bartas flashed in his head... *The Major. Happy-go-lucky Major. He and Antonelli always joking and kidding each other and now they are both dead. Fat, jolly "Major" Bartas... He was married. His wife came to Wolters to see him... a widow now. The Major's gone and Antonelli's gone and I don't know where Barrella is or if he's alive and I wonder how the Barracuda is doing and if he's okay...* A cluster of jeering soldiers continued to shout encouragement to their comrade somewhere beyond the balcony's shadow, but Barkley's mood had shifted from amused onlooker to a morose, sullen state as he brooded over the memory of fallen comrades.

After wasting four or five days at the replacement depot, the red tape had again unraveled and Pfc. Barkley and a number of other men heaved their barracks bags into six-by-six trucks and struck out for their respective units.

Unknown to Barkley, they motored not east towards Germany where the enemy awaited the final Allied assault, but west. West, across France and nearly five-hundred miles behind the fighting front was the Brittany Peninsula where the U.S. VIII Corps was battling for the by-passed port city of Brest. The port, with its ample dock facilities, would be a vital asset to alleviate the Allied logistical problems. The 2nd, 8th, and 29th Infantry Divisions had been engaged in a bitter, protracted struggle, comprised of savage house-to-house fighting, street by bullet swept street. After nearly a month of fanatic resistance, the Germans finally capitulated on September 18th. But it was a Pyrrhic victory; the dockyards were completely destroyed, rendered useless for months to come -- too late to overcome the acute supply shortages that hampered the Allies' momentum. Consequently, the swift advance which began with the breakout from St. Lo ground to a halt on the German frontier, impaled on the Dragon's Teeth of the Siegfried Line. The Allies were literally "out of gas".

The truck squealed to a halt and Barkley was dumped out at St. Divy on the Brittany Peninsula where he found his battalion bivouacked in open fields. It had been a pleasant journey, as far as riding in rough-benched army trucks goes, passing miles and miles of green fields and quaint French villages seemingly untouched by war. It was nothing like the devastation he had witnessed in Normandy. *The Germans must have pulled through here in a hurry*, he reckoned. He and others shouldered their barrack bags and paraded to Battalion Headquarters. After processing his papers he was eventually reunited with Company G, now recuperating from the recent battle.

Barkley discovered that the company had suffered heavily after his departure in July. A few familiar faces remained, but there were far more new ones than old. His old friend, Frank Balchunas, the Barracuda, was no longer among them. The few remaining friends sadly disclosed that Frank had been struck down by mortars as the division closed in on the town of Vire back in Normandy. His wound seemed severe.[*] Sergeant Blackmore, who had been wounded

---

[*] After Barkley had been wounded, Company G continued attacking through the hedgerows. By August 14th the company was pressing hard on the town of Vire where Frank Balchunas' platoon had been ordered to hold up. Frank had just begun digging in when enemy mortars began falling all around. Frank dove for cover, but too late. He was struck in the wrist by one piece of shrapnel and two others lodged in his back. Numerous other splinters riddled his backside. Sixty years later his body still evicts slivers of steel. No sooner had he been hit, than First Sergeant Imbody hoisted Frank onto his shoulder and took off for the rear. Frank's head bobbed precariously above a hedgerow as the sergeant ran, and Frank thought for sure a sniper would nail him. But Imbody deposited him safely at the aid station. To this day Frank regards Percy Imbody as "The Man". He remains forever grateful for the sergeant's courage and devotion to his men and accredits him with saving his life. Frank recovered in England where he had a chance meeting with one of his brothers, John, who was in the newly arrived 95th Infantry Division. After surgery, Frank Balchunas, too, was eventually returned to Company G in time to participate

alongside Barkley, was conspicuously absent, as was Sergeant Parker who had been hit a second time, July 29th. Bell was no longer with them -- no one knew exactly what had happened to him, but he was gone, as was the second scout, Hinson, who was hit a day or so after Barkley was wounded.

Joe Benavidez, who had been wounded the day before the squad encountered the tank in the wheat field, was among those returning to the company, as was Barkley's scrounging buddy, Joe Guajardo, who had been wounded the day after Barkley was hit. And Junior Rollings was back, too. Barkley recalled that Rollings had been wounded that fateful day when Lieutenant Pray got shot in the ass and bled to death.

The casualty list went on and on. As it turned out, Company G had suffered horrendously as the division broke out of the hedgerows at St. Lo. Casualties and extreme fatigue reduced the company to a skeleton force. Although replacements were received, more savage battles at the Falaise Pocket followed by the assault on Brest culled out more of the original men. Of the first parcel of replacements who had arrived on Omaha Beach June 9th, virtually all had been either killed or wounded -- and a few of these, like Barkley, had been patched up and recycled to their companies. Barkley was back in Company G. He was home.

The rest at St. Divy was too short for the battle weary men of the 2nd Infantry Division. The gods of war had beckoned and the division mobilized to re-enter the fray in Germany. On September 26th, after only eight days of rest, elements of the division commenced re-deployment to the vaunted Siegfried Line on the German frontier. The war and suffering would continue.

However, a wild rumor began to circulate among the ranks. Scuttlebutt had it -- from a reliable source, of course -- that the 38th Infantry's Second Battalion wouldn't be going to the front. Instead, they were going to be assigned as train guards in Paris. *In Paris! My God, what a dream!* Daily, other battalions were departing for the

---

in the Battle of the Bulge. But that is another story.

front and men only half-heartedly believed the story. Reality tempered their hopes. Why would they receive such a gravy assignment while the remainder of the division goes off to the shooting war? Guarding trains seemed an unlikely chore for a battle hardened infantry battalion. After all, some reasoned, isn't that what the Military Police are for? *Paris? Naw, can't be true.*

But it was true.

The supply routes to the attacking armies were rife with corruption. Thugs and AWOL soldiers working as black marketeers were relieving some supply trains of as much as 95% of their cargoes before they reached the supply dumps at the front. Regular Military Police at the various stations were not prepared for the monumental task of securing all of the trains that departed the marshalling yards of Paris. The trains made frequent stops between Paris and their destinations, and during these halts gangs of black marketeers swarmed the tracks, broke open the cars and stole anything and everything of commercial value. Needless to say, in war torn Europe, everything was in short supply and in great demand. Frontline troops were being denied everything from cigarettes to soap to winter clothing. Something had to be done.

That something came in the concept of pulling an infantry battalion from the line to provide armed guards on every train departing for the front. In theory, veteran infantrymen would understand the needs of fellow infantry. They knew what it was like to live in deprivation and would cut the black marketeers no slack.

Since the VIII Corps had just completed its mission at Brest and was temporarily idle hundreds of miles from the front, it was decided the troops would come from one of its three divisions. So the 2nd, 8th, and 29th Infantry Divisions conducted a series of lotteries to determine which unit would supply the guard battalion and the Second Battalion, 38th Infantry came out on top. What luck! "Paris here we come!"

First week of October, 1944 -- The big army truck careened around a corner and entered a broad avenue that cut through a canyon of aged and majestic buildings. Trees lined the boulevard at well regulated intervals and cast shadows on the citizens who gaily went about their daily business. Jubilant soldiers leaned from the sideboards to take in the sights, grinning broadly at their good fortune. They had actually made it. They were in Paris!

They had arrived by rail shortly after midnight of October 1st, and were trucked in the dark to luxurious billets in an old hotel located somewhere in the city. After a day of settling in, First Sergeant Imbody posted the much anticipated duty roster and now the men in the roaring truck were off to their listed assignments. Some men were under orders to escort supply trains to the front. Others would stand guard over massive stockpiles of stores stacked at the various depots, while the remainder received the best deal of all -- time to themselves in the City of Light until their names appeared on the duty roster. It was a dream come true!

Barkley watched in wide-eyed wonder as the truck rumbled along the avenues and boulevards, taking in the sight of beautiful old buildings and glimpses of life in Paris. The streets were teeming with civilians and he grinned as his fellow soldiers cut loose with wolf-howls and cat calls whenever they caught sight of pretty mademoiselles: "Ooo la, la! Look at that one!" "Comment allez-vous?"

The girls smiled sweetly and waved at the passing soldiers, evoking lewd comments from the olive drab passengers. The young men's exhilaration knew no bounds. It was sunny and bright and the air was fresh and clean. Ah, Paris! *"Oui, oui!"*

The truck stopped at a large rail yard and the men dismounted. Barkley was awed by the station's immensity. Track after track after track lay one aside the other, too many to count it seemed. Ranks of locomotives and seemingly endless lines of cars filled the yard. Steam poured from the engines' stacks and sounds of clanging bells and whistles filled the air. This was exciting!

Barkley was posted in an open boxcar along with several others as part of a small detachment charged with the security of their train. They were told that whenever the train stopped, they were to dismount and range up and down either side of the track, ever vigilant for suspicious activity. They were under strict orders to shoot anyone who did not heed warnings to stay clear of the cars, and shoot to kill!

This was serious business. When a whistle shrilled, they were to remount their assigned cars as the train rolled on to its destination.

Upon completion of their mission, the men were at liberty to catch a ride on the next train returning to Paris. In its wisdom, the Army knew that the guards would return as swiftly as possible, for after all, their home base *was* Paris. Sometimes, if their destination was close enough and the rail traffic moved smoothly, the men could be back before the next morning. At other times it might be two or three days before they returned. For the most part the runs were routine and the duty boring and just the presence of armed guards deterred any pilferage of the cars.

Much to the enlisted men's delight, their billet was a large, old hotel with a view of the Eiffel Tower. It was an elegant old place, once luxurious, and still retained much of its grandeur and charm. Lavish guest rooms served as quarters for the men and they loved it. After months of living in the squalor of muddy foxholes they felt civilized again! Perhaps the only drawback was the toilet facilities -- it was an old hotel that had been constructed before toilet stools came to vogue. Barkley noticed that a porcelain hole in the floor served as their toilet. One had to squat above the chasm in order to defecate. Luckily the GIs had their issue toilet paper, for Barkley noticed, much to his disgust, that the previous occupants of *le grand hotel* must have suffered from a paper shortage. The walls of the bathroom were smeared with dark streaks, evidence that the people had obviously wiped themselves with their fingers, then scraped the excess on the wall in effort to clean their soiled fingers. "And I thought the French were civilized!" he remarked. Thank God there was a wash basin.

The resident chefs were tickled to have the Americans as their guests. Through years of Nazi occupation the citizens of France had been deprived of simple pleasures such as coffee and had been compelled to drink an ersatz concoction brewed from chicory to satisfy their caffeine cravings. The boarding of a battalion of U.S. Army soldiers proved to be a windfall for the Frenchmen. After befriending the Army cooks, they were allowed to take away all of the used coffee grounds after the men had been served. The French cooks took their treasure to the hotel's roof where they spread the wet grounds upon the tiles to dry in the sun. Once dried, the recycled grounds were wrapped in paper packets and sold as fresh coffee on the Black Market. The Parisians were weary of chicory and willfully paid the price. As a consequence, the hotel cooks turned a handsome profit.

By now Pfc. Barkley was considered one of the "regulars" of the company, having survived the grueling battles in the hedgerows of Normandy. As he settled into his new quarters, the Brest veterans entertained him and the others with incidents that occurred during his absence. Although little was said of actual combat, men took great pleasure in relating other episodes that occurred during the battle -- stories laced with the black humor of war.

The soldiers lounged on beds or straddled chairs as they exchanged their varied stories. Barkley discovered that during the battle for Brest, the company had learned early to avoid advancing down the streets of the city. The Germans were crafty adversaries, skilled at defense. Their machine guns ruled the streets, often firing from shelter of curbside sewer openings. The bullets came skittering along at ankle level, dropping men to the pavement where the gunners would finish their job. As a counter-measure, the men learned that the best way to clear a block of buildings was to blast holes through successive walls as they advanced, thereby avoiding the streets. By this method they stymied the enemy's advantage and cleared their objectives one building at a time. It worked well.

At one point, an American tank had blasted a hole through one building with its cannon. After tossing in a few grenades, a platoon charged through the gap only to discover that they were standing on the stage of a theater with the enemy occupying the gallery and lobby before them. The GIs opened fire. The Germans beat a hasty retreat through the lobby only to come under intense machine gun fire from another platoon that covered the front of the theater. Rushing back inside, they were again fired upon by the platoon that had entered via the stage. Again they attempted to escape through the entrance, but it was no good. They were caught between a rock and a hard place, bouncing back and forth between the two American forces that closed like the jaws of a vise and the comic opera came to an abrupt end.

Another fellow related how his platoon had liberated a great store of liquor. The next day, after being told to hold up, they decided to sample their booty and became incredibly drunk. They drank all day and into the following night, having a rip-roaring time. The following morning everyone suffered from the effects. It was only then that they discovered that the Germans had occupied the building across the street and had witnessed the drunken festivities. As luck would have it, the fight was out of them and they quickly surrendered as soon as the neighboring platoon moved up.

Then another fellow interjected with a story of how they had just received a new replacement lieutenant who was appalled by the men's slovenly appearance. He ordered them to clean up and even ordered close order drill in sight of the enemy! A responding barrage put an end to the marching as well as the lieutenant's brief command. He was relieved and reassigned. Such were the incidents that occurred during the Battle for Brest.

Barkley and the others laughed as the Brest veterans recounted their escapades. Then the doorway darkened as a large, raw-boned man leaned against the door jamb and glowered at the men. He stood with arms folded across his chest, revealing a pair of sergeant's chevrons. "Well, what do we have here?" His voice dripped with sarcasm. It was Sergeant Gascon, the assistant squad leader.* Barkley had first encountered Gascon when he returned to the company from the replacement depot. Gascon was one of the original members of the company, an Old Army man who took pleasure in running rough-shod over the younger men. He had been wounded during the division's first action at Trevieres in Normandy and had returned to the company some time after Barkley had been hit outside of St. Lo. Now, in Paris, they met for the first time. Already he didn't like the man.

Unfolding his arms, Gascon swaggered into the room and stopped before one of the new men. "Who the hell are you?" he gruffed. The soldier gave his name. "Well, no shit. My name's Gascon. I'm told that you're assigned to my squad, so I'll tell you this: You'd better get your act together or I'll come down on you

---

* As with Sergeant "Fretwell", I will use the fictitious name of "Gascon" to protect this man's identity.

hard. Do you understand that?" The youngster's eyes widened at the unexpected assault. "Yeah… yeah, I understand," he stammered.

Good Lord! thought Barkley, *just my luck to have this bastard in my squad.* Now he had Fretwell for his squad leader and this blow hard as second in command. Sometimes you just can't win.

While some men served their stints as train guards, others were detailed to stand guard over the various supply dumps situated near the rail yards. One day, while Barkley was standing his post, he was approached by a Frenchman wanting to know what he had to offer. Although there would be severe repercussions for anyone caught dealing with Black Marketeers, Barkley sensed an opportunity for profit. At this stage of the war anything and everything could be bartered for in some manner and Pfc. Barkley saw his chance. Although he didn't have anything of value, he recalled that he had a tin of impervious salve for water-proofing shoes in his pocket. Retrieving the ointment, he opened it to reveal its gelatin-like contents. The Frenchman looked at it inquisitively, not knowing what it was. Since the Frenchman spoke little English, and Barkley spoke even less French, a communications gap ensued. Still, Barkley was determined to make his pitch. He held out one palm and acted as if he were spreading the gel onto a piece of bread. "Mmmm!" He mimicked the act of eating.

Understanding the pantomime, the Frenchman's eyes lit up. "Cent francs! One-hundred francs!" he offered.

Barkley grinned gregariously as his head bobbed up and down. "Oui, oui!"

Delighted, the Frenchman pulled out a wad of banknotes which was exchanged for the waterproofing gel. Barkley, felt a bit ashamed of himself as the Frenchman walked away. *Poor bastard!* he thought, *He thinks he just bought some sort of jelly.*

On another occasion, Barkley was again standing guard when an automobile squealed to a halt before his post. A man stepped from the car and indicated that he needed gasoline and would gladly trade some cognac for it.

Hell, thought Barkley, *I could use some cognac, it's as good as money around here.* He motioned for the Frenchman to wait while he searched for some fuel. Of course, he had no intention giving this fellow the gas, or least not much -- after all, he could be court-martialed for such an offense. Still, he had a plan. After finding an empty jerry can he walked to where the gasoline was stored and bled a little from a number of other cans so that the quantity would not be missed. He didn't intend on taking much, however, and only filled the can about one quarter full, if even that, then located a water spigot and topped off the remainder of the can with water.

The Frenchman grinned deviously when he saw Barkley approaching with the heavy jerry can. After giving quick, sneaky looks to left and right, he opened the car door and extracted a large bottle of cognac. Both men beamed at the prospect of their acquisitions. Barkley grabbed the full bottle and the Frenchman placed the can of "gasoline" inside his car and sped away. Barkley was pleased with his swindling.

Later, Barkley opened the bottle to sample his prize. He took a swig, anticipating its hearty flavor. "Phhht!" A fine mist jetted from his lips. "Why that sonovabitch!" he exclaimed. The Frenchman had given him a bottle of water with only a few ounces of cognac added for flavor. Then Barkley grinned sheepishly at the revelation. *Well, I guess we each got what we bargained for*, he reasoned.

The chief benefit of being stationed in Paris was Paris itself. When not placed on duty rosters, men eagerly applied for passes to explore the wondrous city. They had been paid for the first time in months and now the money burned holes in their pockets. Many had only two goals: to get drunk and get laid. Rumor had it that both could easily be achieved at a legendary district called Pig Alley, or more formally, Place Pigalle.

Pig Alley was a haven for prostitution where men could easily release all their tension and anxiety in a flurry of wanton passion. Dimly lit streets and smoke filled bars created a seedy atmosphere. "Zig-zig, Cheri?" the girls would softly coo from the shadows of alleys and dingy doorways, enticing prospective customers to their sanctuaries where the deal would be consummated. It was a sordid place, a wild place where unruly GIs looked for trouble and found it, often culminating in fistfights which drew a phalanx of MPs. Billy clubs thumped heads. Blood spilled and teeth vacated jaws before the policemen untangled the antagonists and hauled them away. Still, Place Pigalle had its allure, an exotic charm that drew men like moths to a flame -- volatile, exciting, irresistible.

Young Barkley observed his fellow soldiers as they made bold passes at the more prudent mademoiselles of Paris as well, and noted with interest the damsels' fiery outrage at the blatant propositions. It didn't take him long to work out a short poem commemorating his buddies' endeavors. It was entitled "Wrong Question", and went like this:

"Combien franc?"
Said a fellow Yank,
And the girly slapped his face.
He rubbed his jaw,
And with a Southern drawl
Said, "I don't like this place."

Other soldiers resisted Pig Alley's incendiary charm and sought other forms of recreation. One youngster of Company G was Bill Dudas, another product of Camp Wolters, Texas. Bill's family was of French descent and still had kin – the Beauhowers and DuCastles --living in Paris. He promised his parents that he would look them up. He and Walt Popham took the metro to a poor part of town to search for them. Although they never found the Beauhowers, he and Walt were welcomed by the DuCastles and Bill enjoyed several subsequent visits throughout his stay in Paris.

Another teenage warrior was John Savard, who also trained as a replacement at Camp Wolters and Wind Whistle Hill. His father had been a doughboy with the 42nd Division in the First World War and had cautioned his son of the inherent evils of Paris. Nonetheless, the youngster bucked up his courage to attend a couple of burlesque shows at the Folies Bergere and Casino de Paris. It was the first time he had ever seen a naked woman in his life and he was amazed by what he saw.

Like Barkley, both Bill and John had been wounded in Normandy before being reunited with Company G.

There was so much to see in Paris. Barkley never was one for rampant drunkenness and lewd behavior so opted to take in the sights. Since their initial billet was not very far from the Eiffel Tower he found it an easy walk to view its splendor. He saw the palaces of French kings and of Napoleon who succeeded them. He visited the sites of the French Revolution when tumultuous mobs topped the totalitarian rule of Louis XVI. It didn't take much imagination for Barkley to depict scenes from "A Tale of Two Cities", a book he had read in his youth. He sensed a time when rabid revolutionaries infested the streets and blood flowed freely as heads were lopped off by guillotines. The peasantry would roar their satisfaction with each beheading, a gruesome spectacle... Barkley saw it all in his mind. This was history!

Moving on to other sites he marveled at the magnificent Arc de Triomphe, that spectacular gateway constructed by Napoleon to celebrate the victories of his Grand Armee. And, as in London, there were museums. Barkley always enjoyed a good historical museum and Paris did not disappoint him.

He discovered that the best way to navigate around Paris was by the metro, an efficient subway system that linked the entire metropolitan area. In time, Barkley became quite adept at its use, figuring out which station changes were required to get to his destination. He felt like a tourist whose meals and lodging were all pre-paid in advance. For the first time since his induction he was enjoying Army life. Paris was wonderful.

Barkley and his buddy, Joe Guajardo, exited the metro at a Vincennes station and stepped into the sunlight. It was a beautiful fall day with warm blue skies that matched the spirits of the two young soldiers. They strolled along streets filled with a throng of citizens going to and from their errands. Barkley's steps were lively, springing with the vitality of youth. For the first time since joining the 2nd Infantry Division his jacket bore the bold Indianhead patch upon its shoulder. He was justifiably proud of it -- it was *his* outfit; in his opinion, there wasn't any other that could match it.

As they walked, children tugged at their trouser legs and held out their palms. "Chocolate?" they pleaded, "Cigarette?" A particularly forlorn urchin looked up with haunting eyes and they had no recourse but to offer a coveted Hershey bar. The waif regarded it briefly, then snatched it away before scampering through the crowd. The buddies looked at each other and shrugged nonchalantly, as if to say, "What the hell, they've had it rough with the Nazi occupation."

Not far from the station was a small café wedged amidst a row of stores and other businesses. "Café Tabbac" read the sign above its entrance. The two soldiers ducked inside. It was a quaint place, simple with a few chairs and tables placed closely across the floor. They ordered something to drink and relaxed in the friendly atmosphere. Then Barkley noticed a girl sitting with another at a nearby table. She appeared to be about his age and he was taken by her charm and manner. She glanced up and offered a smile.

Barkley nudged Joe and indicated their presence. Soon, the two GIs were awkwardly trying to communicate with the pair, thumbing clumsily through an English-French dictionary to chose their words as they tripped over the intricate nuances of the strange language. In frustration, Joe blurted a Spanish oath and one of the girls came alive with a stream of the same. It just so happened that the girl spoke Spanish as well as her native French. Joe was amazed and the foursome now had a means of communication with Joe and the Spanish-speaking girl acting as interpreters for Barkley and the other.

Their names were Elaine and Paulette. Elaine, being the Spanish speaking girl, took an immediate liking to Joe, while Barkley seemed to get alone famously with Paulette. In time they were engaged in lively conversation with much laughter and life was very good. They learned that both girls were in their teens and lived in the immediate vicinity. Before leaving, Barkley and Joe had asked the girls to meet them again and they agreed to rendezvous at the very same place at a time in the near future.

As they departed, Barkley turned to memorize the name of the place: CAFÉ TABBAC. He'd remember that. It wasn't far from the metro station and would be easy to find. The two soldiers strolled away, grinning at their good fortune. Little did Barkley know that "Café Tabbac" was a general declaration placed above many shops indicating that it was a coffee house as well as a tobacco shop. But for Barkley it would always remain "Café Tabbac", a place unto itself, the scene of a pleasant afternoon encounter.

Barkley gazed out the boxcar door as the train rattled past the picturesque French landscape. He had again drawn duty on a supply train which now snaked towards its destination somewhere near the front. The train swayed lazily as it negotiated a curve, or lurched and jolted as it increased or decreased its speed, but for the most part the motion was monotonous, a subtle statement on the duty itself.

A daydream played through Barkley's mind and he smiled inwardly as he recalled his and Joe's encounter with the girls in Vincennes, allowing the warmth of the moment to seep through his flesh and nourish his soul. It was a pleasant memory. The other guards chatted among themselves, bored, and smoked cigarettes to while away the time. There wasn't much else to do while the train was in motion. A Belgian conductor shared the car with them and listened intently to their bantering, smiling obligingly whenever he picked up on an American phrase he recognized. He wore the blue uniform common to his trade, now frayed with age but kept in some semblance of repair.

Heavy wheels sang a high-pitched song as they glided along the rails and clattered in metered time as they passed over each rail joint and the gentle swaying of the boxcar all but lulled the men to sleep. A chill breeze whistled through the car, a reminder that colder weather was close at hand.

Bored, one of the men grinned mischievously, the impish smirk of a schoolboy who had just been struck by a devilish thought. He held up a shiny brass cartridge. "A-P! A-P!" he hollered above the incessant rattling, indicating that the round was an armor piercing bullet.

Barkley and the others gathered round him, curious as to what he was about to do. The soldier emitted a roguish leer as he chambered the cartridge into his rifle and declared that he was going to have some fun by shooting armor piercing bullets at the rails. He then leaned out of the boxcar and took aim at a length of parallel track. The others craned their necks to watch while the Belgian, who longed to be part of the gang, leaned farthest from the open door to witness the game.

K-Pow-Zing! Splat!

The Belgian's head shot back as the bullet ricocheted off the rail and tore through his jaws. He staggered a step or two, spewing a gout of blood. His face was frozen in shock as blood dripped from crimson lips.

"Jesus Christ!' cried Barkley.

"Oh, C-Christ," stammered another, "We'll be c-court-martialed for sure."

The perpetrator blanched white. Everybody felt bad about it. The GIs eased the conductor to the floor, offering a flood of apologies and did everything in their power to alleviate his suffering. The bullet had pierced one cheek and exited through the other, taking a few teeth with it. Miraculously, no other damage had been done. Still, it could have been a disaster -- the poor fellow could have been killed.

One fellow applied a field dressing from the first aid pouch attached to his belt, but other than that, there was little they could do. Fortunately they weren't too far from a station and when the train stopped, the stricken man was carried off the train to be sent to the nearest medical unit. All the while, the concerned guards tried to explain what had happened. Surprisingly, the Belgian was very supportive of the shaken GIs and bore no hard feelings towards them. He even upheld their allegations.

Although the men involved worried about the incident for days, no charges were ever brought against them.

One day a ripple of excitement swept the hotel. A flustered soldier approached Barkley and blurted, "You hear about Popham?"

"No. What?" Barkley had befriended Walter Popham in Normandy after discovering that he, too, was a scout in another squad of his platoon.

"He fell asleep and accidentally killed himself. Shot himself in the belly."

The words struck Barkley like a sledge. The story was that Popham, weary with fatigue, had slumped over his tommy gun while on a train and inadvertently triggered the weapon. Several bullets ripped into his abdomen. Barkley felt a sense of loss. There was a strong bond between the two soldiers by rite of sharing the unique position of scout. They both knew the dangers each faced while in combat. It just didn't seem fair. How could a man make it through so much hell only to be killed by accident just because he was tired? It just wasn't fair.[*]

Guard details took up most of Barkley's time and long days were spent riding the rails or standing under arms over stores. No one attempted to shoot at the rails anymore and the matter of the Belgian was best left unmentioned. Strict adherence to duty was the order of the day. No use tempting trouble. They were damned lucky not to be in the stockade busting rocks.

When the opportunity arose, Joe and Barkley made their way to Café Tabbac in Vincennes, hoping to find Paulette and Elaine. They were not disappointed -- the two mademoiselles were perched on the edges of their chairs, preoccupied with chit chat until one noticed the two and gaily waved them over.

Joe and Elaine continued to interpret for Barkley and Paulette whenever they stumbled over their rudimentary knowledge of each others' language. At times Barkley attempted to speak French with the aid of his dictionary, thumbing through the pages before stumbling over the difficult phrases as Paulette giggled at his horrid pronunciation. Again Joe and Elaine came to his rescue and tutored him in diction while Paulette waited patiently for the words. In time all were quivering with mirthful laughter as Barkley murdered another sentence and finally gave up, opting to write the words on a notepad. He looked at Paulette with a bashful grin and received an endearing smile in return -- a smile to match the warmth of sunlight that filtered through the window panes.

---

[*] In reality, Popham had not been killed. That was only a rumor. What had happened was that Walter did trigger his weapon, but a bullet drilled a hole in his buttocks, not his gut. He was evacuated and treated and eventually returned to duty at a later date. But as far as Barkley knew, his friend had become another casualty of war, killed in the line of duty. He never knew the truth until fifty years later.

PARIS

They were in Paris and the war was far away. Barkley and Joe had found themselves wartime sweethearts and life was good.

The following day Barkley began a letter home, expounding the merits of duty in gay Paree. "Paris is a alright place and is 20 times better than London or any place in England," he commented. "Yesterday Elaine, Paulette and I went to the Eiffel Tower, Paris Opera and took the metro (subway) all around Paris." He was having a good time.

As often was the case, he lodged his usual complaint: "I hope I begin to get some mail from home soon as there isn't much to write unless I get some mail to get some questions to answer." Since his return to the company, the Army Postal Service had his mail all screwed up again.

The night was pitch-black. The rail yard was illuminated at measured intervals by parallel rows of towering lamps that cast cones of light onto silvery tracks. Beneath the garish light the myriad of rails appeared like bands of silvery ribbons that faded into the shadows long before the opposite rank of lights picked them up to again wash them in soft, flared beams. Long columns of freight cars crowded the peripheral tracks, waiting their turn to be coupled to other cars which would form the embryonic stage of another supply train destined for the supply dumps, far, far away. Armed guards paced up and down the rail yard, alert for black marketeers, or perhaps Nazi saboteurs who might attempt to wreak whatever havoc they may bestow. The guards were all business with orders to shoot to kill.

Barkley and Joe and another soldier lurked in the shadows at the edge of the yard, wary of the guards who walked their beat. One by one, each prowler slipped between the darkened boxcars. A shiver of excitement shot up Barkley's spine as he sprinted from one car to the next. They were playing a dangerous game. They were searching for one train in particular, a captured German train that supposedly was filled with contraband goods, merchandise and personal things stolen from the French during the Nazi occupation. Allegedly the

229

train was being spirited out of the country when it was captured by the Allies and sidetracked here at the Paris yards.

The stranger who accompanied Barkley and Joe had told them that one of the cars was filled with furs and he hoped to swipe some for his girlfriend. After considerable scheming, the trio decided to heist some of the furs themselves. Like their new accomplice, Joe and Barkley knew they would make a very welcome gift for their girlfriends in Vincennes. Such luxuries were all but non-existent in wartime Paris. The girls' families would be able to make fur-lined winter clothing from whatever they brought them.

They reasoned it was not like they were stealing military items for resale on the black market. These were furs stolen from the people of France by the Nazis, therefore they were merely liberating them and returning them to their rightful owners, so to speak. Besides, they truly believed much of it would be confiscated by high ranking officers anyway. It all seemed justifiable at the time.

So now they crept in the cool, damp night, keeping to the shadows as they closed on their prey. It was like a game, in a way, much easier than the combat patrols to which they were accustomed. By avoiding the crisp edges of light cast from the towering rail lamps, they easily avoided detection.

Finally they arrived at their target train, sitting silently on a dark side track. Barkley and Joe acted as lookouts while the other broke open the car and slid the door aside. They were not disappointed. The car was stuffed with what appeared to be rabbit pelts strapped together in large bundles. The men excitedly helped themselves to one bundle each and stole away into the night. It was a highly successful operation.

Throughout the night the three men stalked the dark streets and alleys until each arrived at his destination. When the ladies of Paulette's home saw the bundle of furs their eyes lit up like Christmas trees. They jabbered excitedly and showered Barkley with kisses and praise. To Barkley it was very satisfying to see them so happy and believed it well worth the risk.

Although Barkley enjoyed whatever time he had with Paulette, he was a free spirit. He belonged to no one and no one belonged to him. By chance he had met another girl, a young lady whose charm and wit had taken him by storm. She also lived in the Parisian suburb of Vincennes, residing in a large manor house with her parents and sisters. Her father was a man of some influence, being the Governor-General of Corsica. Her name was Catherine Orlandetti.

When invited to their house, Catherine's mother would offer Barkley cognac or wine, but he would always politely decline the alcoholic beverages in favor of lemonade. The house was magnificent. Before the occupation the family had obviously lived in opulence. Catherine and her sister, Audree, were accustomed to graceful living and carefree play which included mutual competitions in tennis as well as going to the stables to mount their favorite horses. Being in her teens, Catherine attended classes at a school reserved for the more prosperous citizens of Paris. Her sister taught elsewhere at an academy.

Whenever Barkley got the chance, he'd pay them a visit. Catherine was wonderful. She spoke English fluently, which greatly eased the communications problem, but she also took an interest in educating young Barkley in the nuances of the French language. She displayed much patience while administering to his linguistic education, being tolerant of his errors while encouraging him to try the difficult pronunciations again until he got them reasonably right.

Just being with Catherine was a joy in itself. They'd go for long walks through the parks of Paris where swans glided gracefully upon mirrored ponds, and beautiful trees and shrubberies graced the landscape. In the evenings they'd sometimes take the metro to central Paris where they'd catch a movie at the cinema. Although the dialogue was in French, Catherine proved to be a most able translator. She'd take him to the Paris Opera or perhaps view some other famous attraction. At other times they'd simply sit in the parlor and talk. For whatever reason, the entire family seemed charmed by the shy young soldier and the sisters all but fawned over him. For Barkley the experience was intoxicating. He could hardly believe his good fortune.

In unison the men of Company G moaned. They had just been told that they were to conduct daily sessions of close order drill in preparation for an Armistice Day parade through downtown Paris. It had been a long time since any of them had been subjected to such nonsense and none regarded the order with any enthusiasm. Still, orders were orders and men were forced to spiff up their uniforms, shine their boots and fall in for hours of dull, mindless drill. A nearby park served as a parade ground.

During one drill session, Barkley was suffering from a rare encounter with too much wine the previous evening. Every time the platoon sergeant barked an order, Barkley was half a step behind the others. His head throbbed. He felt as if he'd puke.

"To the rear…MARCH!"

The ranks spun abruptly on left heels and stepped off in the opposite direction. All but Barkley. Numbed by his hangover, he failed to comply with the order and crashed chest to chest with the man who had only a moment ago been marching smartly in front of him.

"HALT!" The sergeant's voice was steeped in rage. "Barkley! What the hell do you think you're doing!"

"Sorry, Sarge. My head hurts so much I can't think straight."

The sergeant looked Barkley up and down, then turned away, saying, "Get the hell back to the hotel. You're useless today."

As it turned out, events proved that the battalion would not participate in the parade after all. The Army had other plans for them.

The pleasant duty of guarding trains was coming to an end. The pilferage of supply trains had been reduced to nil and the battalion was soon to be relieved. As a consequence, the entire battalion was assembled in a large auditorium to be briefed on their next assignment. A colonel stepped to a podium and addressed the men. He told them they had done a superb job safekeeping the front-bound supplies and even read a commendation awarded the battalion for their professionalism while undertaking what he called a difficult task.

Then he got to the meat of the assemblage. He told them they were rejoining the 2nd Division on the fighting front. The vacation was over. "Men," he trumpeted, "Half of you sitting here today will probably not make it back. We're going to crack the Siegfried Line!"

You could have heard a pin drop.

After the shock wore off, Barkley nudged Joe Guajardo who occupied the seat next to his. He nodded towards the other half of the battalion seated across a central aisle, then quipped, "I wonder which half he was talking about?"

Joe laughed, but the gallows humor did not escape him.

CHAPTER 15

SIEGFRIED LINE

November 10, 1944, Montparnasse rail yard, Paris -- The company queued up trackside and awaited orders to board the train that would take them far from Paris. Barkley held his place among his squad mates and, as was practice in the Army, stood and did nothing as one minute crawled into the next and time dragged interminably slow. The entire battalion was present, standing restlessly beneath a pleasant sun, destined for a reunion with the rest of the division and the shooting war on the Siegfried Line and no one was in much of a hurry to rush that unhappy event. Then a whistle shrieked and sergeants barked and the lines began to move.

Some men grumbled and swore beneath their breath as they were herded like cattle into boxcars while others joked and indulged in light-hearted antics, acting more like children boarding a bus for summer camp than soldiers bound for war. Every man carried the panoply of gear associated with the combat infantryman and one man's equipment tangled with the next man's pack, and rifles banged irksomely against another's helmet as they jockeyed for foot space within the confines of the musty car, just as their fathers had been crammed into the "40 and 8" cars of First World War fame.[*] After pushing and shoving one another to accommodate a few more soldiers they were finally allowed to settle down and try to find a place to sit or lay upon a floor littered with an assortment of military equipment.

Then a whistle wailed and the powerful locomotive emitted a superfluous *Whoosh* as pressure was released from steam lines. Cars bumped and jostled one another as they lurched forward, resisting the engine's inescapable pull as if they, too, were reluctant to make this journey.

Again the whistle shrilled, and as if that was a prearranged signal the festive atmosphere dissipated and the men found themselves packed in the stifling confines of the box car and now everyone seemed ill-humored. Men grew surly. Tempers flared. If one fellow encroached into another's space a sharp exchange of foul language ensued before ruffled feathers were smoothed and bruised pride restored. The specter of battle lay before them and worked on their minds, gnawing at their inner fears as they dwelled on the coming fight. *"Half of you sitting here today will probably not make it back,"* the colonel had prophesied. The words echoed in their ears and promised insufferable hardships and a lifetime of nightmares.

The train worked its way out of Paris, then steamed east, across France and into Belgium where the terrain gradually changed from pastoral elegance to rugged hills and thick fir forests. The weather grew progressively colder as the train wended through drab scenery made even more bleak by overcast skies, asserting that the good times were indeed over. No more Pig Alley. No more wine, women and song. Farewell to sweethearts and lovers. Good-bye to all that.

---

[*] Forty-and-eight – forty men, eight horses.

November 13, 1944, Early morning -- A leaden sky posed the threat of snow as the train wheezed to a halt at a dreary little station at the edge of a town called Bastogne. The men disembarked into a gloomy morning chill and looked at the dingy town with disgust. It seemed dull and lifeless after Paris. A couple of citizens stared somberly at the GIs who stared back and sized them up, regarding them as being coarse and backward compared to the lively Parisians.

Companies were formed and the men shuffled off the platform only to be crowded into waiting six-by-six trucks which took them north and the men became aware that a chilling mist was falling and the roads became slick. An icy breeze whipped through the trucks and the men shivered as they gazed morosely at the dismal scene and scowled at the sight of snow and cold, glutinous mud.

Mud. The same mud that would squish into the seams of their boots and soil their clothing. The same mud that would clog every pore of their skin and mat their hair. The same mud that would form the floors of their foxholes and become their dank, clammy beds. It would permeate everything they owned and even their rations would seem to take on the unique texture and taste of mud. It would cling to their boots in ugly clumps, making each step heavier than the last until one felt as if he couldn't muster the strength to carry on. Mud would clog the mechanisms of their weapons, requiring tedious hours of maintenance to ensure they would operate properly when the time came to kill again. Mud -- the foot soldiers constant companion. How they hated mud!

The motor column rolled on. Dark forests covered the nearest hills, appearing thick and impenetrable. It seemed as if the slate gray sky had absorbed all the colors from the landscape and left it as faded and bare as the first wash of an unfinished painting. After a few hours the convoy passed through the town of St. Vith, then drove on for a short while longer before skidding to a halt in a tiny hamlet called Born. The men tumbled stiffly from the tailgates, aching from the cold ride, and were formed up and marched to houses where they were billeted to await their turn on the front line.

The Second Battalion had been divided between the Belgian towns of Born and Medill which were regimental reserve areas located only a few miles north of St. Vith. About eight miles to the east lay the German frontier and the battle front where the bulk of the 2nd Infantry Division had been deployed since early October. Their assigned sector was known throughout First Army as the "Ghost Front", a quiet front in the rugged Ardennes Forest which was much less active than other sectors of the Siegfried Line to the north and south. Battered divisions were sent here to recuperate after prolonged periods of bitter combat in order to re-group, absorb replacements and receive a much needed rest. The 2nd Division had been constantly employed in combat since coming ashore on June 7th, earning a reputation as a top notch fighting unit after excelling in tough assignments in Normandy and at Brest and was due for a break. Not that the Ardennes wasn't dangerous, for anytime men faced enemy guns they were in danger, but the chances of getting killed or wounded here were much slimmer than at the active fronts where offensive operations were being undertaken. This was a defensive sector and the chief dangers lay in the incessant patrolling or reception of incoming artillery fire.

A brand new division, the 99th, was also assigned to this quiet front to undergo its combat shakedown. Here they would become accustomed to working in battlefield conditions while experiencing actual enemy fire, "bleeding" their green troops so they would be able to stand the test of more arduous combat later on a "hot" front. These men who wore the Checkerboard shoulder patch were entrenched to the north of the veteran 2nd Division. In all, four divisions were deployed along the "Ghost Front". Each division held a broad front that stretched their lines thinly over the eighty mile width of the Ardennes Forest -- lines far too thin to repulse a determined enemy attack. But that wasn't expected to happen. The German forces opposing them were weak and seldom launched any sort of attack on this front, and if so, only of a probing or harassing nature. They just didn't have the resources to sustain anything more vigorous. The Ardennes Front was considered a "rest camp", a rehabilitation center for worn out units as well as a training camp for new ones.

November 16, 1944 -- The men of Company G assembled in a cold morning fog and loaded into trucks which joined an eastbound convoy of other Second Battalion troops. They had stayed at Born for only a couple of days while battalion and company officers were briefed on the situation and reconnoitered their assigned positions before being ordered to relieve the First Battalion somewhere on the Siegfried Line. The trucks rumbled over winding roads that twisted between tree-capped hills whose thick coniferous branches muffled the engines' roar. After an hour and a half they squealed to a halt in the middle of seemingly nowhere. The men bailed out and shouldered their weapons and formed long lines of platoons that marched silently up a tree-studded hill toward the fighting front. The faint rumbling of artillery echoed beyond the trees, a distant, hollow complaint. They were in Germany -- the Monster's lair.

November 19, 1944 -- Barkley sat in his foxhole and considered his new environs. The company occupied prepared positions on a forested ridge that overlooked a broad, rolling plain. They hadn't moved since their arrival two days earlier. The position had been previously occupied by Company B which had fortified and improved the defenses on the heights over the past month or so. Their foxholes and dug outs were well constructed and reinforced by log roofs piled high with mounds of earth and were all but impervious to shrapnel, excepting, of course, a direct hit. Deeper to the rear, squad huts had been constructed and life was relatively comfortable for a fighting front. It was a good position.

Below them stretched the Siegfried Line -- Hitler's vaunted West Wall. It was ominous. It was studded with camouflaged concrete pillboxes and gun emplacements, all perfectly situated to offer mutual support if attacked. Barbed wire entanglements bristled across the front and land mines of every type were known to be strewn generously throughout the area, placed in such a manner as to channel attacks into flat naked killing zones, devoid of any cover where carefully sighted weapons could create devastating fields of fire.

But most striking of all was the dragon's teeth. These wedge shaped concrete anti-tank obstacles snaked across the entire front in an unbroken chain. They were awesome, lined up in thick waist-high ranks, appearing as blunt saw-toothed barriers four rows deep that meandered endlessly along the German frontier. They were sinister symbols of the German peoples' tenacity, their determination to defend The Fatherland to the death, to stop the invaders at the very threshold of the Reich and slam the door in their faces. Behind the rows of dragon's teeth, barbed wire, mines and pillboxes sat a small town -- Brandscheid. Barkley didn't know its name, he only knew that it was on German soil and would be stubbornly defended if attacked.

There had already been excitement in the area. A patrol had ventured forth early on their first morning on line and had captured a prisoner. And random mortar fire had fallen in the area all day, wounding two men, one seriously -- reminding the others that although this was a quiet front, it was still a shooting war and men got killed and injured. Although mortar and artillery fire was generally sparse and caused little harm, incoming rounds of various calibers and quantities would continue to fall throughout their stay on the Siegfried Line. They weren't heavy concentrations, nothing like the sustained bombardments experienced in France, but it wasn't wise to stray too far from one's hole as harassing fire could drop in at any time. Men remained in or near their shelters, ready to drop into them at the slightest provocation. They also took precautions to avoid being observed while moving in the open, for the Germans manning the distant pillboxes would periodically open fire at anyone exposing himself in daylight. It was a quiet front alright, but it wasn't safe and memories of the good life in Paris slipped away as if only a dream.

In the following days life boiled down to a measured routine of guard duties and patrols. A series of log covered foxholes ringed the perimeter, giving the sentinels protection from enemy shell fire as they guarded the position. Other men were rotated to the more remote outposts located farther down the slope. Exposed to enemy observation, these men were to keep their eyes and ears open and report by radio any unusual activity. They'd call in sightings of enemy movements, be it vehicular or merely an individual stepping from a bunker, and call in the co-ordinates so Captain Skaggs could call down artillery or mortars upon it. Even sightings of smoke became suspect and drew fire missions. At night the lightly manned outposts were pulled back closer to the main line where they maintained their vigil against German patrols that sometimes probed the lines.

American patrols were conducted around the clock, regardless of weather. Barkley often found himself on small patrols of three or four men that probed the German lines to discover any changes in the enemy's disposition. He no longer carried the Thompson sub-machine gun as it was a short range weapon and would be no good in the open country of Germany. Instead, he now packed the M-1 rifle which offered greater range and increased accuracy.

The patrol missions varied. Sometimes they'd lay in ambush and try to capture an enemy soldier who, hopefully, would spill his guts to the intelligence boys at headquarters. Such information helped to determine what type of units opposed them and hint of their quality. Contact patrols ranged out across the wide gaps that existed between adjacent units, prowling over wooded ridges and through brushy ravines as they searched for signs of enemy infiltration. On a rare occasion they'd have the hair-raising experience of encountering a German patrol. Then gunshots shattered the serenity of the forest, compelling men to hit the dirt and scurry along ravines, desperately seeking cover as bullets whistled past. A brief exchange of gunfire usually settled the matter and the weaker of the two forces would withdraw to the safety of their own lines as parting shots echoed off the hills. Once a patrol was compromised, it was imperative to pull back quickly before enemy mortars hit them or a larger force was dispatched to take them prisoner.

Occasionally Barkley would come across fresh tangles of barbed wire or recently placed mines. The patrol leader would note their location and report them upon their return. They had been told that the Germans sometimes attached land mines to trees which would be detonated by trip wires, so Barkley was constantly alert for taught strung lines. While moving to or from a patrol destination he kept a keen eye for German ambushes or outposts, too, for an oversight on his part could lead to the death or capture of the entire patrol.

But detecting hidden enemies was not an easy thing. One day the Germans had slipped a machine gun into a camouflaged position and opened fire as Barkley's patrol stepped into its sights. The lightly armed patrol was compelled to fall back to their own lines where they reported the gun's location. But Barkley thought this was nearly useless information since the gun was obviously in a temporary ambush sight and would surely pull out before countermeasures were taken. Nonetheless, mortar fire would usually be called upon the coordinates after such incidents to dissuade any further actions.

On another occasion, a patrol led by Sergeant Gascon had stopped in a tree line to take a breather. They crouched beneath the branches and waited, keeping a sharp eye for enemy activity. Barkley had developed a painful cramp in his leg and it began to knot up. Just as he stretched out the afflicted limb to ease the pain Sergeant Gascon drove him to the ground with a forceful thump to his back. "Don't you *ever* move when we're halted," he hissed.

Barkley was furious -- it was only a slight motion. "I had a cramp in my leg," he explained. Gascon only glowered at the response. *You sonovabitch*! thought Barkley, *I've got enough sense not to foul up a patrol*... Pushing him down like that created more commotion than any stretching of his leg. He already hated Gascon. He was sick of his blowhard stories and his overbearing presence where he ran rough-shod over the newer men and reveled in his lies about his lavish lifestyle before entering the army. But Gascon was now the assistant squad leader, being subordinate to Sergeant Fretwell, whom Barkley also disliked. He longed for leaders like Blackmore and Parker, but they were no longer with them, or at least not in his squad. Now he had to put up with all this crap from Gascon who he already determined would probably be next to useless in combat. He, like Fretwell in Normandy, always sent Barkley or one of the others forward if there were any chances to be taken.

Night patrols seemed more successful. Under cover of darkness, Barkley patrolled up to and through the great concrete dragon's teeth that guarded the open plain, finding them good cover

from observation. At times he crawled up to rows of barbed wire and
slithered beneath them, tearing his clothing and slicing his hands and
arms on the sharp tines. Once in enemy territory they'd lay in
concealed positions and watch for any movement and listen for
voices or gunfire, recording their locations before slinking silently
back to their own lines. A sense of fear and foreboding accompanied
every patrol and it was always a relief to return to friendly lines.

Each patrol seemed plagued by consistently foul weather, too.
Dense fogs shrouded trees and sunk thickly into deep ravines,
concealing objects near and far. Demons lurked in the gloom. And
there was always mud -- cold, viscid mud that clawed at their boots
like gummy fingers intent on dragging them down. Struggling
through the cold muck was tiresome and wore Barkley out.

And then it would snow as it was prone to do in the Schnee
Eifel, the Snow Mountains. Then the patrols navigated through
hushed, snow laced forests, boots crunching audibly in the crusty
snow, offering advanced notice to any enemies within earshot. Men
lost their footing on slippery banks and skidded heavily down the
slopes, arms flailing as they tried to snag bushes or branches to arrest
their fall. At times they crossed half frozen creek beds and plunged
through the icy slush, hoping that it would not seep over their boot
tops or penetrate the leather before they reached the opposite bank.
They were always chilled to the bone when they returned to their own
lines and could hardly wait to exchange their wet socks for dry ones.

Time and again Barkley found himself called for such patrols,
always taking the point as a scout was supposed to do, gambling on
experience and good fortune to see him through. But for the most
part, the patrols were without enemy contact and became tedious,
tiring affairs.

Back on the ridge, Barkley adjusted to the monotonous life on
a defensive front. Since moving around in daylight drew enemy fire
he learned to remain in his foxhole or dugout to pass boring hours of
nothingness. If in a dugout, Barkley would often shoot the breeze
with his buddies, reliving experiences shared in Paris, but even that,
in time, grew to the point of redundancy. He could write letters to
while the time away, but really didn't have much to say since

incoming mail was slow and he had nothing to respond to. He always feared that if he wrote anything about the front the censors would blot it out anyway and might even return the letter for re-writing. Paper was too scarce to waste. So, in the end, boredom prevailed and men were engulfed by brooding silence… and time stood still.

The shriek of incoming artillery violated the solitude and the earth shuddered as a few shells slammed into the company area. Concussion pressed on ear drums as particles of earth sifted through the log roofs, but the men were well protected and the shelling did no appreciable harm. Usually it was only harassing fire, yet at times the company received sporadic mortar fire all day long as shells dropped here and there among the foxholes and dugouts, forcing men deeper into their holes where they'd judge each shell's caliber and distance as they calculated their chances of receiving a direct hit.

On other occasions the Germans in the pillboxes below seemed to get a wild hair and sprayed the area with long range machine gun fire, just to let the Yanks know that a war was still on and they were watching. The American response was often a hail of retaliatory mortar or artillery fire called by the captain who was determined to let the Germans know that the 2nd Division held the upper hand and artillery was trump.

When darkness came, it came quickly, and the night was filled with all the uncertainties and anxieties born of unforgiving blackness. The boogey-man of childhood dreams again became reality. The forward outposts withdrew to the perimeter where guards remained alert and prayed for a quiet night. Patrols slipped silently through the lines and disappeared into the gloom, hoping that their night, too, would be uneventful. Bleary-eyed guards kept vigil while the remainder of the company nested in dugouts or curled up in foxholes cushioned by beds of soft pine needles and tried to get some sleep. Frigid air seeped into their holes and wrapped icy fingers about their necks, as if Death itself was tucking them in, counting his wards and ensuring each was present and intact. Breath escaped in vaporous trails.

Their sleep was often interrupted by a few rounds of mortar fire that flashed brightly and set hearts thumping and sometimes tracer bullets darted across the black abyss as German gunners cut loose from the pillboxes far below. Occasionally German patrols probed the lines until challenged by out guards, and when the countersign was not given the guards tossed grenades at them and sometimes received a quick burst of burp gun fire before the enemy vanished in the fog. Again startled soldiers sprung awake and remained alert until they were certain that the intruders had gone away and would bother them no more. But their rest had been disturbed and it would take time before unsettled nerves were quelled and they resumed fitful sleep. Again black frost claimed the night until another round or two of mortar fire jerked them from their slumber.

Varied colored signal flares sizzled across the heavens and outposts would report the incident to the weary men manning the night shift at the command post because the flares were believed to control the movements of enemy patrols. As a consequence, other tired, worn-out men were sometimes roused from their holes to check it out, cursing and muttering beneath their breath as they abandoned their blankets and grabbed their rifles and stepped into the cheerless night. They were tired and cold and only wanted to go back to sleep. And so the night passed on the "Ghost Front" where the men felt blessed not to be making the promised assault on the Siegfried Line. For this was a quiet front -- a piece of cake.

Morning came and men stirred and pulled blankets from their heads before peeking at the frosty scene outside their holes and burrows. If they were lucky hot food would be waiting for them, brought up to the line by the company cooks who had spent the wee hours preparing a breakfast for their battlefront comrades. It was the highlight of the day. Barkley, like the others, appreciated the cooks' efforts and was grateful to receive whatever they had prepared. It was always pretty good fare, served from steaming pans that were set up in the shelter of the woods a short distance to the rear. A few men at a time were allowed to leave their positions to receive their food, then return to their holes while others trailed back for their share. If possible, hot meals were provided every day for the company. But if the company was being shelled the hot chow would have to wait and the men would rummage through their packs for their staple diet -- K rations.

Yet, even a simple chore such as eating could prove fatal. One day Barkley's squad had assembled before the cooks' steaming pans when one of the fellows dropped his mess kit. Everyone jumped as it clattered noisily to the ground.

"Watch what the hell yer doin'!" came a gruff reproach. Tense moments passed as eyes rolled skyward while ears attuned to the forest ceiling, hoping against hope that the Germans had failed to hear the clash of metal on frozen earth from across the vale. But it was too late. Within minutes mortar shells began slamming all around, snapping tree tops and spraying shrapnel in every direction. Fortunately no one was hit. But still, it could have resulted in disaster and the poor soul who dropped his kit was held in contempt for the duration of the day. And every time afterwards, whenever someone rattled his mess kit, Barkley became extremely agitated. "Goddammit! Watch what the hell you're doing!"

Mornings were cold and damp and often shrouded with fog, creating a spooky atmosphere where trees appeared as vague shadows that loomed in the swirling mist. Sometimes a dusting of snow covered the ground and the forest appeared as a story book picture with powdered sugar coated boughs until the temperature rose sufficiently to melt the snow and then all was brown and muddy again in a world without sunshine where every day was dank and cold.

Winter was fast approaching. Although Barkley wore a woolen overcoat, the wet chill penetrated to his bones -- it was difficult to keep warm when living day to day in a hole in the ground. He had already burned the few letters he received to warm his hands and feet, feeding them page by precious page to a tiny fire built on the floor of his shelter. As in Normandy, he wasn't able to change clothes while on the front nor did he expect to. Dry socks remained a luxury. They had been warned that improper foot care resulted in trench foot and that men with trench foot would be severely dealt with -- it was considered a self-inflicted wound. However, the frequent rains, snows and damp weather insured that whatever pair of socks he wore would soon be wet. He'd massage his feet before swapping his extra pair for the sodden ones he just peeled off, hoping the old pair would dry before the filthy, holey coverings he just donned were again wet and mildewed. It was a losing battle.

Nothing else to do, he sat in his hole, bored beyond belief.

Artillery rumbled in the distance as Barkley ambled across the reverse slope of the company's position. Before long, he came upon a dozen soldiers who were heating their rations over a small fire built in the woods. As he approached them, one of their number yelped sharply and fanned his fingers. An officer had sliced his finger on the ragged edge of a ration can. It was only a minor cut.

Closer now, Barkley overheard another officer remark, "Hey, I'll put you in for a Purple Heart."

The injured officer sucked his wounded finger and laughed. "Yeah," he said, "you ought to."

"No. Really," the other persisted, "This is a battle front and I can recommend you for a Purple Heart."

The injured officer seemed incredulous at the offer.

Barkley was disgusted by what he heard. The officer seemed serious about putting his buddy in for a citation. *How the hell are they going to explain that?* he wondered as he walked away, *The artillery isn't even falling close enough to have caused any harm.*

"Mail call! Mail call!"

Jubilation! Mail! A morale booster of the highest order. Just when he thought he could stand no more, boredom's relief arrived. Barkley received a small bundle of letters and a couple of packages battered beyond recognition, yet he hoped to salvage what contents he could, anticipating candies or other goodies from home. He was quickly disenchanted to discover that one box, like the one he received in the hospital, was several months old. Where the hell it had been was anybody's guess. Still, any sweets would be a welcome treat and he eagerly tore open the wrapping only to discover that the contents were stale and hardly edible. Downhearted, he opened the other box which, while not fresh, contained treats made more recently by his mother and he was glad to get them.

Then his attention was drawn to the compact bundle of letters. Several were from his parents. There was also letters from Marilyn and her brother, Loren, as well as a couple from neighbors or friends back home. But one caught his eye and made his heart leap. It bore a French postmark -- "Vincennes". It was from Catherine. He hadn't been sure whether she'd actually write, or not. He anxiously tore the envelope and devoured every line of her stylish penmanship, savoring every word as she declared how much she had enjoyed his company while in Paris and how she hoped that he would write to her. She encouraged him to write in French if he could, but it would also be okay if he felt more comfortable writing in English. It was a wonderful letter and Barkley longed to return to the City of Light. He read it again, then ripped open the other envelopes.

Marilyn's letter was cheerful and also helped buoy his morale. He was glad to hear from her and felt fortunate to have two girls writing him -- one at home and one in Paris.

Loren's letter, while not as exciting, filled him in on what the other kids were doing back in Quincy.

The letters from his parents were almost always written by his mother, with his dad occasionally adding a line or two. As usual, she expressed her concerns for her son's safety and well being and hoped that he was doing all right. She seemed to always add some bit of sage advice that she felt a mother owed her son. To be careful and not take any chances… to stay clear of immoral girls. This brought a chuckle to Barkley. *She must be referring to Paris,* he thought, *for there sure weren't any girls up here!* She always encouraged him to improve himself in education whenever he could. Another laugh. He was getting one hell of an education on how to stay alive. He learned that his parents were fixing up a rental property they had across the street and also got the usual updates on the welfare of the cat and dogs.

Now that he had read all his mail he chose which ones he would answer. He didn't have an abundance of writing paper, so had to be judicious in his selections. For the moment, Catherine was foremost on his mind. He thumbed through his dog-eared French-English dictionary and struggled with his response. He wrote that he thoroughly enjoyed her company as well, and that if he ever returned to Paris he would surely pay her and her family a visit. The final statement was more dream than reality, for he had no idea when, if ever, he'd make it back to that lovely city.

Another sheet of paper was rationed to answer Marilyn who he hoped would relay his message to her brother. That would save a page and an envelope.

Then he answered the most important one -- his parents'. "Somewhere in Germany," he began. He knew that statement alone would inform them that he was back at the front. Last they knew he was living it up in Paris -- they ought to at least know where he now was. As before, he was reluctant to tell them of the hardships, only that it was pretty cold but that he didn't mind it so much. He knew that they'd only worry themselves sick if he told them anything more. He then sugar coated the letter by saying how he hoped to see Paris again. To answer his mother's plea to improve his education, he boasted of his knowledge of the French language and how he can write it, too. He felt certain that that would please her.

In conclusion he scrawled his name at the bottom, and as he did, he wondered if he'd ever see home again.

Later that evening several salvos of American artillery swooshed overhead to pummel the German lines before Brandscheid. The sound thundered up the heights and the GIs gained a sense of comfort knowing that compared to what they received from the Germans, the Krauts were getting the dirty end of the stick. Then silence prevailed until, as if in retaliation, six rounds of mortar fire plopped defiantly into the company area, followed by another period of silence before the night erupted with shattering flashes as seven heavier artillery shells hammered the slopes before them.

November 23, 1944 -- It was mealtime. The day, like every other, was dreary, cold and overcast. Snow covered much of the ground and where there wasn't snow, ugly mud marred the scene. A frozen mist began to fall and the mist matured to a bone chilling rain. Mortar and artillery shells had been landing at random throughout the morning, gouging black holes and spraying mud and shrapnel, but no one was hurt and the rain continued to fall.

But now it was meal time and as if in compliance, the shelling had stopped and all was still. Barkley was pulled from his hole and sent to the backside of the ridge with a number of others to receive their dinner. Cold mud slopped around their boots as they stood nervously in the chow line, expecting another round of mortars to engulf them at any moment. No one dared rattle his mess kit.

The cooks and cooks' helpers stood behind long, portable tables weighed down by large mess pans, and grinned from ear to ear. *Grinning! What the hell was there to grin about?* With a flourish, lids were lifted, releasing clouds of steam that momentarily screened the proud, gregarious faces of the cooks. Wisps of steam swirled from mounds of moist turkey and heaps of dressing and all the trimmings. Servers peered through the vapor, anticipating a reaction. "Happy Thanksgiving," someone blurted.

The dogfaces were stunned. Freezing rain tinkled on helmets as icy pellets leaped from soiled clothing like dying lice. Filthy, unshaven faces gawked in awe at the spread. It was Thanksgiving Day. No one had realized it was a holiday -- until now. A gamut of emotions swept over the mud-caked infantrymen. Some eyes welled with tears while other faces remained blank, indifferent, as if the concept of a holiday did not fully register.

After receiving a heaping portion of the feast, the men straggled back to their mud holes to sit and wolf down their treat before the artillery began falling again. And it did.

After seven days of living in the dugouts and foxholes on the ridge, word was received that relief was on the way -- they were coming off the line. Although it had been their easiest combat assignment yet, it hadn't been a picnic either. The strain of the ordeal had taken its toll. The constant cold and mud, the random shelling and the incessant patrolling grated on their nerves. Several men had been wounded by shrapnel, but no one had been killed. But still, the stress mounted and fermented until it eventually wore them down, physically and mentally. They were tired and dirty and looked forward to the coming rest.

November 24, 1944, 0915 Hours -- The relief arrived, filing through the trees as silently as the morning mist as they exchanged places with the Joes of Company G. Men gathered their meager belongings and relinquished their holes to the very men they had replaced a week earlier. Few words were spoken.

After hiking down the reverse slope the weary men climbed into trucks which waited in the shadow of the Schnee Eifel. They were in better humor now, free at last from enemy observation, and conversed freely and even managed to crack a crude joke or two, inducing a snort of laughter or at least a grudging smile. Drivers jammed gears and gunned their engines and the trucks lurched forward. Other trucks carrying the balance of the Second Battalion preceded them and soon a convoy was heading for the rest areas far to the rear.

The trucks rattled and rumbled as they splashed over rough rutted roads, jarring passengers' teeth at every bump. Safe now, the men became loud and boisterous and failed to hear the howl of incoming artillery over the heavy engines' roar, and just as the leading vehicles entered a road junction the earth flew up around them. Drivers gunned their engines and raced on as more shells bracketed the crossroads. One truck was broadsided by a hail of shrapnel and there were casualties. Somehow the Germans knew of the troop rotation and which route was being taken. One of their patrols, or perhaps even spies must have infiltrated behind the American lines and apparently observed the movement, then called down the destruction that now battered the junction. The planned relief of the battalion had been interrupted. After some confusion an alternate route was selected for the remainder of the convoy. The joking and smiles had vanished.

Company G had not been part of the ill-fated segment of the convoy and had escaped harm. But the gravity of what had happened did not escape them and men brooded over the event. It just goes to show you, some of them reasoned, you never know when your luck will run out. Rumor already had it that one fellow had been killed by chance when a few rounds of 88 fire hit the regimental command post. The luckless soul had gone to the rear to bathe when a direct hit struck the temporary shower he was using. One just never knew where Death lurked. The veterans were well acquainted with the whims of fate and considered themselves condemned men, as if they constantly wore a noose around their neck and it was only a matter of time before the hangman tripped the trap door beneath their feet. Grimly silent now, the trucks rumbled on until they returned to Born where the men dismounted and quietly entered their billets.

Again in the comfort of houses, soldiers attempted to blot out memories of their ill-fated return and strove to relax. They washed up and shaved and began to feel human again. A new attempt at humor drew smiles from troubled faces and in time all was well. But the respite was short. They only stayed at Born for a couple of days where they not only cleaned themselves, but also their weapons and equipment, for they knew they were going back into the line soon. Too soon, the men thought. They were to relieve the Third Battalion which held the regimental left on the same long ridge of the Schnee Eifel that they had just vacated. The Third was long overdue for a rest. The Second Battalion was going to give it to them.

November 27, 1944 -- Tailgates dropped and men leaped to the ground as Company G dismounted the trucks. Once again they found themselves staring at the backside of a long, wooded ridgeline. Their new destination was approximately two miles to the northeast of Brandscheid and perhaps one mile east of a hamlet called Buchet where the 38th Infantry had set up its command post. As before, the men slung their rifles and shouldered machine guns and tri-pods, mortar tubes and heavy base plates and commenced the familiar trudge to the front, slipping on the muddy track as they bypassed patches of snow. A thick stand of fir trees loomed in the fog, creating an atmosphere of mystery and foreboding as they ascended the hill and no one doubted that evil lurked beyond that sinister veil.

Their new position was more heavily wooded than their previous one, slashed by deep draws and ravines. A number of squat, ugly pillboxes dominated the ridgeline, but gratefully their firing ports stared in the wrong direction, for the Germans had been forced from them in September by another division and were currently in American hands. Their sole purpose now was to act as quarters for the squads that occupied the heights.

From their position the men could gaze across a deep valley, dotted with trees. A creek flowed through its cleft and ambled casually to the south, or right, and meandered past a couple of villages before spilling into a distant river. Beyond the creek the bank again rose sharply until it crested on another wooded ridgeline not unlike the one held by the Americans. That was where the Germans were entrenched in a secondary line of bunkers and pillboxes. If one listened close enough, he could here them talking and sometimes someone sang.

Barkley kicked snow from his boots as he entered a pillbox and was blinded momentarily by the unexpected darkness of the dim lit chamber. It was musty and dark and reeked of kerosene, stale sweat and other odors not readily identified. But still, it was out of the elements and the thick concrete roof offered welcome protection from artillery. They had been told that these fortifications were constructed of steel reinforced concrete poured eight to ten feet thick. They could withstand anything, or so it seemed.

Men spread out to select their personal sleeping areas and Barkley staked his by dropping his pack and bedroll on a slab of floor to claim as his own. As his eyes adjusted to the murky light he noticed that the main cavity was one large room with smaller ones, often no bigger than walk-in closets, at the fringes. A candle burned unevenly from its precarious perch atop an upended crate and flickered uncertainly whenever threatened by a sudden draft. A small stove sat at one end with its stovepipe disappearing into the thick gray wall.

It was a pretty good set up -- warm and well protected. But the men realized that they weren't going to spend all of their time in the relative comfort of the pillbox. It was merely the squad's base of operation and only those not assigned to a particular chore would be allowed to remain inside, so it was not always fully occupied. From here men would be sent out on patrols or to man the foxhole outposts that ringed the perimeter.

As before, Barkley resumed his duties as lead scout as patrols ventured into foreign territory. Always cautious, he crept warily along the creek bed that cut the valley floor then crossed it, utilizing the shrubbery and ditches as screens as he reconnoitered the enemy's lines. They'd find good cover and wait, watching for enemy patrols and sometimes even moved closer to the Germans' fortifications to observe their coming and going. They marked weapon locations. They watched as enemy kitchens doled out their rations and noted the feeding times. When they returned and reported their findings, sometimes mortar or artillery fire would be called upon the locations designated.

After completing a patrol Barkley relished the comfort of the pillbox where he was able to warm up and dry his socks. Sleep was taken on the hard floor, wrapped in his blanket, and while it wasn't exactly toasty, it was a hell of a lot better than sleeping in a cold, muddy foxhole in the snow. It was a godsend by comparison and morale remained high.

His only complaint was Sergeant Gascon. Gascon held the younger men of the squad as his captive audience as he spun his yarns about his wonderful life before entering the army. The stories annoyed Barkley to no end. He knew they were false -- lies invented to impress the more naïve kids in the pillbox. Gascon droned on about the magnificent country estate he grew up in. He spoke of the big bearskin rug that stretched before a massive fireplace -- the site of numerous sweltering romantic encounters. He bragged about his cars and all the beautiful women that adored him.

What a line of crap! thought Barkley. He believed Gascon had been nothing more than a bum who probably rode the rails and lived in hobo jungles by the tracks. If he ever held a job it was probably only a temporary one before catching the next freight out of town. Gascon personified the old Army axiom: "He's found a home in the Army." *He found a home, alright,* Barkley thought, *and he knows it. He was probably counting on doing his twenty years and getting out, gliding all the way, letting others do all the work, just like he does on patrols. But the war came along and spoiled all that, now didn't it? And now you're in a combat zone. Big house, my butt!* At times like these Barkley would turn a shoulder and try to sleep, or maybe write a letter by the flickering candlelight as Sergeant Gascon launched another fantastic tale.

A faint boom sounded and a slight tremor wrinkled the air. Soldiers stopped whatever they were doing and cocked an ear. Another explosion followed by another echoed across the hills, muffled by the dense forest that covered the slopes. One of the neighboring companies was being mortared. The GIs gave it a moment's thought, calculated its distance and tried to guess who was getting hit, then resumed whatever they had been doing. Everyone got shelled at one time or another.

Outposts reported hearing a burp gun firing beyond the company front. There it went again, a faint hollow knocking, like some strange mechanical woodpecker. No answer from American weapons. Officers tried to determine the location by sound, then called for mortars to drop a few rounds in the area.

Barkley hunkered in a frozen foxhole as he and Joe Guajardo stood their turn on the outpost line. Snow covered the ground and it was cold. They took turns standing watch while the other crouched in the hole and tried to keep warm. At the present, Joe stood guard, looking stiff and miserable in his clumsy thick overcoat with a blanket draped over his head and shoulders for additional warmth. Although Joe had participated in the Wisconsin winter maneuvers before the division was deployed overseas, he still was not used to the frigid climate. After all, he was from South Texas. While Joe shivered, Barkley slumped to the foxhole's floor with arms wrapped tightly about himself. There was nothing to do and little to say. If they talked at all it was in a whisper for fear the enemy hear them. Conversation was not a viable option.

To pass the time Barkley decided to read a couple of letters he had recently received. It was nearly dusk and light was even poorer in the depths of the foxhole and he had difficulty making out the words that filled the pages. To remedy the situation he held a page in one hand and struck a match with the other. His eyes quickly scanned the sentences as the tiny flame wavered, then went out. He struck another and continued to read until the flame bit his fingers, forcing him to drop the match onto the muddy floor. Another was lighted until it, too, scorched his fingers... and so it went until he had finished each letter.

A delicate mist sifted from a darkening sky. Nothing stirred beyond the hole, save for the creaking of frozen branches that groaned like the arthritic joints of a tired old man. Barkley glanced up at Joe who stood rigid at his post, looking as if he were made of wood. Joe returned Barkley's stare and shrugged, as if to say, "There's nothing out there."

Again Barkley shivered. Boredom reigned. To pass the time, he decided he'd answer some of his mail. Although soldiers could write home free of charge, he recalled that his parents had sent him some stationary and a few airmail stamps to expedite a response. He knew he'd have difficulty keeping them dry and mud-free, even though he had tucked them inside an overcoat pocket. Everything was coated with mud. He knew the longer he waited to use them, the muddier they'd get so decided to use them now. However, it was much darker now and he feared lighting a match for illumination, so he struggled to make do as best he could in the confines of the foxhole. "Somewhere on the Siegfried Line in Germany," he wrote. "This muddy wet hole I am in is one XX of a place to write letters in…" He went on to acknowledge receipt of the stationary and stamps and explained why he was using them now: "I am writing in half darkness and if it don't look so good the way I am writing it is because I am afraid to build a fire to see as the Germans might see it too and that would be bad (for me). It is cold, wet, damp, muddy -- foggy on some days -- and other things that are equally unpleasant, close, Your son, Bark"

It was short and not so sweet. He was thoroughly disgusted with the entire situation.

Back in the pillbox, Barkley shook out his overcoat and unrolled his blanket. A candle burned shyly from its rustic table, haloed by a dainty areola of shimmering light. Flickering shadows danced among the soldiers, cavorting like lost souls -- soft, vague, yet ever present. Some men snored obnoxiously beneath blankets that rose and fell with rhythmic breathing, offset now and then by an involuntary twitch. The rude blast of a raucous fart fouled the air. But most irritating of all was the grating voice of Sergeant Gascon as he capped yet another incredible lie.

Barkley stretched out on the floor and pulled his blanket over his shoulders as he wriggled to get more comfortable. All the while, Sergeant Gascon held court in the center of the room and regaled his audience with a continuous stream of boisterous, self-gratifying fabrications. His voice boomed across the room: "Why, I tell yuh, I never saw such a woman as that an' I jus' knew I had t' have me some."

Annoyed, Barkley rolled to face the dark, sooty wall and thought of home. *What am I doing here?*

Gascon's voice intruded on Barkley's thoughts: "… so I took her up t' my lodge up in the mountains, uh, now like I said, we wuz drunk an' she really wanted it, y'know?…"

Barkley's inner voice screamed defiantly, *Shut up! SHUT UP!* But it was a silent protest, for he knew it would bode him no good to speak up. After all, a sergeant can get you killed easily enough -- on a patrol… in battle. Just about anywhere he can order you out to certain death and there's nothing you can do about it. *Nothing!* If he doesn't like you, he can kill you one way or another and no one will be the wiser. You'd be just another battle casualty. How he hated the loud-mouthed Gascon!

December 5, 1944 -- As before, their relief arrived and once again Company G rotated back to the village of Born for rest and recuperation.

The welcome cry of "Mail Call," sent the men scurrying. Another bundle of mail had caught up with Barkley, a fat packet tied up with string. He culled them and sorted them in the order he wanted to read them. One was from Catherine and he struggled through her taxing English translation, trying to decipher certain phrases and understand what they meant. Parts of her letter were in French and he puzzled over the strange words, consulting his GI French-English dictionary until the pages were dog-eared from use. Still, it was a great boon to be receiving mail from a girlfriend in Paris -- a source of pride, something worth boasting about. When time came, he'd answer her in awkward French and hoped that she would understand what he meant. He sure missed Paris.

He got other letters as well. It was always great to see a letter from Marilyn. She still wrote fairly regularly and he never failed to answer, if at all possible -- war permitting. Other friends from Quincy wrote, too, but it seemed that they were less frequent than they used to be, or maybe the mail system was still screwed up. But most important of all were the letters from his parents. His mother worried incessantly, and rightfully so. Barkley never wrote about what he was doing when in combat, for he knew it would worry her sick. She knew he was in the infantry and that was more than enough. The newspapers and radio probably told her more than she should know. He always told her he was alright and doing fine -- nothing more, no details.

Indoors again, Barkley soaked up the warmth and decided to answer some of the mail he had received over the past few days. He began with his parents. Fingers no longer stiff from the cold, he began to write long, superfluous sentences that flowed from page to page. The letter in itself became an outlet, a dream world in which he could escape for as long as his mind permitted. He wrote of what he hoped to do when he returned home. His pen described plans for remodeling his room and even outlined a budget. He knew exactly where he'd set up his pinball and slot machines. He envisioned a room furnished with an overstuffed sofa and chair set with a nice rug spread across the floor. There would be a radio for music and venetian blinds would govern the lighting. He fantasized of time spent with his friends again, playing his various machines for hours on end. And there would be other activities, too. "Jack Bosse has a dance floor built in his basement," he recalled. "Ernie has a car and a big printing press, Fritsmier has a motorcycle *and* a car and I have a hunting camp in the Ozarks and a game room full of amusement machines... What a time we'll have when the war is over," he declared.

He reminisced about the good times he had while working in the candy factory in Davenport, Iowa. Sometimes, if he was lucky, he'd receive a box of candy from his co-worker, Henry Lefrense, who'd be sure to add a few of the nickel nougat nut rolls, his favorites.

"I am writing a slightly long letter today. One reason is that I am warm and had enough sleep," he confessed. And it was a long letter -- ten pages of copious script filled with dreams and hopes for the future. The only complaint concerned stories of civilians back home earning good wages, then going on strike for more money while he and all the other Joes did the fighting and dying. He hoped that all the soldiers and officers received a bonus when the war was over as compensation.

He always expressed concern for his mother's health and asked if his father was doing okay at the factory.

"Well, it is almost chow time and unless something happens to me while I go to chow, I'll return and write some more. We always have pretty good food for chow." However, after his return, he could not think of anything else to write so closed the letter, then sought his squad mates to shoot the breeze and evaluate the latest rumors.

There was one incident that truly upset Barkley while at the rest area of Born. Higher command had decided that one man from each platoon of the division would be granted ninety days temporary duty back in the States in recognition of honorable service while overseas. It was determined that the only fair method of choosing who would go would be by drawing lots among the qualified personnel. To Barkley's disgust, it was bull-shitting Sergeant Gascon who received the honor. Gascon crowed victorious and boasted of what a time he'd have with all the women when he got home. He was told it would only be a matter of time before the orders were cut to release him from divisional command. Barkley was incensed.

Once again the rest was brief and the men returned to the line. Snow now became the rule rather than the exception, for it was early December and very cold and winter had come to stay. Faces had weathered brown as leather from the cold and despite one's age, no one was young anymore.

CHAPTER 16

THE BATTLE OF HEARTBREAK CROSSROADS

December 11, 1944 -- Snowflakes slashed the darkness, driven by a bone-chilling wind that stung the faces of the lowly infantrymen manning the defenses facing the Siegfried Line. The Regiment had been alerted that they were to be relieved by elements of another division and the men had taken the necessary preparations to facilitate the exchange.

For days rumor had it that the 2nd Division had been selected to spearhead a new assault, a fresh penetration of the Siegfried Line in another sector. It was a highly plausible rumor. The Division had held this "quiet" front for two months and the men were fairly rested after the ordeals suffered in Normandy and at Brest. They knew that their luck wouldn't hold forever.

So they waited, remaining in the relative comfort and warmth of their log dug-outs and cabins as long as they could. Then terribly excited voices from the outside filtered through the walls. Something was really working up the men who were outdoors. Curiosity swelled among the inhabitants of the log huts and soon all were outside, standing in the snow with mouths agape. An incredible spectacle lay before them.

To the west, from the general direction of St. Vith, was an unbelievable sight: a promenade of headlights as a convoy snaked through the forest towards the front. Headlights! At the front?! The veterans of the 38th Infantry were justifiably excited. Barkley and his friends in Company G couldn't believe it! It was suicidal to strike a match in the dark, let alone shining bright headlights! They expected a barrage of artillery to annihilate the column of trucks at any moment.

The snow, trapped in the bright beams, sparkled like diamonds. On they came, relentlessly winding towards the incredulous, gawking soldiers on the ridge.

"Where in the hell do they think they're at?" asked one GI as the vehicles drew closer.

"Jesus!" cried another, "The Germans will slaughter them!"

Several jeeps, carrying officers, roared into the camp and slid to a halt. Truckloads of troops, headlights burning defiantly, followed the jeeps and crunched through the snow as they filed into the company area.

A plethora of voices bombarded the newcomers. "Put out those *damn lights*!! Get off the trucks!!"

Other than the rumbling of the trucks and the clamor of the flabbergasted veterans, no other noise was heard. Artillery should have been raining down on them, indiscriminately destroying jeeps, trucks and men. It seemed very odd to the men of the 38th. Something strange was going on here -- nonetheless, the lights had to go!

Barkley, Joe Guajardo and a few others ran out to the convoy and exhorted, "Get those lights *out*!"

An officer stepped from a jeep into the snow and addressed Barkley, who was nearest him: "Where's the PX?"

Stunned, Barkley was nearly speechless. "You're on a front line!" he answered, "There's no PX. The Germans are on the next hill across the way." He jabbed a finger in an eastwardly direction to make the point. "We may be under attack at any time!"

The officer was appalled by such insolence from an enlisted man. "Where's your salute, soldier?" he demanded.

"Sir, we don't salute officers up here," Barkley answered, then added rather indignantly, "If you want to die sooner than you expected, just let soldiers salute you. German snipers are looking for officer targets. In fact, they *prefer* them!"

Meanwhile, chagrined soldiers of the convoy began to switch off the incriminating headlights.

"Where in the hell did *they* train?" scoffed one of Barkley's squad mates.

As it was, the relieving command was a brand-new division, the 106th Infantry Division, The Golden Lions, fresh from the States. They had never seen a day of combat or had any frontline experience at all. The veterans of the 2nd knew that the Germans would notice this immediately and hit them with probing patrols and vigorous forays to "feel them out" and test their mettle.

The green 106th had been sent to the Ardennes front, the "Ghost Front", to gain a little experience, to get "blooded" before being sent to a more active front.

The active front -- that was the destination of the 2nd Division.

The Battalion mounted trucks and motored west, splashing through the streets of St. Vith, several miles to the rear. When the Americans had first entered St. Vith months earlier, the townspeople had greeted the liberators enthusiastically, cheering and waving home-made American flags. But no one celebrated now. The Stars and Stripes still draped several buildings and fluttered limply in the breeze as the motorcade roared past, but other than that, the streets were all but vacant. Barkley noticed that some houses displayed very small flags, crudely stitched facsimiles of the U.S. colors.[*]

The convoy rumbled steadily into the gray hours of the afternoon and continued on a northerly course. Snow covered hills rose silently to either side, resembling the pale wholesome mounds of virgin breasts, now violated by the serpentine column of vehicles that snaked through their cleavage like the bane of Eden. The dismal weather matched men's spirits and suggested a fate as vague and mysterious as the dim horizon that easily blended with a lead colored sky. Men hunched shoulders against the icy breeze that whipped through the truck beds and cursed as they turned their faces to escape its vicious sting. The convoy slipped along treacherous roads, passing acres of gloomy black forests, more hills and ever deepening snow until it came to rest at a place called Elsenborn.

Company G disembarked in the dark and was assigned billets and felt blessed to be out of the elements, quartered under roofs with stoves and real beds to sleep in. It was wonderful! Yet it only presaged hard times ahead.

While the Allied armies were engaged in the protracted stalemate along the German frontier, the weather had steadily worsened. As the winter intensified, the infantry faced a new enemy - - a serious foot disorder commonly called "trench foot". A soldier acquired this malady by spending continuous days and nights in damp, wet foxholes, unable to dry his feet or change his socks. In time a man might discover that his aching feet had swollen well beyond their normal size, painfully trapped within his boots. After pulling off his boots he was often shocked to discover that his feet and toes had turned blue or even an ugly purple. Sometimes the only recourse for serious cases was amputation. Whatever the degree of the affliction, a soldier was removed from the front by medics and

---

[*] Later, when the Germans broke through during the Battle of the Bulge, the American flags quickly disappeared and were replaced by German banners. The citizens greeted the Germans with the same enthusiasm as they had the Americans. Such is the way of survival.

listed as a non-battle casualty and his loss cut into his unit's fighting strength as surely as if he had been wounded in action. To remedy this situation, vast stores of winter overshoes were brought forward from supply dumps. Until now the supply shortage had been acute and although all of the men possessed overcoats and gloves, only a portion of the front line troops had been issued overshoes.

A big truck from the Quartermaster Company roared into Company G's area and squealed to a halt. The supply personnel who accompanied the truck began to toss out large quantities of overshoes until a heap of them cluttered the ground and the infantrymen scrambled to cull out a pair for themselves. There was no orderly line where a supply sergeant issued boots as men declared their sizes. Instead it was catch-as-catch-can and the men rifled through the pile of boots searching for a pair that would fit.

Barkley joined the teeming throng and snatched up a likely pair. Sauntering off to try them on he soon realized that they were too small, so he returned to rummage through the fast diminishing stockpile. Selecting what appeared to be the next best fit he slipped them over his boots only to discover that they were too large. No one else had a pair to trade so he returned to the dwindling pile and dropped the overshoes among the few remaining pairs. The remnants were pretty well picked over by now and none were his size. He would have to do without winter overshoes.

The arrival of the overshoes dashed one rumor and fanned the flames of another. While reveling in the comforts of Elsenborn, some men had been lulled into believing that the war was all but over, that the 2nd Division had done its share and was being shipped home. After all, the Germans were whipped, weren't they? But now, as men tried on the winter footwear, other, more cynical soldiers soured their enthusiasm. "What need would soldiers returning to the States have for overshoes?" they asked. And besides, hadn't they had it too easy, comparatively, while on the Ghost Front of the Ardennes? They were infantry, they affirmed, they were going nowhere but to more battle and suffering. Now the arrival of winter footwear seemed to guarantee that this latest rumor was true -- they would be attacking the Siegfried Line soon. The overshoes were a bad omen, symbolic of things to come and again some of the men recalled the colonel's apocalyptic prophecy when they departed Paris: "Half of you sitting here today won't make it back. We're going to crack the Siegfried Line!"

The 2nd Infantry Division was about to initiate an assault on a heretofore unbreached segment of the Siegfried Line. The attack would be made through the Monschau Forest, a lower reach of the dreaded Huertgen Forest, in an effort to capture the strategic Roer River dams in Germany. As long as the Germans controlled the dams they were capable of releasing devastating flood waters that would hamper future Allied offensive operations to the north, trapping the lead elements of attacking divisions on the east side of the Roer where they could easily be chewed up and destroyed by German counter-attacks.

The 2nd Division would attack north, then northeast toward its objective. Their assault was to be made in concert with the untried 78th Division which would make a simultaneous attack approximately ten miles farther north. The 2nd Division would attack through a narrow corridor that bisected the lines of another new division, the 99th, which would provide limited supporting attacks to protect what would become the 2nd Division's exposed right flank. First U.S. Army had already suffered horrendous casualties in the Huertgen in exchange for negligible gains -- the dogfaces who fought there had long since dubbed it "The Death Factory". It was expected to be little different for the men of the 2nd Division.

The 9th and 38th Infantry Regiments were to make the initial assaults for the 2nd Division with the 23rd held as divisional reserve. Due to the secretiveness of the attack, the men of the division were ordered to cut off the Indianhead shoulder patches from their jackets -- a ludicrous order to the infantrymen, for they had learned way back in Normandy that the great white star that bore the chief's profile made a perfect target for snipers. By now few, if any, frontline soldiers retained the proud insignia.

December 13, 1944, 0745 Hours -- The men of Company G were again ordered into trucks and began a discreet movement eastward. Heavily armed infantrymen crowded the benches that lined the truck beds and shivered as fresh snow feathered silently to the frozen landscape. It was a short journey, perhaps ten miles, but took better than two hours to complete and the men were thoroughly chilled when they piled from their transports at a Belgian village called Rocherath. They were quickly assembled and commenced a northerly march down a narrow road that disappeared into a distant, snow frocked forest. Morale sank. They were well acquainted with the Beast that lurked beyond the tree line and had no desire to meet it again.

Earlier that morning, as the 38th Infantry departed Elsenborn, the 9th Infantry had already begun its meticulous, fog-shrouded advance northward from the twin Belgian farming villages of Krinkelt and Rocherath near the German frontier. The 38th was to follow in its wake. The going was slow as the GIs slogged silently through deep snow. About a mile north of the villages the solitary road knifed through the forest and wormed directly to their objective several miles away. The men avoided the road, however, as it was known to be heavily mined, thus forcing them to struggle through the thick brush and fir trees that crowded it. Each step was an effort and sometimes the men sank knee deep into the snow.

The 9th Infantry had the mission of capturing a fortified customs station at a Y-shaped road junction called Wahlerscheid, deep in the forest. Once this strategic point was taken, the 38th Infantry would pass through the 9th and make the main effort toward the dams to the northeast. That was the plan anyway.

The 38th Infantry began its march later that morning, trailing the last battalion of the 9th. The leading element for the 38th was the Second Battalion - Barkley's battalion.

Barkley plodded through the deep snow. The weather had warmed a bit and the snow capping the trees melted and showered the GIs with its constant drip, drip, dripping as they pressed through the forest. The fir trees grew thick and the wet branches were often meshed together, like interlocking fingers, forcing the men to physically push them aside time and again in order to proceed. Occasionally large clumps of snow cascaded from the boughs of the towering pines and plopped ungraciously into the snow or splattered down the necks of unsuspecting GIs, evoking curses and oaths from men already wet from previous snow showers. The column splashed through icy slush as they traversed rugged ravines. Soon all were wet. Barkley's leather combat boots absorbed the moisture and already he regretted not having any overshoes.

The cold, miserable march continued towards the road junction, now under attack by the 9th.

The men of the 38th reached a forward area near the front and were ordered to halt beneath the dripping pines. Worn out from the arduous trek, they hunkered in the snow and waited. Now that they had stopped marching, the warmth generated from the demanding hike dissipated and sodden clothing clung chilling to their skin, increasing their misery. Icy water continued to leak from above, marking the passing of time with every drop while the muted rumbling of artillery pierced the heavy canopy of thickly entwined conifers and sounded for all the world like the never ending peal of a distant thunderstorm. It would only be a matter of time before the men of the 38th were committed to the battle. A few rounds of enemy artillery crashed out of sight, somewhere in the forest. The concussion shook loose clouds of snow that sifted through the branches and generated a degree of anxiety among the men below. Tension mounted as they nervously waited their turn. Before long, stories filtered back of tough opposition for the 9th.

The stories proved to be true. At noon the 9th Infantry had run into a wall -- not a real wall, but a more foreboding one all the same, and it was terrifying. While the remainder of the regiment struggled through the dense forest, the lead elements emerged into a wide clearing and were stopped cold by a devastating stream of machine gun bullets. About 200 yards of flat, open terrain stretched before them. On the far side of that expanse sat squat, sturdy, concrete pillboxes, too many to count it seemed, spaced 20 to 30 yards apart. Between the edge of the forest and the pillboxes ran a parallel anti-tank ditch followed by masses of barbed-wire entanglements, sometimes as many as ten rows deep. It was a formidable obstacle.

The men of the 9th continued their attack and soon discovered that the field was not only covered by interlocking machine gun fire, but was also thick with land mines, interconnected by trip wires hidden beneath the fresh blanket of snow. And when the doughboys exposed themselves in the open, a storm of German artillery and mortar shells pounded them incessantly. More shells pummeled the forest that concealed their comrades. They had run into a wall, alright -- a wall of concrete and steel and imminent death. It was hell.

The 9th Infantry was bogged down before the Wahlerscheid defenses. Throughout the day they threw themselves at the fortifications and bled, yet the Germans clung tenaciously to their positions. The crossroads' capture seemed impossible.

Meanwhile, the 38th Infantry remained in its reserve position a short distance behind the front. As daylight dimmed, the growl of engines heralded the approach of vehicles and soon several jeeps emerged from the trees, rocking and lurching as they negotiated the rough, snow covered terrain, then skidded to a halt in the company areas. Blanket rolls were tossed out, then the jeeps roared off to the rear as those left standing in the forest were ordered into bivouac. The infantrymen were left to their own devices to make themselves as comfortable as possible. Not having any pup tents, the men draped their blankets over their shoulders and settled as best they could, nestling into the deep snow. With the coming of night the temperature plummeted and it became much colder. Wet clothing froze stiff while men attempted to sleep.

The following morning the 38th Infantry began to move forward from reserve, accompanied by the howl of artillery shells that swooshed overhead in support of the 9th's attack. Numbed from the cold, the men slowly traced the snowy path of the 9th towards Wahlerscheid junction and the shooting war.

The Second Battalion, which was leading the 38th's march, was halted just short of the junction, ready to exploit any success achieved by the hard fighting 9th. But it was not to be. The 9th still faced fierce resistance and was kept at bay, not making any progress at all. Casualties soared. Still waiting for the front door of the

Siegfried Line to be kicked in by the 9th, the 38th once again was ordered into bivouac in the forest.

Towards late afternoon visibility dimmed, rendering trees, snow and men into vague images of black and white. Occasionally, stray rounds of German artillery crashed like errant fireballs in the treetops above the battalion, snapping branches and flinging shards of shrapnel upon the men cowering below. The tormented cry of "Medic! Medic! Over here!" echoed through the failing light, planting the seeds of misgiving among those that survived and the jitters spread through the ranks like a contagious disease. The veterans bucked up their courage and accepted their fate -- there was nothing they could to about it, anyway. If your number's up, it's up.

The last vestige of light quickly vanished in the heavily shrouded forest and soon all was black. Again men curled beneath the stiffening folds of their blankets and tried to escape their misery through sleep.

The morning of December 15th brought no change to the routine. The men arose, wet and cold and ate their rations. The bloody 9th still battered at the impossible fortifications at Wahlerscheid and the Germans continued to defend them with maniacal determination. The men of the 38th waited impatiently, biding their time before their inevitable commitment to the slaughter.

To bolster the men's spirits and restore warmth and strength, a hot meal was brought forward. To the veterans it was like the Kiss of Death. Although delighted to wolf down hot chow, they knew that this gesture only meant one thing: They'd be going into action -- soon! They never received a feast like this in the field without paying a price for it. The price was generally the "privilege" of making an assault on the enemy. So the men of the 38th gulped their treat with trepidation. The Last Supper. It would soon be time to give the devil his due.

The bitter forest was black and silent as Company G was aroused from its frigid bivouac. Cold, stiff-jointed men grasped their weapons and formed up to join Companies E and F as the Battalion prepared to move out. Barkley clutched his rifle with numb fingers. He was freezing! They had been living in the snow without shelter for three days and he was thoroughly chilled. His toes ached. *I wish I had some damned overshoes*, he thought as he stamped his feet in effort to restore circulation to his numb, lifeless toes. The rough outer leather of his combat boots seemed to act like wicks that absorbed moisture rather than repel it. An uncontrollable shiver ran up his spine. Was it the cold, or fear of the coming battle?

His helmet sat heavily upon his head like a cold steel pot. He was encumbered by his field pack and cartridge belt which constricted tightly around his thick wool overcoat. The heavy coat was damp, but being wool, still helped retain some of his body heat. In its pocket tugged the weight of a grenade launching device which could be attached to the muzzle of his rifle. Previous to departing Elsenborn, someone had decided that he would also be the squad's rifle grenadier, and the launching device would enable him to propel a rifle grenade towards the enemy -- sort of a poor man's mortar. Maybe, just maybe, it might prove useful in attempting to knock out a machine gun emplacement. *Maybe.* Several finned rifle grenades contributed to the weight of his pack. A bandolier of extra rifle ammunition slung across his chest added even more weight. The going would be hard and tough.

The long lines of soldiers began to move out. It was still dark and the thickly matted branches blotted out all traces of star- or moonlight, if there was any, causing the groggy GIs to stumble blindly toward the muffled sounds of a ferocious battle which grew ominously louder at every step.

The racket intensified, now accompanied by wicked flashes of light that slashed through the gallery of trees, briefly illuminating the tense faces of the soldiers as they neared the front. Then, quite suddenly, the forest ended as abruptly as if a monstrous knife had been drawn sharply along its edge, trimming back its ragged fringe until only a well defined line remained, separating forest from open field. There, in the gray light before them lay the stark, hellish battlefield of Wahlerscheid, resounding in cataclysmic explosions. The distant pillboxes. The wire. The wide open, snow covered plain between them and their objective. The stories of the 9th's disastrous initiation to this horrifying obstacle became all too clear. It looked impossible.

Company G was ushered into the battle line as renewed assaults stormed forward in vain attempts to break through the masses of barbed wire that protected the approaches to the pillboxes.

A deafening cacophony of battle sounds filled the air. Machine guns minced human beings while artillery and mortar shells crashed into a scene that challenged Dante's descriptions of Hell. More explosions erupted with ear splitting blasts, giving violent birth to thousands of steel splinters that hissed in every direction while waves of concussion pulsed through the haze and washed over terrified, cringing men.

Squads sprung forward in pitiful attempts to penetrate the wire. Sometimes a lone soldier would run, bent double, leaning into a hail of bullets, only to fall dead or dying amidst the bristling, razor sharp wire.

Back in the forest, German artillery burst high in the treetops, splintering branches as shrapnel rained straight down upon the hapless men below. It was nearly impossible to take shelter from these deadly tree bursts -- laying flat, as they had learned to do, only increased one's chances of being hit since the explosions were directly overhead instead of on the ground. The best bet was to remain erect and hug close to a tree and pray that you didn't get hit by a jag of scorching steel. At Wahlerscheid, Death reigned supreme.

Bullets cut a swath inches above Barkley's head as he slithered through the snow. Prudence had dictated that the squad drop to their bellies as they emerged from the forest and now they forced their way forward in a slow, meticulous crawl. Men grimaced as gleaming tracers darted overhead in neon flashes, causing them to plunge their faces into freezing slush as machine guns spit death from three pillboxes to their front. The ground heaved as sickening explosions belched fire and steel and ripped loose chunks of frozen earth that jettisoned skyward, then cascaded onto the men as they inched forward. Desperate to gain the protection of a ditch to their front, they pressed on.

Barkley literally hugged the ground, pressing his body hard into the dingy snow as his platoon crawled deeper into the inferno. His heart pounded wildly. It seemed as if an iron fist twisted in his guts while frenzied demons clawed at the fragile veneer of armor that guarded his will to go on. Their unholy talons slashed at the very core of his soul in attempts to rip it to shreds and allow his courage to seep into the tainted snow like blood from a fatal wound. He fought off the assault and resolved to push on.

Eventually the platoon tumbled into the ditch and deployed parallel to the enemy line. Row upon row of barbed wire separated them from the menacing pillboxes that guarded the barren field before them. Barkley's squad, and the remainder of the platoon, lay prostrate, strewn out to his right. To his left stretched another rank of frightened GIs who cringed below the parapet of the ditch. Barkley didn't recognize them. He was the last man in his company's line, or the first, depending on how one viewed it, and the men to his left were strangers from some other company.

The battle raged in a hell-fired fury.

Barkley scrutinized the scene with horror. Company G and the neighboring companies had crept forward as far as they could go and were now in the ditch, pinned down by intense machine gun fire. The masses of barbed wire were only yards beyond their makeshift trench. The entire approach to the fortifications was sown with deadly land mines which were concealed beneath the snow -- their interconnecting trip wires were equally invisible. The assault companies simply couldn't go any farther. It seemed hopeless.

Interspersed among the forward riflemen were snipers who tried valiantly to ricochet bullets into the narrow firing slits of the pillboxes, but to no avail. German machine guns continued to sweep back and forth along the line of desperate GIs, forcing them deeper into the ditch. The never ending crash of artillery and mortar shells reaped a deadly harvest.

It was pure hell. Barkley couldn't fathom how the high command could expect them to take this seemingly impregnable line of fortifications. The 9th Infantry had been at it for days with no success whatsoever, yet the Division persisted by sending up the 38th.

Then, through the dim light of the nightmarish scene, awkward movement on the left caught Barkley's eye. A lone soldier sprung from the ditch, hunched forward as he raced toward the coils of wire. He clutched a set of wire cutters. To Barkley's amazement, the soldier flopped before the wire and frantically worked the cutters as bullets zinged through the wire all about him. The audacious fellow had managed to snip one or two strands before a burst of gunfire ripped through his body. His lifeless form hung limply in the wire, absorbing more bullets as machine gunners zeroed in on this threat to their defenses.

My God! thought Barkley, *the poor bastard!*

But then, incredibly, another GI dashed into the open, sprinting headlong toward his dead comrade. He collapsed in the snow beside the corpse and wrestled the cutters from dead fingers. Then, with frenzied motions, he too began to cut at the wires. Within seconds he met his fate and slumped into the wire -- the wire cutters dropped to the blood stained snow.

Barkley watched in horror. Now his head jerked to the left again just in time to see an officer order another soldier out into the killing field. The doomed man staggered to his feet and stumbled forward. After a few faltering paces, his figure was obliterated by a brilliant blast as he tripped a land mine. His charred body lay in black and red snow, writhing, screaming in agony.

Oh, Jesus!

To the left, the officer touches the next man, and he too vaults the parapet, silhouetted against a background of flashing explosions. As this man rushes forward and is gunned down, Barkley realizes the officer is working his way, one by one, toward him. *Oh, my God!* he thought, *the sonovabitch is coming my way! Does he have the authority to send me out there? He's from another outfit... but still, he's an officer...*Dire anxiety filled Barkley's heart. His attention was drawn back to the wire as the last victim, though wounded, stirred, then lifted the cutters with strained, deliberate motions to snip a few more wires with his last scrap of strength. Barkley's eyes were riveted to the scene until the man's body jerked and danced from the impact of more bullets and it was over. The wire cutters lay among the slain and beckoned the next sacrifice.

Another GI is condemned as the maniacal officer orders him out. At the wire the soon-to-be-dead man fumbled with the cutters and succeeds in snapping a couple more strands before bullets shred his body.

The Servant of Death spoke to the next man in line and he dutifully rises and charges towards the wire. He doesn't make it.

Only a few men separate Barkley from the Servant of Death.

Sheer terror gripped Barkley. His gut twisted in a sickening knot. He felt drained, weak. His legs quivered as if made of gelatin and he wondered if he'd even be able to gain his feet when ordered to go. But he supposed he would. Hope was a fleeting thought. The officer would be at his side soon. *Maybe, just maybe, if I'm* _lucky,_ he thought, *Maybe I'll only get a leg blown off.*

The staccato hammering of machine guns rose above all other sounds and another doomed soul falls.

For a brief moment the whole scenario is played out in Barkley's mind: His leg is severed in a searing blast… the evacuation to a hospital… crutches… life after 19 years with only one leg… *If I'm lucky.*

As quickly as it came, the vision vanishes. Barkley found himself staring into the face of the soldier to his immediate left. Only two men remain in the doomed squad. The officer's hand rested heavily on the shoulder of the next victim. Only two men left -- then Barkley goes.

Again Barkley focused on the face of his soon-to-be death mate. The poor wretch bore such a grave expression that it surpassed hopelessness. His eyes were filled with utter terror, despair, suffering with no chance of redemption. Barkley had never seen such a face -- the haunting face of the condemned. Silently they gazed at one another in stark mutual terror, unable to speak. Each face seemed a mirror image of the other, contorted and twisted in sickening expressions -- death masks. They were Forlorn Hopes cast into a sea of despair.

Again machine guns hammered like nails sealing a coffin. *Only one man left, then I go.* Death breathed coldly down Barkley's neck and he abandoned all hope.

Then salvation came. Like a saving angel, a runner appeared and crawled up the line. He singled out the officer and gave a report. Word was passed down the line that a group of Americans had somehow infiltrated behind the fortifications and was engaging the

Germans in tough fighting, blasting in the back doors of the pillboxes with satchel charges and killing every defender that refused to surrender. In that manner this small section of the Siegfried Line was breached and the 2nd Infantry Division's attack passed into the sinister forest beyond.

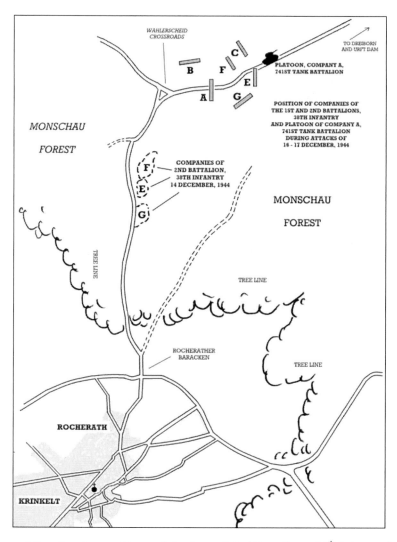

Map showing positions of the 1st and 2nd Battalions, 38th Infantry during the attack at Wahlerscheid, Germany (Heartbreak Crossroads), December 13 - 17, 1944. (Map by C. Barkley, based on actual map at National Archives.)

CHAPTER 17

THROUGH THE FOREST EVIL

December 16, 1944 -- in the Monschau Forest, German Frontier. While battalions of the 9th Infantry fanned out toward the towns of Monschau and Hoffen in the northwest, the First and Second Battalions of the 38th Infantry pushed eastward into Germany proper.

The Second Battalion had been spearheading the 38th Infantry's attack with Companies F and E abreast, advancing astride the road that cut through the forest and led east to Dreiborn, their first objective some five miles distance. Initially, Company G was designated battalion reserve and trailed close behind the fighting front where they endured a recurring series of tree bursts that sprayed shrapnel like rain upon petrified soldiers. But other than that, they were spared the immediate dangers that faced the assault elements and their role as reserve passed relatively uneventful.

The ordeal of the pillboxes was behind them now, a nightmare forever etched in their minds. Before them lay the hidden terrors of the unyielding forest, dark and menacing. They had been advancing since dawn when they had passed through the smoldering hell of Wahlerscheid's fortifications and plunged into the forest to its rear. The leading companies had gained almost immediate contact with the enemy, but resistance had been light for the most part; at least nothing like Wahlerscheid. Apparently the Germans' backbone had been broken when the 9th Infantry captured the crossroads pillboxes.

Yet still, the enemy was out there, lurking somewhere in the forest. Progress was slow. Men still bled and died. As resistance stiffened, it became necessary to deploy Company G which was ordered to sweep through the forest on Company E's right. No other troops extended beyond that point -- Company G was now the end of the line, the open flank.

"Scouts out." Lieutenant Welch's voice carried crisp and clear on the frigid breeze.

Pfc. Barkley rose from the snow, kicking up wispy clouds as he reclaimed his solitary march through the haunting silence of the fir forest. After a moment's hesitation, the second scout struggled to his feet and plodded a measured distance behind Barkley, stepping high to negotiate the deep snow. The balance of the platoon followed, weapons held ready to respond to any trouble encountered by the lead scouts who slipped between rows of sagging evergreens, then vanished, engulfed by a sea of green that swallowed them as easily as the walls of a house possessed absorbs its ghosts. The towering pines loomed overhead and seemed to glower at these interlopers, these foreigners who dared to tread on the sacred soil of The Reich. The men pushed on, ducking beneath the heavy, snow encrusted boughs in effort to catch a glimpse of what lay ahead. The forest remained silent, a stern barrier that refused to reveal its dreadful secrets.

Slowly, methodically, Barkley advanced. It was midday, yet only dim light managed to filter through the dark green canopy. And it was cold. Not as cold as the shivering, teeth-chattering frozen nights, but cold all the same; cold enough to cause each exhalation to explode in clouds of vapor as breath was snorted through raw, red nostrils. Still, despite the frigid conditions, what snow remained in the upper tier of branches melted and began its inexorable descent towards the earth. One by one, each pristine bead slipped from branch to branch until each droplet dangled from the last bough, clung to the last slender needle before releasing its grip to join its predecessors in an omnipresent drip, drip, dripping onto the GIs below. The soldiers were already miserable from the previous days spent in the damp forest -- the steady weeping of the trees ensured they'd remain that way.

The overbearing silence was violated only by the sound of the scouts' boots pressing into the snow: *Crunch... scrunch... crunch.* The sound seemed to be amplified by the stillness and each step became a perceptible warning to any Germans who may be laying in ambush, poised like some wounded animal waiting to pounce out and maul its pursuer -- perhaps at the next brush row, or maybe the next firebreak. Barkley's eyes strove to penetrate the dense foliage, searching for possible enemy positions. His ears strained to hear the slightest sound -- the metallic slide of the bolt of a weapon being cocked or perhaps some vague rustling beneath the shadowy branches. All the while the sound of his own boots crunching in the snow betrayed his every step. It was tense, nerve-wracking work.

At times a brushy draw or suspicious clump of trees would cause him to raise an arm in a signal to halt and those behind him would freeze and drop to the snow, weapons ready. Initially, Barkley, too, would sink to a knee. His eyes probed the forest before him as if he possessed x-ray vision, dissecting every branch, every lump of snow. He took a long silent scan, holding his breath lest the sound of his own breathing cloak some tell-tale noise.

Nothing. There seemed to be no danger ahead. Yet, still, he knew it was up to him and his fellow scout to conduct a more thorough investigation. That was their job. His head swiveled to locate the second scout. Their eyes locked in unanswered question. With a shrug, Barkley's attention returned to the front. Silence. A faint whisper of wind. Snow sopped his pants legs and for an instant he was painfully aware of how cold his feet were. Again he searched the trees and scrutinized every snow laden bough. There seemed to be nothing up ahead, nothing out of the ordinary. The forest leaked around him: plop... plop-plop. *What the hell.* Barkley released a long-held breath as he rose to his feet, intent on physically investigating the suspicious terrain. The muzzle of his rifle nosed before him, ready to snap into action at the slightest provocation. The second scout's finger tensed on his trigger, ready to riddle the brush with a full clip if necessary as he covered Barkley's route. Timeless moments passed as Barkley closed with his goal and gingerly nuzzled the branches with his rifle. It was clear. He blew a sigh of relief then signaled forward as he resumed the point and plodded on. The second scout rose and followed... then the platoon. The somber silence of the forest closed heavily around them.

Barkley's sluggish pace defied the cadence of his pounding heart as he proceeded towards his next dilemma. He pushed aside an impeding branch, and as if that simple act signaled some gross violation of nature, the sky wailed in protest and someone yelled, "Hit it!"

Barkley was already balled at the base of a tree when the first shell struck. Hell incarnate manifested itself high above as one treetop after another exploded, flinging torrents of shrapnel upon hapless, cowering men. Splintered branches followed every burst, thumping heavily into the snow, and sometimes entire trees snapped and crashed to the ground, threatening to crush anyone unfortunate enough to lay within their reach.

A second salvo followed by a third ravaged the towering firs until all below quaked with fear and someone unleashed a scream of unbearable agony, a plaintiff howl drowned by the maelstrom that swirled around them.

And then it was eerily still.

Ears rang in the haunting silence. Lingering battle smoke wended through branches and clung to the forest floor where the smell of fear and death and sweet evergreens mingled with the acrid odor of cordite. The smoke drifted aimlessly between splintered trunks and sank to stain black a pristine floor now littered with greenery and pitted by the impact of innumerable shards of sizzling steel. A moan seeped from the haze, drawing eyes to a comrade who lay stunned and helpless in a pool of crimson snow.

"Medic! We need a medic up here."

An aidman struggled through the snow and knelt beside his patient and did his best, working with frozen fingers until a litter team arrived to haul the heap of mangled flesh away. A bright red stain was all that remained to mark the spot where a comrade had been.

And then the lieutenant took control. "Okay, Barkley. Move out."

Adrenaline pumped fiercely through Barkley's veins as once again he pressed through the now silent forest. Snow crunched noisily beneath his boots. His eyes searched every possible source of danger before taking his next step. *Crunch.* He knew that somewhere out there a man with a gun was determined to kill him. He swallowed hard and moved on as he tracked the rabid Beast of War. *Scrunch, crunch.* White-capped branches brushed his shoulders... deep snow impeded every step, wearing him down. The perpetual cadence of his boots crunching in the snow announced his approach: *Scrunch... Scrunch... Crunch!* He might as well have been marching through the forest banging a bass drum.

Physical contact with the enemy was imminent. Resistance to the Americans' advance, if not directed specifically at Barkley's platoon, would be wrought on other weary, cold and scared GIs who forged through other parts of the snowbound forest.

The abrupt stutter of a burp gun would shatter the silence as a lead scout and his squad stepped before its sights. Perhaps that would be the extent of the contact -- a quick burst that sent the GIs diving to the snow, allowing the Germans time to melt deeper into the forest where they'd regroup, coiled and ready to strike again.

At other times the Germans made a more determined stand, intent on stopping the Americans' relentless drive. Then the initial shock of gunfire would be supplemented by other weapons as bullets lacerated tree trunks and clipped whisks from fir branches that tumbled to the snow. GIs would scatter and form a battle line which soon came alive with the harsh *BAM! BAM! BAM!* of rifles and the rapid clatter of a BAR as they returned fire.

The Germans were virtually invisible in the dense foliage. Sometimes their riflemen and machine gunners fired from camouflaged slit trenches or well constructed log bunkers that protected them from U.S. artillery. From such sturdy emplacements a handful of dedicated men were capable of holding up an entire column of advancing Americans.

As the action developed GIs advanced by fire and maneuver tactics. It was an old story to the veterans -- it would take time, skill and unwavering resolve to dislodge the enemy from their positions. GIs slithered desperately through the snow to lay down fields of fire as incandescent tracer bullets flitted overhead. Others scrambled to their feet and sprinted, bent double as they closed in for the kill. Grenades wobbled through the air. *WHAM! WHAMM!* Another clatter of covering fire preceded the next series of grenades as other GIs darted forward, ever cautiously, to inspect the enemy strong points. The Germans were gone.

But one could tell where they had been. Well camouflaged slit trenches and fighting holes defiled the pristine snow. Their log roofs bore fresh bright slashes where shot and shell had taken their toll. Spent cartridges littered the area -- virtually hundreds of them where a machine gun had been. Repulsive, mangled corpses sprawled here and there -- "Gott Mit Uns" declared their belt buckles -- "God With Us". The dead lay in their own filth and dirty red snow.

And one could tell which direction the survivors had gone, too. Trampled snow trails led through the trees then vanished beneath heavy ice-encrusted boughs that drooped like curtains to the forest floor. Some were bloody trails -- the trail of the wounded beast.

The Battalion pushed deeper and deeper into the heart of the Monschau Forest. Progress had been good by military standards, gaining 1,500 yards on the 16th of December. However, the deeper they penetrated the stiffer the Germans resisted. Incoming artillery became more and more prevalent as mortar and artillery shells snapped tree tops and sprayed shrapnel on the weary GIs, further delaying their progress. The lead elements of the Battalion became enmeshed in fierce firefights. Making any headway became increasingly difficult and as night approached -- and darkness came quickly in the forest -- the American attack ground to a halt. The infantry had gone as far as they dared.

The men of Company G prepared to dig in for the night. The forward perimeter was established and outposts were placed, providing security against counter-attacks. Beneath the twilight, a supply jeep worked its way as close to the front as the driver dared to replenish ammunition and rations. Everyone feared that the sound of its engine would draw another barrage. But none came and the jeep drove away unmolested into the night.

The struggle through the deep snow combined with the fear and tension of combat was enough to wear down any man. The troops were dog-tired. Their long day had begun on the night of the 15th when they had marched through the frigid forest to reach the stark, open killing ground before the murderous pillboxes at Wahlerscheid. The bloody battle for those fortifications was followed immediately by an attack through the snowy forest. As the day developed the men found themselves fighting their way through the dense, dripping forest, incurring additional casualties from resistance that was sometimes quite fierce. The dreaded tree bursts were a constant threat and caused additional strain on threadbare nerves.

And the weather took its toll, too. The men had been living in the forest for days without basic shelter. They only had their overcoats and blanket rolls to stave off the elements and all suffered from the harsh winter cold -- some more than others -- and some of these were evacuated with frozen feet or cases of crippling trench foot. No matter what the affliction, the line companies were weakened by these non-battle casualties as much as by deaths and wounds.

So now, in the waning light, weary men tried not to think of how cold they were, or how scared they were as they prepared to bed down for the night. Barkley pulled out his GI shovel, scraped away a foot of snow and began to chip at the frozen earth. Blue Eyes, the replacement, hugged his body as he squatted nearby and shivered. His pale eyes watered with despair, almost to the point of tears.

"I'm cold!" he complained.

Barkley looked up. "Dig," he grunted as he chunked his shovel into the frozen earth, "Dig to keep warm."

"It's too cold."

Barkley studied the pathetic boy. *My God,* he thought, *where do they get them? He's barely out of high school. He doesn't belong here.* "Dig, dammit. The work will keep you warm."

Pale streams of vapor snorted from red nostrils, then billowed like clouds from an overworked steam engine.

Blue Eyes stared incredulously at Barkley, wavered for a moment, as if teetering on the brink of some momentous decision, then took up his shovel and hacked furiously at the snow packed earth, venting all his anger and frustration with every stroke. He was livid.

Satisfied, Barkley resumed his own work. *Where do they get them? He'll never make it.*

After a great deal of effort, Barkley had gouged his own meager hole -- more of a slight depression than foxhole, actually. He was wet and cold, so was grateful for the body heat generated by the labor -- one sure couldn't build a fire without drawing enemy fire. His shelter, however, wasn't quite complete. It required thick, heavy branches to deflect or absorb any shrapnel that was sure to come howling from above. Fortunately, downed branches were plentiful, compliments of the German and American artillery bombardments. The big German guns were sure to speak again, yielding more branches, and perhaps casualties, before the night was through. In short order Barkley was dragging battle scarred timbers to his nook to employ as shields, angling them so as to provide access to the hole and afford a firing port in event of a German attack. He suggested that Blue Eyes do the same. Satisfied with his temporary shelter, he unfastened his blanket roll from his pack and crawled into is den. He was home.

Silent now, he thought of Blue Eyes shivering in the next hole. *Dumb kid will never make it,* he repeated. Actually, he bore no malice toward the boy. It was just that he was so young and fresh, so green. He was reminded of young Willie back in Normandy. Like Willie, this was his first attack. Fretwell had paired Blue Eyes with Barkley so the kid could watch and learn. Barkley didn't want to shepherd over him and almost resented his presence, because the new kids always got hit, coughing up blood as they called for their mothers, then died. At least a few of the old hands remained, stalwarts like Joe Guajardo and Hoernke, veterans of Normandy --

reliable, steady men, proven in battle. They were the "old men", old at nineteen and twenty-some years of age. And at nineteen years, he too, was one of them -- an "old hand".

But being experienced was no talisman from danger. Their buddy Joe Benavidez was no longer with them -- victim of a tree burst earlier in the day -- another old Normandy man gone.

A pang of hunger stabbed his gut and prompted him to rummage through his pack in search of a K ration. *The kitchen trucks won't be up tonight*, he reasoned as he worked open a meat can. The contents resembled greasy dog food -- and it was cold. He forced down the gelatinous mush one spoonful at a time, then settled in for the night.

As he curled beneath his blanket he was aware of a disturbing resonance, a steady rumbling of artillery somewhere far to the South. It was a heavy bombardment. Someone else was catching hell. Well, that was their problem, he had enough to worry about and he pulled his blanket tighter and attempted to sleep.

The night sky shrieked. Explosions cracked like thunderclaps as fireballs blossomed among the tree tops. Shrapnel clattered onto log roofs while severed branches crashed heavily all around. No one slept. In the dark someone whimpered.

Later that night, Sergeant Fretwell roused Barkley from his nest and summoned him for a patrol. It was incredibly still. The harassing bombardment had ceased. Bleary eyed, Barkley rolled from his hole, threw off his blanket and grabbed his rifle. His overcoat was stiff from a glaze of ice that shattered and tinkled at every movement. Cold air pierced his lungs, then exploded in a constellation of mystic crystals as his breath collided with the frigid air. As he walked, he became acutely aware of just how noisy his footsteps were. The melting snow refroze in the night, forming a brittle crust which crackled and crunched at every step. The stillness of the night enhanced the noise. *How the hell can you patrol in this!?*

It was a small patrol, only four men or so, and their mission was to infiltrate enemy territory and take a prisoner. They stumbled blindly through the alien forest, heading in the general direction of the German lines. They had no idea where the enemy would actually be. Despite the darkness, their silhouettes contrasted sharply with the snow, making them easily recognizable as human beings as they moved from tree to tree, a threat to anyone watching for hostile activity. After floundering in the snow for a length of time they decided to lay in ambush, hoping to catch a German patrol off guard, and thereby seize a prisoner.

An icy breeze lacerated their faces as they lay motionless beneath the trees, waiting for an enemy that never came. Body warmth melted the snow where they lay and the moisture saturated their clothing, adding to their misery. After a prolonged period of shivering it seemed obvious that the Germans weren't moving -- they would not be able to nab a prisoner. Fretwell decided to return to their own lines. Barkley took the point.

The patrol lost its bearings in the dark and unfamiliar terrain and became lost. It was a hell of a predicament and gave birth to a serious quandary: What if they blundered into the Germans? They stumbled on in the direction they believed would lead them to friendly lines. Barkley cautiously eased aside another branch when suddenly the stillness was shattered by a shrill, panicky voice: "Halt!" It sounded American.

Immediately Barkley dropped and froze in place, then called out, "American patrol!" Hair raised on the back of his neck.

"Sunset," came the challenge in anticipation of the countersign.

Barkley was silent. *The password... just what the hell is the password?* He had forgotten. He whispered to one of the other patrol members, "What's the password?" This man, too, couldn't remember. Neither could Fretwell.

"Sunset!" repeated the sentry. This time the voice had an icy edge to it. He hoped to hear the proper response of "Rain".

"Look," cried Barkley, "we forgot the password."

"You'd better give the goddam password!" The voice was now rattled, alarmed that this could be a German trick.

The patrol muttered among themselves. None of them knew or could remember the countersign. They lay in the snow, fearful that the startled outpost might toss a grenade or open fire on them.

Again Barkley claimed that no one knew the password but they were an American patrol from Company G. As it turned out they *were* lost -- the outpost was not of Company G. The decision as to whether the alerted outpost would open fire or not relied on the patrol's knowledge of American sports trivia, a subject of which Barkley knew virtually nothing.

The cross-examination boiled down to a litany of baseball questions.

"Who won the World's Series in '43?" continued the interrogation.

Oh, for Christ's sake, thought Barkley, *I don't know who won the goddam World Series.* One of the young privates of the patrol frantically pondered the question and begged support from the other members, "It was the Yankees, wasn't it?" he whispered. No one knew for sure. "I'm pretty sure it was the Yankees," repeated the youth. But his voice lacked confidence.

"It was the Yankees, wasn't it?" Fretwell finally blurted. His face remained burried in the snow. The response didn't suit the outpost. It sounded like just what it was: a guess. Unconvinced, more sports questions followed.

This line of questioning was getting nowhere. Fretwell lay paralyzed in the snow, fists balled in fear and frustration. He was no help. It was Barkley who decided to act. "Now look!" he began, "We're an American patrol! We're an American patrol! We're coming in. Don't shoot! We're coming in," and he slowly rose to his feet with is rifle held high over his head in a non-threatening manner. "We're Americans. We're Americans", he cautioned as he slowly advanced. Fortunately, no shots were fired and the excited outpost reluctantly allowed the lost patrol to pass.

Returning to the Company area, Barkley was again lost in the dark. His sense of direction was all fouled up. *Where in the hell's my foxhole?* he wondered as his eyes searched the snow. Other GIs were hunched in their shallow dens with blankets pulled tightly around them, shivering and twitching in fitful attempts at sleep.

Barkley stopped and looked about. It was very dark beneath the pines. He was in his platoon area but was disoriented. His body sagged with fatigue. He was wet and cold and miserable. The weather was freezing.

He wandered among the shadows of the other holes, searching, silently cursing to himself. *Goddamit! Where's my blanket?* He knew he had dropped it outside the entrance to his foxhole to mark its location, but where was it now? Then, by pure chance, he stumbled, litterally, on his own blanket in the snow. He picked it up and shook it, knocking snow from its stiffening folds, then swung it over his shoulders before ducking into his crude shelter.

His wet clothing clung chillingly to his skin. Since he hadn't any overshoes, melted snow had soaked through his combat boots and saturated his socks -- he hadn't been able to change them for days. *How in the hell do I keep from getting trench foot?* he mused bitterly.

Unable to build a fire, he had to rely on his damp overcoat and GI blanket for warmth. He curled into a ball, trying to concentrate his body heat by knotting the blanket at his throat with numb, bleeding fingers. His teeth chattered fitfully. Quivering and shivering, he fell asleep from pure exhaustion.

Ice covered branches creaked in the breeze.

By daylight of December 17, the haggard men of the 38th Infantry prepared to continue the attack towards Dreiborn and the vital dams beyond. A faint but continuous rumbling could be heard to the South. Artillery. Someone was *still* catching hell, and plenty of it! It was ominous. But the doughboys of the 38th had their own problems -- they were still engulfed in the dense, evil forest, confronted by a cunning enemy whose only desire was to annihilate them to keep them from defiling the soil of their beloved Fatherland.

Whereas the men of the 38th thought they had their problems, they didn't know the half of it. Unknown to them, German Field Marshal Gerd von Rundstedt had launched his massive counter-offensive on the morning of December 16th, striking the thinly held American lines to the south of the 2nd Division with a ferocity heretofore unseen on the Western Front. (This accounted for the steady rumbling of artillery heard by Barkley and his comrades.)

Three entire German Armies surged through the Ardennes Forest. Nineteen divisions, two independent brigades plus attachments were in the first wave alone! 250,000 men comprised the initial assault elements, spearheaded by hundreds of tanks and supported by masses of artillery. Many more would follow. The surprise was complete and the thinly spread American defenders were chewed up in the Schnee Eifel and thickets of the Ardennes.

Opposing the Nazi juggernauts were only four U.S. infantry divisions supported by scattered elements of an armored division. Two of these, the 4th and 28th, were experienced combat units that had been badly mauled in the vicious Huertgen Forest. They had been sent to the relative quiet of the "Ghost Front" to recover, rest up and take on replacements. The remaining two divisions, the 99th and 106th, were new, "green" divisions, having been sent to the Ardennes to enable them to adjust to combat conditions on a less intense sector before being fed into the major battle fronts elsewhere. The Ardennes front was an ideal site for this, where combat was limited and the threat of serious enemy countermeasures was believed to be almost nil.

The 99th Infantry Division had arrived in the Ardennes in mid-November and held the northernmost sector of this front. While still "green", the men were beginning to "ripen" and elements of this division were supporting the 2nd Division's attack towards the Roer River Dams.

The fourth division on the Ardennes front was the newest U.S. division on any front, anywhere. These were the naïve, inexperienced youngsters of the 106th Division, "The Golden Lions" who had taken over the 2nd Division's positions east of St. Vith only a few days earlier. Many of them were still sick from the rough passage to Europe followed immediately by a bone chilling journey to the front. They had been expecting nothing more than light action as they eased into combat in a quiet zone. When the German panzers came roaring out of the snow-clad forest to their front they were square in their path and were caught completely unprepared and were subsequently overwhelmed.

The storm of German tanks and infantry pierced the "Ghost Front" at multiple points. Stunned defenders fell back in confusion, leaving only pockets of desperate, yet determined GIs fighting for their lives in last ditch efforts to hold the line. The Ardennes front was crumbling fast and the threat to the entire First U.S. Army was severe. Nazi tanks were rolling westward!

Meanwhile, General Robertson, the 2nd Infantry Division commander, suspected the worst on the morning of the 16th when he received reports of strong enemy penetrations to the south. His division was on the offensive and he had two regiments, the 9th and 38th, far to the front, piercing Germany like a razor sharp stiletto. Now this new development to the south threatened to sever his narrow supply route on the only road to and from his attacking troops. He could loose two entire regiments if this road was cut. He made plans for the immediate withdrawal of the 9th and 38th Regiments, but his corps commander, General Gerow, insisted the attacks continue on the morning of the 17th. However, he did approve of Robertson's withdrawal plan in event the situation to the south worsened. Nonetheless, the attacks through the Monschau Forest were to continue with caution. Reluctantly, General Robertson concurred.

December 17, 1944, Monschau Forest -- The Second Battalion was still spearheading the 38th Infantry's attack and Company G was expected to keep up the pressure on the right flank. When orders would come to move out, as they surely would, Pfc. Barkley would once again find himself on point as lead scout for his squad. He had endured a freezing night, gaining only a few restless hours of sleep beneath his frosty blanket. His breakfast of cold rations, intended by the Army to provide nourishment for the coming ordeal, rolled in his stomach like a great ball of grease and only exacerbated the uneasy feeling that gripped him. The exertion of struggling against the snow, the cold, and the ever present threat of machine guns and artillery grated on his nerves and was wearing him down, both physically and mentally. Still, he resolved to remain alert, if not for his own life then at least for the benefit of the others who trusted in his sharp vision to keep them safe from harm.

It was now the 17th of December. Barkley and his comrades had been living in deplorable conditions since the 13th and had been in combat since the night of the 15th. (The poor dogfaces of the 9th Regiment had been in battle since the 13th!) The advance through the forest was as depressing as ever. Death lurked behind every tree, crouched in every gully, and peered from the branches above, biding its time until overwhelmed by an insatiable hunger which compelled it to lunge out and claim its ghoulish feast of human flesh and slake its thirst with warm red blood.

The strain on Barkley's nerves was growing. The company had already sustained a number of casualties over the past couple days and this battle of attrition was claiming one man here and few others there. It would be only a matter of time before his own luck ran out. Still, progress was being made and the Battalion inched deeper into the forest.

Just when it appeared that the Battalion was on the verge of breaking out of the forest and into the open ground beyond, the attack was abruptly halted. The men were ordered to dig in.

Heavy artillery rumbled in the distance as members of the attached machine gun section set up their weapons and began erecting mini-forts of fallen timbers. Barkley and his buddies, too, began to drag logs and branches for their own protection when the platoon sergeant approached and told them to prepare to move out. "We're pulling back," he said, "There's been a breakthrough to the South and we gotta pull back fast or we'll be cut off."

As the words sunk in, the distant thunder took on a more foreboding tone. Unknown to the men, the entire Battalion was about seven miles deep into German territory and was about to be surrounded. Without hesitation, the men gathered their equipment and waited for the word to fall back. No one relished the idea of a rapid withdrawal. They had been trudging through deep snow for days, often under a hail of shrapnel and were dog tired.

They waited apprehensively, fearing the worst. The forward outposts still had to be called in. Eyes and ears strained to detect movement in the tangle of vegetation before them. Minutes ticked by, then an hour. Machine gunners sat tensely behind their weapons, ready to spray death among the branches while riflemen crouched behind their half-finished breastworks, hoping that the enemy would never come. *If we're pulling out*, they thought, *let's do it!* The waiting was torturous.

Dimming light indicated that it would soon be dark. An air of urgency prevailed.

Men nearly jumped from their skins as a sudden exchange of gunfire erupted somewhere to their left. Company E was entangled in a hot firefight. They gripped their weapons and monitored the battle as it ebbed and flowed. Shadowy figures appeared in the tree line before them. Fingers tensed on triggers. *Who are they, friend or foe?* was the universal question. The answer came as the branches parted and the outpost guards came staggering through the snowy boughs with bewildered looks upon their faces. Sighs of relief rose from the ranks. Now no friendly troops should be to their front unless it would be a patrol from E Company -- any further movement in the forest would probably be hostile.

Night came, swift as death, and with the night came another sharp clash of arms to the left. Apparently the Germans were feeling out the Battalion's defenses, searching for a weak point, and Company E was catching hell.

The metallic cough of American mortars sounded from a clearing to the rear as their shells pooped from their tubes in effort to stop the attack. Soon, bigger guns of U.S. artillery battalions thundered from afar. Death screamed overhead and smashed the forest with blinding flashes as the massive shells joined the mortars in attempts to thwart further advances of German infantry and screen the ensuing withdrawal.

And then the guns were still. Bands of smoke drifted through the trees as if carrying the ghosts of the dead, and the blackened forest was filled with a tense, sinister silence -- the uncanny silence of the unknown. And still the men waited.

At last word came: Fall back. The Battalion was finally organized and the withdrawal had begun. Company E was assigned the unenviable task of rear guard while the remainder of the Battalion commenced its hasty retreat, surrendering all of their hard earned gains without a fight. However, if they didn't hurry, they might be cut off and surrounded. Silently, Company G disengaged and withdrew in the dark. Not one shot was fired.

What had happened was that General Robertson had correctly assessed the rapidly deteriorating situation to the south and deemed it necessary to call off the attack in the Monschau Forest. He had decided to pull back his attacking battalions to plug the gaps appearing in the 99th Division's lines. In so doing he had to form a hasty defense line from his uncommitted units to hold open the retreat route of his attacking forces as they disengaged and withdrew down the only road available to them. His foremost attacking units began to peel off piecemeal from their assault. The 2nd Battalion of the 38th Infantry was spearheading the entire thrust and would be the last unit to return to the twin villages of Rocherath/Krinkelt on the Belgian border where Robertson hoped to stem the German tide. The situation was critical.

The Second Battalion was strung out in column as it retraced its path through the now dark forest -- the gravity of the situation pushed them along at a frantic pace. Artillery thundered steadily from afar, seemingly louder, closer and more menacing at every step. Vicious firefights flared along the route as the rear guard parried determined thrusts of advancing enemy infantry. Flanking squads were attacked and overrun.

At times, the men of Company G were compelled to trot, on orders, to expedite their withdrawal and they became winded. In the course of their harried counter-march they passed the rows of pillboxes at the Wahlerscheid road junction that had been so bloodily captured two days earlier. Abandoning these hard won prizes was a bitter pill to swallow. The men of the 2nd Division referred to them ever after as the "Heartbreak Crossroads", having been forced to relinquish them without a fight. Someday they may have to try to take them again, and that was not a pleasant thought.

But the problem at present was returning to the twin villages as quickly as possible before the Nazi hordes pinched off their retreat route and swallowed them whole. The situation was worsening. Artillery fire increased in volume and intensity, crashing continuously in the direction in which the GIs marched. German artillery and Nebelwerfers, the multiple-barreled rocket launchers known as "Screaming Meemies", showered large caliber shells and 150mm rockets onto the desperate GIs who hustled between the pines. Soldiers looked up and flinched as the big rockets screeched overhead with their demonic howls, striking fear into hearts and plucking at already high-strung nerves. Another volley crashed with the force of a train wreck among the trees somewhere to their front. Shimmering flashes lit the sky. Prodded by the savage shelling and urged on by officers and sergeants, the soldiers quickened their pace. German infantry continued to threaten their flank and rear as the panting GIs fled through the darkness of the forest evil.

Having gained Wahlerscheid junction, the column surged southward down the solitary road that cut a narrow corridor through the firs. Company G was ordered to halt and take up defensive positions at a firebreak. A platoon was ordered to act as the new rear guard and fanned out to entrench along the tree line. The remainder of the Company sank to the snow in support and took a brief breather beneath the boughs to await the passage of Company E, the old rear guard.

Men lay in the snow, chests heaving from the exertion of their forced march. Their equipment and heavy, damp overcoats had been impeding their progress. The thick wool was saturated by melted snow and seemed as heavy as lead. To remedy this, Lieutenant Welch moved down the line and ordered his men to shed their overcoats and blankets -- warmth must be sacrificed for speed. Barkley quickly peeled off his web battle equipment and unbuttoned his coat, then pitched it and his blanket onto one of the fast growing piles of garments that littered the snow. He then re-strapped his pack and ammo belt, having only his light battle jacket to ward off the bitter cold and awaited their next move.

The sound of artillery reverberated through the forest and seemed to be falling everywhere. Now and then neon tracers stitched the darkness as machine gun bullets ripped through the branches.

Eventually, Company E passed through the lines. Company G remained in place, hearts pounding as the world collapsed about them, waiting for the word to pull out, to join the exodus to God-knows-where. Finally, Captain Farrell of Battalion Headquarters arrived and ordered the company to pull out. The men resumed their retreat, striving to leave the black horrors of the forest behind them. They were now the last unit of the 2nd Division to withdraw from the forest -- the rear guard. As they marched, another blood-chilling salvo of Screaming Meemies screeched overhead, grating like a thousand witches' fingernails scraping across Satan's blackboard. The sinister rockets struck farther down the road, exploding with a wicked crash that resounded with the promise of more to come. The harried column plodded on.

Suddenly, the distraught men of Company G emerged from the forest and entered open terrain. The scene before them was terrifying, almost mesmerizing after days of being blinded and smothered by the claustrophobic forest. The men now found themselves in open country, racing for the twin villages only a mile or so away. To their left the blackness was pierced by rampant, flashing explosions that mushroomed brilliantly in mounting fog. Tracer bullets criss-crossed the sky in graceful arches as they sought their targets, and pinpoints of light blinked sporadically in the darkness where individual riflemen blazed away.

Before long, the column approached an intersecting road clogged with long rows of stationary American trucks. Barkley noticed that not one of them was moving. Many had doors flung wide open, an indication that their drivers had panicked and abandoned their vehicles during the chaotic withdrawal. Apparently they had run for their lives. Off to the right, at the head of the motionless convoy, an intense fire blazed. As Barkley drew nearer he recognized the burning object to be the hulk of a knocked out tank -- an American tank. It seemed to be positioned in such a manner as to make the road impassable. It would have been difficult for a truck to maneuver around it in the snow and apparently the drivers had taken to their heels, not wanting to meet the same fate as the blazing tank.

The flames illuminated a macabre, chilling scene. Flickering shadows danced among the motionless, mud-splattered vehicles that stretched into the darkness to left and right, solemn reminders of the horror and panic that took place here a short time ago. Long lines of grim-faced soldiers trod down both sides of the slippery southbound road, a road that had been rendered into an obscene smear by the boots of a thousand others and various vehicles, all fleeing for the questionable safety of Rocherath and Krinkelt, now within sight.

Although snow still clung doggedly to the earth, random patches of soil began to appear as a chilling mist began to fall.

Coatless soldiers cursed their misfortune as the drizzle pelted their faces. The mist, augmented by a growing fog, presented a dismal picture, offering scenes thought nearly impossible a couple of months previous. Discarded equipment littered the route now pitted with craters from the intense shelling. Scattered corpses blended into the roadside mud, marking the route like gruesome milestones while others appeared as dark lumps in the snow -- unfortunate victims of the hellish bombardments that tormented the harried column. Other soldiers leaned over the fallen and seemed confused, as if deciding whether to leave them or carry them away. The passing soldiers stared at the slain with horror and shuddered, knowing that they could be the next to fall. The war definitely would *not* be over by Christmas! The suffering seemed immeasurable.

The dual towns, too, suffered from war. Artillery shells rained liberally upon the farmers' homes, and despite the distance and the thickening fog, one could clearly see that several buildings had been set ablaze, glowing softly, like candles in the gloom. Flames cavorted wildly among roof tops and threatened to spread to neighboring structures. The community, if given its will, would surely have uprooted its foundations and fled the unholy destruction that was rapidly descending upon it.

Meanwhile, twin files of soldiers sloshed down the road now littered with the ruin of war. The mist escalated to a fine, cold drizzle that soaked their jackets and splashed their faces to mix with the grime and sweat of their grubby beards, anointing them like the oils of the last rite.

Soon the frazzled men of Company G reached a clump of farm houses just north of Rocherath. Other companies of the Battalion had already been deployed as they arrived to defend the northeastern approach to the hamlet. The Second Battalion, being the leading element of the 38th Infantry's assault earlier that day, was now the last of the 2nd Infantry Division's units to be extracted from the forest. The entire attacking force of the division had been pulled back, having disengaged from actual contact with the enemy, then withdrawn across the face of a crumbling front to arrive, more or less intact, to set up a defensive position to repel a major enemy offensive. It was a close call -- an achievement that many military experts would have said could never have been accomplished. All of the attacking battalions of the division had run the Nazi gauntlet and had survived, but not without cost -- the casualty toll was mounting. If Barkley had taken a head count he would have noticed that not only was Joe Benavidez no longer with them, but that Frank Santone had disappeared, too, lost sometime during the retreat. Was he wounded? Dead? All they knew was that he was MIA, missing in action.

CHAPTER 18

INTO ROCHERATH

Rocherath, Belgium, was a tiny farming hamlet latticed by a few muddy streets which merged with the lanes of its sister hamlet, Krinkelt. Butted together atop a gentle mound, Rocherath and Krinkelt appeared as a single village, thereby acquiring the American nickname of "The Twin Villages". If anything distinguished one from the other, it was that perhaps the houses of Krinkelt were situated closer together than those of Rocherath, thereby giving it a more urban appearance. The inhabitants of both communities dwelled in sturdy, two-storied stone or brick houses built to last for generations. The approximate dividing point of the twins was a gray stone church that sat on the eastern edge of the community and served parishioners of both villages. Its towering steeple loomed protectively over its faithful flock and kept stern vigil over the village which, surrounded by its fields and ringed by snow-frocked forests, made for a setting of pastoral simplicity. But now, in the winter of 1944, the Devil was hosting a ball in Rocherath and all the demons of Hell had been invited.

Late evening, December 17, 1944 -- After completing its harrowing withdrawal from the Monschau Forest, Company G arrived at the Second Battalion Command Post just north of Rocherath where Captain Skaggs reported for orders. Instead of receiving a much needed rest, his company was ordered to continue marching into town to assist in the defense of the Regimental Command Post which was under attack by infiltrating tanks and infantry. The situation was critical, not a moment was to be lost. Captain Farrell was to continue with them as a guide to their new position.

The night sky shimmered and thundered as the company departed the Battalion area. They marched in a staggered column of twos, one on each side of the road with Captain Skaggs leading one file while Captain Farrell led the other. A perpetual chorus of small arms fire swelled from the darkness and sometimes bright streams of tracers skipped across the very road they were expected to travel. Regardless of the danger, they pushed on, placing blind trust in the judgment of their officers.

They entered the town and followed a street believed to be the most direct route to the Regimental HQ. The steady drizzle mingled with an ever thickening fog to reduce visibility to a matter of yards. At one point the company was just about to pass between two rows of houses when a voice called from the dark, "Get the hell out of there or be cut to ribbons." Startled, the men dove spontaneously into the snow-packed ditches on either side of the road.

Captains Skaggs and Farrell conducted a quick reconnaissance and were shocked to discover that enemy troops occupied the houses on one side of the street while Americans held those on the opposite side. For a moment, an uneasy stalemate existed between the opposing forces and no one controlled the intervening street. The voice in the dark had saved Company G from ambush. After consulting with the officer in charge of the area Skaggs and Farrell decided that an alternate route to Regiment would be more prudent.

The company resumed a more circuitous route to the Regimental CP. Barkley had no idea where they were going, or why. He only followed orders and plodded on, as if in a trance, trailing those before him as they retraced part of their route before trekking off in yet another direction.

It was a confusing, unsettling march. Gunfire rattled from every direction as the column stumbled blindly through the fog shrouded streets. Artillery thudded randomly throughout the village and men winced as subsequent concentrations drew ever closer. Here and there a house burned wildly, lighting the damp, dismal streets like torches set to illuminate the path to Hell. The distinct stutter of a burp gun echoed from some distant alley as another shell screamed in close and crumbled the corner of someone's home. Instinctively, several new men bunched together and were subsequently chewed out by sergeants: "Keep your interval, godammit! Keep your interval!"

As the column approached an intersection a sudden burst of gunfire sent men diving for cover as bullets whipped through the lead platoon. Heads bobbed from roadside ditches as men tried to locate its source. Others peeked from house corners. Several GIs sprinted across a street, bent low, and were chased by a stream of tracers that lashed from the dark. Other soldiers located the tracers' source and returned fire and the gunfire escalated as the leading squads zeroed in on the tell-tale muzzle blasts that betrayed the enemy positions.

Farther back, Barkley had rolled into a slush filled ditch along with his squad and waited for things to develop. Cold mud and snow soaked his clothing, forcing an involuntary shiver to ripple beneath his skin as he stared into the void.

More gunfire shattered the darkness and then as quickly as it had begun, the firing ceased. A squad dashed forward and disappeared in the dark. All was clear. Apparently the company had chanced upon a small group of infiltrating infantry for they were soon driven off, and the column reformed and cautiously resumed its march to relieve the beleaguered headquarters.

It was after midnight when the company finally reached the Regimental Command Post near the center of town. The men deployed among the houses, employing the sturdy structures as strong points and braced for the coming attack. "We'll hold here," they were told, "There'll be no falling back. We'll fight and die here if need be!"

A grim resolve gripped the men. The GI grapevine had worked overtime since their departure from the forest -- scuttlebutt had it that American wounded and prisoners were being summarily executed by rampaging storm troopers. The 2nd Division was up against fanatical Nazis again, this time the dreaded SS. Their villainous reputation as a ruthless, bloodthirsty lot preceded them. Old hands of the 2nd Division bitterly remembered that the same circumstances existed while fighting the German paratroopers in the hedgerows of Normandy. The GIs resolved to reciprocate -- there would be no quarter given -- no prisoners taken. A venomous blood feud was reborn. The mood for the battle was set -- it would be a fight to the finish.

Men kneeled behind windows or peered from doorways as they monitored the struggle that raged elsewhere in the night. Artillery shells screamed overhead and fell in thunderous concentrations wherever some commander or the other deemed it necessary to repel or aid an attack. Small arms fire crackled incessantly from various quarters of town and when one wild firefight died down in one sector another erupted elsewhere. And even more foreboding, word was passed to be on the alert for marauding enemy tanks that had penetrated the hastily placed outer defenses and now lurked somewhere in the town.

Barkley's squad occupied a house that formed part of the defensive perimeter that ringed the Regimental Command Post. Sergeant Fretwell cursed and swore epithets as he posted his men at windows and doorways and cautioned them to remain alert, not only for the enemy but also for stragglers from the battered 99th Division who were allegedly falling back in disorder. "Be damned sure of who you're firing at... could be GIs," he snarled.

Barkley crouched near a shattered window and listened to the battle sounds that drifted through the broken frame. He was cold, dog-tired and scared. The past five days had been exhausting, physically and mentally. *How much more can be expected of us?* he wondered as he resisted the iron weight of fatigue. He glanced around the room, searching for the comforting sight of old comrades like Joe

Guajardo, or Earl Hoernke, or even young Blue Eyes -- men bonded by the misery of war. Others, like Joe Benavidez who had been wounded in the forest and Frank Santone who had disappeared during the withdrawal, were conspicuously absent. *What had happened to them? Dead?... Maybe lost or captured?... No, not captured -- they're shooting prisoners, aren't they?* His eyes snapped back to his window and peered into the drizzly fog, searching for the enemy he hoped would never come.

A variety of colorful flares streaked sharply in the distance, shimmering softly in the mist as they arched ever higher, reached their apex, then plunged with deliberation somewhere beyond the rooftops -- red ones, green ones -- signals and acknowledgements from German assault troops. The enemy was still out there, scheming in the dark, plotting their next move to eradicate the vermin that dared to infest their beloved Fatherland. They would not allow the hallowed soil of Germany to be contaminated by the tainted blood of the American schweinehunds! The very thought was repulsive. To the young German soldiers it was a holy war, a war to preserve the pureness of the Germanic race, and they were more than willing to sacrifice their lives for Germany and their Fuhrer. They were the SS, the pride of Germany. "Meine Ehre Heisst Treue" ("My Honor Is Loyalty") had been engraved upon the blades of their presentation daggers -- "Blut Und Ehre" ("Blood And Honor") embossed upon belt buckles. "Sieg Heil!" they had chanted in unison, "Hail Victory!" "Sieg Heil! Sieg Heil!" over and over until the words thundered and echoed in their ears forever.

By and large, it was eerily still in Barkley's sector. However, the flares, the burning buildings, the encircling battle sounds, the cold foggy streets made for a decidedly haunting atmosphere. On occasion small groups of Germans emerged from the fog, moving ghostlike among the shadows and prowled the streets like wolves closing in for the kill. Alert GIs swallowed their hearts as they leaned into their windows and doorways, leveled their rifles and took aim. The ensuing volley exploded like a thunderclap, startling everyone, especially those who were blind to the action. Echoing shots faded in the mist. Pulses quickened, temples throbbed. All eyes strained in the dark. Men in other houses, those who didn't know what was happening, stood at their posts, alarmed, hearts pounding as they tried to determine what was going on. *Is this it? Is this the big attack?* Gloved fingers tightened on rifles, tensed for another round -- and they waited. But nothing happened. Only the freezing drizzle and fog remained, punctuated by the occasional distant flare and the echoes of remote combats in other parts of town. Time passed slowly. Eyelids grew heavy. Artillery rumbled incessantly beyond the limits of their domain.

Again suspicious movement in the shadows caught the eye of one soldier who alerted the others with a nervous whisper. Everyone watched attentively. *Who is it? Who is it?* Fingers curled around triggers. Dark figures stirred in the shadows across the street, creating anxious moments for the men as they tried to decide whether the specters were GIs or Germans. Suddenly the mysterious figures bolted into the street and someone cried, "Halt!"

"Don't shoot! Don't Shoot!" came a frantic plea. They were Americans.

A half-dozen men were waved into a house. They were forlorn soldiers from the haggard 99th Division -- several were without weapons and a couple had no helmets. They had seen Hell close and up front and didn't want anymore. They were completely demoralized.

"For God's sake get outa here!" one shrieked in wild-eyed terror. "There's thousands of 'em out there. Thousands! And they got tanks, too."

The poor fellows had had one hell of an initiation to battle. Unknown to the 2nd Division men, they had put up a good fight in the forest to the east and had held longer than anyone could have expected. But now they were looked upon as beaten men, totally unnerved by what they had experienced. An officer sent them back to the CP where, hopefully, Regiment would deal with them.

Then all was still again. *There's thousands of 'em* -- the words rang in their heads, creating doubts as to their own survival. The men of Company G tried to settle their rattled nerves while listening to other combats that erupted to the east, north and south, allowing them time to contemplate their own fate on this black winter night. They could only guess who was winning or whether they'd be cut off from friendly troops at any moment, forced to fend for themselves, to fight to the last. *We'll hold here. We'll fight and die here.* That was the word.

It wasn't until the wee hours that the rattle of gunfire sputtered, popped, then petered out. The fighting had ended -- for now. Barkley gripped his rifle and waited. Who knows what will come next? Then an officer appeared and told the squad to follow him. The men struggled to their feet and soon the survivors of Company G were being led through the dark streets only to be ushered into another house deeper in town. They were told to catch what sleep they could.

Bone-tired, Barkley stumbled upstairs with others and was soon bedded down on a floor crammed shoulder to shoulder with rows of GIs. Barkley squeezed between two men and tried to get some sleep. It was awfully uncomfortable. His ammunition belt cut into his back and he had to cradle his rifle in his arms. The men were sandwiched so tightly that he was unable to turn over to get more comfortable -- his muscles knotted in a painful cramp.

The abandoned houses hadn't any heat. Every window had been shattered by concussion, granting winter access to every room. Curtains fluttered limply in the breeze. The men were exhausted, wet, hungry, and cold -- their overcoats and blankets lay in the snowy forest miles away where they had dropped them to lighten their loads. Men shivered uncontrollably. Fingers were stiff and brittle from the frigid weather and throbbed painfully from a profusion of splits and bloody cracks. Some men suffered severely from nearly six days of constant exposure to the harsh winter elements endured during the forest fight and subsequent withdrawal through snow, slush and rain. Their feet were wet and blue toes ached painfully in icy boots. Many wheezed with every breath or hacked raspingly, spewing up gouts of phlegm from congested lungs, further irritating throats already sore and raw from chronic coughing. Fevers were common, yet few riflemen were considered sick enough to be relieved from duty and pulled from the line. Only those clearly diagnosed with frozen feet were evacuated. Barkley, who had never received overshoes, was miserable. His feet felt as numb as blocks of wood. But he knew that his squad was already short-handed from casualties and every man was needed. He wasn't going to let down his end of the bargain and resolved to tough it out. Worn out, he fell asleep.

Sleep, the first since the few hours of the previous night in the forest, would be very short and not so sweet. It was the early hours of December 18th. The men of Company G had precious little sleep since rising on the night of the 15th to assault the pillboxes. They would receive even less in the days to come.

General Robertson, commander of the 2nd Infantry Division, made it clear to his subordinates that it was imperative that the twin villages be held. They sat directly astride a major east-west road network leading to the massive supply base at Liege some thirty miles to the rear. The loss of Rocherath and Krinkelt would enable the German armored forces to streak westward to take these supplies, then wreak havoc in the rear of the entire First Army. By stopping the Germans here, General Robertson would be able to buy time to build a stronger defensive position on Elsenborn Ridge, a natural strong point a couple miles to the rear of the villages. Here he would concentrate his forces, massing vast numbers of artillery and have his infantry dig in. Elsenborn Ridge dominated the entire northern approach.

But, before he would be able to accomplish the mission of fortifying Elsenborn, he would have to hold Rocherath/Krinkelt. To do this he selected Colonel Boos' 38th Infantry Regiment. The 38th would be virtually sacrificed in an effort to buy time for other elements of the 2nd and 99th Divisions to secure Elsenborn. The 38th would not be entirely alone, however, as it was supplemented with a battered battalion of the 9th Infantry holding a vital road junction about one-half mile east of Rocherath, as well as fragments of the 23rd Infantry which had fought with valor while aiding the 99th Division during the primary phase of the German counter-offensive. The defenders would also be bolstered by elements of the 741st Tank Battalion and 644th Tank Destroyer Battalion to counter the inherent threat of the abundant German armor. The remainder of the 2nd Division would fall back to Elsenborn Ridge. The stunned survivors of the 99th Division were to pass through the Twin Villages and join the men preparing the Elsenborn defenses. Some stragglers from that organization, like those of the 23rd Infantry, were merged into the units holding Rocherath and Krinkelt.

All of this required Robertson to hold a disintegrating front under heavy attack while withdrawing his attacking forces at Wahlerscheid parallel to the front of the advancing enemy, then reposition those forces withdrawn to defend the villages while the remainder of his units reformed on Elsenborn Ridge. To accomplish these goals was a tactician's nightmare. For those selected to defend the villages, it was to be an ordeal they'd never, ever forget... if they survived.

For the Germans, the taking of Rocherath and Krinkelt was the highest priority for the Sixth Panzer Army's initial assault. The villages were the linchpin to their success. Their capture cleared the route to Liege, then on to the ultimate objective far on the coast, Antwerp. The villages were to have been taken on the first day of the offensive, December 16th, by infantry. However, the green U.S. 99th Infantry Division had put up a terrific fight and, aided by elements of the 2nd Division's 23rd Infantry, had stalled the thrust long enough to allow General Robertson to pull his attacking units from the Wahlerscheid assault.

Frustrated by this early setback, the Germans threw in their best troops to carry out the mission; they were determined to take the towns. The Waffen SS were tossed into the fray. The 1st SS Panzer Division ("Leibstandarte Adolf Hitler") jabbed from the south while the vaunted 12th SS Panzer Division ("Hitler Jugend") reinforced the thrusts of the 277th Volksgrenadier Division aimed directly at Rocherath/Krinkelt.

The 12th SS Panzer Division had a reputation for daring and brutality. During the Normandy campaign they became notorious for their slaughter of Canadian prisoners. They were equipped with the very best tanks the Nazi arsenal could offer and were highly confident of their assignment. Their tanks included not only the reliable Mark IV panzer, but also the excellent 47-ton Mark V "Panther" with its deadly 75mm gun. Each tank's cannon was complimented by two machine guns. The Mark IV was equal to the American Sherman, while the Panther far outclassed anything in the U.S. arsenal and was much feared by American tankers and was sheer terror to the U.S. infantrymen. A variety of armored assault guns, mean and lean in appearance and resembling low slung tanks, were also tossed into the fight and were just as menacing to American infantrymen as their panzer cousins.

The youthful members of the 12th SS Panzers were highly trained and indoctrinated far beyond the point of fanaticism. Brutal killing was all they knew. Their divisional commander, Hugo Kraas, addressed his troops before the battle, evoking them to give their all for the Fatherland. He pressed the point with this chilling sentence: "I ask of you, and expect of you, not to take any prisoners with the possible exception of some officers who might be kept alive for the purpose of questioning." They eagerly complied.

December 18th, 1944 -- The half-dawn came, foggy and cold. Inside the houses men lay on the floors in rows, resembling cadavers laid out in an over-crowded morgue instead of soldiers asleep in their ersatz barracks. Red-eyed sentries kept vigil from doors and windows and wished that they, too, were among the prostrate bodies packed tightly across the floor, lost for the moment in the vacuum of slumber.

As gray light seeped through windows, sergeants entered and rudely kicked dozing men's boots, breaking the bonds of cherished sleep. "Get up! Let's go! Everybody up." Soldiers stirred and grumbled and coughed as they disentangled their bodies and cursed the day they were born. A scarecrow of a man rose and stepped over his prostrate comrades, then exited the room and entered another where he unbuttoned his fly and urinated in the corner of someone's parlor. It was morning, December 18th.

Barkley awoke, feeling thick with fatigue and shook his head to clear the cobwebs that muddled his senses. He was vaguely aware of where he was... the crowded room... the soldiers in various stages of wakening, some supported by an elbow, yawning, blinking. Others remained still as death, unwilling to rise. Sergeants strutted about, imploring the men to rise and Barkley rose slowly, stiffly, an automatic reaction to orders given.

Awake now, he became aware of the sounds of a furious battle raging somewhere to the east and he knew the nightmare was real and not some abomination from his dreams. The ordeal was far from over.

The company was to resume its arc of defense around the Regimental Command Post. Sergeant Fretwell assembled his squad and led them downstairs where he ordered them outside to take up positions among the neighboring houses. As Barkley pushed past the door he entered a world thick with fog. Even nearby houses appeared soft and indistinct.

No sooner had the first few soldiers entered the street than a deafening burst of gunfire erupted from the opposing houses. Bullets snapped past their ears and splattered into the wall and door behind them, compelling those in the lead to dash for the shelter of the nearest dwelling while the others, reeling from the storm, clambered back inside. Although fired point blank, none of the men were hit as far as Barkley could tell. Unknown to the Americans, the Germans had spent their night in the houses directly across the street. Apparently the Germans had been just as startled by the sudden appearance of the Americans as the Americans had been of them.

Barkley had been the third man to exit the house when the firing began and chased after the other two who ran a veritable gauntlet before dodging behind a neighboring building. Bullets smacked savagely against its walls as they skittered around the corner. At the same moment, a fusillade of gunfire exploded from the house they had just vacated as the occupants returned the fire. The Germans responded with every weapon they had, igniting a wild, close quarter firefight.

Sheltered now behind the house, Barkley's group kicked open a back door, then cautiously entered. A quick reconnaissance ensured the house was vacant and they quickly joined the fray, taking pot-shots at muzzle flashes and vague shadows that appeared in the widows across the street.

The maddening burr of enemy machine guns rent the air as tracer bullets ripped up one house then skipped to the next, intent on suppressing the American fire. In an instant, a cluster of enemy soldiers dashed from the fog and into the street but a withering volley caught them midway and all tumbled to the pavement and were still. And with that, the gun firing ceased. Gun smoke seeped from bolt-open rifles as defenders jammed home fresh clips and braced for the next assault.

Barkley sat on his haunches near a window and kept watch on the house across the street. As he squatted, he listened to other, distant, combats that resonated from the fog. Rifles and machine guns blurted sporadically from other sectors where comrades fought for their lives. Grenades thudded dully in the distance, adding impetus to others' desperation.

Rrrrrp! The harsh burr of an enemy machine gun reclaimed his undivided attention as tracer bullets flashed close by. A second burst swept the edifice of his own house and he was down in a heartbeat as the window sill disintegrated in a shower of splinters. Bullets thudded savagely against an interior wall, gouging great holes in the plaster. On his belly now, he scrambled to another window to peer gingerly into the street beyond.

Roiling smoke and fog restricted his vision to a matter of yards. A steady drizzle continued to fall, cold and relentless -- a weak attempt by nature to dilute the blood that leaked from still warm bodies. Meanwhile, the battle ebbed and flowed in violent impulses, accented by the occasional thud and flash as grenades were hurled from one house to the next, a prelude to a final, vicious assault. Again bodies fell in the street as battle sounds rose to a deafening crescendo.

Suddenly the back door burst open and in came Sergeant Fretwell. "Follow me," he panted, "We're gonna try to flank the sons-a-bitches."

Barkley and the others joined him behind the house where they edged their way towards a corner. Four of them now, they pressed their bodies hard against the house's outer surface as they neared a street they hoped to cross. Battle sounds came from all directions, but their immediate concern was a bright stream of tracers that flashed down the length of the street they wished to cross. Fretwell was in the lead, inching slowly along the house in effort to take a peek around the corner. Barkley edged cautiously behind him with rifle at the ready. All the while, bright tracers shot down the street at regular intervals, glowing vividly in the fog about five feet off the ground.

Fretwell glanced quickly around the corner then suddenly jerked back as another stitch of tracers snapped past. *Oh, shit!* thought Barkley, *How in the hell are we going to get across?* Fretwell faltered, fidgeted. What to do? He originally wanted to take the squad across the street to a more advantageous position, but the machine gun fire presented a definite deterrent.

Again a string of tracers streaked past, cutting the same path as the previous bursts, about shoulder high. Fretwell studied the line of fire, then spoke: "Barkley, do y'think we can get below that an' on to the other side?"

Barkley was dubious. It looked too risky and he said so. Fretwell wasn't big on taking chances himself and Barkley was afraid he'd do as he'd done in Normandy -- order his scout out first.

As Fretwell and Barkley pondered their options, the other fellows kept watch on nearby houses, alert for enemies, for no one knew just which houses held GIs and which held Germans. Suddenly one fellow caught sight of movement across the street and warned the others. They could see that it was another GI doing the same thing they were doing: peeking around a house corner to observe the same glowing line of tracer bullets.

Barkley and Fretwell watched the lone soldier as he intently studied the tracers. The intermittent bursts remained at a constant height above the surface of the street. It seemed as if the enemy gunner was firing from a fixed position on some distant target with short, rapid bursts. The lone soldier monitored the fire a while longer, then started across. Apparently he came to the same conclusion as Fretwell for he ran stooped double, figuring he'd stay out of harm's way by keeping well beneath the line of fire. He had barely entered the street when he suddenly dropped hard to the surface. *Oh, Christ*, Barkley thought, *He slipped!* But no! He hadn't slipped, he'd been shot! The soldier shuddered as more bullets slammed into his body and he was dead, a crumpled heap in the middle of the street.

Barkley was stunned. The bright stitch of tracers remained well above the man when he was hit. Then a grim realization dawned on him: another machine gun must have been working in concert with the first. The second gun was firing at a much lower level, using the first gun to lure out unsuspecting soldiers. The second gun wasn't using *any* tracer ammunition, thus seemingly "invisible". The poor GI walked right into it.

"Neat trick!" Barkley grimaced. He'd remember that one.

Fretwell paled. "The hell with this!" he cried as he inched away from the corner and took his men to the rear of the house to find another route. They would *not* be crossing *that* street.

In time things quieted and they rejoined their platoon which occupied several adjacent houses. An unknown number of Germans still held the houses across the street and everyone was cautioned to remain alert. Barkley eased up to a window. Before him the street was heavy with fog. Disfigured bodies lay scattered between him and the enemy, appearing as shapeless piles of rags. Only the appearance of a hand or boot or bloody head indicated that these things once were human. Barkley contemplated their pitiful forms. *There are so many ways to get killed and you never know that the breath you just took may well be your last. A sniper could take me right now. The roof might cave in. Or maybe the next burst of machine gun fire has a bullet with my name on it. An artillery shell might be in the air right now, plunging towards this house, destined to destroy this very room. There are so many ways to die. And death can come so quickly.* The incident involving the tracers in the foggy street still troubled him. *That could have been **me**!* He longed for a cigarette.

It was still early morning, yet save for a series of explosions and a riot of small arms fire that sounded from elsewhere, all was unexpectedly quiet in the immediate vicinity. Then someone heard it.

It was faint, but distinct -- there was no doubt as to what *that* sound was.

"Tanks!" someone shouted, "Tanks!" It was a woeful plea, more a cry of desperation than warning.

Barkley paused and listened. There it was -- the unmistakable squeal and clank of heavy treads clattering over bogey-wheels. Electric shivers raced up his spine. The last time he squared off with a tank, back in Normandy, he barely survived. Now they loomed out there again somewhere, a nightmare lurking in the gloom. Apparently they had overrun the outer defenses and now intended to annihilate the remaining defenders.

The sound grew louder. Eyes and ears strained and the world stood still for a long, intolerable moment as the inevitable drew closer. The earth trembled, and then there they were. Barkley's blood ran cold as the first monster emerged from a swirl of fog, grinding down the street with evil intent. It was huge, massive -- a gigantic Panther. Its long cannon protruded menacingly, as if searching for trouble. German infantrymen clung like parasites to its deck, whooping and cheering as they rode their machine into battle. They acted as if they were drunk. Then to Barkley's horror, another tank followed the first, and then another, each swarming with howling, jubilant panzer grenadiers. More infantry trotted alongside and behind the iron beasts. Barkley's heart pounded wildly as he checked his weapon to ensure it was loaded, then quickly pushed off the safety.

With a crash, a devastating volley of small arms fire exploded from American strong points as each tank ran the gauntlet of houses. The young panzer grenadiers seemed oblivious to the volumes of gunfire that poured from the houses and cheered lustily as bullets slashed through them and clanged off the armor of their wildly careening mounts. When hit they tumbled to the street, fully ignored by their comrades who laughed maniacally as they aimed and returned the fire. It was madness! It was terrifying! *They must be hopped up on dope*, Barkley thought as he aimed his rifle at the crazily laughing madmen and triggered round after round. They were so close he could hardly miss. It was like shooting ducks in a shooting gallery. Other GIs did likewise and the tank-borne soldiers were caught in murderous cross-fires. Sheer bedlam filled the street. Dead and wounded Germans spilled from their charging battle wagons and dropped heavily to the street as their tanks churned on. The survivors leaped off and scurried into nearby houses and began to spray the American houses with automatic weapons. It seemed as if they all had burp guns. Gunfire rose to a deafening roar.

From his window Barkley noticed that several dead and wounded Germans lay directly in the paths of their own tanks. The wounded flung up hands in weak attempts ward off the closing behemoths, then screamed horribly as the heavy treads smashed them flat. Others struggled to gain their feet in pathetic attempts to join their comrades in nearby houses but were gunned down by cold-hearted Americans. "Shoot them! Shoot them!" someone had cried, recalling the tales of wounded GIs murdered by Nazis earlier in the struggle. The Black Flag had been raised -- no prisoners would be taken.

Two more tanks emerged from the fog and trailed the others. Now five Panther tanks converged on the Regimental Command Post, firing their cannon at suspected American strongholds as they came. Brilliant explosions engulfed several houses, pitching masonry into the streets like stones from volcanic eruptions. Desperate GIs fired volley after volley at the soldiers that accompanied the tanks, forcing them, like their predecessors, to take refuge in the houses on either side of the street. The tanks, however, were unstoppable. A few daring soldiers flung hand grenades at the steel hulks, but to no avail -- the grenades simply bounced off the thick armor and exploded harmlessly in the street. Seeming irritated at these futile attempts, the tankers cranked their guns in the direction of their tormentors and let fly with a round or two of high explosives before moving on. Black smoke poured from several battered houses, drawing bright flames that flickered from roofs and windows.

Meanwhile, bullets by the hundreds flew in every direction. Tracers skipped off pavement and splintered woodwork and pocked stone walls as machine guns cast their webs, making streets all but impassable. The smoke of burning buildings blended with fog so thick that it became difficult to tell if a knot of crouching, running soldiers was friend or foe. At times it was discovered only too late that the ghostlike figures were German assault troops. Such an error could prove fatal. Once again, nobody knew who held which house and the struggle degenerated into a chaotic free-for-all.

More panzers entered the villages where lanes and alleys seethed with unbridled savagery. German tanks lumbered at will through the streets and seemingly unopposed, raising hell among the houses as they moved from one to the next. Their great gun turrets swept from left to right and back again, as if sniffing out targets before blasting American strong points.

Barkley watched in horror as a tank poked its long cannon through a window down the street and fired. A fireball burst from the house as debris clattered to the pavement. Clouds of black smoke poured from the window and before the smoke had cleared the tank moved on to the next building and fired again. Flame and smoke and wanton destruction filled the house, surely killing or maiming anyone unfortunate enough to have remained inside. Satisfied with its devastation, the tank moved on and disappeared in the fog.

A couple of American tanks blundered onto the scene, appearing weak and inadequate for the task before them. Outgunned and under-armored, the U.S. tanks were no match for a head-to-head confrontation with the mammoth German panzers. Their only chance was to play a lethal game of hide-and-seek among the ruins and hope to get off a round or two through the thinner armor plating of their rear, or possibly score a lucky side shot. No sooner had they arrived, it seemed, than the American tanks pulled out. The infantry were on their own.

From his window, Barkley watched spellbound as the panzers negotiated the narrow streets. The shrill squeal of tracks passing over bogeys set his hair on end. The heavy treads grated on the pavement, crushing anything and everything in their path. Rubble from crumbled walls was ground to dust beneath forty-seven tons of pressure while the odd piece of furniture that had spilled from ruptured homes was splintered beyond recognition. Time and again tanks aimed their cannons at individual houses, fired a shell or two, then moved on to create havoc elsewhere. Barkley knew he couldn't stop a tank with his rifle, but at least he could keep the German infantry at bay. Keeping one eye on the marauding armor, he scanned the neighborhood for likely targets and triggered a round or two whenever the opportunity arose.

Soon, another German tank appeared in the street with machine guns blazing. It grew larger and larger until its mass seemed to fill the street. It drew abreast of the house that held Barkley's squad and suddenly lurched to a halt and began to crank its gun in their direction.

"Jesus Christ!" someone cried, "Get out! Get out!" A panicky GI scrambled up a nearby staircase while Barkley and several others dove for the cellar in a madcap dash to escape the blast that was sure to come. The cannon's muzzle pointed at a window -- then fired. The foundation shook. Chunks of masonry, splintered wood and shrapnel flew in every direction. Gritty smoke rolled down the stairwell like an unholy specter and embraced those who cowered there with its terrifying shroud. Deafened by the blast, men cringed in horror as the malevolent cloud reached out to them, as if straining to touch their very souls and claim them for its own. Men gagged and choked and were shocked to discover that they were still alive, that the house hadn't collapsed upon them. Anyone remaining upstairs was surely dead -- the concussion alone could snap one's neck!

The tank gunned its engine and rumbled off to seek another target. Men hacked and gagged as smoke and dust filled their lungs and someone yelled, "Get up there! Now!" Immediately a bevy of soldiers raced upstairs, desperate to reach the main floor before SS troopers stormed the house. Lingering diesel fumes blended with the pungent odors of cordite and smoke, burning nostrils like acid and caused eyes to weep and stomachs to sicken. A drab-clad body lay sprawled across the floor, covered with dust and debris.

A gust of bullets whipped through a window, smashing everything in their path. GIs dropped to their hands and knees as they scrambled past shattered furniture and heaps of plaster just in time to push their rifles through windows and release a galling fire. Storm troopers tumbled like tenpins. Those not hit reeled as if struck by a gale force wind, then teetered in a moment of indecision before falling back amidst a hail of bullets. Spent cartridges tinkled to the floor as an empty clip pinged from Barkley's rifle. He rolled away from his window and pulled another clip from his belt while others took the lives of several young Germans who writhed in the street. A half-dozen or more of Hitler's supermen lay scattered in the muck outside their house. Some were within spitting distance.

Another clutch of storm troopers burst from a swirl of fog to the left and swept like a whirlwind across the street. Startled riflemen responded with a few rapid shots but none were hit and the enemy disappeared behind a distant house. "Watch that flank! Keep yer eyes on 'em!" came a sharp command and a couple GIs scuttled, bent double, to seek windows on that side of the house just as another flurry of gunfire erupted from their front. A few GIs returned a desultory fire. Ammunition was getting low.

Meanwhile, three Panther tanks planted themselves at an intersection a couple hundred yards distance, each pointing in a different direction and began plastering the American houses with high explosives. Then a lone Panther roared through a nearby intersection, disturbing a cloudy bank before disappearing deeper into the village. An explosion soon followed and echoed among the houses. Another clatter of small arms fire rose from the same direction, muffled by the chilling mist and fog that permeated the streets and alleys. A column of black smoke rolled high above the site.

The rampaging panzers seemed invincible. The tanks and fanatical SS men pushed hard on the Americans and closed in from every direction. It appeared as if this would indeed be Company G's last stand. But, unknown to the GI behind the rifle, it was no longer a combined effort by the enemy. The tanks, now denuded of their infantry, were acting on their own. American riflemen kept the tank commanders buttoned up beneath their hatches which restricted their vision so that they roamed the streets like nearsighted rhinoceros' -- extremely dangerous, but nearly blind. The SS grenadiers, no longer riding jubilant on their armored vehicles, were being held at arms' length by desperate GIs who believed, rightly so, that they were fighting for their lives. And furthermore, the defenders benefited from the excellent fire support given by the American artillerymen. Devastating concentrations of high explosives pummeled the Germans' line of advance and stifled the flow of reinforcements. The tenuous defense was holding.

Eventually, as these actions unfolded, the seemingly unstoppable panzers began to fall victim to the close confines of urban warfare. A handful of intrepid GIs armed with bazookas stalked the streets to ambush passing tanks from cellars and alleys. Others did the same from second story windows. Most of their rockets simply glanced off the thick armor plating, but occasionally one struck home and ripped off a track or managed to penetrate a weak point.

The few American tanks and tank destroyers that dared to challenge their more powerful German counterparts nested in barns or backed down narrow cul-de-sacs to await the prowling panzers that would eventually cross their sights. Firing from seclusion, they managed to account for others before clattering posthaste to the next possible ambush sight. The tankers, too, were fighting for their lives.

Whenever a German tank was disabled it would jolt to a halt, as if something powerful had reached deep inside the beast and ripped out its guts. Escape hatches clanged open, releasing rolls of fuming smoke that drew up black clad crewmen desperate to escape their burning vehicle. American riflemen took aim from nearby houses and gunned them down as they scrambled for their lives. It was a regular turkey shoot. Those not hit clambered from their hatches and scurried like rabbits as bullets pinged off the armor and skipped along the street. Few, if any survived. Sometimes the first German to expose his head from a hatch would be killed outright, falling back inside where his lifeless body hampered the escape of his comrades. Bright orange flames lapped the air as black, oily smoke boiled from the flaming coffin. Blood curdling shrieks rose from its depths as men roasted alive and soon only the sickening stench of burning flesh was all that remained of young men once bold and strong.

But the valiant effort of the Americans was not without cost -- dead GIs lay crumpled where they fell. Destroyed U.S. armor burned like torches in people's yards or clogged the streets with their charred, dormant hulks, holed through and through by powerful armor piercing ammunition. Crews were dismembered or incinerated. Undaunted, others continued to fight tenaciously, hiding among the ruins and alleyways, waiting for the odd chance to score a kill.

The remaining panzers now lacked proper infantry support and had lost their initiative. Unable to maneuver among the narrow streets and being fired upon at seemingly every turn, they quickly succumbed to desperation. Bazooka teams popped from windows or dashed from behind houses to release their rockets, then vanished before machine guns could cut them down. American armor waited patiently and continued to chalk up scores. Eventually, five Nazi tanks sat motionless in Company G's area, surrounded by their dead crewmen. Others blazed elsewhere throughout the town and surrounding countryside. The tide of battle was turning.

Sensing a death trap among the narrow, blinding avenues, the surviving German tanks withdrew from the cauldron of smoke and fire and killing steel. Without armored support, many of the German grenadiers abandoned their houses and melted to the eastern fringe of town where the fighting tapered to a few parting shots, then ceased altogether. Company G had won its battle.

Knocked out Panther tank in Rocherath, Belgium. The tank's cannon barrel has been completely blown away – bearing testimony to the ferocity of the battle.

CHAPTER 19

WELCH'S DEFENSE

Late morning, December 18, 1944 -- The clamorous din of battle surrendered to a strange, unsettling stillness. A tense atmosphere prevailed where unbound violence simmered just beneath the surface, ready to boil up at any moment and once again spill onto the streets and alleys of the smoldering villages. Dead men and wrecked machines were everywhere, strewn amidst the ruined and battered homes.

Deep within the shadows of a house, Pfc. Barkley unscrewed the cap from his canteen and took to a celebratory swig. He had been in many battles before, but none as savage as this. Exhausted, he sat against a wall and closed his eyes. But rest was not to come. It was discovered that several pockets of Germans remained in the vicinity and someone had to evict them. Since Company G was not presently engaged, the job fell to them. Platoons were assembled, then set out on their assigned missions. As Barkley's squad filed out a door, a sergeant stood beside a kitchen table piled with ammunition and stacks of D-bars. Soldiers stopped to fill ammo pouches while the sergeant handed out as many of the sickening sweet chocolate bars as one cared to take. Barkley took two.

Barkley's squad advanced down a street, alert for snipers as they worked from house to house. Before long, gunfire erupted from the mist somewhere to the front. BARs and light machine guns laid down suppressing fires while squads assaulted individual houses. Grenades were tossed through windows, exploded. Assault parties burst through doors, screaming like madmen as elusive shadows slipped from room to room or dashed for back doors in attempts to escape the sudden fury that fell upon them. Teams of soldiers moved warily up staircases to search for hiding enemies who sometimes rolled grenades upon them. Vicious combats unfolded at close quarters, leaving dead and wounded men sprawled in bedrooms, kitchens and parlors. Others, those who had escaped the houses, were gunned down as they ran through neighbors' yards. The once peaceful Belgian homes had become charnel houses, places of chaos, destruction and death. Warm blood sopped decorative rugs or stained the hardwood floors.

Grenades boomed dully a block or so away as Barkley's squad leap-frogged another. A guttural burr sent bullets ripping down the street as a burp gunner cut loose from a nearby house. Men dove for cover as bullets knifed past them. Rifles popped rapidly as one soldier covered another's advance and the attack proceeded from one house to the next.

At one point, Barkley came across a soldier cowering behind a wall. It was Sergeant Gascon, the loud-mouthed braggart so despised by the younger privates of the squad. Much to Barkley's satisfaction, Gascon's stateside leave had not come through before the Division set off on its attack some days earlier. Now Gascon cringed behind his shelter, flinching at every sound. He trembled violently, sobbing incoherently. He acted as if he didn't know what to do and refused to participate in the action and Barkley hated him for it. He hated him not only for all of his bullshit stories and bullying he had done in the past, but also for being a sergeant and not acting like one, allowing all the others to do his fighting for him. Disgusted, Barkley moved on. Later he heard that Gascon was eventually wounded or evacuated as a combat exhaustion case, but whatever his circumstances, Barkley did not feel sorry for him.

After a series of wild, close quarter actions, the Germans were finally pushed from the center of town and the squads once again occupied houses lining the streets of central Rocherath. All was quiet, the battle won. Again each squad's strength had been whittled by casualties as they lost a man here, and another there. Some squads could barely muster half strength.

The survivors collapsed within the ruins. One hardly noticed the howl of passing artillery anymore -- it had become commonplace. Only the crackling of burning buildings disturbed the brooding silence as flames lapped at rooftops and danced lightly along exposed, charred beams. Rolls of smoke boiled from the clutter of crumbling homes and darkened the streets now clogged by rubble and the hulks of scorched tanks and demolished vehicles. Dead Germans lay everywhere -- in the streets, in the buildings and the muddy, snow-slushed yards. Several smoldering corpses dangled grotesquely from knocked out tanks where the crews had met their fate by bullet and fire. The pathetic personal effects of residents had spilled from homes and lay strewn across muddy yards, debouched by the tempest of war. Fences were broken and trampled down. Trees laid bare and felled. It was as if a monstrous tornado had devastated the town and left it for dead.

It was the same within the houses. Every room had been ransacked by battle. Broken glass and scores of spent cartridges littered floors smeared by muddy boots and blood. Curtains had been ripped from windows. Wallpaper hung loosely from plaster that had been blasted, holed and lacerated by explosions, bullets and shrapnel. Furniture had been smashed and overturned. It looked as if a herd of wild animals had stampeded the place, crashed through it, then left, leaving a path of destruction in their wake.

The moans of the wounded disrupted the silence, aggravated by the haunting sobs of a soldier huddled in a corner, teetering on the brink of complete and total psychological breakdown. A medic entered the house, burdened by his satchel of sulfa powder, battle dressings, morphine syringes and other medical paraphernalia and quickly made his way to the wounded. The medics were life savers, angels of the highest order and highly revered by the combat soldiers. After stanching the leaking blood and sometimes performing rudimentary surgery he attached evacuation tags to each casualty, listing the nature of the wounds and which life saving measures he had taken to stabilize his patient. Litter bearers were summoned to evacuate the worst cases. Those with less severe wounds, the walking wounded, were given directions to an aid station and hobbled out of the house, trying to gain their bearings among the ruins and devastation. Others, those who bore minor scrapes, cuts and superficial wounds, ignored their injuries and remained on duty.

The medic moved on to visit the next house and the room was consumed by the whimpering of the poor fellow sobbing in the corner. His nerves were shot. He knew he couldn't be spared -- every man capable of wielding a weapon was desperately needed. In a gesture of compassion, a soldier tried to console his trembling buddy, looking helpless as he gently patted his comrade's quaking shoulders, massaging them while cooing soothing words: "It's alright. It'll be okay." But everyone knew it wasn't. The poor fellow shivered and wept unto himself, oblivious of a world gone mad. Others dared not look at him, as if his affliction was contagious and could be transmitted simply by sight. They turned their faces, half embarrassed for themselves and half for the wretched creature trembling in the corner. The soldier's comrade draped an arm around his buddy's heaving shoulders and glared hatefully, not so much at the others, but more at the monster of war, the beast that had sucked the very soul from his friend, his buddy, the man once sound and robust who had shared foxholes and rations with him in deplorable weather conditions. They had exchanged ribald jokes and tales of home and recognized each others loved ones by the photos they carried. They were as close as brothers, comrades in arms who had shared countless dangers on many fields of battle. But now his buddy was gone, lost to a world none of them could fully comprehend -- not fully. He had simply reached his breaking point. It was heartbreaking and it could happen to anyone -- and that was the true horror of it. No one dared to look at him except in fleeting glances, for they feared they may be looking at a mirror image of themselves. No one wanted to admit it could happen to them and they diverted their attention to the ruined streets beyond their windows and doors.

The dead lay where they had fallen. There was no time to remove the dead. No one cared to look at them either, and finally some soldiers yanked draperies from windows or swiped quilted coverings from inhabitants' beds to hide the corpses from view. They were grim reminders of what lay in store for the survivors. *No one really expected to survive the war, did they? Not in one piece, anyway.*

Barkley slumped against a scrap of plaster that once was a wall and probed a pocket for a cigarette. Muddled by fatigue, he tried to digest what had just happened. Already it all seemed a blur, a wicked nightmare to be shoved into a dark corner and forgotten. *It couldn't possibly get any worse*, he thought as he regarded the devastation. He took a long drag on his cigarette and exchanged incredulous looks with the grubby, battle smeared faces that shared the room. No one spoke, for there was little to say. A few puffed absently on their own cigarettes, drawing numb pleasure from the anesthetizing effects of tobacco.

As they dwelled on their circumstances a sudden outburst of gunfire rippled a few blocks away, creating anxious moments among the house's inhabitants. But it remained a distant quarrel, someone else's fight and didn't concern them, not for the moment anyway, and again they eased against battered walls to rest.

As they waited for things to develop, they counted heads and each wondered -- *How did I ever survive?* Fortunately, casualties had not been as severe as one would have expected --the houses had been stout enough to absorb much of the punishment dealt by the Nazis. But nonetheless, the ranks had been whittled little by little. Squads that boasted a dozen men when they began their forest attack on December 15th were now down to seven or eight. All the same, they had held against the terrible tanks and fierce enemy attacks. They had stood their ground and some of them were even a bit elated at their achievement, satisfied that they had done their part in beating back the German assault.

But the elation didn't last for long. A runner stumbled into the house and spoke rapidly to Sergeant Fretwell, then darted out the door. Fretwell looked sick as he turned to the squad and grimly told everyone to be ready to move out. There would be no rest. They were under orders to move to a new location. Some other outfit was in dire straits and needed help.

As the gravity of the order sunk in, spirits sagged to a new low. Men stared blankly at Fretwell as he spoke and they hated him for it. They muttered and swore as they rose to their feet, automatically checking their weapons and adjusting equipment as they prepared for battle, then shuffled outside to join others of their platoon.

Only their platoon, the Third, was being called out. The balance of the company would remain in place as guards for the Regimental Command Post. Lieutenant Welch, Barkley's platoon leader, had drawn the unenviable assignment of assisting the decimated First Battalion which was barely holding its own against repeated impulses of enemy armor and infantry on the eastern fringe of the twin villages. A squad of heavy machine guns was to accompany them.

The platoon marched south, boots crunching on rubble strewn streets as they passed between rows of battered houses. Sounds of a terrific battle wafted from somewhere to the east where someone was catching pure hell. Barkley's feet were cold, numbed to every step and he was exhausted, worn out from days of relentless combat and lack of sleep and living without the barest comforts of civilized life. But he kept going, plodding along as he always had. *Pick 'em up and set 'em down.* It was habit, the cruel ritual of the infantry, this marching, marching, marching. How long had he been marching? It seemed like a lifetime since he had marched out of Camp Wolters only to march up the gangplank of a ship bound for Britain. He marched up and down Wind Whistle Hill until they marched up another gangplank only to be ferried across the Channel to Omaha Beach and now he had marched clear across France and on into Europe, and on and on and on. Well, no. He hadn't really marched through France. No, he had crawled and slithered and run hunched over, dodging bullets and God knows what else to escape the clutches of Death. He had struggled through mud, mud, and more mud -- always mud! Oozing mud, claylike mud that clung to one's boots like parasites bent on sucking life from its host, making each step heavier than the last. There was cold mud, slippery mud, gummy mud, frozen mud. *How many kinds of mud can there be?* God molded man from clay and now it seemed as if the clay was dragging man down to reclaim him as its own. How he hated mud! And he was so tired... his legs quivered from exhaustion. His frozen boots clumped heavily on the icy street, moving him forward as if they, and they alone had control of his zombie-like body and he had no choice but to follow the steps of the dirty GI Joe that trudged before him. They marched as if in a trance. *Pick 'em up and set 'em down.*

As they marched, artillery continued to sough overhead and crashed with authority somewhere beyond their sight. The mad rhythms of distant, dueling machine guns underscored the artillery's thunder and blended with its deep, resonating rumblings to create a symphony of destruction, an ungodly accompaniment to another tragedy unfolding a short distance to the east.

The spire of a church steeple loomed ahead, jutting high above the smoke and mist like an aiming stake planted to aid the enemy guns. The bedraggled column homed in on it, as if it were a magnet and the men were slivers of steel. As they drew closer, Barkley could see that even the House of God was incapable of escaping the ravages of war. Its gray stone walls were battered and marred with untold numbers of bullet and shrapnel scars. Its steeple was riddled with gaping holes and part of the church's roof had been blasted away, revealing the skeletal ribs of its structure. Flames flickered on blackened beams, cavorting like imps celebrating the arrival of Hell on Earth. Destroyed tanks of both armies clogged the streets that converged upon the chapel, looking enormous and inherently evil, even in death. Mud spattered bodies were strewn helter-skelter in the streets and nearby yards, some half buried beneath heaps of rubble, looking as if a giant hand had scooped them up, crushed them, then dropped them like so much waste. It was evident that one hell of a battle had taken place here. More would surely follow.

In time the platoon arrived in another part of town that looked just as forlorn and beaten as the rest of the village. Lieutenant Welch conferred with the A Company commander and then, with the aid of a guide, led his men to the north. His platoon was to plug a gap between Company A, which faced the fields to the east, and the unit somewhere to Company A's left.

Again Barkley followed, not caring where they were going, for he knew wherever it was, it would be cold and he'd be miserable and he'd probably meet his death because he no longer believed he'd live through the remainder of this fight. It went on forever. He slogged on as if in a daze.

As they approached their assigned position the harrowing burr of an enemy machine gun broke the spell. In an instant, the column was down. Men scrambled for the ditches that lined their route while others sought refuge in nearby houses. Again the machine gun rattled. It sounded close. Earlier, Lieutenant Welch's guide had advised him that he'd encounter several enemy tanks stranded on a road as he approached his designated sector. Now the tanks were making their presence known. The lieutenant made a cursory reconnaissance and quickly assessed the situation. Before him six German tanks sat upon a road only a few hundred yards away. A drift of smoke leached from the lead tank. It seemed apparent that it was out of action. The remaining five were stacked up behind it, unable to maneuver around their crippled leader due to the steep, slippery ditches that flanked the road. Although a couple of them also bled smoke, the others, like any trapped beasts, were full of fight and were the source of the intermittent machine gunning. Closer to his present position were several farmhouses that sat on the fringe of town and dominated the road that bore the tanks. He noted the advantage offered by the houses and decided to utilize them as strong points from which he'd conduct his defense. He issued orders. Sergeants responded -- and men moved.

Soldiers crept forward, ever conscious of the tanks that menaced their approach. At times the panzers snapped off a burst or two whenever men exposed themselves. Tracers flashed brightly as GIs sprinted from cover to cover, but in time the squads arrived at their designated positions and the gun firing stopped.

The orphaned platoon settled into the battered houses and waited. Barkley eased to a window to steal a peek. *Oh, Christ!* he thought as his eyes locked on the enemy armor, *More tanks!* They simply sat there, huge and menacing, as if a row of pillboxes had been plopped precipitously upon the battlefield. The lead tank continued to leak smoke into a cast iron sky. He concluded that it was definitely out of action, as was another, but the others he wasn't entirely sure of. One seemed particularly contentious and sprayed the houses with short clips of machine gun fire whenever targets presented themselves.

Farther out, a dark forest girdled the front, appearing every bit as dismal and foreboding as the forest they had left the day before. *Was it only yesterday?* It seemed ages ago. Snow mottled fields eased from the forest, then rose gradually as they neared the twin villages. About a hundred yards or so down the slope from Barkley's window lay a series of dun colored hedgerows that divided the fields that served the farmhouses now occupied by the Americans.

Plumes of black smoke rose from the fields and roads before him, marking the death sites of a dozen or more tanks that had been knocked out in previous engagements. And as far as the eye could see, the landscape was defiled by hundreds of ugly, black blotches where artillery shells from both armies had cratered the land. And scattered between these vile cankers were scores of dark shapeless lumps, the abominable remains of the dead.

Battle sounds waxed and waned in varying degrees as the struggle seethed in other parts of town, but for now all was still in Barkley's sector.

Sergeant Fretwell returned from having council with the lieutenant, then moved among his men. The platoon's disposition was not a good one, he told them. Their left flank hinged on one of the major roads leading into the twin villages, a route used repeatedly by German armor in their desperation to break through the American defenses. So far, the Americans had held, but just barely, allowing only a few rogue tanks to break through. These had been the tanks eliminated by the tank destroyers and bazooka men earlier in the day.

In addition to the tanks on the road to their front, they were also to be alert for enemy activity from the tree line on the far side of the field to the east. That, they were told, was from where the

Germans had launched their attacks. More tanks were sure to come down the road that pierced their left.

Although an entire company had been overrun and all but wiped out in this very area the previous day, the order still stood: Hold at all costs. There would be no falling back. Fretwell reminded them that they were up against the hated SS. Death or capture seemed inevitable. It was expected that the enemy would pilfer the dead in search of valuables and the lieutenant didn't want to give the Germans any unsolicited gifts. Seemingly unimportant personal correspondence might prove a boon to enemy intelligence, so he advised anyone still bearing papers or letters that may somehow aid the enemy to destroy them now.[*] He went on to say that although their circumstances looked bad, they had to hold -- it was their lot to get the job done.

The veterans took it for what it was -- another shit detail. Still, they knew that every other outfit had their share of troubles, too, so they submitted to their fate. After all, they were infantry. They were expendable. The newer replacements, those who once believed that the war would be over by Christmas were greatly disillusioned and were justifiably worried.

In compliance with the lieutenant's orders, a small fire was built behind the house and men began to feed pages of letters and envelopes to the flame. Young Blue Eyes stood mutely near Barkley and gazed forlornly at a photograph. He looked up and with a long face asked: "You don't think I'll have to burn my picture of my mother, do you?"

"I don't know," Barkley answered, "Does it have a name or address or anything on it?" He knew the Germans might use that against the kid if he were taken prisoner and interrogated -- if they didn't kill him, that is.

"Yeah. Yeah, it has my address on the back."

"Yeah, you'd better burn it."

---

[*] This order may have stemmed from the fact that during the previous night, Germans tried to infiltrate American positions masqueraded as GIs, saying that they were from such-and-such company -- information that may have been gleaned from personal correspondence found on dead or captured soldiers.

The kid gazed fondly at the image, then pitched it into the fire. Flames darkened its edges. The corners curled as the fire took hold, the gloss blistered, then burst into flame and mother was no more.

Fretwell's squad was distributed among the rooms of a sturdy house that overlooked the road. Although they were again behind walls, a frosty breeze swept through broken panes and penetrated every room. Men hugged their bodies for warmth. Perhaps it was easy to feel sorry for oneself. *If only we had our overcoats!* If only... *If only our outfit had been in some other sector we wouldn't be in this mess. If only I'd been placed in the Quartermaster Corps instead of the goddam infantry... If only I hadn't been drafted. If only... If only... One could wish a million "if only's" and it'd get you nowhere.*

Barkley peered through a glassless window and shivered as he gazed at a cheerless sky. A thousand thoughts tumbled through his mind as he surveyed the frigid landscape and then it suddenly dawned on him that he had a quandary of his own. He had forgotten that he still carried the letter of commendation from the War Department concerning the tank invention he brainstormed back at Camp Wolters. He had carried it in his pack as a keepsake and source of pride, but now he debated whether to keep it since the situation looked so grave. The fighting had been severe, the worst he'd ever seen. He hardly knew how he had survived this long and now even the lieutenant wasn't exceedingly optimistic about their future. His imagination raced. If he were to be captured and the letter discovered, as it surely would be, he probably wouldn't be shot on the spot but taken instead to some Nazi headquarters for questioning. He feared that they might think he had other ideas and inventions which would introduce him to hideous tortures to extricate more information. He knew that he didn't have any more inventions, but the Nazis wouldn't know that and might think he was just being stubborn and torture him even more to break him. The thought was enough to move Barkley to his ultimate decision. He pulled the dog-eared envelope from his pack and looked at it a moment, then stepped outside and tore it into small pieces before flinging them to the breeze. The scraps fluttered like confetti to the icy mud below.

Back in the house, Barkley lit a cigarette as he gazed across the room and conducted his own, personal, roll call. Fretwell now had sole command of the squad since his assistant, Sergeant Gascon, had disappeared -- and in Barkley's opinion that was of little consequence since he considered Gascon as next to worthless. Then there was Hoernke, looking weary and disheveled as he hugged his BAR and snuggled against a wall to catch some shut eye. He, too, had come a long way since Normandy; had been in some tough scrapes. Joe Guajardo was still with them, standing watch through a shattered window. Broken glass crunched beneath his boots every time he shifted. Joe was one of the few original members of the company remaining, having come ashore on Omaha Beach, and had as much combat experience as anyone. Joe and he had had some good times in Paris after both returned to duty from wounds received in Normandy. And then there was Blue Eyes, the wide-eyed replacement, unsure of himself or what to do. *My God! How'd the kid make it this far?* He was, like so many kids before him, an enigma to Barkley. Some of them fell apart at the first shot, while others stood the test and became good soldiers. So far, despite his baby-faced appearance, Blue Eyes was holding his own. The others in the house, sprawled in various stages of repose in efforts gain some sleep, were empty faces, strangers whom he hardly knew. *Why bother to make friends?* he thought, *when they'll only wind up dead or horribly maimed.*

Twilight neared. In the distance, a house burned brightly, casting brutish shadows across unwashed faces, defining every crevice and blemish that scored their features, rendering bearded mugs into haunting masks, alter images of the men they once were. The devilish glow flickered and consumed several men who lay sprawled across the floor, lost in nightmares unresolved. Numbed of emotion, Barkley pitched the stub of his cigarette, then curled against a wall and instantly fell asleep. Outside, the continuous thunder of artillery failed to wake him. He slept like the dead.

It seemed as if he had just nodded off when he was awakened by loud voices and much clambering of boots and equipment. "Let's go. We're moving out. Let's go." It was Fretwell. With him was the platoon sergeant. Fretwell's squad had been given a mission. They were going down the forward slope to provide an arc of security for the others. Groggily, Barkley grabbed his rifle and slowly gained his feet. The room was almost dark.

Led by Fretwell, the squad exited the house and vanished into a bank of mounting fog. Distant features were soft and indistinct. A stream of tracers fluttered brightly in the twilight and arched towards the town. It was long range fire, harassing fire meant to keep the Americans holed up in their houses and foxholes. The sputter of the gun echoed like a taunting laugh.

As the squad descended the slope, they were aware that the tanks were no longer visible, swallowed by the fog, and that was good, for if they could not see the tanks, then the tanks could not see them. Only the sound of their boots crunching the snow could give them away.

It was nearly dark when they arrived at a low hedgerow a hundred yards or so down the slope. The hedgerow, if one could call it that, offered little in the form of concealment. It was nothing like the thick, shoulder-high dikes Barkley had encountered in Normandy. Instead it was a meager earthen ridge less than two feet high crowned by a sparse tangle of barren branches -- scant protection from bullets or shrapnel. Upon arrival, one man was planted behind the low embankment and told to dig in. On all fours now, Fretwell turned and crawled to his left, leading the others farther down the line. The plaintive chopping of the abandoned soldier's shovel echoed eerily in the fog behind them. He was on his own.

After crawling another fifteen or twenty yards, Fretwell stopped and again ordered a man to dig in. Satisfied with the interval from the first soldier, Fretwell moved on, dragging the others in tow.

In time, only Fretwell and Barkley remained. "Keep yer eyes peeled," the sergeant warned as he indicated Barkley's post, "They pushed patrols all night last night." And with that Fretwell turned and crawled away. Barkley was the last man deposited on the line. He held the far left.

The entire squad had been dispersed across a wide front, spread far too thin to hold off anything more than light patrol activity. It was obvious that they were being sacrificed for the security of the others. If circumstances dictated, they would initiate a firefight, a brief firefight to be sure, but enough to alert the men in the houses of an impending attack.

Darkness fell. Isolated now and blinded by thickening fog, Barkley crouched behind the frail excuse of a hedgerow and studied his position and was not pleased. He knew that somewhere beyond the hedgerow lay an open field and beyond that the column of dormant tanks remained on the road. The branches and twigs before him were so thin that German eyes could easily pierce its skimpy veil to observe every move he made. He needed to get deeper into the earth. Hunched low, he began to dig.

How in the hell are we supposed to hold here? he thought as he thrust his blade into the earth. *We are dead men.* Another jab at the mud. *We're spread out so far apart a Kraut patrol could easily knock us off.* He pried his shovel free from the clinging mud. *This is suicide.* His tool rose and fell again. *We'll all be killed for sure.* He hacked savagely at a tangle of roots, chopping like a man possessed.

As he dug, distant explosions boomed and flashed in the mist before him. The big shells crashed continuously as American gunners tossed shell after shell upon the enemy, providing the forlorn hopes of the foxhole line their only consolation.

A machine gun ratcheted in the distance. Barkley ducked instinctively as a string of tracers flitted high overhead, then disappeared in the fog behind him. He tensed and waited. Beyond the hedgerow he knew The Beast prowled -- the source of a thousand nightmares. Again the big guns rumbled. Flashes shimmered against the clouded sky. Shivers shinnied up his spine. *It's spooky out here, alone in the dark.* He resumed his digging. His shovel caught on another web of roots. *This damned hedge ain't no protection at all!* The blade broke free and he continued his silent tirade. *This is suicide.*

It was well past dark by the time he completed his foxhole. It was a reasonable piece of work, several feet deep and enhanced by the low parapet before him. But there was always room for improvement -- the deeper the better, but he was exhausted. He took a breather.

The work had been strenuous. His underclothing was soaked with sweat and now that he had stopped digging, the damp air seeped in, causing his muddy clothing to cling chillingly to his skin, adding another degree of suffering to his misery. It was not just the simple cold of winter, but the bone-chilling cold associated with the nearly unbearable combination of being cold *and* wet in winter. As hours passed, the temperature dropped, resuming the cycle of thawing days and freezing nights. His teeth rattled. *Goddam!* he swore. He had been cold and wet for days, but now he no longer had his overcoat -- or blanket -- and he pondered the wisdom of discarding them in the forest the evening before. Only his damp and mud slimed battle jacket remained to stave off the frigid air. He shivered continuously. His stomach rumbled. When had he last eaten? He couldn't remember. Whenever it was, it was only cold, greasy rations spooned from a can. What little water remained sloshed icily in his canteen. And what about ammo? Only a few clips remained in his belt. And he was tired. They had had so little sleep over the past few nights -- almost none. Not near enough rest to restore strength and fortify one's spirit. *This can't go on much longer.*

Again a machine gun stuttered as artillery illuminated the fog.

When will they come? When, not if -- for everyone knew this fight was far from over. The squad was under orders to hold the line until relieved. There was only one man to a foxhole, so there would be no taking turns on watch, and as a consequence no one would be allowed to sleep. *If only Mother knew...* and he was glad she didn't.

While the American artillery kept up its constant battering, the German guns responded in kind, dropping round after round throughout the night. New fires were kindled among the buildings. Occasionally a stream of long range machine gun fire arched gracefully overhead, glowing softly in the fog as the bullets knifed towards unknown targets in the twin villages.

The fog grew denser, thick as murder, blotting out trees and buildings and even the closest objects seemed to evaporate before one's eyes. It muffled the battle sounds and cries in the dark and the only thing clearly audible was the distant thumping of artillery that rivaled the pounding of one's own heart. Soldiers stared intently into a night filled with a conspiracy of secret movings and phantom footsteps. Every sort of horror imaginable lurked just beyond sight, ready to pounce upon them and rip them to shreds the moment they lowered their guard. *I must stay awake. I must stay awake. I must stay awake.* There would be no relief from the terror. There would be no sleep this unholy night.

Barkley adjusted his grip on his shovel and again plunged the blade into the soil. He was grateful for the warmth generated by the work.

Again the artillery rumbled. Men stood their posts and stared into the thick and impenetrable fog, ears straining like those of blind men entrusted to defend the palace gates, and fear filled their hearts.

CHAPTER 20

THE HOUSE

December 19, 1944 -- Dawn came, soft and gray, and with the dawn came a warming trend -- the weather had taken a turn for the better, or so it seemed. But the warming brought on a thaw and now Barkley's hole was being encroached by streams of water that flowed from melting snow. It began sometime during the night, the trickling of water that grew increasingly steadier, and by daybreak an inch or better of icy water pooled on his foxhole floor. Since he hadn't any overshoes, his boots were absorbing every ounce of moisture they encountered. "Sonovabitch!" he muttered as he crouched in the muddy soup. Water glistened like rippled glass as it dribbled down the foxhole wall.

Then, just when it seemed as if things could not get worse, a husky growl broke the morning stillness and rumbled across the plain

-- German tanks were revving their engines. They sounded close. Again they roared, resonating from somewhere beyond the hedgerow line, and Barkley's blood ran cold at each ominous snarl. The deep throated gnarl reverberated time and again across the fog shrouded fields and immediately Barkley's concern over the rising waters vanished. *Those damned tanks are still out there*, he thought, *biding their time until ordered to lunge out and finish the job.* Again a Nazi tanker gunned his engine, causing the hair to bristle on the back of Barkley's neck. *Maybe they are doing that to scare us*, he reasoned. If so, it was working. He didn't want to tangle with any more tanks. The menacing growl echoed across the field like a lion's roar, unraveling strand after strand of Barkley's frayed and threadbare nerves.

Despite the harrowing sound of revving tanks, it remained relatively quiet in his immediate sector until another fierce battle erupted a short distance to the north where again German steel and iron men grappled in life-and-death struggles among the ruins. Climactic battle sounds erupted from the fog as Barkley hunkered in his hole, witness to an endless litany of gunfire and explosions that told of the terrible struggle and he waited for the brawl to spill into the fields surrounding him but it did not, and in time the battle subsided and again all was still.

Minutes crept slowly, yet the fog refused to yield.

Nowhere to go, nothing to do, he squatted in squalor as a fine mist caressed his face. He shivered and wondered how the others were faring. They were out there, somewhere, burrowed in foxholes strewn to his right. He realized that they were spaced so far apart that it would be virtually impossible to carry on any semblance of conversation, so resigned to his fate and mulled over the coming fight.

As the morning aged the fog grudgingly gave way and lifted ever so slightly, like a curtain teasing the audience of a much anticipated play. Vague images began to take form and congeal. As if coaxed by the growing light, the melodic gurgle accelerated as water pooled at Barkley's feet.

Again an engine roared, setting his teeth on edge. Frightened, he hunkered lower and studied the water as it trickled over his foxhole's rim. It flowed from only one direction and he guessed correctly that his foxhole was situated on a downward slope and melting snow was being channeled directly towards it. Lucky him. How fortunate.

His belly grumbled. To appease his hunger, he nibbled on the last decimated scrap of a D-bar.

Again an engine roared.

Another hour elapsed. By now ice water lapped well over the toes of his boots and penetrated the porous leather, sending sharp pangs shooting up his legs. *Damn it all to hell!* he thought as his boots sloshed obscenely in the mire, *I gotta do something.* After a moments thought, he unsheathed his trench knife and began carving niches into the foxhole wall. In short order he had fashioned a pair of footholds several inches above the water line. By inserting his feet into these makeshift stirrups he was able to elevate his body by pressing his back firmly against the slimy wall while lifting his buttocks above the icy pool.

He didn't know how long he remained that way, straining against the muddy walls in effort to keep dry, but in time the posture proved too strenuous and before long his feet splashed down and again he squatted in frigid mire. *Shit!*

Then a more sobering dilemma claimed his attention. A machine gun opened up and began raking individual foxholes with sweeping fire. It sounded so close that Barkley assumed it came from one of the tanks out on the road before him. At the same time, flat trajectory artillery began ravaging the nearby houses. Barkley presumed it too, came from one of the immobilized tanks, but it was only a guess, for he was unwilling to risk raising his head to verify his assumption. It seemed as if the houses behind him were the recipients of most of the action as the gunner vented his anger against the thick-walled homes. Explosions resonated across the mud-slicked fields.

Then, as if awakened by the tanks, the sky released an ugly moan as German artillery fluttered overhead. Salvo after salvo dropped hard amidst the battered houses, flashing brightly in the burgeoning light. A flurry of automatic fire clattered in the near distance, punctuated by the sharp crack of M-1s, but for the moment, none of the action seemed to affect Barkley's squad and he remained in his hole, blinded by the slippery wall. Was the enemy breaking through the thin line of defenders? Would he and the others manning the foxhole line be cut off, surrounded, annihilated? Or were the men in the houses holding, fighting desperately to repulse yet another assault on the crumbling town? Battle sounds rose to incredible heights and blended into one cacophonous roar.

Peeking over his foxhole's rim, Barkley attempted to assess the situation. The tanks were still on the road before him, now visible in the chilling mist. Although immobile, one of them kept up a steady fire upon the distant houses. Behind him, to his left rear, a sturdy farmhouse stood like an indomitable fortress. Sheets of flame lashed from seemingly every window as the defenders fired at a horde of German infantry closing in from the snow mottled fields before them. A Panther tank closed in and tossed shell after shell into the house, ripping great chunks from its stolid walls. Smoke poured from several windows. A second tank, barely visible in the fog, drew ever closer to the town, firing its cannon as it trundled down the road. Others followed, each crowded with panzer grenadiers. More enemy soldiers trailed on foot. A smattering of gunshots flashed in the dim gray light as defenders responded from other dwellings. Then vengeance fell with the wrath of avenging angels as American artillery found the range. Volley after volley engulfed the attacking tanks, clearing the riders from their decks and the infantry went to ground.

Although others were engaged in savage combats, nothing stirred in Barkley's immediate sector. Expecting the worst, he shoved his rifle onto the muddy parapet, swallowed hard, then crouched and waited.

Bullets snapped overhead or plowed up muddy furrows while artillery crashed all about, and all the while the sharp crack of the panzers' cannons punctuated the clamorous din as shell after shell smacked against the sturdy homes behind him. The occupants resisted with tenacity born of desperation, unleashing a flurry of small arms fire.

Again Barkley's eyes searched the murky field before him.

The fog only added to the confusion of battle. Unknown to Barkley, much of the German armor was stalled upon the road leading into town, impeded by the disabled tanks that cluttered it. Unwilling to risk getting mired in the muddy fields to either side, they simply sat there and fired in support of the assault. Lined up like sitting ducks, they presented luscious targets for American artillery observers and soon an avalanche of high explosives fell upon them like an iron fist. Black eruptions sprouted all around, but still the tanks kept up the fire.

With their armor stalled upon the road the German attack began to falter, then wilt beneath a perfect storm of fire and steel. The stationary tanks seemed frustrated juggernauts that lashed out at their tormentors with unbound fury -- stubborn combatants that refused to yield. Then suddenly one shuddered and burst into flames as a shell struck home. Shell after shell threatened the remaining tanks and before long they seemed to recognize their plight and spun around and churned away. A wealth of bursting shells escorted them from the field of battle. Sensing that they were being abandoned by their iron guardians, the infantry, too, withdrew, leaving their dead to occupy the mud-choked fields that bound the smoldering village and soon all again was quiet.

The enemy gone now, an unsettling stillness claimed the scene. New fires blazed among the houses, sowing smoke and cinders across a dismal sky. Out on the road the stricken tank blazed brightly amidst other hulks, roaring testimony to the devastating effects of American artillery.

The German attacks seemed unimaginative, utilizing the same head-on tactics that resulted the same consequences with armor and men falling back to reform and try again. The troublesome tank remained on the road, flanked by its dormant brethren that stood like silent sentinels, menacing giants that continued to threaten the defenders of the dying village. More blackened wrecks clogged the streets or desecrated the surrounding fields. Some of these still smoldered, leaking contrails of smoke that smudged a cast iron sky, offering startling evidence of several days' savage fighting.

Barkley crouched in his hole and waited for whatever next may come. Although they had managed to throw back every attempt, the German attacks showed no signs of weakening. Surely they'd try again. He inventoried his ammo in anticipation of another attack. Only a few clips remained. He had no idea when, or even if, he'd be re-supplied.

Meanwhile, the water flow escalated. He now squatted ankle deep in freezing water. Desperate, he pulled out his canteen cup to use as a bail and pitched cupfuls of water over his foxhole's rim, but could not keep pace with the steady flow and in the end the effort proved futile. He considered his footholds again but immediately dismissed the idea. No one can stay in that position for any length of time, levitated above the water by sheer muscle power. The strain was just too much. *I've gotta do something*, he thought, *I can't go on like this.*

Disgusted, he decided that maybe he'd best abandon his watery sump in favor of one of the farmhouses behind him. He knew that the one over his left shoulder was occupied by GIs because a veritable storm of gunfire had poured from its windows and doors during the last attack. If he could just make it that far without getting shot he could continue the fight from there. But that was the problem. The house was a good hundred yards or more from his hole. How to get there in one piece? He wondered if the Germans were still monitoring the foxhole line. Perhaps they had only fired randomly when they machine gunned his hole earlier in the day -- maybe they only caught him by chance. To test his theory he removed his helmet and placed it on the blade of his shovel, then gingerly raised it above the foxhole's rim. *Rrrrrp!* Helmet and shovel came clattering down as bullets splattered all around. *Sonovabitch! The bastard's got me dead to rights!* He was trapped in his flooding hole. He hugged his body and shivered. Time dragged.

He wasn't sure what to do now. He realized he couldn't stay in the foxhole much longer. Ice water sopped his trousers and soaked his boots and socks. Every inch of his body ached from bone crushing cold. His feet seemed numb as stone. *How long has it been since I had dry socks?* he wondered. *Four days? Five? Too long. How the hell* **do** *I keep from getting trench foot?* Water dribbled steadily down the foxhole walls. *Jesus Christ,* he moaned, *It's up to my goddam boot tops now!*

That was it. That was the last straw, the one that broke the proverbial camel's back and forced his inevitable decision: "Hey!" he hollered to his right. He had to shout because their holes were spaced so far apart. "Hey! My hole's filling up with water. I can't stay here. We're gonna die anyway, I'm going up to the house to die."

No response.

"Hey!" he repeated even louder, "Did you hear me? I'm going up to the house to get out of this goddam water."

Still no answer. *Aw, shit. Maybe he's dead. Or did the squad pull out without my knowledge, leaving me here all alone?* He didn't know. All he knew was that his hole was filling with ice water and no one seemed to be in the next foxhole. His boots were totally immersed now and he shivered uncontrollably. His clothing clung chillingly to his skin. Hunger gnawed at his belly. Except for nibbling on the remnants of a D-bar earlier that morning, he wasn't sure when he had last eaten. Fatigue held him as if in a vise grip -- sleep was non-existent, a fairy tale. He was a filthy, mud-caked animal that harbored no hope of survival. He knew that German machine guns had fired at his hole before, but he just didn't care anymore. He decided to move. Mustering his strength and courage, he sprang from his pit and sprinted for the safety of the farmhouse. To his amazement, he arrived unscathed.

The house was a depressing ruin occupied by a dozen GIs. Several soldiers peered intently beyond shattered windows, ever vigilant for approaching enemies, while others sat with backs against the walls and rested. Three stranded tankers in coveralls huddled in a darkened room and talked softly among themselves, and in another a soldier applied a battle dressing to a comrade's bloody wound. All were under the command of a lieutenant who listened to Barkley's story, then incorporated him into the house's defense. The officer and his men must have been from some other platoon or company, for all were strangers to Barkley.

He hardly had time to study his new environment than incoming artillery rocked the house. More shells sailed in, splattering shrapnel and mud against the walls, and then a guard called out: "Here they come!"

Men once lethargic scrambled to doors and windows and watched with terminal interest as another file of German tanks plunged down the narrow road that knifed directly towards them. As before, the armored column was restricted to the pavement, unwilling to maneuver in the soft, thawing fields that bound them. Each tank swarmed with heavily armed panzer grenadiers. As was practice, more infantry followed, hunched over in their long gray overcoats, weapons held at the ready as they trod heavily towards their goal.

As the panzers approached the bottleneck of wrecked armor that clogged the road the awestruck Americans fully expected them to stop as they'd done before. But expectation quickly turned to dread as the lead tank nudged past its disabled comrades and came barreling directly down the lane. The accompanying infantry deployed to left and right and quickened their pace. The die was now cast, and the defenders steeled their nerves and waited for the hell that was sure to come. But fortune, as fortune goes in war, can quickly change and grace arrived from high above.

As if on cue, a counter-barrage smashed into the advancing enemy, dropping many, but the tanks came on and crawled inexorably closer. As they neared the village, their hulls twinkled brightly as machine guns came to life. The desolate GIs in the foxholes could do nothing to stop the panzers so concentrated their fire on the infantry that accompanied them. Rifles popped continuously all along the outpost line while a machine gun chattered defiantly and knocked off several grenadiers with one extended burst. Unfazed, the remaining grenadiers clung to their mounts and turned their weapons upon their tormentors and released a deadly stream. One tank leveled its cannon at the foxhole line and fired a round or two.

Barkley watched from a window, helpless now to aid the poor souls in the rifle pits. His good friend, Joe Guajardo, was still out there, and all the others, too. Joe, whom he had known since Normandy and who had shared in his Paris escapades. Poor Joe.

The lead tank drew closer, then lurched to a halt, allowing its infantry to leap away, and at the same time its big gun swung towards a target and cut loose. *Wham!* A thick cloud enveloped a nearby house. The tank fired again while its machine guns rattled in support of the dismounted infantry. Other tanks followed and aped their leader, firing round after round as they passed the outlying houses. Meanwhile, the infantry crept closer and all the while U.S. artillery rained down and chewed the earth around them.

Barkley and several others dashed upstairs to gain the advantage of second story windows and sniped at enemy soldiers that lay in the ditches or crouched behind the low dikes that hemmed the fields.

"Make every shot count!" a sergeant cautioned as bullets chipped stone from a nearby window. Soldiers aimed deliberately, ever conscious of their dwindling ammunition supply. Barkley's rifle bucked hard against his shoulder as an empty clip pinged away and he pawed automatically at his ammo belt for another. Only a couple of clips remained.

As he pushed the clip into his rifle, the leading tank fired again, knocking loose another piece of their fortress wall. For a moment their view was obscured by clouds of smoke, but everyone knew the enemy was creeping ever closer. Taking a deep breath, Barkley spun to the window and aimed at the soldiers accompanying the tank.

To Barkley's horror, the behemoth lumbered directly towards them.

The lieutenant, who was only a few feet to Barkley's left, briefly monitored the tank's approach then grabbed his radio. "We need tank support up here!" he pleaded as a stream of bullets flashed through a window and powdered the wall behind him. The radio crackled a weak response and an expression of disbelief came over the lieutenant's face. "What do you mean tanks can't maneuver in this terrain?" he replied as bogey wheels squealed below, "The German tanks sure as hell aren't having any trouble -- they're rolling right beneath my window!"

Exasperated, he turned to his men. "Anyone got any rifle grenades? I'll give the Silver Star to anyone who knocks out a tank."

Barkley remembered he had been issued a couple before their attack through the woods. He still had them in his pack, but he no longer possessed the device to launch them. It had been in his overcoat pocket -- his overcoat now lay somewhere in the snowy forest where they had discarded them during their hasty withdrawal two days earlier. The irreparable oversight now came back to haunt him.

WHAMM! Another explosion rocked the house as bullets hammered an outside wall.

"Oh, Christ!" someone bawled. "Here comes another one!"

The second tank burst through a swirl of smoke and aimed its cannon directly at them. *WHAMM!* The house shuddered as if possessed.

Barkley staggered through blinding smoke and dust to glance out a street-side window in time to see the tank grinding ever closer.

Like its predecessor, it had to pass directly beneath the upstairs windows on its route to Rocherath.

Frantically, he ripped off his pack and extracted both of the finned grenades, then pressed his back hard against a wall near the window and waited.

Again a string of bullets clattered against the edifice. Rifle shots popped in reply.

Barkley's fingers trembled as he worked loose the safety pin of the first grenade.

The house vibrated with terrifying effect.

"Now!" someone shouted, "Now!"

Barkley spun to the window and dropped the grenade as the tank rumbled past, then cringed and waited. Outside, the noise of battle was so deafening that Barkley wasn't even certain if his grenade exploded or not, but the tank rolled on unscathed.

More explosions wracked the house, tearing away great chunks of masonry as the shooters dodged from window to window in their desperation to keep up the fire. And then another tank lumbered into view. "Oh, Christ," someone wailed as it neared the house. Barkley grabbed his last rifle grenade and pushed towards the window and flung the bomb even harder than the last as the tank clambered below -- but the grenade simply glanced off the angled armor and exploded harmlessly in the mud and that was that. He had no more grenades.

Then things worsened.

As if annoyed by Barkley's action, the tank jolted to a halt and a motor whined as its turret rotated towards their house. Faces blanched white as its great cannon gaped directly at a window. "Look out!" someone screamed as men scrambled to clear the room. And then it fired.

Chaos engulfed the house. Walls quivered from shock as smoke billowed from room to room. Stunned men gawked incredulously at each other, choking, hearts raging, expecting the end to come with the next blast, but none came and the tank moved on.

Another man was dead, a shapeless heap piled against a wall.

"Get up there!" someone shouted as he pointed towards the windows. "Get up there, goddammit! Keep up the fire!"

The survivors floundered through a cauldron of boiling smoke to man the windows of their besieged fortress, and the battle continued in hell-fired fury.

Barkley jammed home his last remaining clip. That was it. Eight more rounds and he would be out of ammunition. He fired repeatedly until the exhausted clip sprang from the receiver. "Out!" he cried, "I'm outta ammo!"

Others had been robbing the wounded and dead of their ammunition and now Barkley was compelled to do the same. He scrambled beside a corpse and rummaged through its bloodied ammo belt until he found several fresh clips. Re-supplied, he rejoined the shooters at the windows.

Another flurry of bullets powdered the stone surrounding a window and a body pitched backwards and slammed to the floor. Blood seeped across the boards. Elsewhere someone shrieked while another sobbed uncontrollably, yet still they continued to fight. Others seemed more berserk than sane, howling, yelling, laughing like lunatics as they fired their rifles.

Barkley, too, fought maniacally, racing up and down the stairs, laying down fire as actions warranted. He had given up all hope of surviving this, his personal Armageddon. He felt hollow, worn out. He had been pushed beyond human endurance and his emotions raged out of control. His hands trembled continuously now. Whenever he spoke, his voice broke into a high, frantic pitch that rose, then fell in timbre, and he could not control it and that bothered him, for he knew he was nearing the end of his tether. It seemed as if everyone had given up hope of ever surviving this fight. Their only desire was to kill as many Germans as possible before being killed themselves. But Death, so omnipresent and absolute, could be exceedingly cruel in its patience and would not yet claim them. Their fate was not quite sealed.

Outside, rifles and machine guns continued firing all along the line and all the while artillery and cannon fire took their toll on the houses and buildings of Rocherath.

A massive detonation came from above and at the same instant a trio of beams crashed through the attic and pierced the ceiling to dangle precariously like unstable stalactites. A sea of smoke and dust boiled through the gap to explore the halls as if ascertaining the extent of the shell's destruction. Shaken, the defenders ignored the wreckage and renewed their desperate action.

Another tank rumbled beneath a window just as a tremendous explosion brought it to a standstill. Apparently it had fallen victim to a bazooka team, or perhaps one of the hidden Shermans. It simply sat there for a long moment, seeping smoke from a fatal wound. And then its hatches clanged open.

"Kill them! Kill them!" someone roared as the crew exited their crippled tank.

Soldiers leaned from upstairs windows and fired down upon German boys as they scrambled for safety. They were so close it seemed as if the muzzle blasts of their rifles would surely singe their clothing. It was impossible to miss and soon all five lay dead around their vehicle.

Eventually, somehow, the tide of battle began to shift. Despite several armored breakthroughs, each American strongpoint managed to hold firmly and kept the panzer grenadiers at arm's length. Unsupported by their infantry, the panzers were vulnerable to any number of American anti-tank weapons and soon pulled back lest they join the ever mounting number of smoldering wrecks that filled the streets and roads of the smoldering villages. As the tanks withdrew, the infantry seemed to loose heart and their fire crackled feebly, then dwindled to nothing. Once again the battle was over.

It was now late afternoon. Dimming light failed to penetrate the veneer of battle smoke that shrouded a dying world. Artillery continued to crash in the distance and somewhere a machine gun clattered restlessly, but for now, the relentless assaults had ceased.

The house was ominously still now. Gun smoke sifted lazily through every room, wending among the dead and dying soldiers as if curious of the spectacle of war. From somewhere outside a fire crackled, spitting cinders upon the street while wisps of smoke drifted past windows to veil the soldiers' view.

Barkley studied the devastation wrought upon the house. The sturdy home had taken a beating and was reduced to a battered ruin. Shattered beams jutted from a gaping hole in the roof that allowed daylight to seep into the house, revealing chunks of plaster strewn across a floor littered with spent cartridges and the clutter of broken furniture. Shards of broken glass glinted dimly in the waning light of a winter's afternoon.

His gaze shifted to his new found comrades and he was appalled by what he saw. Numb, slack-jawed beings dressed in mud caked uniforms slumped heavily against the walls, appearing more dead than alive. Red eyes glowered from blackened faces that bristled with wild whiskers, resembling Emmett Kelleys in sagging battle dress -- carbon copies of Mauldin's Willie and Joe, or something worse.[*] Few men remained to continue the fight. The others were dead or wounded horribly.

As Barkley surveyed the carnage, the lieutenant pleaded on his weak radio link for reinforcements. The answer was discouraging. He was told that no help was available -- that the Germans were not taking any prisoners and he must hold at all cost. The last message was chilling, a call for desperate men to take desperate actions. It seemed evident that no one was going to survive this fight.

Downstairs, the tank men conversed in conspiratorial tones, then announced arbitrarily that they were leaving to find their unit and quickly left the scene. Barkley wasn't sure what to think of their departure. He truly doubted they were going to find their outfit, but thought that saying so gave them validity to escape a hopeless situation. They hadn't been much help anyway, he reasoned, as they only kept to themselves while the dogfaces did all the fighting.

As the tankers ducked out, the lieutenant roamed from room to room to check on his men's disposition. As he counted heads he appraised their ammunition supply and asked how they were holding up. His inquiries were met with grunts of guarded acquiescence. After all, what could they do? Their orders still stood: Hold at all costs. *At all costs! -- to the last man.*

Weary, Barkley slouched against a tattered wall and nervously fingered his rifle. His hands trembled slightly as he stroked the wood and he was overcome by a queer sensation that left him indifferent towards his own survival, as if it really didn't matter anymore, for he truly believed that this was it. It was over, or would be soon, for this

---

[*] Emmett Kelley was a comedian whose character was a dirty, unshaven hobo. Willie and Joe were cartoon characters who, through their wry foxhole humor, personified the dog-faced infantrymen of World War II.

battle never ended and only worsened at every turn. He realized he'd never see home again, and again his thoughts turned to his mother and dad and he thanked God that they'd never know how miserably he died. *How the hell did it come to this?* he wondered as he tried to track the events that led to his present predicament. Jumbled images of Camp Wolters, and Normandy and the induction station in Chicago tumbled through his head. But he was too exhausted to place the circumstances in their proper chronological order and in the end the effort proved futile, for it really didn't matter anyway, for he was *here* and there was nothing he could do about it. *Hell, I made it pretty far*, he reasoned and forced a dead man's laugh. All of his buddies from training days were long gone now -- dead or seriously wounded. *Why should it be any different for me?* Accepting his fate, a bitter hatred overwhelmed him and he resolved to go down fighting, to take as many of the Nazi bastards as he could before he fell.

Again his hands quavered and his breath came shallow and weak. He was so tired. It had been days since he'd had any decent sleep. His head nodded with fatigue, then sunk to his chest.

He didn't know how long he rested that way, with his chin anchored upon his chest, but before long, a woeful cry brought him back to life: "Oh, Christ... HERE THEY COME AGAIN!"

Barkley moved lethargically towards his post and stared numbly out the window and his heart sank. More tanks approached from afar-- nine of them this time -- all in column, barreling directly towards them. Again each crawled with panzer grenadiers. There was a sense of finality in the manner in which they advanced, as if failure was no longer an option and it had its effect on the handful of men who remained to defend the house. It was like a recurring nightmare. Someone muttered an oath as dark as the room itself, then spat thickly upon the floor. Barkley said nothing, but simply glared at the daunting host as he pushed his rifle through the window. It looked as if this, indeed, would be their last stand.

But the lieutenant had other plans. He realized that his meager force was far too small to provide an adequate defense. He had more dead and wounded men than those capable of fighting. The house was crumbling around their ears and had become untenable -- it was now more mausoleum than impregnable fortress. Perhaps the strain of fatigue, constant combat and responsibility of command hampered his ability to think clearly, but ultimately he came to a painful decision.

"Gather up!" he hollered as artillery screamed overhead.

Only two other soldiers besides Barkley joined the lieutenant downstairs.

"Listen up," he began, "We're going to break out of here and join up with some other outfit. Give what ammo you have to the wounded... they'll provide covering fire."

So it's come to this, Barkley thought, *We're going to leave these poor bastards to the enemy.* Everyone knew the Germans weren't taking any prisoners. The wounded were doomed. They were incapable of making the exodus and would have to sell their lives as dearly as possible so that others may live, and that was a hell of a thing to ask.

Barkley's heart hammered violently as he handed over his few remaining cartridges to a condemned soul -- all but one. He saved the last bullet for himself because he knew those SS men were big bruisers -- vicious, hard core Nazi fanatics. He only weighed 145 pounds and did not relish the idea of grappling hand-to-hand with one of Hitler's apes. He'd have one last surprise for him. His hand trembled as he chambered the solitary round, and then he was ready.

Outside, the earth leaped and shuddered as incoming artillery intensified. More shells howled overhead to erupt in salvos as American gunners played their role to perfection, and all the while the house continued to disintegrate around them as the several tanks stranded on the road cut loose with the occasional shell.

Inside, the four survivors exchanged sickened glances as they assembled near the back door and readied for their escape.

Another explosion shook plaster from the walls, and then it was still.

"Go!" the lieutenant croaked.

The leading soldier lunged through the door and was promptly knocked backwards as machine gun bullets splintered the frame. His riddled body thumped heavily to the floor. The others recoiled in horror. "Oh, Christ!"

After a moment of panic and indecision, the lieutenant's eyes darted nervously about the room, then regained control. "Alright," he rasped, "Alright, we'll go out this way," and jerked a thumb in the direction of another room. As they assembled by the door, the lieutenant gave that archaic order: "FIX BAYONETS!"

Jesus Christ! thought Barkley, *Fix bayonets? Fix bayonets!? There're tanks and machine guns out there!* It was the dumbest order he had ever heard. Nonetheless, he deftly drew the blade from its scabbard and snapped it onto his rifle.

Outside the battle raged. Smoke drifted across the room to sift up raw, red nostrils and once again Harold Barkley stood in Death's dark shadow.

One last look around. A deep breath, and then the lieutenant gave the classic infantry command: "FOLLOW ME!"

In an instant the lieutenant was gone. Barkley and the last remaining soldier sprung after him, and as they did a deafening blast flung them both back inside and slammed them hard against a wall.

Barkley was down on his back. Dazed, he shook the cobwebs from his head and tried to evaluate what had happened. Apparently one of the tanks on the road had thrown a shell at them, striking above the door the very moment they exited the house. His right hand ached, and as he sat up he was shocked to discover that his hand was nailed to the stock of his rifle by a long jag of sizzling steel. He rose unsteadily, and as he did he released his grip, allowing six inches of shrapnel to pull through his hand as the rifle clattered to the floor. Blood dripped steadily from trembling fingertips. Glancing around, he noticed the other soldier was dead, a shapeless sack slumped against the wall.

The room spun and again he shook his head to gather his wits. He had to get out of this death trap. As he took a step towards the door, a sharp pain radiated from his left knee, and as he looked down he noticed another slender needle jutting from his trousers. Reaching down, he winced as he plucked the narrow, imbedded shaft from below his kneecap and then darted through the splintered door frame.

Outside, the earth quaked with fiery explosions as tracer bullets stitched the dimming light. Not far away, the lieutenant was still running and Barkley chased after him and soon both crashed feet first into a board fence that paralleled a muddy, sunken road. They lay there for a moment, panting, and then the lieutenant said, "C'mon, let's get outa here," and rose to follow the muddy track which led to God knows where, and it really didn't matter, as long as it took them away -- away from the sights and sounds and smells of battle. Away from the ill-fated house. Away from Death and Hell on Earth.

They slipped and stumbled the length of the muddy trough, anxious to find friendly faces. Artillery continued to shriek overhead and exploded brightly in the thick battle haze where machine guns rattled and ripped as the two armies tore at each others' throats. Flames flickered and snapped as the twin villages burned beneath a pall of black, billowing smoke. Abandoned military equipment was scattered everywhere, mingled with the pitiful personal items of the villagers. Wrecked vehicles and tanks clogged the streets and burned in people's yards where the dead of both armies were strewn with alacrity. The waste of war polluted the soil and tainted the sky.

Barkley and the lieutenant ran as if escaping the gates of Hell. Before long, they chanced upon another group of haggard, dirty GIs who appeared to be preparing to make an attack. They looked scared as hell. An aid man wrapped a battle dressing around Barkley's wounded hand, tagged him, then sent him deeper into town where other casualties were being assembled.

He splashed through chilling mud, sometimes running, sometimes crawling as bullets snapped and whined overhead. He passed piles of broken furniture that had spilled from rubble that once was homes and everywhere lay the dead in twisted, mangled lumps, mute testimony to three days of unbridled mayhem.

In time he came upon four or five big deuce-and-a-half trucks with sideboards parked along a rubble strewn street. Dozens of injured men were being helped aboard by a team of overworked medics-- the more seriously wounded being lifted up on stretchers. More wounded trickled in. In short order, the trucks were filled beyond capacity and Barkley and the other walking wounded were forced to stand to allow room for the litter cases.

It was nearly twilight when orders came to move out. Powerful engines growled deeply as the drivers worked their gearshift levers and the big trucks lurched forward. The convoy rumbled past scenes of utter devastation as it traveled west and soon the dying villages were behind them, a flaming tribute to an insatiable orgy of blood and gore. And then they were in the open, jolting roughly over a deep rutted road.

En route, someone suddenly pointed skyward and cried, "Look!" Others glanced up and saw several parachutes floating from a darkened sky. Curious, the drivers stopped their vehicles to gawk at the spectacle.

Barkley was horrified. He had heard rumors of German paratroopers infiltrating behind the US lines and now feared the worse. He knew that all of the wounded had been stripped of their weapons when loaded onto the trucks and were virtually defenseless. Leaning over the rail, he called to the gawking drivers, "Got any guns? Those aren't ours." The drivers stared back, seemingly perplexed. "Get the hell outa here!" Barkley shrieked. Un-nerved, the drivers quickly complied and the column roared ever westward and disappeared in the darkness.

Barkley was taken to a field hospital overflowing with butchered men. Every type of suffering surrounded him. His own wound, while painful, was minor compared to many others, so he waited his turn for treatment, but in due course his time came and a surgeon removed another splinter of steel buried deep within his hand. The tendon leading to his middle finger had been severed when the shrapnel nailed his right hand to his rifle stock and now the digit stuck straight out as if making an obscene gesture. There was nothing to be done about it for now and the wound was re-bandaged with a thick swath of dressing that encased his hand like that of The Mummy. Barkley did not even mention the slight wound to his knee. It had only been a slender piece of steel which he had removed himself before he ran from the house. Somehow, it did not seem like a legitimate wound to him and the injury was not recorded.

Meanwhile, as he waited transfer to yet another hospital farther to the rear, Red Cross personnel provided stationery for wounded soldiers to notify their loved ones that they were alright. The only problem for Barkley was that he could not use his damaged hand. His dilemma was solved when another soldier volunteered to write the letter in his stead. Barkley gathered his thoughts and began to dictate:

"Dear Mother and Dad," he began. The soldier scribbled, then waited. Barkley continued: "Do not write to this address until you hear from me. Will probably be evacuated to another hospital and will send new address in next letter." Again he paused. "Was shot in right hand and small piece of shrapnel in left knee. Cannot bend fingers to write. After operation I hope my fingers will not be stiff. Tell Ernie will write soon." Then as explanation for the strange, crisp handwriting he added: "A friend of mine is writing this letter for me. Will write particulars later."

Completed, the writer placed the letter before him so that he could sign it himself. With painstaking effort, he scrawled his signature, the lines and curves appearing erratic, but legible: "H. Barkley".

By now it was December 20th, 1944. He knew that he had narrowly escaped from Hell on earth. Although now safe, part of him would remain forever in that smoldering cauldron of boiling blood and bones called Rocherath. He never wanted to do it again.

Postscript to the Battle for Rocherath and Krinkelt

The Battle for Rocherath and Krinkelt in Belgium was one of the crucial events of the opening stages of the great German Ardennes Offensive -- The Battle of the Bulge. It was here that the beleaguered Americans made their stand against the seemingly unstoppable onslaught of German armor and men that poured from the forest before them. Through their sacrifice, they bought time for other elements of the American command to consolidate their positions on strategic Elsenborn Ridge where they held firm for the duration of the month-long Battle of the Bulge. The brawl at Rocherath and Krinkelt was a desperate action resulting in many casualties and many harrowing events. Every company that participated in this bloody fracas had stories of courage and *desperation in the face of nearly insurmountable adversity. Many others went unnoticed, or unsung. The following are but a few such actions recorded of men of Company G, 38th Infantry during those trying days.*

After their withdrawal from the Monschau Forest late on December 17th, 1944, Company G was immediately sent to aid in the defense of the Regimental Command Post situated in the heart of Rocherath. Enemy tanks and infantry had penetrated the tenuous lines and roamed freely through the streets. In the darkness, First Sergeant Percy Imbody, of Perkiomville, Pennsylvania, was sent to check on the disposition of the Second Platoon. In the confusion, he got lost and was captured by fifteen Germans. Percy Imbody was a big man. Knowing then that the Germans were not taking prisoners, the sergeant flung his weight behind his fists and punched it out with the three closest captors, then bolted for the Second Platoon yelling for them to open fire. They did. Imbody survived.

The following morning, December 18th, was the high tide of the German effort. Again tanks had penetrated the outlying defenses and entered the fog-shrouded village. A tremendous battle ensued. Despite the chaos, a number of Company G men stepped to the fore and made significant contributions to the battle. A bazooka team consisting of Pfc. Samuel Distefano, of Cannonsburg, Pennsylvania, and Pfc. Joseph Nemec, of Chicago, Illinois, knocked out two Panthers that crossed their sights. Two more tanks were disabled by the bazooka of Pfc. Eugene Gillen, of Jersey City, New Jersey, and Pfc. Albert Bruner, of Evansville, Indiana. A squad leader, Staff Sergeant Alfred Maddux, of Trio, Georgia, accounted for one more Panther, giving a total of five enemy tanks for the company that morning. Knocking out the massive German tanks was not an easy task and took incredible nerve and courage to do so.

Another incident during the savage fighting highlights the cold-blooded attitude of the young killers of the 12th SS Panzer Division. At one point it appeared as if a number of Germans were willing to surrender. Young Brady Nelson, who spoke some German, eased into the street and approached the house to take them in. Just as he neared, an SS man stepped from the doorway with a flame *thrower and torched young Nelson. It was Brady Nelson, who during the attack through the forest two days earlier, had laid with his squad in the snow before a fire break. Gazing across the void, he turned to Pfc. John Savard and said, "I wonder what would happen if I asked if there are any Germans over there? Would I get a 'Nein' in response?" At the time it was funny. Now young Brady Nelson was dead. His squad would no longer take prisoners.*

Later, after Lieutenant Welch's platoon had already been assigned to help the First Battalion, the balance of Company G was relieved of its duty defending the command post and returned to its parent Second Battalion, now fighting desperately on the northeastern fringe of Rocherath. In darkness they dug in around several farmhouses that guarded a crossroads. A three-man patrol was sent out to locate the German lines. None of them returned.

In the early morning fog of December 19th, the Germans sprung another attack under cover of darkness. A number of Germans had penetrated the foxhole line and ran rampant behind the company front, spraying defenders with automatic fire. Potato Masher grenades laid out most of the company mortar men. Seeing that the situation was rapidly deteriorating, First Sergeant Imbody took matters into his own hands and organized a counterattack from personnel from the company command post and killed most of the Germans who had managed the penetration. For his actions of the previous day and this one, Percy Imbody was awarded the Silver Star Medal. The few survivors of the bold German patrol had taken refuge in a barn. GIs from a nearby house closed in. None of the Germans survived.

The action that morning was so touch-and-go that Captain Skaggs actually called artillery down on his own men to stabilize the line -- a desperate measure, but it worked.* Heavy attacks continued

---

* This is similar to an incident that occurred during the First Battalion, 9th Infantry's desperate battle at Lausdale Crossroads, just to the east of the Twin Villages on the morning of December 18. Here the fighting was so desperate against an onslaught of panzers and hordes of infantry that their commander, Lt. Colonel McKinley, ordered the American artillery to fire upon his entire battalion, as the enemy was intermixed with his own men and threatened to break through. When finally allowed to withdraw, the battalion was nearly annihilated. Company A came out with only five men. Company B, nineteen; Company C, forty; Company D, the weapons company, had lost its machine gun and mortar platoons; and the attached *throughout the day and bazooka teams from Company G hunted down the few enemy tanks that managed to enter the town. At one point, nineteen year old John Savard, of St. Paul, Minnesota, turned a corner just in time to be staring straight down the cannon barrel of a Panther tank. He dove for cover just as the cannon blew the corner off of the house. Savard suffered from frozen feet and was evacuated a couple of weeks later.*

Another teenage warrior was Bill Dudas, of Benton Harbor, Michigan. Bill was also a member of the Third Platoon (Barkley's platoon). He had been an athlete in high school and was called "Muscles" by his squad mates. He well remembered the harrowing withdrawal from the forest where he had been a member of a special reconnaissance patrol. During the bitter fight for Rocherath, he recalled how the German tanks came barreling down the road and fired directly into the houses. He learned to lay low near the foundation where the house was sturdier to escape harm. He did not like it when a bazooka team was near, for the enemy always noted the flash of the weapon, which drew a flurry of return fire. He also recalled an incident when about six Panther tanks rumbled down a road and began opening fire on their position. It became clear that one of them was going to fire at the house he was in. There were three men downstairs and two up in the attic, and Dudas yelled at the attic men to clear out fast, but too late. The tank fired its cannon and tore out the entire attic. The two men up there were surely killed.

When several tank men were inside the house he was in, their commander asked if anyone could operate the 37mm gun of a light tank. Dudas, like Barkley, had trained as an anti-tank man at Camp Wolters, Texas, and said he could do so. The tank commander took note, but never called for his services. When the battle was over, Dudas suffered from severe frostbite.

Both Dudas and Savard were veterans who had been wounded in Normandy.

Another veteran of Company G was Lieutenant John Wheeler, of Cincinnati, Ohio. It was two of his men, Distefano and Nemec, who had knocked out a couple of Panther tanks on the morning of

---

Company K walked away with only one officer and ten enlisted men. McKinley began his defense the previous evening with 513 soldiers.

December 18th. Nemec loaded while Distefano fired from a window as the first tank passed between two houses. He fired so hastily that he failed to note if all was clear behind him and the backflash of the bazooka's rocket brushed Wheeler's leg. The tank ground to a halt and partially blocked the road. Later Distefano and Nemec repeated their feat.

Later, when the company returned to Battalion control, it was Wheeler's weapons platoon that was so shot up during the early attack of December 19th. The action was so hot that two of his machine guns overheated and burned out their barrels during the two-hour battle. It was his mortar crews that had been eliminated during the brief German breakthrough.

Within a month the 2nd Infantry Division resumed the offensive and Lieutenant John Wheeler had a foot blown off by a land mine hidden beneath deep snow on February 11, 1945.

After three days of nearly non-stop battle, Company G was withdrawn with the rest of the 38th Infantry to the defensive positions prepared on Elsenborn Ridge, some two miles to the rear. They had accomplished their mission, and done it well, but the cost was high -- better than fifty per cent of its men were casualties.

Every battalion of the 2nd Infantry Division that participated in the defense of the Twin Villages received the coveted Presidential Unit Citation for extraordinary heroism in action -- a description that well describes the men who earned it.

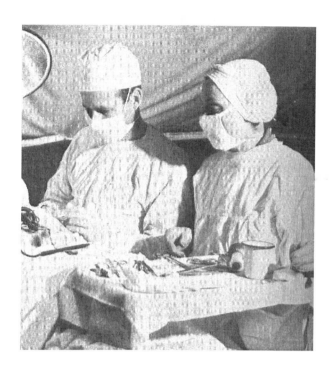

CHAPTER 21

LIEGE

Late December, 1944 -- Barkley had been taken to a U.S. Army hospital in Liege, Belgium, where his wound was re-examined to determine the extent of damage that had been done by the shrapnel. The severed tendon still needed to be re-attached and another operation was scheduled from which he emerged with his right hand wrapped in a wad of heavy gauze. His splinted middle finger jutted straight from the bandage while his thumb remained exposed. It was a curious design, one which forbade him the use of his dominant hand except for the most menial tasks.

Although his hand had been punctured through and through by shrapnel, the wound was not large and the healing process was expected to be swift and complete.

The doctors also noted that Barkley's nerves were shot. He winced at every unexpected noise. If someone dropped a bedpan, for instance, he'd plunge to the floor as if a mortar shell had struck. Although this was a conditioned response from months of combat, it was hardly necessary at the hospital and the medical staff was concerned. His speech pattern was highly erratic, as well. Each time he spoke he stammered slightly and his voice rose shrilly then fell, as if he had no control of its volume or rhythm. Doctors took notes and scheduled future sessions with the hospital psychiatrist, for it was determined that Barkley was suffering from some sort of shock. He was diagnosed with combat exhaustion.

Being ambulatory, Barkley was free to move about at his own discretion. At times he'd explore the various wards in search of familiar faces, but there were so many and some of these were swathed in bandages rendering them unrecognizable. He wandered as if in a daze as he strolled between rows of bed-ridden patients. Suddenly a distant voice called his name.

Barkley jumped as if struck by a cattle prod.

"Barkley!"

There it was again. His eyes swept the ward in search of the source of his name calling. *Who the hell knows my name?*

"Barkley, for christsake, I thought you were dead." It came from a young Mexican face. Joe Guajardo beamed brightly as he lay in a bed with his hands clasped upon his chest. His severely swollen feet poked obscenely from beneath the covers. They were an ugly purple color.

Barkley's head swam. Everything was as if in a dream -- sluggish, thick. "Joe..." he mumbled as he shuffled awkwardly towards his friend. *My God, it's Joe!* He was thrilled to see his buddy, grateful that someone else had survived. They quickly exchanged stories of how each wound up in the hospital. Joe Guajardo, being raised in southern Texas, had suffered horribly from the frigid weather and wet conditions of the harsh European winter. His feet were a mess. He had hobbled painfully the last few days of their ordeal in Rocherath, clumping along on frozen feet until they had no more response than blocks of wood and in the end they simply gave out. He could walk no more. As a consequence, he was evacuated to the rear for treatment. That was on December 19th, the same day Barkley was wounded.

Joe went on to say how the whole squad, what was left of it, believed that Barkley had been killed in the foxhole line.

Barkley explained how and why he went up to the house, and at that very moment he realized what Joe had just told him -- that everyone thought he was dead.

"M-my God," he stammered, "S-somebody better tell them differently before my folks get a telegram saying I'm dead."

Alarmed, Barkley notified hospital personnel of the mix-up and could only hope that the record would be set straight before a Western Union messenger gave his mother a heart attack.

Later, Barkley returned to Joe's ward to reminisce about the good times they shared in Paris the previous fall, but a stranger lay in Joe's bed. Joe had been moved to another hospital, and maybe even back to the States. Once again Barkley was left without a friend in the world.

"Hey!" someone cautioned in a hoarse stage whisper, *"Listen!"*

The ward fell silent and everyone cocked an ear and listened intently. Eyes rolled to the ceiling as if searching for the source of the soldier's concern and soon all heard the faint droning that hummed from afar. *Buzz bomb!* The Germans had been launching the large robot bombs with some degree of regularity and now another approached from the East to terrorize the city of Liege. The droning increased, sputtered, and then cut out completely. Eyes grew wider in the ensuing silence, anticipating the plunge of one ton of high explosives that now descended somewhere upon the city. Finally, a dull thud sounded far in the distance and all released a sigh of relief. Once again one of Hitler's secret weapons had missed them.

Although he suffered from combat fatigue, Barkley managed to find the experience almost amusing. Having survived countless barrages from artillery and mortars and the terrifying tree bursts in the Monschau Forest, he saw no reason to be alarmed. They were lodged in sturdy buildings and the bombs flew over blindly. It was only by chance whenever they struck and Barkley knew the odds of getting hit by a single flying bomb were slim. But the others, especially the hospital personnel, did not share his rationale and were nearly paralyzed with fear every time a buzz bomb crossed the horizon.

Still, Barkley knew that at that point in his life that his own luck was all but used up. He was certain that if he went back into combat he would not survive. There was only so much a fellow could take and he was now a very different man than the youth that climbed over the hedgerows of Normandy so many months ago. He had witnessed the unfathomable horrors of war and had been a willing participant in the wholesale slaughter himself. He had endured the rain, mud and summer heat of France where he had been wounded, patched up and returned for more. Upon his return he had been sent into Germany where he suffered from the intense cold. He'd fought for the pillboxes of Heartbreak Crossroads and had barely survived the recent breakthrough in the frozen hell of the Ardennes and now he was done, hollow, only a shell of a once robust and vibrant young man. And he was plagued by the realization that all of his friends were gone -- dead or severely wounded -- and this troubled him deeply. It was just too much and went on too long. Even now, days after his arrival at the hospital, he remained extremely nervous. He just knew he'd never be able to return to combat.

December 25, 1944 -- It was Christmas day. Barkley lay on his bed, devoid of thought until a chorus of mild cheers and applause broke his trance. Soon, a group of Red Cross volunteers paraded through the ward, passing out brightly wrapped packages and each wounded soldier beamed broadly as he accepted his gift. Then one soldier nudged Barkley and said, "Hey, buddy, look at that." Barkley looked in the direction of the patient's finger and his jaw dropped. Not only were the Red Cross men handing out presents to the Americans, but also to the several wounded Germans who were lodged in the hospital. What troubled him was that while each American received a small package, every German received a much larger gift. "Well I'll be damned!" Barkley said.

January 4, 1945 -- The hole in Barkley's hand healed nicely and his rehabilitation began in earnest. The severed tendon had been successfully re-attached, but as a consequence it was somewhat shorter. The ligament pulled tightly on his middle finger, causing it to thrust straight out from his hand and it would not bend.

To remedy this, he underwent daily therapy where tiny weights were attached to his finger via a pulley device. He'd sit through his sessions, lifting and releasing the weight to stretch and strengthen the truncated tendon. It was easy therapy, but progress was slow.

One day a bevy of officers came trooping through the wards with much pomp and ceremony and presented Purple Heart Medals to a number of patients who had been wounded in action. They passed out a lot of them, and some, like Barkley who had been wounded before, were handed tiny bronze oak leaf clusters to pin to the medals they had received earlier. Barkley attached his to a piece of Red Cross stationary and mailed it to his parents with detailed drawings on how to attach it to the ribbon of the medal he had sent home from England some five months earlier.

The hospital was a pleasant enough place and Barkley was tickled to be sleeping beneath clean, starched sheets every night. Everything smelled pure and sanitized. And it was so quiet -- no explosions, no machine guns, no mud or snow or rain. It was dry and warm and life, for the most part, was good.

He was now allowed passes into town and took advantage of them, exploring the city at his leisure. He could come and go as he pleased, as long as he was back in time for bed check. He nosed through the bars, cafes and shops of Liege, which gave him the opportunity to practice his rudimentary French. He had little money but managed to purchase a few items to send home. He bought a silk handkerchief for his mother as well as another and an ornamental bracelet for Marilyn. On a rare occasion, he'd enter a pub and have a drink, but not often, for a shot of cognac was going for as much as one dollar in some establishments.

At meal time Barkley would join other ambulatory patients as they made their way to the mess hall located across the hospital grounds. Crisp winter air stung their lungs as they queued up at the entrance and it was then that Barkley noticed a peculiar sight -- several patients bounding from tree to tree as they worked their way towards the mess hall door. Each would peer cautiously around his personal trunk, then dash to the next tree as the fellow before him vacated his position. They would continue this bizarre game until they reached the building housing the cafeteria. Barkley was told that they were combat exhaustion cases. Although they were safe well behind the lines, each believed he was still in combat. The non-combatant patients pointed and laughed at the spectacle, but Barkley knew what they were experiencing and had genuine pity for the poor souls. For them the war was far from over.

Entering the mess hall, Barkley received his meal and set his tray upon a long table. As he sat he looked at the man sitting across from him his gaze froze. He didn't mean to stare, but each of the poor fellow's ears looked as if they were molded from scraps of raw hamburger. Ugly red scar tissue marred his face and each side of his head. Barkley's stomach churned.

As he attempted to eat, he listened to the fellow's story. He had been an air crewman whose bomber had been shot down. Flames had swept through the fuselage and seared the fellow's face before he could bail out and now, after much reconstruction, it appeared as if his face would heal, but his ears still looked as if slabs of raw meat had been hung on either side of his head. Barkley did not finish his lunch.

Barkley's physical therapy progressed satisfactorily. Each day saw minor improvement and in time full use of his damage hand was restored. But there still remained the unsolved mystery of his chronic nervous disorder. If someone came up behind him and slapped him on the back in casual greeting, he'd jump like a cat. His voice still quavered when excited.

He sat through a number of grueling sessions as the psychiatrist questioned him about his combat experiences. Barkley did not want to remember as much as the doctor wished, and unconsciously blocked the images of death and destruction that plagued his memory. They were his own, personal nightmares and he wished to keep them locked away. But in time he was scheduled for a final evaluation to determine if he was fit to be returned to duty. Barkley perched uneasily on the edge of a chair centered before the doctor's desk.

The doctor began with a general review of their progress, then leaned forward with his elbows propped upon his desk. "Are you ready to return to the front?" he inquired casually.

Barkley glared at him as if the doctor didn't fully realize the absurdity of his question. "Y-you send me back to combat and you've killed me," he stammered and again his voice began to rise. "I'll be a dead man." He was deeply agitated by the question.

The doctor eased back in his chair and clasped his hands behind his head. "Why, I've been over here for seven months and it hasn't bothered me."

Seven months? Barkley thought incredulously, *Seven months of what? Sitting on your ass in a hospital miles from any action? Seven months of sleeping beneath clean sheets in a warm bed? Eating three square meals every day? Of course it hasn't bothered you!*

"Do... do you know what it's like out there?" Barkley blurted, fully knowing the good doctor had no idea what he was talking about. As he completed his sentence, an orderly entered the room and dropped a stack of books directly behind him. *BAM!*

Startled, Barkley sprung from his chair as if shot from a cannon and lunged across the desk to throttle the doctor before the doctor could react.

Realizing his mistake, Barkley released his grip and returned to his chair, visibly shaken. His hands trembled violently.

The terrified orderly shied away.

Wild-eyed, the doctor regained his composure, then quickly scribbled a note on a piece of paper and slipped it into Barkley's file. Rewinding the tab, he handed it to Barkley. "Take this to Major Gilkens[*]," he told him as he gently rubbed his neck.

Still trembling, Barkley rose and left as the orderly nervously collected the books from the floor. In the hall, Barkley was curious as to what the doctor had written so ducked into a restroom to sneak a

---

[*] Major Gilkens is a fictitious name.

peek at the message. Entering a toilet stall, he unwound the tab and read the note: "Recommend indefinite re-assignment for rest and recuperation." A sense of relief washed over him. It was as if a massive weight had had been lifted from his shoulders.

It was January 30, 1945.[*]

---

[*] To this day, Harold Barkley does not know if the dropping of the books was an accident, or pre-arranged to see how he would re-act. Either way, his reaction proved that he was not ready for combat duty.

CHAPTER 22

CASUALTY OF WAR

Late February 1945, Longuyon, France -- Barkley dropped his barracks bag on the floor of the orderly room and stood before the First Sergeant. "Private First Class Barkley reporting for duty," he recited.

The sergeant relieved him of his orders. "Okay, stand easy."

The faint whistle of a locomotive sounded from afar. Outside, foot steps rushed past, and there was the sound of strange, heavy things striking other heavy things and the general bustle of manual labor.

Barkley listened to the hubbub with disinterest as the sergeant read his orders. He had been transferred to a Railway Operating Battalion, the 712th, for extended duty until his nervous condition was rectified. First Sergeant McGuire, who presently sat behind the desk, was less than pleased to have Barkley as a member of his Headquarters Company. Barkley was a combat exhaustion case. McGuire had received other combat exhaustion cases over the past months and they proved to be misfits, square pegs to be fitted into round holes. They knew nothing about railroading and never would as far as he was concerned. He cursed silently beneath his breath as he pondered where to place this latest arrival and finally decided to pawn him off on the communications detachment as a telephone operator. He couldn't do much harm at a switchboard, could he?

Barkley was given to another sergeant who was to take him to his new quarters. As they proceeded down the tracks a nearby locomotive released pressure from its break line -- *"WHOOOSH!"* Immediately Barkley dove to the ground. The escaping steam sounded just like an incoming artillery shell.

Several railway men standing nearby laughed and pointed at the prostrate soldier. Chagrined, Barkley looked about sheepishly as he rose to his feet and dusted himself off. His heart pounded like a jack-hammer.

"It's okay, son," chortled the sergeant, "It's okay. You don't have to do that anymore." He knew what had happened, why the young soldier had hit the dirt, and now he made an awkward attempt to comfort and reassure him.

Upon arrival at his new quarters, Barkley was pleased with what he saw. His new home was a sidetracked rail car, similar to a caboose, which held four bunks, two to a side. In addition to real beds, it had a roof, and windows and even a small stove. It sure beat the hell out of a foxhole! Barkley smiled inwardly. Already he began to like his new assignment.

Headquarters Company, to which Barkley was assigned, was charged with the administrative functions of the battalion and also provided contingents of supply, mess, signal, and dispatching personnel. The other companies did the labor. Company A maintained the track. Company B operated roundhouses and kept all the equipment in good working order, while Company C was the operating company that provided the crews that actually ran the trains.

Many of the battalion had been genuine railroad men back in the States before being drafted. Their unique backgrounds placed them in the Army's Transportation Corps where they quickly put their expertise to practical use. Dozens of Railway Battalions shuttled every type of supply from seaports in France, Belgium and The Netherlands to the big supply depots closer to the front in Germany. It was these same type of trains that Barkley and his buddies had guarded during their detached duty in Paris so many months before.

That evening, Barkley was taken to the communications room where he stared in wonder at the tangle of cords and flashing lights that made up the switchboard. He knew absolutely nothing about telecommunications, but another soldier gave him brief instructions as to what his duties were, and they seemed simple enough. His only chore was to plug the wire cables from one caller to the next into the proper receptacle on the board to make a connection. Since there was only four officers present, it wasn't too difficult, but as it was, he was a poor candidate to serve as telephone operator. Having the company officers so close at hand made him jumpy as a cat. He'd often make the wrong connections, linking incoming or outgoing calls to the wrong line. He'd study the board, unplug the cord and re-insert it, hopefully into the correct inlet. The officers, knowing his nervous condition, were patient with him, but it seemed at times that he was more a liability than an asset to the headquarters' operation.

Trains passed all through the night, and calls concerning the same were routed through Barkley's switchboard. Much to his relief, another communications man was present to guide him through his duties. He didn't work too hard at it, though. Since he was a combat exhaustion case, he was under orders to rest and recuperate and was excused from the rigors of a regular work schedule. He was only required to work one day out of the week, which no doubt irked some of the regular railway soldiers who put in long hours every day. But Barkley didn't really give a damn. He felt that after all he had gone through, that he was going to take it easy, if he could, and dedicated himself more to goofing off than applying himself to any degree of physical labor. He had it made and was going to make the best of it.

By daybreak his relief arrived and he was free to do as he pleased. He was intrigued by the bustle of the rail yard. Trains came and went, huffing and chugging, bells clanging as they rolled heavily along the rails. Massive engines strained against the drag of heavily laden cars and shrilled their whistles as if in complaint.

Down the line, a squad of "gandy-dancers" plodded beside the tracks, tools angled like rifles upon their shoulders as they marched towards a handcar that would take them to their next job. Another crew was already aboard a work train that sat idly upon a siding, waiting its turn to take to the rails. These men would travel farther down the line to work on a trestle, or a bridge, or perhaps to spread ballast as they maintained the way.

From the shops came the clanging of huge hammers and screeching of metal grating upon metal as damaged cars and locomotives were repaired. Sparks flashed brightly as welders plied their trade and all the while the voices of men at work filled the air.

The sky was bright and the air was crisp and life, for once, was good. For Barkley it was a happy time -- a time of honest toil instead of the Devil's work that he once knew where men killed men for the sake of God and Country.

Grateful to be alive, he strolled leisurely to his quarters and fell asleep.

Barkley struck up workable friendships with several of the railroad men, especially those that shared the small car they called home. Private First Class William Green, from Klamath Falls, Oregon, became his best friend and occupied the bunk opposite his in the car, as did Technician Fifth Grade Jack Yaryan, a full-blooded Indian from Hope, Idaho, who also became a close friend. Another Pfc. was a fellow of French descent named Edward Rougeux who hailed appropriately from Frenchville, Pennsylvania. Others were Technician Fourth Grade Joe Henley of Georgia, Pfc. Loyd Boren of Wichita, Kansas, and a private named Usealman from Indiana. His non-commissioned officers were Staff Sergeants Richard Binkley of North Carolina, and Emilio Compagnoni of Reno, Nevada. All-in-all, everyone got along swell.

CASUALTY OF WAR

Barkley discovered that he wasn't the only soldier transferred from the battlefront. There was a sprinkling of other combat exhaustion cases just like him, men such as Marshall Cole, who was a former rifleman from the 26th Infantry Division which had also fought in the Battle of the Bulge. Having undergone similar experiences, he and Barkley quickly bonded. One thing that none of them could readily adjust to was the harrowing sound of the engines releasing steam. Every time, all of the ex-combat soldiers would dive in unison to the ground, much to the amusement of the regular railroad soldiers, for as had happened to Barkley earlier, the whoosh sounded like the rush of an incoming artillery shell.

There was another combat exhaustion case, an ex-paratrooper, but he didn't last long. One day they found his jacket folded neatly alongside a bridge that spanned a deep gorge. His body was found smashed upon the rocks far below. It remained a mystery why he did it. Noting that he still had on his paratrooper boots, some speculated that he simply snapped, that he must have decided it was time to make a combat jump and dove off the bridge as if from a plane. But, of course, no one really knew what tragic event pushed him to the ultimate act. But he was dead, and that troubled everybody that knew him.

One of the benefits of being assigned to the Railway Battalion was that each member was issued a rail pass that allowed free passage on any train under the battalion's jurisdiction. Barkley took full advantage of this unforeseen boon. Since he only worked one day each week, he had plenty of time to explore the French countryside. By now the war had long since passed the region and he could roam the area at will.

One day, to kill time, he and a friend decided to investigate the nearby fortifications of the Maginot Line. The Maginot Line was France's answer to Germany's Siegfried line, and Barkley, realizing its historical significance, wanted to see it. His buddy brought along a camera so they could record their trip on film. They wandered among a continuous string of concrete pillboxes and emplacements, searching for the perfect place to take their pictures. Finding a suitable backdrop, they took turns posing besides the concrete emplacements, holding souvenir German helmets as props as each stared grimly into the lens.

As Spring neared, the weather improved, but the nights remained cold and all the while trains steamed to and fro in a perpetual parade of forward moving munitions, supplies and troops and rearward bound cars crammed with prisoners destined for the POW cages. And still other trains rolled solemnly westward, hospital trains, filled to capacity with broken men from the fighting front. And the war dragged on.

Back at the rail yard, Barkley and several others strolled leisurely past a locomotive. *Whooosh!* Again the ex-combat men dove to the ground. As before, the others burst into riotous laughter, immune to the curses cast upon them by the grim-faced men who slowly rose to their feet. It was a strange sensation -- for all the world the steam still sounded as if a large shell was coming in. The ingrained reaction of self-preservation was a hard habit to break. But as time passed, Barkley became accustomed to the sound of escaping steam and would catch himself in mid-dive, then draw upright, saying to himself: *No. I don't have to do that anymore.*

One morning, an inspection team entered Barkley's four-man barrack. "'Ten-shun!" someone bellowed and the men sprung to their feet -- all but one. Barkley remained sprawled on his bunk, feigning sleep as an officer and his entourage walked in. While the others stood stiffly by their bunks, Barkley lay as if oblivious to the ceremony. The officer noticed him, but said nothing, for he was aware of Barkley's exceptional circumstance and proceeded with his inspection, then left without saying a word.

Barkley's buddy, Green, fidgeted as his eyes followed the officer, then turned uneasily to Barkley and blurted, "Jesus, Barkley! You're going to get a court martial."

Barkley rolled over and grinned, "Naw, they can't bother me. I've got a medical condition! I've got it in writing that I'm excused from all that military crap."

CASUALTY OF WAR

By now, Barkley realized he could get away with about anything short of murder. His orders were clear -- due to his nervous condition, he was exempt from any and all military protocol. He no longer had to appear for roll call or stand any formations. He didn't even have to salute officers! And that, in the Army, was a cardinal sin. Another provision was that he was only required to perform light duty on a limited number of days and he continued to do so, putting in his time at the switchboard whenever scheduled, and little more. Barkley had it made. For once the joke was on the Army.

Late March, 1945 -- Finally! Mail! As a consequence of his frequent movements -- from combat to the hospital to the Replacement Depot to his current station -- Barkley's mail never caught up with him and that had been his greatest complaint. Now he received a large bundle of envelopes and carried them away as if guarding something precious. One of them was dated August 2, 1944. Now where the hell *that* one has been he could only guess, but he poured over every sentence as if it were fresh news, then ripped open the others. He learned that his parents had received his letter from the day he was wounded and how grateful his mother was to get it, for it was much better than receiving the visit from the Western Union man, who did, of course, arrive at a later date. They also received the oak leaf cluster for his Purple Heart Medal which they displayed alongside the ETO ribbon attached to his framed photograph.[*]

His mother lamented the fact that her son was not allowed to return to the States. "Why can't they let you come home to train troops? You have been facing death and have been wounded twice."

He was assured that his father was still working and his mother continued to gather eggs from her hens, although she had suffered a leg wound from an ornery rooster. She acknowledged that the rooster was mean and was close to becoming dinner.

His mother informed him that the pup now sleeps in a box on the porch and "is so sweet and cute, I think he takes after us. Ha!"

---

[*] Although Barkley was entitled to the European Theater Campaign Medal, he had only been issued the ribbon bar until the actual medal could be awarded. Tiny bronze "battle stars" were attached to either the medal or the corresponding ribbon to denote participation in a particular campaign of the European War.

She also had time to take in a movie downtown, "Going My Way", which was the first movie she had seen in a long time.

And there was sad news, too. Ernie Hemmings wrote that his cousin's husband had been killed in action.

Barkley also received a couple of letters from Catherine and her sister, Audree, in Paris. The girls were doing fine and Audree was soon returning to the university as an instructor. Catherine implored Harold to return to Paris, if he could, and visit again. She'd like to take him riding, to which Barkley had to laugh, for he'd never ridden in his life.

The following day he received another bundle of mail and he was satisfied that the mail jam had, at last, been unclogged. But he still hadn't seen any of his Christmas packages and he couldn't understand this, for by this time, all of the other soldiers had long since received theirs. Later, in explanation, he had been told that the 2nd Infantry Division's APO[*] had been overrun during the German's breakthrough in December and that many Christmas parcels for the division had become war booty.

The battalion remained at Longuyon for only a short period after Barkley's arrival. By March the last barrier guarding Germany proper, the Rhine River, had been breached and American divisions began pouring through the bridgehead at Remagen. As the front pushed deeper into Germany the base of supply also advanced, compelling the 712th Railway Operating Battalion to pack up, lock, stock, and barrel, and move to Luxembourg City where they arrived on the first day of April. To Barkley's delight, headquarters was set up in a stately old hotel located near the tracks where he continued to put in his time, but little else.

Barkley really liked Luxembourg City. It was a clean, modern city that had everything a man could ask for. The people were very sophisticated and truly appreciated the Americans' presence and best of all, it seemed as if everyone spoke passable English. He flirted with the girls and frequented the Red Cross canteen and occasionally patronized the restaurants and bars with his newfound buddies where he sampled the sweet burning nectar of cognac.

---

[*] Army Post Office

CASUALTY OF WAR

About this time he noted a disturbing difference between himself and the original men of the Railway Battalion. Everyone but he wore his campaign ribbons on his uniform whenever they went out on the town. As a combat infantryman, Barkley never wore anything but the blue and silver Combat Infantry Badge, for that was the only award that truly meant anything -- a true badge of honor and he wore it proudly as a member of that exclusive club. All the others ribbons and medals, said combat men, were simply chicken-shit, everyman awards and they refused to wear them.

But now, whenever Barkley went into town he noted that the mademoiselles fawned over the multi-colored ribbon bars that adorned his buddies' chests. Save for his Combat Infantry Badge, his own uniform was barren, for he had mailed his Purple Heart Medal, its oak leaf cluster, and his ETO ribbon to his parents each time he received them. Feeling left out, he soon wrote home asking his parents to return them since everyone else was wearing theirs. Until then, he'd have to be content with his CIB.

After two weeks in Luxembourg City the 712th was on the move again, crossing the Rhine at Mainz, Germany, before rolling on to Gross Auheim, east of Frankfurt, on the Main River. Headquartered at Gross Auheim, the elements of the battalion were distributed among towns all along the line. Barkley's detachment set up shop some thirty rail-miles farther up river, at Lohr.

Lohr, like virtually every other city in Germany, was a wreck. Most buildings were little more than piles of rubble, destroyed by bombs and shells. It seemed that any remaining civilians lived in cellars of those structures that had not completely collapsed. For the first time, the battalion found itself in occupied enemy territory. No one was allowed to communicate with the German citizens and a strict order of non-fraternization was enforced. Unlike France and Luxembourg, the GIs were now looked upon as conquerors rather than liberators and the mood quickly changed from joyous to tense.

April 13, 1945 -- Word passed swiftly through the ranks: President Roosevelt was dead. He had died the previous day -- victim of a cerebral hemorrhage. The men were stunned. It was as if a dark cloud had swept over them and swallowed them whole, for Roosevelt was the only president that many of them ever really knew, having been sworn into office in 1933 when most of them were mere boys.

At that time, the nation suffered from dismal economical conditions wrought by the Great Depression. Unemployment was rife. But Roosevelt's New Deal policy put Americans back to work and slowly but surely set the nation back on its feet. After Pearl Harbor, he had unified the country and galvanized it for war. Roosevelt was revered by many as the nation's savior.

Barkley, too, was saddened and wrote a short letter home to express his sorrow, for he believed that Roosevelt had made a good president.

Meanwhile, Barkley continued to do next to nothing while serving his time as telephone operator. He still had difficulty with certain connections, but managed to get by until one day he somehow re-routed one officer's call directly back its originating point, and that was the end of that. Soon Barkley was packing his bag. His days at the switchboard were over. He was reassigned to the signal crew.

At first Barkley was disappointed, for he believed he had a good thing going as a telephone operator. Although he barely knew how to handle the switchboard, he knew even less about being a signal man. It sounded like manual labor, and he worried he might really screw things up.

Barkley peered out the window of a two-storied building and stared into the darkness beyond the tracks. He had been assigned to the night shift where he and another soldier awaited the arrival of passing trains so they could set out the proper signal lamps to instruct them on their approach. Red lanterns meant "stop"; green meant "go". It was as simple as that.

It was all on-the-job training and Barkley was doing his best to learn. *Who knows?* he thought, *Maybe this will lead into a good job when I get home.* He only needed to know just when a train neared so he could place the lanterns, and the trains came frequently, as many as sixteen or more in a twenty-four hour period.

CASUALTY OF WAR

The battalion now operated in occupied enemy territory. Being unfamiliar with the German rail system, the Army saw fit to employ a number of German railroad men to assist in the daily routine at each rail yard. Their intimate knowledge of each station's operation would prove invaluable to the American railroaders and a number of them were allowed to resume their old jobs under the watchful eye of their soldier counterparts. Many of these were engaged as switch controllers or signal men.

Although citizens of Germany, these men seemed harmless enough. They were all middle-aged men, and although age had never stopped Hitler from conscripting older men into the army, these men were rail workers and the railroads had been a vital part of Germany's war effort. Their status exempted them from military service, and they were glad about it. The Americans recognized their skills and quickly put them to use. The Germans knew their craft and took pride in their work. The GI railway men saw no reason to suspect their German counterparts and took to them right away, and before long bonds of friendship formed by virtue of sharing a mutual trade.

For Barkley, their arrival was an unforeseen boon. No longer a switchboard man, he continued his watch in the tower one night out of seven, but the longer he worked, the less he liked it. But now, thanks to the arrival of several Germans, things became even easier than before. The elderly Germans were eager to please and Barkley took full advantage of their enthusiasm. While he goofed off in or around the signal room, the Germans did most of the work. Before long Barkley relied on them to notify him if an approaching train was to halt, or pass on through. Barkley would acknowledge their tip, then saunter out to set the proper lantern in place. His work ethic slipped for the worse and he became lazy.

For their effort, the Germans were richly compensated. Through rude communication, Barkley discovered that they and their families had been living chiefly on potatoes and bread for the last two years. In return for their work, Barkley would sneak them scraps of food from the kitchen or sometimes give then a box of rations. One morning, he and several others were frying several pounds of bacon at the conclusion of their shift. All of the Germans present watched intently, eyes riveted on the bacon as it sizzled and popped in the pan.

The aroma filled the room and it was all they could do to keep from drooling.

Although they fully intended to share, the GIs ignored the Germans and made out as if they were going to eat it all themselves. After each soldier filled his plate, there was still plenty remaining. At last, Barkley pointed to the bacon and said, "Here, help yourself." He reinforced his statement with motions of eating. After a brief hesitation, the Germans fairly leaped at the pan. But to Barkley's amazement, none of them took a bite. Instead, each wrapped their portion in newspaper and started out the door. Seeing the puzzled look upon Barkley's face, one commented, "Fuer meine Frau. Meine Frau!" He was taking it home to his wife. Their beneficiaries were exceptionally grateful.

Meanwhile, the war was going well -- the Germans were on the run on every front. On April 25th, elements of the First Army had linked up with the Russians on the Elbe River and other Allied Armies were pursuing the Hun as fast as they could travel and everyone knew it was only a matter of time before the final shot was fired. In Berlin, the Red Army has overrun all but a few blocks of the great city and by nightfall of April 30th Adolph Hitler put a pistol to his head and committed suicide. It was Spring 1945, and the world was about to make a turn for the better.

May 8, 1945, Luxembourg City -- Barkley grinned broadly as he was jostled by a crowd gone wild. Pure jubilation filled the air as shouts and singing rose above the clamor created by an enormous crowd. Thousands of people had poured into the street in spontaneous celebration, for this was the day of Germany's unconditional surrender. It was V-E Day -- Victory in Europe Day. Everyone was delirious with joy.

Soldiers and civilians locked arms and swayed to and fro as they paraded the breadth of the streets, singing and laughing with unbridled joy. It seemed as if everyone had received the word simultaneously and all poured into the street by the thousand, by the tens of thousands and the party was on.

CASUALTY OF WAR

Barkley was having a great time. He had, by chance, been in the city when the news of Germany's capitulation came and now he was caught up in the middle of a celebration like he had never seen before. He and a buddy bought a bottle of champagne and drank it, then worked their way downtown in time to see a large bridge illuminated by hundreds of lights and the crowd pointed and laughed and everyone was happy. Everyone was kissing everyone else and Barkley and his friend encountered a pair of girls they did not know and the foursome marched with thousands of others to the Royal Palace to await the appearance of the Duke and Duchess of Luxembourg. When the royal couple stepped onto a balcony the crowd went wild and commenced singing and the royals simply waved but made no speech and the people cheered again.

Then Barkley and his girl departed and ducked into a café where they had a faltering conversation in French with neither understanding the other but both smiled and that was communication enough. After each downed a glass of wine they re-entered the throng that filled every street and walked until midnight, then each went home.

The following day the celebration continued as if it would never end. Barkley and his buddy stood outside the Red Cross canteen where they could now drink all the Coca-Cola they wanted for free -- a savings of five francs apiece. Before long a band set up in a public square and began to play all the national anthems of the Allied nations and again everyone cheered and sang and tears flowed shamelessly. As the band struck up "The Star Spangled Banner" Barkley dutifully stood at attention until the final strains were swallowed by the gregarious roar of the crowd. Relaxing again, he began to take another sip of his soda pop just as the band broke into "La Marseillaise" of France, and again, because he was in uniform, he was required to stand at attention and then the band blared the national anthem of Luxembourg. Those who knew the words sang with fervor and then it, too, was over and Barkley reached for his Coke. But before he could lift his glass, the pompous strains of "God Save The King" soared above the cheering crowd and once again Barkley faced the bandstand and stood erect. And so it went, anthem after anthem and then they were repeated time and again and it was very difficult to take advantage of the free Cokes.

377

Later, as the celebration continued, Barkley and his friend picked up a couple of girls and they shared a quart of ice cream before forcing their way into a bar to order more champagne. The bubbly wine tickled as it sloshed down Barkley's gullet and he had more and even danced with girls he did not know, and that in itself was rare, for Barkley had never learned to dance. Then they ordered another round and by evening he was decidedly drunk. The war was definitely over.

The following morning Barkley's head felt as if struck by an eighty-eight.[*]

---

[*] German Eighty-eight millimeter artillery shell.

CHAPTER 23

ARMY OF OCCUPATION

May, 1945, Lohr, Germany -- Now, with the war over, the high command instituted the third and final phase of the Transportation Corps' mission in mainland Europe. Phase III called for a gradual return of all rail operations back to the Deutsche Reichsbahn -- the German State Railway. Whereas a few essential workers had already been engaged, more and more former German railroad employees were being called back to work under Allied supervision.

The arrival of additional German workers pleased Barkley. Although still delegated to light duty, he did even less than before and now only went through the pretense of work. Much of his time was spent sitting in the signal shack while the Germans did virtually all the labor.

Another German indispensable to the operation was the ex-station chief, the Bahnhofmeister. Although the policy of non-fraternization was still in effect, it became harder and harder for the GIs not to carry on casual conversations with any Germans they encountered. The local Bahnhofmeister was jovial and outgoing in his manner and seemed more than accommodating to his new masters. He was friendly to all the Americans, regardless of rank, and enlisted men were no exception. One of Barkley's co-workers, Berriman[*], was having intimate relations with the Bahnhofmeister's fifteen year old daughter. Once, he engaged her father in conversation, struggling through a mixture of French and English, highlighted now and then with a few newly acquired German words. Berriman boasted that he, too, was a "chef de gare" -- the French phrase for station chief.

"Ja?" the Bahnhofmeister queried. "Du bist ein 'chef de gare?' Ein Bahnhofmeister?"

"Ja, ja," Berriman answered without batting an eye, "Ja, in der States before the war -- before der krieg." Which of course was all bull-shit.

Later, Berriman wanted Barkley to accompany him on a visit to the Bahnhofmeister's home so he could see his young girlfriend. The Bahnhofmeister resided in a well appointed apartment above the station house in Lohr. It was immaculate. It was obvious that he had been a man of considerable substance and had carried much weight in the community. While Berriman sat with the buxom young girl on his lap, Barkley played the part of conqueror and made himself at home, snooping into whatever nook or cranny met his fancy. All the while, the girl giggled gleefully at Berriman's bold advances.

In time, Barkley came across a set of photo albums and casually leafed through the pages. What he saw stunned him. Page after page depicted groups of uniformed men smiling as if at some formal affair. Each wore a swastika armband. Many of the photos portrayed the Bahnhofmeister himself, resplendent in his uniform, smiling gregariously as he clasped other uniformed Nazis by the hand as if they had known each other for years. Other pictures were panoramas of the massive Nazi Party rallies such as those staged in Munich and Nuremberg, and some of these featured close-up shots of Hitler and none other than Barkley's most unwitting host. The

[*] Berriman is, in this instance, a fictitious name.

Bahnhofmeister was a Nazi. Now, with the U.S. Army occupying his home town, he acted the humble and submissive public servant. It sickened Barkley and he even considered turning the bastard in to the authorities in Frankfurt.

On the final day of the war, the German armies had surrendered en masse, and as a consequence vast amounts of weapons, vehicles and war materials fell into the hands the victorious Allies. Near Lohr there was an arms depot where captured German weapons were stored prior to their disposal by the proper authorities. Every type of infantry weapon imaginable was stockpiled there, under guard of a detachment of Military Policemen. It was a treasure trove for souvenir hunters who, under certain circumstances, were allowed to rummage through the depot in search of genuine war trophies. The only stipulation was that their selection be limited to small arms and could not be fully automatic, such as a machine gun. All one needed was a permit from his commanding officer allowing him to take the weapon of his choice.

At one time, Barkley had a number of battlefield trophies he had acquired in France. After being wounded he had lost track of them and assumed that they had been stolen by rear area personnel or lost when the Germans overran the Divisional rear area during the Breakthrough in December. He longed to find replacements to send home. He applied for a permit from Colonel Doud.[*]

Barkley's permit allowed him two firearms. Upon arrival at the depot, the MPs verified his authorization, then allowed him to enter and he was stunned by what he saw. Every type of weapon imaginable was stockpiled there -- row upon row of rifles, machine guns, pistols, mortars -- you name it, it was there. After rummaging around, he eventually found a pair of rifles he'd like to send home. His father would be delighted to receive them, he thought. But when he returned to the gate, the guards stopped him, looked over his selection, then tempted him with a bribe. They'd give him a good sum of money if he'd stash the weapons outside the gate where they could pick them up later. If he'd accept, they'd still allow him to re-

---

[*] Lieutenant-Colonel Forrest R. Doud, commanding 712th Railway Operating Battalion.

enter the facility and choose two more firearms for himself. They seemed confident about their offer -- apparently they had done this before. Perhaps they had aspirations of selling them on the Black Market, or offering them to rear echelon soldiers for a stately profit. Whatever the reason, Barkley agreed and took the cash.

Back in the compound, he continued to scavenge for himself. In time he came upon a true prize -- a sniper rifle exactly like one he had taken from a dead paratrooper in Normandy. It was a beauty! He also picked up one of the famous P-38 semi-automatic pistols. He believed he needed a hand gun for self protection when he went into town, for things could get rough in some areas and he wanted a little something to persuade an antagonist to back off.

Later, when he went for some target practice, he was disappointed when he discovered that his pistol had a slight malfunction. Whenever he pulled the trigger, the weapon refused to fire. It always took a second tug on the trigger before it went off. At first Barkley believed it may have been a fluke, or perhaps faulty ammunition, but time and again the same thing happened and he became accustomed to pulling the trigger twice before it fired. He decided the problem stemmed from a weak firing pin.

Having so much free time, Barkley had ample opportunity to explore his new environment. Lohr was a fair sized town that sat on the right bank of the Main River and he saw no reason not to investigate the community. He'd often go with a couple of workmates to prowl the bierhauses and bars on a regular basis. Sometimes he'd go alone.

By now he had taken to drinking liquor more often than usual. Although not a drunk by any means, he came to appreciate the taste of cognac. Whenever he went into town it seemed as if he was half-drunk, half of the time, and the drink made him bitter. A deep hatred raged within him. It was something he could not explain, but it chewed at his gut and in time the liquor changed his disposition. Once he had been an amiable young man, easy to befriend. But now, after living through the horrors of combat and watching so many friends slaughtered he became angry, and at times was down right mean.

By early June, the non-fraternization rule was weakening and it was not uncommon to see GIs escorting Frauleins in public. One day, Barkley was sitting at a café table, chatting quietly with a girl when two brawny soldiers swaggered in. They were boisterous and talked roughly as they grabbed a nearby table. They each looked natty with their pants legs bloused in their boot tops and several ribbon bars pinned above their jacket pockets -- the American Defense ribbon, the American Campaign ribbon, the new European Campaign ribbon.[*]

In no time, they noticed the wiry young GI sitting with the pretty fraulein and began to leer at her while making snide remarks. Soon, one bellied up behind Barkley and said, "What'll you do if we take her from you?"

"*What* did you say?" Barkley spat over his shoulder. He had heard him alright, but he wasn't going to take any crap from any rear echelon bastards strutting around with their cheap ribbons pinned to their chests, acting like genuine heroes.

"I *said*, what're you goin' to do if we take your girl from you?"

"Now you hear me," Barkley hissed as he turned to face his antagonist, "I'll take one of you and he won't make it. I may not get both of you, and I really don't care what happens to me, but one of you won't be walking away." The inflection of his voice gave no doubt that he meant what he said, that he was just crazy enough to go all out with them.

Just then, the other soldier noticed the silver and blue Combat Infantry Badge on Barkley's chest and the Second Infantry Division patch on his right shoulder and pulled his buddy by the arm, saying, "Come on. Let's go." And they departed.

About mid-June, Barkley received word that he had been recommended for the Good Conduct Medal. In light of what he was presently doing, it seemed a good joke on the Army, but when he later heard that it was being awarded to any infantryman who

---

[*] American Defense Medal for any military service two years prior to the attack on Pearl Harbor. American Campaign Medal for one year's service in the continental United States after Pearl Harbor. European, (African, Middle Eastern) Campaign Medal for service in those named theaters of war.

faithfully fulfilled his duty while in combat, he realized it was a legitimate award. He wrote home to his parents, explaining that with this latest decoration, plus his qualification for another battle star for his European Campaign ribbon, he would now possess sixty-one points.

The point system was something new in the Army, and everyone kept close track of his personal score. When the magic number of eighty-five was reached, a soldier was eligible to be sent home. One point was awarded for each month spent in the Army. Another was given for each month served overseas and a coveted five points was awarded for each campaign served in as well as for each decoration received. After that, the un-married men were at a disadvantage, for the married men got an additional five points just for being married. They also received five more points for each dependant child they had, up to three in number. Therefore a man married with children could reap as many as twenty points in one swoop! That was quite a windfall. Plus, many of the older men, such as those in the Railway Battalion, had been in the Stateside Army for a considerable length of time before their unit was shipped overseas. Whereas Barkley had spent only five months in the States, some of the older men had been in the Army since the draft of 1940.

While Barkley had, at this time, been in the Army for only a year and eight months, he had accumulated sixty-one points, and had earned most of them the hard way. Like many a young man who had been drafted at eighteen years, that was about as many points as he was going to see for quite a while. He would be stuck in Germany.[*]

But still, the system was as fair as could be hoped for, for a married man should get home as swiftly as possible, and any man who had been in the Army since 1940 had probably had his fill of it. Barkley had no real complaints.

---

[*] In reality, Barkley actually qualified for seventy-six points at this time. But poor record keeping had a tough time keeping up with his frequent movements each time he was wounded, and failed to award him the other decorations due him. Of these were the Bronze Star Medal for action in Normandy; The Presidential Unit Citation for what his battalion had achieved during the Battle of the Bulge at Rocherath, Belgium; and another bronze campaign star for participating in the Battle of the Bulge. All of these were awarded him twenty years later after some diligent clerk found the missing records in Washington, D.C. They arrived in his mail box without fanfare in 1964, and were a complete surprise.

June 18, 1945 -- It was a sunny day. Troop trains continued to pass along the lines operated by the 712th Railway Operating Battalion, carrying entire divisions from vanquished Germany to ports on the French coast. Here the unfortunate passengers were destined to return to the States en route to the Pacific Theater of Operations, for the war in the East still raged and many more men were needed for the upcoming invasion of mainland Japan. It was expected to make the bloody D-Day landings look like a cake walk.

Barkley was milling about the rail yard when one such train screeched to a halt to allow its passengers a chance to stretch their legs. He thought little of it, for he had seen it a number of times before. But then his eye caught sight of their unit insignia. Each soldier sported a black shield shoulder patch bearing an Indian head centered on a large white star. *My God! It's the Second!* The men were from his old outfit, the 2nd Infantry Division.

He pushed his way toward them, asking, "What regiment? What regiment are you with?"

"Thirty-eighth Infantry," came a surly reply. *The Thirty-eighth!* It was the very organization he had been assigned to in Normandy nearly a year to the day earlier.

Now he was very excited. "Where's Company G?" he asked anxiously as he moved among the ranks. "Do you know where Company G is?"

A soldier nodded farther down the tracks. "Down that-a-way." Barkley took off at a rapid clip.

He wormed through the teeming crowd and then stopped cold as he recognized an old comrade in the distance. "Blackmore!" he called as he thrust up a hand, waving. "Blackmore!" He could hardly believe it. It was Sergeant Blackmore, his old platoon sergeant who had been wounded beside him in Normandy so many months before.

Excited, he began to shove his way towards his friend, calling his name until a tough young infantryman grabbed him by the arm and sneered, "That's *Lieutenant* Blackmore to you!" He said it with such contempt that it was obvious that he believed that Barkley was just another rear echelon soldier who had no right to be among real combat men, let alone *talk* to them. But by then Blackmore arrived on the scene and intervened on Barkley's behalf.

"It's okay, Hoffman," he said as he patted the soldier on his shoulder, "This is Barkley. He was with the company in Normandy." Hoffman gave Barkley a final appraisal, then decided if his lieutenant said it was okay, then it was alright with him, too, and walked away.

The two veterans were delighted to see each other. Barkley was amazed that Blackmore could even walk, let alone continue with active service, for he believed that he had been shot through both knees in that wheat field in July of 1944. But Blackmore told him that his wounds had been clean, that no bones were hit, and after his recovery he had been reassigned to the company. Later he won a battlefield commission, thus the lieutenant's bars.

Barkley quickly told his old sergeant how he came to be in a railway outfit, which drew a snort and a quick smile and then the whistle sounded and the re-union was over. Lieutenant Norman Blackmore hollered at his men to "mount up", and then with a wave, bid Barkley adieu. And that was the last Harold Barkley ever saw of the best combat soldier he had ever known.[*]

Germany's defeat proved to be a dream come true for Barkley. Previously, he had traveled to various parts of liberated Europe by way of his battalion rail pass. But now, with victory declared, he made plans to tour the rest of the continent.

One of the other signal men was another "eight-ball" sent to the battalion to recover from combat exhaustion. Since each only had to work one day out of the week, they agreed to cover one another's shift. That way each would have two weeks off duty for every two days of work.

---

[*] In the course of assembling documentation for this story, Barkley's son, Cleve, made several attempts to locate Norman Blackmore, but to no avail. Percy Imbody, Company G, Thirty-eighth Infantry's First Sergeant, told him that Blackmore received a battlefield promotion in Germany to Second Lieutenant. Blackmore stayed in the Army and was last seen by Imbody at Fort Lewis, Washington, before the Second Infantry Division departed for another combat tour in the Korean War. That was the last he saw of him.

Taking advantage of his rail pass, Barkley traveled to nearby Aschaffenburg, some twenty-five miles to the west, and farther up the line to the big city Frankfurt.

In Aschaffenburg he met a German woman named Emma. She was considerably older than Barkley, he just turned twenty, and she thirty-six, but she was attractive and sociable and Barkley desired to get to know her better. Although she only spoke German, conversation was completed through use of a friend who spoke tolerable English. He discovered that Emma lived with her mother in an apartment in town; that she was married; that her husband had been somewhere on the Eastern Front, although he could well be dead for all she knew; her brother had been an ace in the Luftwaffe. Despite all this, she took to young Barkley and they became friends. At every opportunity thereafter, Barkley boarded the next train west and stopped at Aschaffenburg.

Post-war Europe was a chaotic place with homeless people wandering the length and breadth of the continent. They were known to the Allies as "DPs" -- Displaced persons -- refugees trying to find their way home. Many had lost track of family members and were desperate for reunion. Most wore only whatever clothing covered their backs. They were penniless, hungry and scared. By the tens of thousands, and then thousands more, they created a constant flow of humanity that shifted from one part of the continent to the other in a world filled with turmoil and fear.

Most traveled by foot, utilizing carts and even bicycles to transport their meager belongings. Occasionally one would see a family piled into a farm wagon drawn by a plodding, swaybacked horse. Sometimes they attempted to snatch a ride on the German run trains, stuffed tightly into boxcars and some even clung to the roofs of the clattering cars -- a dangerous practice. For them it was a time of poverty and despair. Hope was only a faint, faltering light, but at least there was hope and hope, as they say, springs eternal.

And there were others, as well. After the cessation of hostilities, hundreds of thousands of German soldiers were being released from the prisoner of war cages. All had to find their own way home by whatever means they could. One of these methods was by rail.

Once, while traveling to and from his various destinations, Barkley noticed a young German woman in uniform, perhaps twenty-two years old, sitting with several ex-German soldiers. It was rumored that she was a doctor who had served on the front with a medical detachment. The Germans chatted quietly among themselves.

Barkley, who had been drinking, noticed that the woman was rather attractive and decided he'd engage her in conversation. The Germans fell silent as the American soldier approached. "Guten Tag," he addressed the woman in his most cordial manner. She ignored his advance and stared coldly out the window. The German soldiers looked away, as if nothing was wrong.

Barkley was infuriated at the snub. He was bitter about everything and everyone these days, especially German soldiers, and her reaction pissed him off. It didn't help that he had been drinking. "I know you all hate Americans," he spat. "You've been trying to kill me for a year!" The Germans didn't even look at him, but stared blankly, as if in a trance.

"You want to kill me now?" Barkley shouted as he pulled the P-38 from his waistband. "Here!" He thrust the pistol butt first toward the woman. "Shoot me if you want to."

Wide-eyed now, she shrunk away. Her companions did nothing.

Barkley persisted and offered the pistol to all of them. "Go on!" he roared, "Shoot me!" He knew that it always took two pulls of the trigger before the weapon went off due to its weak firing pin. He hoped one of the Germans would try to grab it, and then he'd beat the crap out of all of them before the culprit would be able to try again.

Wisely, no on accepted his offer. Then, as if trying to ease the tension, the woman spoke. In faltering English, she mentioned that she didn't want trouble and was simply on her way home to Frankfurt. In time she even revealed her name and offered Barkley a chance to visit her if he ever got to Frankfurt.

Satisfied, Barkley continued the conversation. But he never intended to see her again.

On another occasion, Barkley noticed a pair of young Germans trying to steal a ride on the last car of an Army train. They had jumped aboard just before the train was scheduled to depart and now stood on the rear deck with their meager bed rolls lying at their feet. Barkley knew it was strictly forbidden for anyone but Army personnel to ride on any train operated by the U.S. Army, so leaped aboard to confront the wartime hobos. Both were clad in bits of Wehrmacht uniforms, apparently recently released POWs.

Barkley approached them in a menacing manner. "Aussteigen!" he ordered as he pointed forcefully to the siding, demanding they get off the train.

They stared back dumbly, as if they did not understand his meaning.

"Get off! Raus!" Barkley snarled, pointing again as the train lurched forward and began to move. The stubborn Germans refused to yield.

"Get OFF!"

The Germans glowered indignantly at the American's outburst and stood their ground, which further enraged Barkley. "RAUS!" he bellowed as the train gradually picked up speed. But still they refused to budge.

Incensed, Barkley jerked his P-38 from his jacket and in one motion poked it directly into one's face and snapped the trigger. Blood drained from the wide-eyed soldier's face as he leaped backwards off the train. Barkley feigned surprise at the "misfire", then glared at the other who took the hint and quickly followed his comrade's lead. By now the train had gained momentum and both tumbled roughly into the ditch that flanked the track. Still angry, Barkley kicked their bundles after them.

Kraut bastards! Who the hell do they think they are?

Meanwhile, Barkley continued to escape every chance he got. Aschaffenburg had now become a routine destination, for he and a buddy each had a girlfriend there.

Aschaffenburg had been bombed mercilessly during the war. The damage was so extensive, so complete, that the town was now called "The City of the Dead", and not without reason. The rail yard was a disaster. A number of tracks had been blown and twisted by bombs and dozens of destroyed cars had been pushed aside in tangled heaps. It seemed that every passenger car had been riddled by bullets. Hardly a building remained standing and many of these had been gutted by fire. Wherever one walked, he was forced to skirt the ubiquitous craters that now marred the city like some monstrous pox. The Germans, being an industrious people, had cleared the rubble from the streets and created avenues of passage through the debris, but everything else remained in ruin. Families now lived in damp cellars, or nested in bomb ravaged apartments of those buildings that hadn't crumbled. The simplest niceties were scarce and begging was not uncommon.

Emma and her mother resided in a barren apartment. Like every other German family in the aftermath of war, they had very little to live on. But having young Barkley as a frequent guest had inherent advantages, for he'd arrive with such treats as canned spam or some other tinned meat from Army issued rations. It was no burden to him, for he always took his meals in the mess hall and had no use for bland rations. But still, bringing the occasional gift of canned meat was not enough to alleviate their hand-to-mouth existence, so Barkley devised a plan to ease their constant hunger.

Returning to Lohr, he cornered a friend who had a full case of spam hidden away. Knowing that a full case of canned meat would be a real treat for Emma and her mother, Barkley quickly cut a deal with his buddy then departed immediately for Aschaffenburg. But now he had a problem. It was late by the time he arrived in the city. A curfew existed and the MPs had orders to shoot violators on sight. The trick now was to get his booty to his girlfriend's home without being seen. But after combat, evading the MPs seemed like child's play and Barkley easily slipped through the dark streets to deliver his treasure to Emma and her mother. And they were extremely grateful.

Now, with the war over, Barkley became more tourist than soldier and traveled to cities throughout the continent. His excursions took him farther and farther from Lohr. Although he still visited Emma and her mother in Aschaffenburg, he also returned to Luxembourg City and traveled as far as Brussels and Antwerp in Belgium.

Once, while walking the streets of Luxembourg City, he noticed two young women standing idly as he approached. One nudged the other as he passed and nodded appreciatively. "Tres physique!" she cooed in French, "What a figure!" The remark was inspired by Barkley's tight-fitting Ike Jacket. The newly issued garment was cropped close at the waist, accentuating the wearer's figure. Barkley had broad shoulders and narrow hips and the new jacket exemplified the effect, much to the ladies' delight.

On a train in Brussels, an attractive young lady sat opposite him and smiled politely whenever their eyes met. Before long, they were engaged in conversation with Barkley struggling with his elementary French and she stumbling over a few choice phrases in English.

In time she pointed to his jacket and indicated that she'd like to have "un souvenir Americain." Barkley didn't fully understand her meaning until she touched the badge and ribbons upon his chest. "J'ai besoin d'une decoration," she pouted. She wanted either his Combat Infantry Badge or Purple Heart ribbon.

"No," came a sharp reply. Apparently she did not realize what the shiny blue badge or the simple purple and white ribbon with its tiny oak leaf cluster meant to the young soldier. But she insisted, and in time Barkley grew impatient with her pleading. "Here!" he blurted at last, "You want a souvenir? Take this!" And he pulled a half-carat diamond ring off of his finger and handed it to her. She forgot about the ribbon.

Barkley enjoyed visiting all the cities, but best of all he returned to the crown jewel of Europe -- Paris! He had received a number of letters from Catherine imploring him to return to the City of Light for a visit. Now, with the war over he saw no reason not to see her again. He still enjoyed the luxury of having nearly two weeks off of work and quickly made his plans.

Paris was immediately familiar to him -- the broad avenues, the landmarks, the metro -- it all came back to him as if he had never left. First and foremost on his agenda was a reunion with Catherine. Upon arrival at their home in the suburb of Vincennes, her mother was delighted to see the sweet young soldier they had entertained six months earlier. Barkley was seated in the parlor and Catherine and her sister, Audree, were called to the room. Audree was dressed in riding clothes, having just exercised one of their horses. Catherine looked as beautiful as ever in a casual dress.

They had a pleasant reunion, chatting in broken English seasoned with a French phrase or two and everyone laughed and smiled and had a good time. In due course, Madame Orlandetti suggested refreshments and through Catherine, asked young Barkley if he'd prefer lemonade or wine. Barkley declared his preference for wine. The matron was astonished by his reply, for young Barkley never touched alcohol the last time he visited. Non-plussed, she returned with a tray holding a full decanter and several glasses and set it on a table.

Before long they were joined by Catherine's father, the governor general of Corsica. He was tall and held himself very erect and strutted in a stately manner that suited his station, but he was always cordial to young Barkley and even joked with the young soldier through the interpretations of his daughters. He produced a photo album filled with pictures of his family and scenes from Corsica and the grounds surrounding their present home. Barkley was amused when he viewed a photo depicting the governor-general's honor guard in Corsica. They appeared a motley squad attempting to look business-like, but Barkley laughed inwardly, for although armed and uniformed, they hardly qualified as bona fide soldiers. After sharing a glass of wine, the governor departed, leaving the young ones to themselves.

In time, Barkley and Catherine slipped away. They strolled through the gardens and groves of the chateau and made small talk. Although they never rode the horses, they did row in the lake and took her Irish setters for a walk. Returning to the house, Barkley was invited to dinner, and then it was time for him to go. But it had been good to see Catherine again, for she had never given up on her young soldier beau and had written faithfully throughout his service. For Barkley, Catherine would forever remain one of his most pleasant memories of the war.

Back at Lohr, Barkley became impatient with people and was ill-tempered. At times he reported for duty half-drunk and couldn't keep his mind on his work. Although he enjoyed his visit with Catherine, he longed to be with Emma in Aschaffenburg.

Once, after drinking much of the day, he sprang aboard a German locomotive that was getting up steam. The train was scheduled for an eastward destination, but Barkley wanted to go west, to Aschaffenburg, to see his girl. "Sie gehen Aschaffenburg" he demanded as he pointed to the West.

The German engineer put on his stubbornest face. "Nein. Nein," he protested, "Wir fahren nach _____." He was going nowhere but to his assigned destination.

Barkley, however, was also stubborn. Earlier, while snooping around the office, he had used a typewriter to forge a false document stating that he was with the Criminal Investigation Detachment of the Provost Marshal's office. Angered now by the engineer's reluctance to comply with his wishes, he flashed the CID card in the German's face while waving his pistol like a madman. "ASCHAFFENBURG!" he roared. The German's eyes went wide at the sight of the card. To him it was as if a Gestapo agent was standing before him. After a dozen years of Nazi rule, most Germans paled at the sight of the Gestapo and now the engineer believed that the ranting, drunken soldier waving proper credentials was the American version of the dreaded secret police. Immediately, he uncoupled the locomotive from the remainder of the train and turned it around to roar full throttle in the opposite direction. Barkley had a personal rail-taxi all the way to Aschaffensburg. It was a wonder he didn't get court-martialed for his exploit.

On another occasion, Barkley and his buddy were again in Aschaffenburg, whooping it up at a local bierhaus. The place was packed with GIs. In time, several beers had completed the route from mouth to belly to bladder and Barkley rose to relieve himself. He had just staggered through the restroom door when a vague figure lunged from the shadows behind him. A beer bottle rose high above the figure's head and came swooping down. Barkley dodged at the last moment and avoided the blow. Though drunk, he swung a fist with all his might, and after a brief struggle, the mugger bolted out the door.

Barkley staggered after him and sounded the alarm. Other GIs rose to give chase. Then other young Germans got involved and a brawl soon erupted between GIs and a host of bitter young Germans. The brawl developed into a full-fledged riot and earned a column in the GI newspaper, *The Stars and Stripes*.

It was later determined that the instigator who attempted to brain Barkley with the bottle must have been one of the young malcontents called "Hitler's Werewolves". The Werewolf movement was meant to be a nationwide guerilla insurgency intent on driving the occupation forces from Germany. Fortunately for the Allies, and Germany, too, it never took hold.

On another night, Pfc. Barkley was returning to the station after spending time with Emma at her mother's apartment. The streets were dark and foggy. As he strolled leisurely towards his destination, he became aware of the faint sound of footsteps tapping somewhere behind him. He stopped. The footsteps stopped. Barkley listened intently, trying to determine if the owner of the hollow steps was nearing, or moving on. Nothing stirred. A sixth sense told him to use caution, for it was not uncommon for an individual soldier to wind up in a hospital, or dead on a night such as this.

Again he stepped off towards the station. Immediately, the phantom footsteps echoed from behind. The hair raised on Barkley's neck. As a precaution, he patted his jacket to ensure his pistol was still there. Upon reaching a corner, he stopped and turned to see who was following him but again all was still. Nothing but dark shadows and ugly piles of rubble. Concerned now, Barkley reached into his jacket and touched the pistol's grip. He moved on a short while longer, then quickly ducked into the shadows of a ruined building and waited. He pulled out his pistol and intentionally pulled the trigger once. The next time he did so, the weapon would fire. He was ready. His nemesis resumed his stalking, then stopped abruptly, as if he was aware that he had lost sight of his prey. Barkley held his breath as his ears strained against the darkness. After a pause, the footsteps clattered in the opposite direction, then faded altogether. The game was over. After a moment of hesitation, Barkley again resumed his stroll to the station and no one followed him anymore.

Late August, 1945 -- Again orders came to move. This time Barkley's detachment was sent to a lackluster town called Laufach, located between Lohr to the east, and Aschaffenburg to the west. It wasn't much compared to Lohr and there was little to do. Barkley did not like it. Bored, cognac became his most willing companion.

August, 1945, Laufach, Germany -- It was a moonless night and Barkley was drunk. He stood on the upper floor of the signal shack, poised like a sea captain on the bridge of a swaying ship as he surveyed the scene before him. A line of pole lamps stretched into the darkness, glowing softly as they lit the rail yard and illuminated tandem bands of silver track that vanished into the night. From below came the sound of shuffling feet as several German laborers disturbed the ballast. Voices murmured in the dark.

Barkley took another swig from his bottle, then nuzzled the butt of his souvenir sniper rifle to his shoulder. He had decided he'd have some sport by seeing how many lights he could take out before his aim failed him.

The rifle weaved and bobbed as Barkley tried to steady his weapon. Bleary-eyed, he found it difficult to focus on the sights that rolled arbitrarily before his eyes.

The tall lamps stretched far into the darkness and burned brightly, as if defying his intentions.

Realizing he'd never hit anything with his weapon swaying like a bough in wind storm, he wised up and propped the barrel upon the closest window sill. Heavy-lidded, he aimed again. *Ka-POW!!* The rifle bucked and a light bulb shattered. A thousand iridescent slivers rained onto the tracks below. Smiling, Barkley worked the bolt and aimed at the next lamp. *Ka-POW!!*

Below, in the darkness, the German workers flinched at every shot and muttered among themselves. *"Verrueckter Amerikaner!"*[*]

Before the night was over, there wasn't a single light shining for hundreds of yards down the track.

One day, Barkley's buddy, Green, borrowed the rifle and shot a fox that was sniffing around the tracks. Green was pleased with his marksmanship, but not as pleased as the German station chief who took the animal home for supper. Meat was scarce and he was

---

[*] "Crazy American!"

delighted to have it. To commemorate the occasion, Green and the station chief held the fox by its tail and posed for a photograph in the rail yard.

Inspired by Green's achievement, Barkley, too, tried his hand at hunting and shot what he believed to be a small deer. In reality it proved to be a large hare. The mistaken identity was caused by a snoot full of liquor.

Earth shattering events occurred in the Pacific theater of war. On August 3, 1945, a single bomb of unfathomable strength destroyed an entire city in Japan. Even after Hiroshima's destruction, the Japanese refused to yield and promised a fight to the finish. As a result, President Truman ordered a second atomic bomb dropped on Nagasaki three days later, which finally convinced Emperor Hirohito to acknowledge the shameful truth, that Japan was soundly defeated. On August 15th the Japanese formally surrendered on the deck of the USS Missouri anchored in Tokyo Bay. Finally, after six grueling years of total destruction and misery, the Second World War had come to a close.

At the conclusion of hostilities, rumors spread like fallen leaves swirling in an autumn wind. Some heard that the 712th was being shipped home. Others said, no, that they were being transferred to the Pacific Theater, while a few disconsolates scoffed at the idea and said the battalion would remain indefinitely in Germany to help get the Deutsche Reichsbahn* on its feet.

In time, orders came for the entire battalion to prepare for the movement to a port in France. Many still held to the second rumor and believed that they were bound for Japan. But Barkley was not going with them. He and a few of the other attached personnel were to be transferred to other units that made up the Army of Occupation.

Initially, Barkley was upset, because he believed if they were indeed going to Japan, he wanted to go along. He knew his present duties were free of danger, and besides, he'd get the chance to see the

---

* German State Railroad.

exotic Orient. But his commanding officer said no, that he would be transferred.

Accepting this, Barkley requested that he be sent to a unit in the immediate vicinity, for he knew the area well by now and had a number of girlfriends in the nearby towns. The captain said sure, that they'd take care of him. When his orders came, he discovered that he was being assigned to the 735th Railway Operating Battalion. He'd never heard of them, but he assumed they must be stationed close by.

September, 1945 -- Barkley was disappointed. Much to his dissatisfaction, he discovered that the 735th Railway Operating Battalion was centered at Linz, Austria, more than three-hundred miles to the east of his familiar haunts. He felt as if he'd been duped by the captain. Maybe it was the captain's idea of payback for his less than stellar performance, but here he was all the same, stuck in unfamiliar territory, among a new set of strangers.

He discovered that Linz sat upon the banks of the beautiful Blue Danube River. The Danube, however, was not so lovely as the popular waltz let on. Instead it flowed sluggishly past the town, a murky, brown watercourse so dull and lifeless that it seemed as if it, too, had been drafted and forced to don military dress. While the Americans sat on the right bank, the Red Army of the Soviet Union occupied the opposite shore. No one was permitted to cross into the others' territory unless on official business.

Upon his arrival, Barkley had once again been assigned as a switchboard operator for Headquarters Company. He studied the board before him, but his thoughts were elsewhere. His mind was on Aschaffenburg, not Linz, and certainly not this damned telephone switchboard with its cords dangling like tentacles of some sub-oceanic creature. He felt as if his old captain had given him a royal screwing on his reassignment.

As Barkley adjusted to his new location, he noted strange things were taking place. It seemed as if all the people of Europe were destitute, living virtually a hand to mouth existence amidst rubble and ruin. The Americans had plenty of everything: food, clothing, blankets, soap -- you name it, they seemed to have it. All of these things were relatively easy to obtain for resourceful GIs. As a result, the Black Market thrived. To his utter amazement, Barkley discovered that certain soldiers were getting the equivalent of $3.00 for a Hershey bar. Cigarettes went for anywhere from $5.00 to $10.00 a pack. Gum, $2.00; blankets, $30.00 to $40.00 apiece. As for clothing, black marketeers could reap $20.00 for a shirt, $15.00 to $20.00 for a pair of pants, and as much as $50.00 for shoes!

The temptation to cash in on the dealings was strong, but Barkley quickly decided against it. He had no desire to spend time busting rocks in the stockade for God knows how long. Although others were growing rich, he'd not take part in the underground enterprise.

Meanwhile, while Barkley worked his switchboard, his commanding officer began receiving letters from his mother in Quincy, Illinois, requesting her son be sent home as soon as possible. She complained that the war was over and that her boy had done his share and there was no good reason to keep him overseas. The colonel read her implorations with disinterest, for he no doubt had a stack of other letters in a similar vein and her pleas were systematically ignored.

As in western Germany, it didn't take long for any GI to become acquainted with at least one girl in Austria, and Barkley was no exception. He had a chance encounter with a pretty Fraulein of Linz and quickly made his play. Her name was Josephine and she was a school teacher. It made no difference to Barkley that she was dating a Polish officer at the time. To her advantage, Barkley was an American, and even though only an enlisted man, he had access to many things her Polish *liebster* could not provide -- things such as cigarettes, or the occasional gift of canned rations. By comparison, young Barkley seemed to have plenty of money to spend. So as a matter of simple economics, she spurned the Polish officer for the American Private First Class.

In time, Barkley's association with Josephine proved beneficial. While other soldiers continued to trade their black market goods to the local Austrians, Barkley noted that no one seemed to be dealing with the Russians across the Danube. He knew a simple pack of smokes was still going for $5.00 to $10.00 a pack. Since his departure from combat, his smoking habit had slackened, and as a result he always had extra cigarettes on hand. As a consequence, he decided to enter an untapped market -- the Red Army. To supplement his meager supply of smokes, he traded a portion of his chocolate ration to other soldiers for additional cigarettes. He planned on turning a decent profit at the expense of the Ruskies.

Using his girlfriend as his go-between, he'd load her up with candy and extra cigarettes and send her across the bridge where she'd barter with the Russians on his behalf. She always returned with respectable profits and would receive just compensation for her efforts. It was a satisfying arrangement for all concerned.

In dealing with the Reds, Barkley noted how incredibly backward many of the Russian soldiers were. They had been impressed into service from the vast steppes and rural areas of the Soviet Union. Most were simple serfs, uneducated peasants who had no chance of ever achieving a decent life under the harsh rule of Stalin's communist empire. He was amazed when he discovered that the "Ivans" were impressed by the novelty of indoor plumbing. Many had ripped fixtures, pipes and all, from walls to take home to their hovels in Mother Russia, fully believing that all they had to do was insert the severed pipes into their own walls and water would pour out like magic! The same went for light bulbs.

Innately ignorant of modern conveniences, the Soviet soldiers lived little better than animals themselves. In battle they were sent in waves against the German machine guns and fell in droves. Their commanders cared not how many were killed, for they knew if they sent wave after wave after wave against the Germans, the Germans would eventually run out of ammunition and their line would break. Life meant little to the common soldier and he fought savagely. And their lives meant even less to the officers who led them, for their commanders, too, fought with the threat of a bullet in the back of their heads if success was not achieved. In light of that, their men's lives were of little consequence. Under such brutal leadership, the

Russian Front was a place of savage, no holds barred warfare. It was a bloodbath. In light of that, the survivors felt justified in taking whatever they wished from the vanquished.

While Barkley did little to aid the efficiency of his new unit, he continued his "playboy" lifestyle while away from his duties. But he now had one problem, and it was a major one. It seemed that the Polish lieutenant who had previously been seeing his current girlfriend greatly resented him for stealing her away. Now and then Barkley would see him lurking close by whenever he was with her, glaring hatefully from the shadows, and he knew nothing good would come from it. In time his suspicions proved true.

One day Barkley was passing out cigarettes to a number of Germans who had assembled behind a line of sidetracked rail cars. He was not charging them for the smokes, but graciously handed out one cigarette apiece to each outstretched hand. They were civilians he had befriended while working in the rail yard.

Suddenly a lone German approached from down the line and breathlessly warned Barkley that the MPs were coming -- that they knew he was dealing with the Germans and were going to arrest him. Although the policy of non-fraternization was hardly enforced anymore, dedicated MPs could still make it rough for anyone who violated the order, if they so desired.

The party quickly dispersed and Barkley scurried for the cover of another car to observe what would happen. Sure enough, along came several military policemen and who was leading them, but none other than the Polish lieutenant! The bastard was trying hard to eliminate his competition.

On another occasion Barkley was walking in the dark when out of nowhere, an electric line crashed to the rail yard. Sparks flashed brightly as the live wire writhed and leaped within touching distance. Barkley's heart sprang to his throat as he jumped back. He had barely missed being electrocuted. There seemed to be no good reason why the line would have broken and he suspected foul play on behalf of the jealous Polish officer. "You missed me, you sonovabitch!" he hollered into the darkness, but no one answered, nor did anyone step forward to claim the deed.

Late November, 1945 -- Barkley's routine continued throughout the fall with him putting in his time at the switchboard while yearning to be free to conduct his personal business in Linz. Meanwhile, his commanding officer continued to receive desperate letters from his mother imploring him to send her only child home. She blatantly mentioned that she was sick and needed him by her side. Then the letters from the Red Cross came pouring in, declaring the same, and tiring of this the colonel cut the orders releasing Pfc. Barkley from his command. It was over. Harold Barkley was coming home.

Battered, but still alive, Barkley would now be able to reap the benefits of survival: reunion with family and friends; a job; perhaps a wife and family -- all the things so many others would never, ever have, for many a young man lay beneath the cold soil of France and Belgium and Germany and cemeteries all around the globe. And untold others were condemned to life in wheelchairs, or had been fitted with prosthetic limbs to replace those ripped off by exploding shells and mines. Others were blind and would live many, many years in total darkness, having to rely on youthful memory of what color the sky is, or how green the grass can be in the Spring. The price of freedom had been exceptionally high. So much tragedy. Most of Europe lay in ruins. People had been displaced by the millions and many had lost track of families never to be re-united again. The horrors of the Nazi concentration and death camps would forever haunt those who had survived them. And the soldiers of every army would forever battle the recurring nightmares that would plague them to their dying days, for they were personal horrors that few wished to share.

As Barkley packed his barracks bag, he was flooded with emotions. He recalled the faces of lost comrades -- the inquisitive expression on Antonelli's face; how "Major" Bartas' belly shook whenever he laughed; Barrella the lover; spooky-eyed Bell; young Willie who trembled so at the prospect of battle. He saw the haggard, battle-worn faces of his fellow scout, Hinson and the two Joe's --

Guajardo and Benavidez. He recounted the courage of Sergeants Blackmore and Parker, as well as big-boned Hoernke. There was "Blue Eyes" and Frank Santone -- and so many more, all wounded or killed.

And then there was the ol' Barracuda, Frank Balchunas. At least Frank had made it home and had even visited with Barkley's parents in the Fall of 1945. With the exception of Frank Balchunas, Barkley would never see the others again, although they had been bonded by blood and fire and had, for a time, been as close as brothers, each looking out for the other until felled by enemy fire.

What did it all mean? Perhaps the world was now a better place to live. Who could say? But at least he knew for a fact that what he and the millions of others had done was good, that they had freed Europe from the twisted aspirations of a madman. Perhaps that was the payoff. Perhaps so many others had to be sacrificed so that good could triumph over evil. But, of course, that was a very idealistic view. Maybe they all died for nothing. Maybe, in the long run, nothing would change and men would always be evil and good ones would always die trying to stop them. Perhaps it was a vicious circle that never ended. What did it all mean?

In the end, Barkley discovered more questions than answers and finally decided it was far above his capabilities of reason and reduced his thoughts to cleaning out his foot locker. At last he strapped his souvenir rifle to his barracks bag and walked away. The war was over. He was going home.

THE FINAL SCENE

Mid-December, 1945 -- Barkley arrived by rail at Le Havre, France, where a troopship, the U.S. Army Transport "Lincoln Victory" awaited him. Its destination was Boston, Massachusetts. As he ascended the gangplank, the souvenir rifle strapped to his bag banged the back of his head as it had done at seemingly every step since leaving Linz, and he grumbled at the wisdom of ever taking the damned thing. Once on deck, he was ordered below with hundreds of other soldiers who were ecstatic at the prospect of going home and the mood was sheer jubilation. On the 17th of December, the ship glided gracefully from port with exceptional ease, offering no inkling of the dangers that lay before them.

En route, the Lincoln Victory, as well as a number of other ships, sailed directly into a North Atlantic storm. Being better than halfway home, they could not return to Europe and had no recourse but to ride out the storm that closed rapidly upon them. The seas heaved and swelled and men became sick, but that wasn't half their problems. In due time, gale force winds blew up and battered the ship and waves lapped over the decks. Orders came to batten the hatches and all personnel not on duty were required to remain below. The ship rocked one way and then the other spilling men from bunks and tossing them like dolls as they attempted to negotiate the narrow passage ways of the lower decks. And then things worsened.

The storm intensified. The Lincoln Victory lurched as if pushed from behind by a violent force then leaped high as if attempting to fly. Daylight peeped from below mid-keel as the prow and stern rode colossal waves which released their grip and the good ship slapped down hard upon the sea. Then massive waves towered on either side as the Victory sank into a vale of parting waters and rolled one way, and then another before rising high again to mount the peak of another wave. The ship shook and rattled at every blow. Outside the wind howled with unremitting force, crying with the voice of a million banshees and everyone feared for their lives. Rumors ran rampant that the Victory Ships were massed produced of pre-fabricated modules and were prone to break apart if caught in such a storm as this. Again the ship shuddered and moaned and everyone just knew the Lincoln Victory would surely break apart and all would be lost at sea.

Before departing Le Havre, the captain had announced that they would be home before Christmas, a statement that had been received with much joy. But now the storm was having its say. The public address system declared that their arrival would be delayed beyond their anticipated date of arrival, but they would still be home by Christmas. But the storm raged stronger than ever.

Like everyone else, Barkley was terrified. He truly feared for his life and thought what an indignity it would be if he perished at sea after all he had been through in battle. It just wasn't fair. But just as in battle, he knew there was nothing he could do about it, so rode out the storm and prayed. And like the others, he was sick. The galley had all but given up on feeding the green-faced passengers that clung desperately to anything they could grasp as they vomited 'til their guts ached. Some began to believe that maybe they'd never make it home at all.

By the third day, December 24, a gallows humor fell upon the passengers and crew of the Lincoln Victory, compelling some wit to unofficially re-christened the good ship "The Bucking Victory". It was now Christmas Eve and everyone realized they would not be home for the Holiday. Their fears were verified when the passengers read the captain's declaration in the ship's newsletter saying the same. The public address system made another announcement, declaring that a traditional Christmas dinner would be served the following day, complete with all the trimmings. No one seemed elated at the prospect of eating.

After several grueling days, the storm finally abated. With calm seas, the Lincoln Victory poured on the steam and navigated post-haste for Boston harbor. They arrived safely on December 27, 1945. They were fortunate. Not every ship that rode out the storm survived. One vessel was known to have sunk with all hands lost, and it was rumored that at least one other had gone down as well. The soldiers and sailors of The Lincoln Victory were very lucky indeed!

Soon after his arrival in the States, Pfc. Barkley had orders to report to Camp Grant, Illinois, for discharge. It was the same camp he had begun his military service nearly two-and-one-half years earlier. But before he was allowed to leave he was ordered for a final physical. Upon its conclusion a doctor told him that he had a slight heart murmur and that they'd have to keep him at the post hospital several more weeks for further tests -- *unless*, of course, he was willing to sign a waiver releasing the Army of any liability in the matter. Like every other veteran, Barkley was anxious to get home. He signed the waiver. His final papers were issued on New Year's Day, 1946. He was given a one-way train ticket to Quincy.

Barkley disembarked from the train at the station at Second and Oak Streets in Quincy, and shouldered his barracks bag. *Thump!* Once again, the souvenir German rifle banged him on the back of his head for the umpteenth time. Readjusting his load, he struck out for his old neighborhood a dozen or so blocks away. Turning onto Monroe Street, he climbed the familiar steps that led from the street to his parents' house, and as he did so, that damned souvenir rifle whacked him on the back of his head for the last time. His dad came out to greet him. His mother remained indoors, veiled by the screen of the kitchen door. Stepping onto the porch, Barkley dropped his bag on the rough hewn boards and stated the obvious: "Well, I'm home."

Epilogue

The same day he arrived home, Harold Barkley took off his uniform and never wore it again.[*] His Army days were over. It had been an experience he would never forget. Many of the details were indelibly burned into his memory, and many of these would produce nightmares for many years to come.

A week or so after his homecoming, Harold's father, Harry, stood at the fence line of his backyard, engaged in conversation with one of his neighbors. Harry mentioned that his son had had a rough time during the war. The neighbor threw up his hands as if in protest and said, "Oh, nobody wants to hear about that anymore. That's ancient history."

Harold Barkley was now twenty years old. Although a twice-wounded veteran of five campaigns and numerous battles, he still was not old enough to vote or legally buy liquor. But that did not dampen his spirit. He immediately found employment at Gardner-Denver Company, a factory that produced industrial compressors. Eventually he became a casting inspector, retiring in 1980.

In the spring of 1946, he met a pretty country girl named Esther Schone, from Golden, Illinois, whom he married on November 10th of the following fall. The union was blessed with four children, the first being a daughter, Esther Jean ("Jeannie"), born in 1949. Sons

---

[*] This statement is not entirely correct. In the fall of 1994, Harold's son, Cleve, coaxed him to don a surplus Ike Jacket and trousers to participate in one of the Fiftieth Anniversary Celebrations honoring those who served in World War II. Wearing his ribbons and Combat Infantry Badge for the first time since January, 1946, Harold danced with his wife, Esther, to the tunes of the reconstituted Glenn Miller Orchestra. The dance floor was filled with other veterans and their wives. Some also wore bits and pieces of era uniforms and a few still fit into their originals. It was a moving sight.

Myron (January 1951) and Cleve (December 1951) followed, with the last, Alvin (August 1956) coming as a surprise.

All through his life, Harold acquired collectables. He made good use of contacts made in England while recovering from his first wound in the summer of 1944 and corresponded regularly with them after his return home. This led to others in Britain, and along with newer contacts in America, Harold gradually amassed a respectable collection of coins, Indian artifacts, fossils, old bottles, etc., etc., just to name a few. Although lacking a high school diploma, Harold possessed an insatiable appetite for knowledge of all things historical. Being self-taught, he gained expertise in many fields -- at one time he had been considered for mention in Who's Who of Indian Relic Collecting and later was instrumental in cataloging thousands of old glass bottles in a nationally distributed bottle collecting guide. For a time he was editor-in-chief of a monthly newsletter regarding the collection of American Indian artifacts entitled "The Relic Collector".

In 1963, he moved his family to Taylor, Missouri, across the Mississippi River from Quincy, where he built a museum in which to display his varied collections. Now, in 2006, he continues to collect the unusual, as well as interesting items, and sells them by mail order throughout the nation.

FINAL HONORS
(added since the first edition)

At age eighty-five Harold Barkley received notice that the French government had bestowed him the prestigious Legion of Honor for his participation in the liberation of their nation from Nazi domination. The honors were consummated on November 2, 2010, at American Legion Post 37 of Quincy, Illinois, with members of the Military Order of the Purple Heart participating. Though feeble, Harold stood proudly as Brigadier General Richard "Hap" Northern, Illinois National Guard, retired, pinned the medal to his chest. Fellow veterans saluted as the stirring strains of *The Star-Spangled Banner* filled the room, followed by a rousing rendition of France's national anthem, *La Marseillaise*. "This is my last hurrah," Barkley somberly told his family upon conclusion of the ceremony.

Eight months later Harold Barkley passed away at the Veterans Hospital in Iowa City, Iowa – it was June 14, 2011. His widow, Esther, poignantly noted that it was Flag Day. He was eighty-six years old. His body was returned to the place of his birth, Quincy, Illinois, and buried with full military honors. He was a hard working, honest man who throughout his life persevered through adversity with characteristic stubbornness, but most of all he bore an unshakable love for his family. He is dearly missed. He was my father... enough said.

FINAL SCENE

IN DEATH'S DARK SHADOW

TELL ME HOW IT WORKS

HOW DO SATELLITES WORK?

DANIEL R. FAUST

PowerKiDS press

New York

Published in 2021 by The Rosen Publishing Group, Inc.
29 East 21st Street, New York, NY 10010

First Edition

Editor: Siyavush Saidian
Book Design: Reann Nye

Photo Credits: Cover, p. 9 Andrey Armyagov/Shutterstock.com; Series Art (gears) goodwin_x/Shutterstock.com; Series Art (newspaper) Here/Shutterstock.com; p. 5 Triff/Shutterstock.com; p. 7 (top) Aleks49/Shutterstock.com; p.7 (bottom) 3Dsculptor/Shutterstock.com; p. 12 IrinaK/Shutterstock.com; p. 13 Stocktrek Images/Getty Images; p. 14 Jose Luis Stephens/EyeEm/Getty Images; p. 15 lavizzara/Shutterstock.com; p. 17 NurPhoto/Getty Images; p. 19 (background) seecreateimages/Shutterstock.com; p. 19 (earth, satellite) aapsky/Shutterstock.com; p. 20 aapsky/iStock/Getty Images Plus/Getty Images; p. 21 Universal History Archive/Universal Images Group/Getty Images; p. 22 SCIEPRO/Science Photo Library/Getty Images.

Cataloging-in-Publication Data

Names: Faust, Daniel R.
Title: How do satellites work? / Daniel R. Faust.
Description: New York : PowerKids Press, 2021. | Series: Tell me how it works | Includes glossary and index.
Identifiers: ISBN 9781725318175 (pbk.) | ISBN 9781725318199 (library bound) | ISBN 9781725318182 (6pack)
Subjects: LCSH: Artificial satellites–Juvenile literature.
Classification: LCC TL796.3 F38 2021 | DDC 629.46–dc23

Manufactured in the United States of America

CPSIA Compliance Information: Batch #CWPK20. For Further Information contact Rosen Publishing, New York, New York at 1-800-237-9932.

Find us on

CONTENTS

MOON OR MACHINE?

Most nights, you can see the moon when you look up into the sky. The moon is a satellite of Earth. A satellite is a body that orbits, or moves around, another larger object. Most of the planets in our **solar system** have moons. Some only have one or two, while others have dozens.

Moons are natural satellites. Some satellites are man-made. We call these kinds of satellites artificial satellites. Artificial satellites are objects that humans have made and launched, or sent into orbit.

The Earth has only one moon. Jupiter has 79 known moons, including the largest moon in our solar system: Ganymede.

5

FROM SPUTNIK TO SPACE STATIONS

On October 4, 1957, the **Soviet Union** successfully launched the first man-made satellite into orbit. It was named Sputnik 1. This satellite, which was only about the size of a beach ball, changed history.

Some believed Sputnik's launch proved that the Soviet Union was more advanced than the United States. In the United States, scientists began studying ways to beat the Soviet Union in what became known as the Space Race. On January 31, 1958, the United States launched its own satellite, Explorer 1.

TECH TALK

Did you know that space stations, such as the International Space Station (ISS), are satellites? They're habitable artificial satellites, which means they're large enough for people to live in.

6

SPUTNIK I

INTERNATIONAL
SPACE STATION

When it comes to satellites, size doesn't matter.
Sputnik 1 wasn't much bigger than a classroom
globe, but the ISS is large enough for several
people to live and work in.

7

PARTS OF A SATELLITE

Satellites have several basic parts. The housing is the outside container of the satellite. The other parts are inside or mounted to the outside of the housing. These parts include radio systems, an onboard computer, and a power source.

Satellites need power continuously, or all the time. The most common power sources are **solar panels** that charge batteries. Solar panels are lightweight and **efficient**. Because satellites may sometimes move out of direct sunlight, batteries are used as a back-up for the satellite's panels.

Satellites can use solar panels like this to draw a lot of power from sunlight. **Engineers** are working on ways to use space solar panels, like those on satellites, to provide clean power on Earth.

A satellite's antenna system receives and sends out signals, or messages, to Earth. Transponders are special machines that strengthen these messages. Satellites also have small **thrusters** that help keep them in position.

One of the most important parts is the command system. This part acts like the satellite's brain. It makes sure all of the other parts are working correctly. It also receives commands from Earth. Finally, the thermal, or heat, control system makes sure the satellite doesn't get too hot or too cold.

> Although they have the same basic parts, not all satellites look the same. Scientists try to make their satellites cheaper or more efficient by putting the parts together differently.

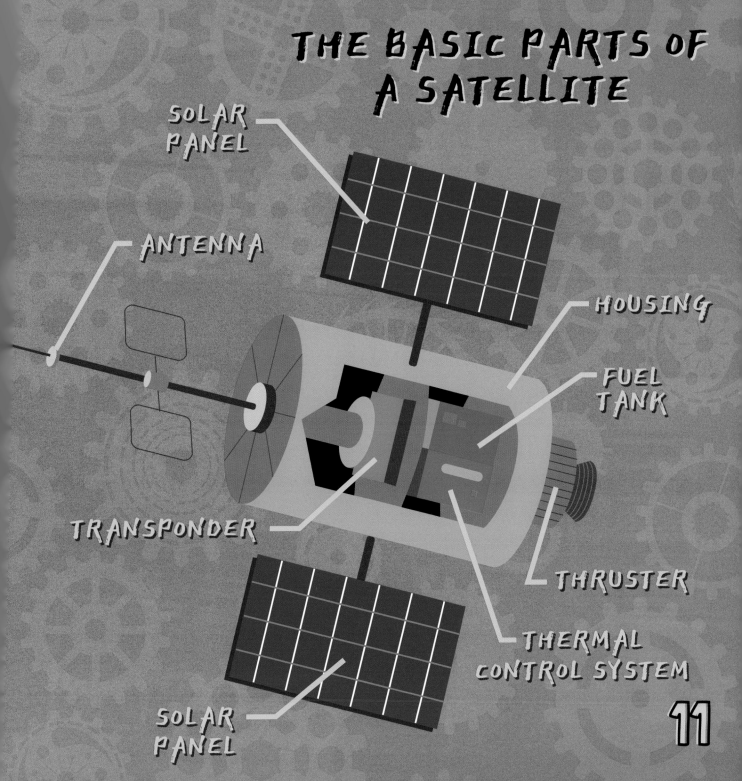

THE BASIC PARTS OF A SATELLITE

SOLAR PANEL

ANTENNA

HOUSING

FUEL TANK

TRANSPONDER

THRUSTER

THERMAL CONTROL SYSTEM

SOLAR PANEL

11

SATELLITE MISSIONS

There are many satellites orbiting Earth, and they all have different jobs. Communication satellites, or comsats, are very important. They allow us to send telephone, radio, and TV signals to any place on the planet.

TECH TALK

Telephone and radio signals that don't use satellites need to be near special towers on land. Satellite radio and telephones can "bounce" signals off of satellites to reach more areas on Earth.

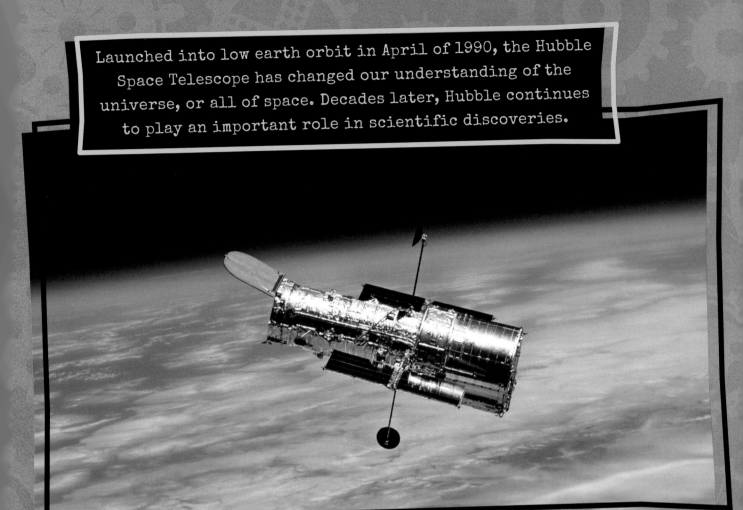

Launched into low earth orbit in April of 1990, the Hubble Space Telescope has changed our understanding of the universe, or all of space. Decades later, Hubble continues to play an important role in scientific discoveries.

Astronomical satellites are like **telescopes** in space. Scientists use these satellites to observe faraway planets and other space bodies. Because these satellites are in orbit, they can provide a clear view of space without being made unclear by the gases surrounding Earth, called the atmosphere. 13

Navigational satellites are able to determine the exact location of someone or something anywhere in the world. The Global Positioning System, or GPS, is a group of navigational satellites that send signals back and forth to locate a person or object.

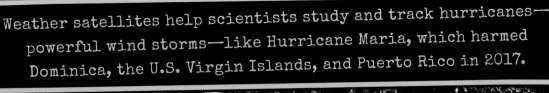

Weather satellites help scientists study and track hurricanes—powerful wind storms—like Hurricane Maria, which harmed Dominica, the U.S. Virgin Islands, and Puerto Rico in 2017.

Earth observation satellites and weather satellites observe data, or facts and figures, about the planet's **climate** and weather. These satellites help scientists forecast the weather and keep track of **climate change** and natural disasters, or harmful natural events, such as hurricanes.

15

THREE... TWO... ONE... LIFT OFF!

In the past, many satellites were carried into orbit by space shuttles. Today, rockets bring them into orbit because rockets run much more efficiently. Many countries and companies can more easily launch rockets into space.

Once the rocket is launched, it carries the satellite into Earth's atmosphere. When the rocket reaches about 120 miles (193.1 km) up, it lets go of the satellite. Small thrusters on the rocket make sure the satellite separates completely.

TECH TALK

Between 1981 and 2011, NASA's space shuttles flew 135 missions, or jobs. Space shuttles carried people into orbit, conducted scientific studies, helped build the ISS, and launched and fixed satellites.

16

Founded in 2002, SpaceX is a private company that builds and launches rockets and other spacecraft. SpaceX has successfully launched satellites and brought shipments to the ISS.

STAYING IN ORBIT

The same forces that keep the moon in orbit also keep man-made satellites in orbit. These forces are gravity and inertia. Gravity is the force that draws two objects toward each other. Inertia is an object's likelihood to remain in motion.

When a satellite is launched, its inertia keeps it going in one direction at a constant speed. However, Earth's gravity wants to pull the satellite back toward the ground. The balance between these two forces keeps the satellite in orbit.

TECH TALK

Some satellites are positioned so they stay in the same spot above Earth. These satellites are said to be in geostationary orbit. Communications and weather satellites are often placed into geostationary orbit.

18

SATELLITE'S INERTIA

THE PULL OF EARTH'S GRAVITY

Satellites, whether they're natural or man-made, remain in orbit around the Earth because of the tug-of-war between the satellite's inertia and the pull of Earth's gravity. This balance is called orbital velocity.

19

FAR FROM HOME

Astronomical satellites, like the Hubble Space Telescope, study the universe from Earth's orbit. We can learn a lot about other stars and planets this way. However, the best way to study another planet is to go there.

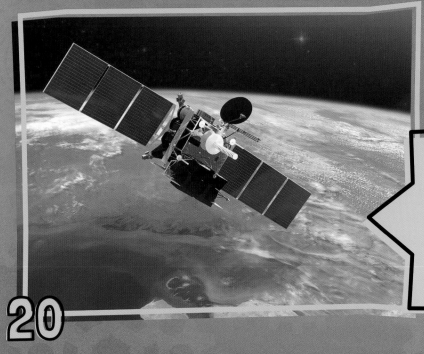

TECH TALK

When most probes reach the end of their lifespan, they are deorbited. This means they are allowed to fall out of their orbit and either crash or burn up in the atmosphere.

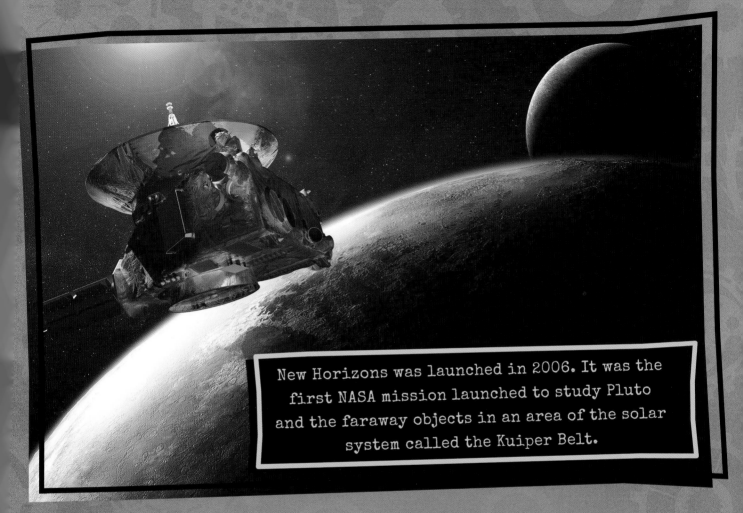

New Horizons was launched in 2006. It was the first NASA mission launched to study Pluto and the faraway objects in an area of the solar system called the Kuiper Belt.

NASA and other groups have launched special satellites called probes. These satellites orbit the planets, moons, and other objects in our solar system and send scientific data back to Earth. Some probes, like Voyager 1, have even gone beyond the edge of our solar system.

SPACE JUNK AND MEGA-CONSTELLATIONS

Since the first satellite was launched, Earth has become surrounded by a cloud of **debris** made of old, broken satellites and leftover rockets. There are also large groups of satellites called mega-**constellations**. This makes the space around Earth very crowded.

Engineers working on new satellites are thinking of ways to reduce space junk and protect satellites in the crowded space above Earth. They are planning to make satellites with better sensors and a machine has even been made to guide old satellites back to Earth.

22

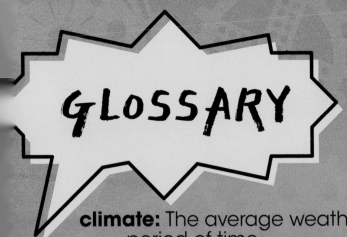

GLOSSARY

climate: The average weather conditions of a place over a period of time.

climate change: Change in Earth's climate caused by human activity.

constellation: A group of stars that makes a particular shape in the sky.

debris: Something that is left behind because it is not wanted.

efficient: Capable of producing the desired result without wasting material, time, or energy.

engineer: Someone who plans and builds machines.

solar panel: A flat system of special cells that use sunlight to make energy.

solar system: The sun and all the space objects that orbit it, including the planets and their moons.

Soviet Union: The Union of Soviet Socialist Republics, a former country in Europe and Asia.

telescope: A tool that makes faraway objects look bigger and closer.

thrusters: Engines that produce thrust by expelling a jet of fluid or gas.

INDEX

WEBSITES

24

Due to the changing nature of Internet links, PowerKids Press has developed an online list of websites related to the subject of this book. This site is updated regularly. Please use this link to access the list: www.powerkidslinks.com/tmhiw/satelittes